METROPOLITAN CORRIDOR

Cover, Railroad Stories, *1937. (Courtesy of* Railroad Magazine*)*

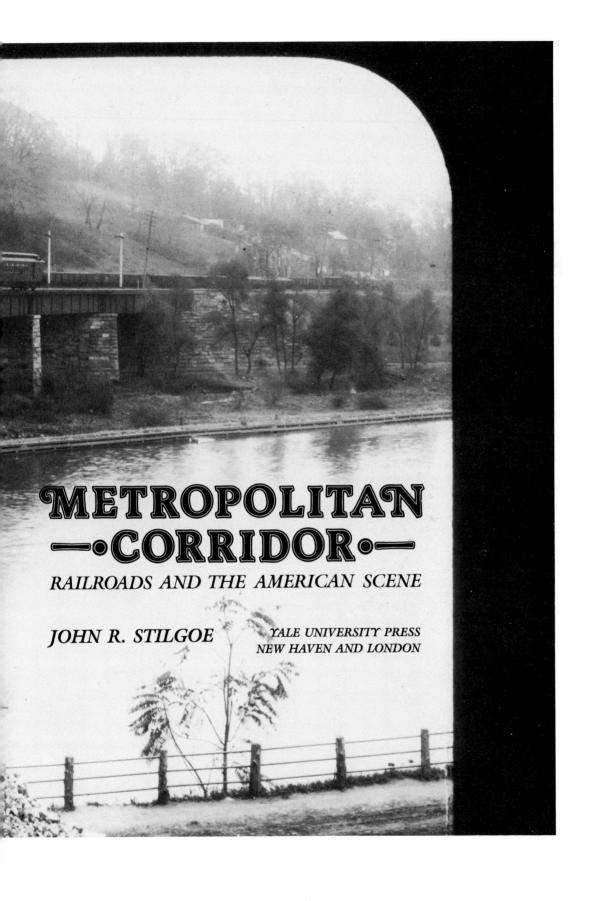

METROPOLITAN
·CORRIDOR·

RAILROADS AND THE AMERICAN SCENE

JOHN R. STILGOE   *YALE UNIVERSITY PRESS*
NEW HAVEN AND LONDON

Designed by Sally Harris
and set in Galliard type.
Printed in the United States of America by
Murray Printing Company, Westford, Mass.

Library of Congress Cataloging in Publication Data

Stilgoe, John R., 1949–
Metropolitan corridor.

Bibliography: p.
Includes index.
1. Railroads—United States—History. 2. Railroads—
United States—Right of way—History. 3. Railroads—
Social aspects—United States—History. I. Title.
HE2751.S68 1983   385'.0973   83–3585
ISBN 0–300–03042–8

1 2 3 4 5 6 7 8 9 10

PRECEDING PAGES: *A short passenger train*
rumbles over a bridge in eastern Pennsylva-
nia. (Collection of the author)

FOR MY PARENTS

CONTENTS

PREFACE

IN THE HALF CENTURY
following 1880, the railroad industry reshaped the American built environment and reoriented American thinking. The luxury passenger express booming over grade crossings and hurtling past small-town depots, the slow freight chugging through industrial zones, even the morning and evening commuter locals shuttling back and forth between suburban stations and subterranean urban terminals operated in a unique environment. Certainly the actual railroad right-of-way of roadbed and tracks, signals and depots, bridges and junctions no longer represented the tentative beginnings of a new transportation pathway. Instead it reflected the power of sophisticated engineering, of heavy industry unknown two generations before. Trains and right-of-way transformed adjacent built environments, modifying them in novel, sometimes startling ways. They nurtured factory complexes, electricity generating stations, and commuter suburbs while enfeebling Main Streets and other traditional places. "Railroad iron is a magician's rod," mused Emerson in the 1840s, "in its power to evoke the sleeping energies of land and water."[1] By the turn of the century, Americans knew that railroad iron meant far more; train travel provided a distinctive, almost cinemagraphic vision of the built environment beyond the plate glass windows. Trains, right-of-way, and adjacent built form had become part environment, part experience, a combination perhaps best called *metropolitan*.

For the small boy grasping his father's hand as the crack express thundered past in a roar of steam, coal smoke, and dizzying vibration, the train existed as fiercely directed energy, as power magnified almost beyond comprehension. For the father, the train represented perhaps nothing more than *The Limited* or *Fast Mail* passing through on schedule; or perhaps it represented something so important that he deliberately brought his child into its presence. In the age of interstate highways and jet airliners, the magnetism of the train and its path can be all too easily dismissed. Today the trains are fewer, the steam locomotives retired, and the once impeccably maintained right-of-way littered with rubbish and overgrown with weeds. But the trains and right-of-way that molded space, structure, and thinking in nearly forgotten ways remain somewhat active nonetheless. Almost but not quite ruins, they stir now with quickened energy. Understanding their half century of importance may indeed facilitate understanding rural, suburban, and urban environments, for trains and right-of-way created a fourth distinctive environment—the metropolitan corridor. And in an energy-short age, parents may bring boys and girls to see the metropolitan corridor restored.

"Readers of poetry see the factory-village and the railway, and fancy that the poetry of landscape is broken up by these," Emerson announced in the twilight of traditional American landscape. Despite his assurance that "the poet sees them fall within the great Order not less than the bee-hive, or the spider's geometrical web," few thoughtful Americans of the 1840s immediately accepted them.[2] As I hope *Common Landscape of America, 1580 to 1845* shows, industrial enterprise disconcerted a nation respectful of agriculture and of tradition.[3] In *The Machine in the Garden: Technology and the Pastoral Ideal in America*, Leo Marx argues that writers and painters worried about the fracturing of tradition and the transformation of the rural countryside.[4] The development of the railroad-shaped environment coincided with other changes, particularly the growth of cities, the spread of heavy industry, and the expansion of "American" civilization across the High Plains, changes interrupted but not stayed by the Civil War. The built environment reflected these developments in the three decades following 1850; a number of scholars have analyzed the import of urbanization, industrialization, and westward migration, and this book deliberately attempts to avoid duplicating their efforts. As John Brinckerhoff Jackson discusses in *American Space: The Centennial Years, 1865–1876*, the late 1870s witnessed the end of a great epoch of spatial transformation and the beginning of a period of consolidation.[5]

In the railroad industry, the period from 1880 to 1930 marked not only the consolidation of lines and expertise, but a sort of prosperous stasis about which remarkably little is known.[6] Historians of business and economic development continue to study the formative years of individual railroad corporations, emphasizing very early eastern firms such as the Baltimore & Ohio or the first long-distance western lines, particularly the Illinois Central, the Union Pacific, and the Great Northern, or else they focus on the Depression-era collapse of prosperity.[7] Two reasons perhaps explain the void in scholarship. On the one hand, by 1880 railroad firms had evolved much of the management and mechanical technique on which they relied for the next fifty years, a reliance that made the industry especially susceptible to the strains and competition created by the Depression, the highway lobby, and the airlines. On the other, the pre-1880 age of entrepreneurial enterprise remains glamorous in ways that the subsequent "managerial era" does not. Only recently have scholars begun examining the 1880–1930 period, and much remains to be done. In *The Visible Hand: The Managerial Revolution in American Business*, Alfred D. Chandler, Jr. scrutinizes the development of the managerial system within and beyond the railroad industry, and Carl Condit, in his magnificent, two-volume *The Port of New York*, analyzes the creation of the rail and terminal systems of greater New York City from the beginning of the rail era to the present, tracing not only financing and design, but the impact of technological innovation.[8] John H. White, Jr., in *The American Railroad Passenger Car* and Michael Bezilla in *Electric Traction on the Pennsylvania Railroad* have deepened scholarly understanding of two facets of the 1880–1930 period of railroad engineering.[9] Nevertheless, the historian of the railroad visual environment, the concatenation of space and structure that comprised so much of the metropolitan corridor, must often work without the reassuring presence of background material.

One question concerning cultural background deserves mention here, for an answer lies at the heart of this book. Did the romantic-era distrust of the railroad and its trains descried by Leo Marx endure in the decades after 1880? Was Emerson an oddity, atypically optimistic about the speed with which Americans would learn to love the train and its right-of-way? Or was he actually quite pragmatic, but wrong about the timespan of the awakening love? As the following pages reveal, my own research strongly suggests that the distrust did not endure. Emerson and his contemporaries knew the train and the railroad as novelties; subsequent generations were born into a world in which trains seemed as commonplace as spiderwebs. An exhaustive analysis of periodicals, including not only mass-circulation magazines but special-interest journals and children's publications, underlies the position taken throughout this book.[10] Certainly, as the text and notes indicate, railroad boards of directors, interlocked financing, and rapacious corporate capitalism all attracted growing public condemnation and eventually public regulation.[11] Interpreting the conflict between admiration of a new terminal building, drawbridge, or express train and hatred of a fare or tariff increase is scarcely straightforward, especially in light of contemporaneous articles that advise setting one railroad corporation against another to insure competition and low rates, blame high passenger fares on government-regulated, too-low freight tariffs, and explain express train collisions in anti-union terms. Several scholars, beginning with Robert Edgar Riegel, who published *The Story of the Western Railroads* in 1926, have addressed the issue of the public perception of corporate capitalism, either by examining the political mood of the nation in the 1880–1930 period or by tracing the roots of such reform movements as Progressivism.[12] The issue in this book is not theirs. The following pages look as closely as possible at the physical presence of the railroad industry and its infrastructure and seek to interpret the public attitude toward them. Dividing object from creating system may be unwise, but to research the origin, growth, and place of corporate finance in this period is to produce another book. Perhaps the typical American saw in the great ocean liner the machinations of the shipping interests; perhaps he saw in the great wheat ranches the fluctuations of the commodities market; and perhaps he saw in the speeding luxury train the intrigues of Wall Street financiers. But perhaps parents showed children steamships, bonanza wheat farms, and great locomotives for the things themselves, in all their magnificent complexity.

What the typical American saw in the metropolitan corridor is intimately related to the photographs and other illustrations in the following pages. The half-century era chosen here encompasses the shift from professional to amateur photography, and the shift away from painting as the dominant form of representational art. In "Beauty in Ugliness," a 1930 *Photo-Era* article aimed at serious amateur photographers, Edward D. Wilson directed his readers' attention to "the scenes wrought by the industry of our modern age" and noted that "they are unsightly, to be sure, at first glance abhorrent; but after contemplation they take on an aspect of most singular beauty." In particular, he focused on the railroad and its trains. "Is not a steam locomotive a thing of most stupendous beauty? It is the very materialization of power, incomprehensible power," he continued with mounting enthusiasm for industrial scenery. "The very age, however, that created the roaring locomotive, the grimy smokestacks, and the filthy, waste-laden river, has created a new form of art," he concluded. "This is photography."[13] The photographs illustrating this book lack grandeur; indeed they are quite ordinary. Theirs is an aesthetic not of the period before 1880, a period characterized by painting and lithography, nor of the years after the Great Depression, when artists turned from the corridor to other environments. Theirs is the aesthetic of the 1880–1930 period—the era of the metropolitan corridor, when most Americans embraced a now half-forgotten environment that reshaped American experience.

This book offers only an introduction, an addition to the vocabulary of visual analysis of the built environment.

ACKNOWLEDGMENTS

MY LONG EXPLORATION OF the metropolitan corridor has profited from encounters with many helpful people. I am indebted to the staff of the Loeb Library of the Harvard University Graduate School of Design, especially to Christopher Hail, Judith Auerbach, Melanie Lewis, and Katherine Poole. For help in assembling the photographs, I am grateful to Jeanne Bartlett, Frederick A. Kramer, Donovan L. Hofsommer, Frank Kurtick, and John White, Jr. Acquisition of the photographs was made possible by a generous grant from the Dean's Faculty Research Fund of the Graduate School of Design. My colleagues and students made many suggestions, as did the railroad employees with whom I spoke in my travels across the country. To Judy Metro, Maura D. Shaw Tantillo, Sally Harris, and Tina Weiner of Yale University Press, I am indebted for meticulous attention to detail. To my parents, who enlivened a rural boyhood with visits to corridor places, I owe a special debt. And finally, I thank my wife, Mary Ann, for the most thoughtful support possible.

Cover, Railroad Stories, *1937. (Courtesy of* Railroad Magazine*)*

INTRODUCTION

METROPOLITAN CORRIDOR designates the portion of the American built environment that evolved along railroad rights-of-way in the years between 1880 and 1935. No traditional spatial term, not *urban*, *suburban*, or *rural*, not *cityscape* or *landscape*, adequately identifies the space that perplexed so many turn-of-the-century observers. Reaching from the very hearts of great cities across industrial zones, suburbs, small towns, and into mountain wilderness, the metropolitan corridor objectified in its unprecedented arrangement of space and structure a wholly new lifestyle. Along it flowed the forces of modernization, announcing the character of the twentieth century, and abutting it sprouted new clusters of building. Its peculiar juxtaposition of elements attracted the scrutiny of photographers and advertising illustrators; its romance inveigled poets and novelists; its energy challenged architects, landscape architects, and urban designers. Always it resisted definition in traditional terminology. And suddenly, in the years of the Great Depression, in the ascendancy of the automobile, it vanished from the national attention. Yet the corridor remains, although now often screened by sumac and other junglelike trees and avoided by highways, still snaking from one well-known, often-studied sort of space to another.

Where is the corridor? To find it one must drive far from the interstate highway cloverleaf, away from Main Street and Second Street; one drives downhill, for the corridor follows the gentle gradients of river valleys, or to the rundown part of town, for the corridor no longer enriches the structures snuggled along it. In the city, one drives away from tall glass-skinned office towers to the grimy factories still watched by thrusting red-brick smoke stacks. In the suburb, one drives along the old parkway, along the former streetcar route leading to the commuter station. In the small town, one drives toward the grain elevator, the coal trestle, the creek bed. In the country one drives toward the line of telegraph poles. Always one drives toward the railroad right-of-way, the energizing spine of the corridor.

Understanding the corridor, indeed seeing the corridor, involves knowing something of the old popular love of railroad trains. By 1880 the train, and particularly the fast express, struck few observers as a monstrous machine soiling a virginal garden.[1] Instead it seemed a powerful, romantic creature inhabiting an environment created especially for it. What little romantic and

Transcendental distaste endured lingered in an atmosphere of public appro-
bation.[2] Despite hideous wrecks, high freight tariffs, and political manipula-
tions, the railroad industry enjoyed a favorable reputation based on such
seemingly insignificant happenings as a businessman sleeping soundly on a
Pullman express racing through a blizzard, a small-town storekeeper glimpsing the headlight of the fast mail speeding exactly "on the advertised," a young
boy falling asleep to the distant, lonesome whistle of the slow freight.

Between 1880 and the Second World War, countless journalists and magazine writers extolled the magic of railroading. Many of their stories, particularly the fiction, appeared in family periodicals like *Collier's*, *Saturday Evening
Post*, and *Harper's Weekly*, often overshadowing muckraking reports of derailments and corporate bribery. In 1900, for example, *McClure's* published three
rousing short stories concerning railroad adventure. "Conductor Pat Francis"
and "The Million-Dollar Freight Train," the work of Frank H. Spearman,
emphasize the heroism of trainmen confronting imminent disasters born of
storms, mechanical failure, and human error.[3] The third, "The Luck of the
Northern Mail: The Story of a Runaway Boy and a Runaway Train," traces a
series of insignificant occurrences climaxing in a young boy's valiant effort to
prevent a mountain-grade collision. "Today he holds an enviable position in
the employ of the great railway system in whose interest he displayed such
masterly courage that morning when he saved the Northern Mail," the story
concludes in an ending that became typical by 1920.[4] Adulthood, for adoles-
cent boys at least, arrived when they entered the employ of the railroads and
learned to master the locomotive, signal tower, or drawbridge.

Spearman, E. S. Dellinger, William Edward Hayes, Harry Bedwell, and
Cy Warman, many of them railroad employees with a flair for fiction-writing,
produced literature of little lasting merit. But their short stories and novels
sold widely, not only to the millions of American families directly or indirectly
involved in the railroad industry, but to millions of others somehow touched
by the "romance of the rails."[5] Among the readers were men whose jobs required railroad travel, farmers entranced by the express train paused momentarily at a small-town junction or by the night flyer tearing across the fields in
the distance, and, perhaps above all, boys anxious for railroad careers. Some
of the writers produced novels about boy life on the rails. Warman's *The White
Mail* of 1899 depicts the adventures of two adolescents employed as bridge
watchers by a western railroad company and explains how one rose to become
president of the line.[6] Allen Chapman's turn-of-the-century series, while infused with a similar Horatio Alger sentiment, emphasizes the intricacies of
railroad work. His *Ralph of the Roundhouse, or Bound to Become a Railroad Man*
and *Ralph in the Switch Tower, or The Adventures of a Young Railroader* and
many subsequent novels introduce young readers to the intricacies of life on
the right-of-way.[7] Most of the adult fiction shares a similar goal, emphasizing
the heroic deeds on stormy nights, accidents averted, and, as in Frank Spear-

man's 1903 novel, *The Daughter of a Magnate*, female hearts won by devotion to duty. Some railroad companies subsidized such romantic fiction; in 1905, for example, the Lackawanna Railroad backed *A Paper Proposal*, a story in which two strangers fall in love on a fast express.[8] Thousands of readers sought out such stories, and in 1906 one publisher began *Railroad Man's Magazine*. That periodical emphasized railroadiana and featured "true-to-life" stories about daily routines, vexations, and adventures, along with non-fiction explicating the meaning of signals, the braking of freight trains, and the fueling of locomotives. *Railroad Man's Magazine* became *Railroad Stories* in 1932, and by 1937 was *Railroad Magazine*; each title sought to attract a wider audience, and each title was more successful.[9] Americans, especially boys and men, found in the literature a gateway into the seemingly romantic life of the railroad right-of-way.

Railroad fiction falls into two broad categories. One, represented by a far greater number of novels and short stories, traces life on the rails, in the process describing everything from air brakes to coaling stations. The other emphasizes the building and management of railroads and unwittingly illuminates a crucial element in any study of the metropolitan corridor. Two sorts of engineer worked on the railroad. About one the public knew a great deal; the locomotive engineer clad in denim overalls, peaked cap, and red bandana peered from his cab in dozens of calendar illustrations, in countless magazine advertisements, and, of course, from hundreds of speeding or creeping trains. About the other—the college-trained intellectual charged with determining alignments and building bridges, signal systems, and tunnels—the general public knew little. Such engineers, armed with slide rules and transits, created the rights-of-way and directed their operation. In railroad fiction, they are men of action, able to think quickly to avert disaster, able to manage work crews of willing if muddle-headed laborers, and able to control capital and so rise to management and ownership positions. In such novels as Spearman's *The Daughter of a Magnate*, Samuel Merwin's *The Road-Builders*, and Francis Lynde's *The Taming of the Red Butte Western*, young engineers build railroads, manage men, machines, and money, and in time advance civilization. Again and again, as in Lynde's 1912 novel, *Scientific Sprague*, educated heroes use mathematics and technology to solve physical and human-relations problems. While these stories are as filled with adventure, technical explanation, and love affairs as the other category of railroad fiction, they emphasize the new nature of the modern railroad. No traditional principles govern its creation, maintenance, and operation; only men familiar with modern forces such as high-pressure steam, steel-beam construction, and electricity can direct it. Not surprisingly, the popular mind confused the two engineers, for both engineman and road-builder shared in the mysteries of the right-of-way.

Out of the confusion emerged an outpouring of literature, not all of it fiction. Grammar and high school textbooks, for example, rammed home the

The 1922 New York Central Lines calendar illustration.
(Courtesy of Consolidated Rail Corporation, collection of the author)

Powerful locomotives and fast passenger trains entranced little girls, too, as this 1920s Otto Perry photograph makes clear. (Courtesy of Denver Public Library, Western History Department)

clear message of the pulp magazines and popular novels. Edward Channing's *Elements of United States History*, a 1919 textbook aimed at sixth-grade children, emphasizes the important role of railroads in "developing" the nation. But by illustrating its arguments with a photograph of a speeding *Empire State Express*, an image certain to arouse the romantic attention of any boy and most girls, it presents its young readers with the two-fold meaning of engineering.[10] In textbooks, children's reference books, and in factual analyses of the industry directed at adult readers, the railroad appears as a romantic, intricate, decidedly modern phenomenon ruled by men more educated, more courageous, more dedicated to duty, and more adventurous than most.

Autobiographies of the period suggest the imaginative impact of the right-of-way, at least on boys. Perhaps the finest is an autobiographical novel, Harold Waldo's *The Magic Midland*. The 1923 work traces the maturation of a small-town teenager torn between the agricultural values of his preacher father and the romance of the railroad. Despite beatings and other punishments, the young man persists in visiting the depot and railroad yard, hooking rides on freight trains stopped at water tanks, and reveling in "the dark arcanum of the caboose, with its bunks, its goblin green and ruby-eyed lanterns, its lurid magazines of railroad amours and derring-do." He learns the mysteries of the railroad watch that must keep perfect time no matter what its position in an overall pocket, and he forever wanders down to the railroad tracks. "There in the chill of dawn they swept away, eight fascinating rivulets of steel, narrowing, curving, sliding away—like a frosty river into the misty morning," writes Waldo of the right-of-way. "There had always been an irresistible attraction in that river of steel which swept from lake to lake across his great old state. And how many times he had thrilled to the idea of sliding out on it—away and away."[11] From his lookout in his barn loft, the young man watches the right-of-way until its pull becomes too strong. Despite his father's protests, he leaves for a life of metropolitan adventure.

Waldo's undeservedly ignored novel examines not only his own boyhood, but a national coming of age. In the years between 1880 and 1920, the nation outgrew its rural, small-town values and way of life and instead embraced a different existence.[12] Men chronicling their awakening into adulthood frequently emphasized the railroad as the place in which they discovered both personal and societal change.[13] "A freight hopper and a man of the railroad world" was no longer only a farm boy or the son of a main-street storekeeper.[14] He was initiated into an engineered world of artificial spaces and structures, a world governed not by seasonal rhythms and democracy but by the meticulous ticking of Waltham and Hamilton watches and imperiously telegraphed orders, a world powered not by sunlight and horses but by steam and electricity.

Not until the mid-1890s did the nation begin to grasp the imaginative impact of the railroad and the corridor evolving along it. As late as 1895,

Railroad employees posed nonchalantly against the most powerful of machines. (Collection of the author)

Advertisement for railroad watches, National Geographic, *July 1912. (Courtesy of Hamilton Watch Co., Inc., Lancaster, Pennsylvania)*

Advertisers associated their products with railroading to capture something of "high iron" glamor, as this 1916 advertisement suggests. (Courtesy of the Archives, The Coca-Cola Company)

Lionel Catalogue for 1929. *(Collection of the author; reproduced with the permission of Fundimensions, manufacturers of Lionel Trains)*

No. 407E "LIONEL STANDARD" 100% "DISTANT-CONTROL" COMPLETE RAILROAD

HERE is the finest gift that any boy could wish for—a complete **Lionel** "Distant-Control" Railroad, containing not only the best trains we manufacture, but a very large variety of Electrically-Controlled and illuminated Accessories. The Passenger and Freight Trains can be started, stopped, reversed and operated at any speed at any distance from the track. The Switch Signal-Tower, shown in the foreground, and the elevated Tower in the rear, enable you to operate all the Electrically-Controlled Accessories at a distance. The specifications of this marvelous model Railroad are given below.

OUTFIT No. 407E—COMPRISES

1 No. 408E "Distant-Control" Locomotive	1 No. 212 Gondola car	38 S Track	1 No. 80 Semaphore	20 STC "Lockon" connections
1 No. 380E "Distant-Control" Locomotive	1 No. 213 Cattle car	18 C Track	2 No. 77 Crossing gates	Wires for making electrical connections, connecting ties for joining sections of track, lamps for headlights, interior of cars and all illuminated accessories are supplied with this outfit. Track layout is 12 feet 10 inches long by 6 feet 4 inches wide.
	1 No. 214 Box car	4 ½S Track	1 No. 89 Flagstaff	
2 No. 81 Controlling rheostats	1 No. 215 Oil car	1 No. 124 Station	2 No. 76 Block signals	
1 No. 418 Pullman car	1 No. 216 Coal car	1 No. 189 Villa	1 No. 69 Warning signal	
1 No. 419 Pullman and baggage car	1 No. 217 Illuminated Caboose	1 No. 191 Villa	1 No. 436 Power house	
	1 No. 218 Operating Dump car	3 No. 184 Bungalows	1 No. 437 Switch tower	
1 No. 490 Observation car	1 No. 219 Operating Derrick car	1 No. 438 Signal Tower	2 No. 67 Lamp posts	
1 No. 431 Dining-car	1 No. 81 Semaphore	1 No. 101 Bridge	1 No. 56 Lamp posts	
1 No. 211 Lumber car with load of lumber	1 Type K Transformer	1 No. 110L Tunnel	2 No. 57 Lamp posts	*Code Word* "ALLY"
	3 pr. 222 Switches	12 No. 60 Telegraph Posts	2 No. 59 Lamp posts	
	2 No. 23 Bumpers	1 No. 78 Train Control		

Price is Listed on Page 45

Edward Bok, the editor of *Ladies' Home Journal*, noted that "of our immense population of nearly sixty-nine millions not more than three per cent of the people go fifty miles away from their homes during a year," and that a third of the travelers went only as far as summer-vacation cottages or hotels.[15] Within a few years, however, other observers recognized that the number of travelers had less importance in understanding the changed national mind than had the sedentary people who hoped to travel. "The farm did not satisfy him," wrote the great agricultural reformer Liberty Hyde Bailey in 1907 of "the experience of many thousands of farm boys" anxious to move on. "The shriek of the locomotive and the roll of the trains suggested a great world that lay beyond his vision."[16] By 1930 the transformation was complete. "It has been said that over this Hudson Division more than twenty-five per cent of all Americans pass at some time or other in their lives," wrote Edward Hungerford that year in an analysis of the main line of the New York Central Railroad Company. "The record shows that in an average year more than four million persons ride up and down this division, all the way between New York and Albany."[17] Of course many persons rode more than once, but the figure of four million includes almost no commuters. In the years between the assertion of Bok and the statistics of Hungerford, Americans—and particularly younger people—had grown familiar with the metropolitan corridor.

Certainly the toy industry reflected and encouraged the staggering change in outlook and behavior. By January 1937, the color cover of *Railroad Stories* featured a locomotive engineer pausing from oiling his own machine to put a drop or two on the toy engine held up to him by a young boy. The cover spoke volumes about the intricate web of railroad affections that directed attention at the metropolitan corridor. The Lionel Corporation had purchased full-page advertisements for its toy electric trains, and the magazine had begun a column devoted to model railroading. Among stories like "Sun and Silence," which told of the boredom endured by telegraph operators in isolated stations in southwest deserts, and "Man Failure," which explicated the loyalty of an unfairly fired engineer, blazed the advertisements for toy trains.[18] Firms such as the Ives Company, American Flyer, and Lionel helped mold the national imagination; since their founding in the first years of the new century, they had exploited the love of railroading, the new force of electricity, and, above all, the power of sophisticated advertising.[19] Even *Fortune Magazine* studied their effect on the national character.

Its full-color, exquisitely illustrated, forty-five-page 1929 Christmas catalogue proclaimed the Lionel Company as the builder of the finest toy trains in the world. Competing firms shared the burgeoning electric train market, but Lionel provided most technical innovation and much philosophy. Founded in 1900, the firm produced ever more realistic and sophisticated models of American steam and electric locomotives, passenger cars, and freight trains while emphasizing the suitability of the hobby it stimulated. J. Lionel Cowan and his executive staff intuitively understood the popular, modern fascination with railroads and trains, and they advertised their products by tapping an almost awesome energy.

"Is there a boy or man who doesn't thrill at the sight of a Lionel Passenger or Freight Train—speedy as a comet—life-like in every detail, flashing by crossings, slowing down to a stop as the automatic semaphore or train control is set against it, and gliding away again as the signal shows 'Clear'?" asks the catalogue in its introduction. The trains receive much attention, of course, but the catalogue emphasizes the creation of a model railroad complete with bridges, stations, signal towers, tunnels, turntables, and houses, all placed among twisting lines of track. Operating such a "layout" proves as much fun as assembling it over the years, asserts the catalogue; Lionel locomotives reverse direction by "remote control" and activate signals automatically, always in approximation to prototype equipment. "There's knowledge to be gained from the study of Lionel Model Railroading and there's realism," announces the large type, "and the thrill that comes from the personal operation and direction of a great railroad system." Given a train, track, switches, and enough "accessories" like signals, a boy with the help of his father could construct an objective correlative of the "romance of the rails." Operating toy trains, in the words of the Lionel Company and its competitors, did more, however. It strengthened father-son relationships, taught boys something of electricity, geometry, and mechanics, and prepared teenagers for responsible positions in the industrial world. "Many hundreds of boys who were Lionel fans years ago are today occupying positions of importance on the great railroad systems of the country, helped forward by what they learned as boys through the operation of their Lionel trains," the catalogue announces in a section entitled "Unlimited Fun for Dad and His Son."[20] The boy who studied Channing's history textbook might come home from school to engage in a hobby as important to his education as anything acquired in class. He could be both locomotive engineer and civil engineer; he could design a right-of-way and operate trains over it. He could familiarize himself with the systems engineering of the future.

The toy train companies sold hundreds of thousands of sets comprised of a train, oval of track, and power transformer, and at least several hundred thousand families erected permanent layouts in cellars or attics. In a long, handsomely illustrated 1932 article, *Fortune Magazine* notes that the Lionel Company's 1931 Christmas sales exceeded all previous records. The article only pretends to recount the financial success of the firm, however. Its real concern lies in describing the toys: "Any man with pretensions to normality knows a lot about toy trains. We may tell him something of their commercial background, but the essence of toy railroading is contained in the nostalgias in his heart." Certainly the full-color illustrations of Lionel trains, stations, switches, and villages reveal the magazine's delight in describing toys it frankly admits fascinate as many grown men as they do boys. "Apparently the toy train is irresistible," concludes the article. "And the moral for economists is clear: there is no depression if your heart is set on owning and landscaping a railroad."[21] For children too poor to afford even the minimum-priced trains sold by the Marx Company, for farm children far from electric lines, the advertisements in *Railroad Stories* and the millions of catalogues mailed gratis kept alive the desire to own a miniature version of the railroad right-of-way, to master the metropolitan corridor.

The 1929 Lionel *Catalogue* hints at the larger significance of the metropolitan corridor, for it depicts not only railroad items, but models of other constituents of the built environment lining the rails. Electricity-generating stations, bridges, suburban houses, and dozens of other items adorn its pages. Such items, advertised as accessories or scenery, enabled a child or adult to locate his toy railroad in the correct larger spatial context. For while the railroad and its glamorous trains formed the spine of the corridor, alongside the tracks evolved a new and unique environment.

Every metropolitan corridor announced novelty. In rural areas, the corridor flaunted agricultural time-keeping; all night, when farm families slept, trains rolled through the electrically lighted darkness. Almost everywhere, except where the latest electric locomotives had replaced steam-driven engines, the corridor smelled not of traditional wood smoke, but of coal smoke. Locomotives, factories, and generating stations burned the modern fuel that suburbanites were only beginning to accept in 1880 but accepted without question by 1925. Corridor structures displayed such new building materials as yellow firebrick, poured concrete, and steel lattice girders, heralding the virtual end of wood-frame building. More than urban areas, the corridor spoke of the power of the new, expert builder, the engineer, the architect, the landscape architect. Democracy ruled little building in the corridor; instead, engineers speaking for private clients directed the siting of factories, the facades of depots, and the planting of station gardens. Unlike cities, which continued to represent bygone ages of traditional building and unplanned development, the corridor announced modernity, planning, and systems engineering.

Every corridor crackled with electric speed. Along the railroad right-of-way appeared first telegraph lines, then telephone wires, and finally electricity transmission wires, some serving railroad dispatching and signal systems—the "remote control" that fascinated children and adults watching signal lights change position or color—and others serving the businesses located along the tracks. Electricity speeded mail trains, the fastest vehicles on earth; electricity timed factory openings, production lines, and furnace grates; electricity powered the trolley cars that sped away from stations into suburbs and rural areas, extending corridor space and time into regions distant from trains. Organized haste, even the comparatively slow haste of the back-country freight train rumbling from town to town, suffused every structure and space of the corridor.

Bank advertising calendar. (Collection of the author)

Magazine cover, 1910. (Courtesy of Harvard College Library)

Passengers in high-speed luxury express trains, and commuters in locals chugging along at forty miles per hour, moved too hastily to realize accurately the new environment through which they rode. While poets, essayists, and filmmakers eventually scrutinized the "view from the train," the corridor received scant attention from those accustomed to walking through cities, suburbs, and rural areas. People walked across the corridor, particularly when roads intersected the corridor and the railroad track at its center, but only hoboes walked along it, and the hoboes rarely commented on their observations. Despite its being the most traveled of American environments, the corridor remained the least known, striking most observers as a conglomeration of new spaces and forms seen too quickly for study.

Out of fragmentary sources, therefore, comes this book, an introduction to the metropolitan corridor as a visual image, an introduction to a distinctive American environment scarcely recognized in its prime and today as little frequented as the great urban railroad terminals that mark its ends.

1. GATEWAY

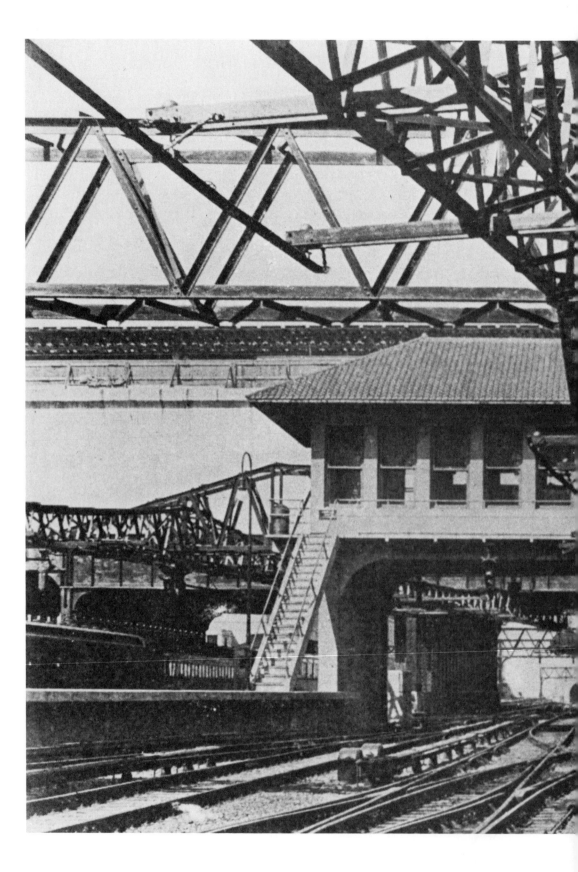

Engineer's view of a terminal-throat signal tower, ca. 1914. (Collection of the author)

❦ISOLATED, WINDSWEPT,

utterly unintelligible to tradition-minded travelers, Manhattan Transfer announced the reach of the twentieth-century urban railroad terminal. Alone in the vast north Jersey marshes, the station served no town, no village. Not even a dirt path connected it with the houses and factories miles away. Essentially several canopy-covered passenger platforms linked by a handful of tiny, brick service structures, it inspired no architectural criticism. But its remarkable and indeed unprecedented function attracted the scrutiny of a nation. "They had to change at Manhattan Transfer," wrote John Dos Passos of two characters in his 1925 novel about life in New York City. "'It's funny this waiting in the wilds of New Jersey this way,'" muses the groom to his bride.[1] Funny perhaps, but to Dos Passos significant. His novel is entitled, simply, almost starkly, *Manhattan Transfer*.

At the turn of the century, the marshes remained an enigma to passengers aboard trains bound for the Hoboken and Jersey City ferry terminals. Approaching New York City from the south and west meant detraining in New Jersey at the edge of the Hudson River, boarding railroad-company ferry boats, and eventually landing at Manhattan piers, a complicated adventure remembered by Edith Wharton in her 1920 novel, *The Age of Innocence*.[2] "It was a sombre snowy afternoon, and the gas-lamps were lit in the big reverberating station," she writes of the Pennsylvania terminus in Jersey City in which a chief character awaits a friend. "As he paced the platform, waiting for the Washington express, he remembered that there were people who thought there would one day be a tunnel under the Hudson through which the trains of the Pennsylvania railway would run straight into New York."[3] Wharton and Dos Passos understood the reorientation wrought in just a few years by the directors of the Pennsylvania Railroad. In the 1920s, passengers crossed the north Jersey marshes anticipating not a time-honored ferry crossing, but an entrance into the future. In the midst of the marshes, at Manhattan Transfer, an age innocent of submarine tunnels, electricity, and systems-designed terminals had encountered a creation almost beyond imagination.

In the last decades of the nineteenth century, Americans learned something of bedlam. Spiraling increases in railroad passenger traffic taxed and

Manhattan Transfer Station, showing Rapid Transit Train New York to Newark, N. J.

MANHATTAN TRANSFER

P-63548

So important was Manhattan Transfer that in 1915 it merited a postcard view of its own.
(Courtesy of the Newark Public Library)

overtaxed urban terminals intended to handle far fewer passengers. In Boston, Cincinnati, Chicago, St. Louis, and particularly in the New York City terminals located on Manhattan Island and the Jersey shore, entering a terminal at almost any hour—especially at the hours newly designated "rush"—meant plunging into chaos.[4] Thousands of passengers jammed ticket windows and waiting rooms and thronged concourses and train platforms; piles of luggage, mail, and express items, perched atop hand-drawn carts, swayed through the multitudes. Above the human and mechanical roar, railroad officials announced trains, offered advice, and attempted to operate trains, switches, and signals. Coal-burning steam locomotives not only added to the racket, but their smoke and steam blasted the hordes scrambling past to coaches and Pullmans and drifted inside waiting rooms to half-choke patrons already nearly insensible from noise. Now and then novelists tried to capture the atmosphere of such crazed places, sometimes detailing their effect on country people arriving in cities, but the chaos defied description.[5] The mad scurrying along dimly lighted corridors and through seeming mazes of booths, gates, news-vendor stands, and doorways gave rise to the expression *rat race*, for at rush hours, the tens of thousands of travelers struck observers as almost feral.

Scurry is perhaps the only word that adequately describes the pace of turn-of-the-century traffic. Continuous jams of drays, carriages, streetcars, and other vehicles slowed transport times, of course, but pedestrians persisted in dashing around such stoppages, and teamsters and coachmen "made time" on back streets, down alleys, and wherever an open vista beckoned.[6] As early as the 1850s, a few far-sighted visionaries saw the potential of traffic development; Frederick Law Olmsted, for example, deliberately designed Central Park drives not only to keep vehicular traffic separate from pedestrians strolling along footpaths, but also to limit the number of vehicles able to use the drives at any one time.[7] By 1900, however, magazine writers inveighed against the scurrying propensity of city dwellers. "Before ten minutes had passed, the old familiar unpleasant sensation of being in a hurry took possession of my mind," lamented Eliot Gregory in a 1900 *Atlantic Monthly* article entitled "A Nation in a Hurry." Gregory recorded the shift in pace as he disembarked from his ocean liner and entered the maelstrom of New York City. "Our transit from dock to hotel was like the visit to a new circle in the Inferno, where trains rumble eternally overhead, and cable-cars glide and block around a pale-faced throng of the 'damned,' who, in expiation of their sins, are driven forever forward, toward an unreachable goal." Suddenly understanding that his European vacation had enabled him to perceive the "curse" of the haste that he had previously taken for granted, Gregory studied the habits of New Yorkers smitten with "rapid transit," rapid eating, and rapid everything else. He scrutinized the dining habits of businessmen in "breathless breakfast" and "quick lunch" establishments, noted

Brooklyn Bridge, quiet at midday, ca. 1906. (Courtesy of Library of Congress)

that one restaurant owner displayed stock-market quotations on a black-board for the benefit of his patrons, and watched New Yorkers scramble aboard streetcars. "The young man who expects to succeed in business must be a hustler, have a snapshot style in conversation, patronize rapid-transit vehicles," and, of course, eat quickly, Gregory noted in an attempt to explain the driving force of the scurry.[8]

Rapid transit appears again and again in magazine articles as the most visible manifestation of urban haste. In 1909, when Edward Hungerford published "The Human Side of a City Railroad" in *Harper's Weekly*, one New York City intersection of three double-track streetcar lines carried six hundred cars in the busiest hour of the day, "ten cars to the minute, a car every six seconds," according to the experts, a "snarl" that reached "about the height of human ingenuity in traffic handling." The master of the intersection, "a stubby little man in a faded uniform," stood in a zone marked by about twelve paving-stones; to step outside it meant the certainty of being struck by a streetcar—to cross the street without much experience and care, and perhaps luck, meant collision with streetcar, automobile, or other vehicle.[9] Henry James blasted such intersections; in *The American Scene* of 1907 he condemned the maiming and death caused by streetcars.[10] But the cars and subway trains sped ever faster, driven by a force summed up in another magazine piece describing the Boston subway system. "It is probably not too large an estimate to assume that on the average each passenger on the Tremont Street route can get to his destination in four minutes less time than was formerly taken upon the surface," gloated George D. Crocker in the 1899 *New England Magazine* article. "As the number of passengers who ride in the subway is about fifty million per year, a saving of four minutes per passenger means a saving of two hundred million minutes, or over three million hours, or three hundred thousand days of ten hours each, or the working hours of a thousand people for a year."[11] The riders of streetcars and subway trains ate quickly, dressed quickly, ran quickly, did business quickly. When streetcar snarls stopped high-speed ground travel, the throngs dashed for subway and elevated trains.[12] The urban public demanded—and usually received—speed in every sort of transportation.

Gregory and other reformers raised their voices against the scurry, but only a few heard and changed their lives. "We are going fast upon our way, we people of the United States," warned a *World's Work* editorial in 1907. "The Pace That Kills" addressed the issue of construction deaths—"every floor of a skyscraper is laid in the blood of a man"—and deaths caused by railroad accidents, but the editors worried about the death of a culture. Americans had discarded traditional agricultural values that prized steady evolution and instead embraced new philosophies of senseless haste.[13] Railroad companies advertised ever faster express trains, limiteds that flirted with collision and derailment every mile of their runs, but passengers wanted to go still faster.[14] "Coming on from Washington the other day, the passengers began to show signs of restlessness near Newark," wrote Gregory of a train approaching the New York City ferries. "By the time Jersey City appeared on the horizon, every man, woman, and child in the car was jammed, baggage in hand, into the stuffy little passage near the entrance, swaying and wobbling about while the train backed and filled."[15] Somehow the passengers thought that such action speeded their journey, although clearly it did not; the ferries left only after all train passengers had boarded. Such frenzy punctuated long-distance passenger-train travel, but it characterized commuter travel.

In the years between 1880 and 1930, hundreds of thousands of Americans moved to suburbs. According to a vast outpouring of magazine articles, the movement freed wives and children from all the unhealthful aspects of urban life, including the pace that killed spirit if not body.[16] Of course, the men lived an even wilder existence, commuting back and forth on crowded trains leaving from ever more crowded terminals. In their mad desire to escape city scurry, families moving to "the country" increased the scurry almost beyond measure. One hundred thousand passengers, mostly commuters, used Boston's South Station every workday; a greater number thronged the Oakland Pier Terminal serving San Francisco. Every twenty-four hours, 779 trains served South Station; 1200 served Oakland Pier. Most of the trains arrived and departed at rush hour.[17] No wonder that articles on improvements in terminals appeared so frequently in suburb-oriented magazines like *House and Garden*.[18] Every improvement meant a more orderly, more efficient scurry, a smoother arrival in the morning and a quicker getaway in the evening.[19] Commuters and long-distance passengers alike welcomed these improvements as the cure for congestion.

Urban congestion preoccupied American reformers, many of whom discovered in railroad terminals instances of chaos equaled—perhaps—only by the mass crowding of New Yorkers crossing Brooklyn Bridge at the end of a workday.[20] Dislike of the congestion in terminals originated partly in the national love of "shaving time," but also in the developing affection for systematized "steady-flow" movement. Manufacturers, engineers, and other experts understood steady flow to be a process in which machines, items, or even people moved through space in an orderly fashion.[21] Certainly a well-regulated railroad line exhibited such a flow, with its impeccably spaced trains following one another on schedule according to rules. The slaughtering of steers and pigs in the Chicago stockyards demonstrated the systematic meat packing that eventually produced the humming assembly line located in a vast, one-story factory.[22] Engineers gradually perceived traffic congestion in mechanical terms and began to make known their vision of the crisis besetting so many cities. Of the turmoil at Brooklyn Bridge, for example, Henry Harrison Suplee, in a 1908 article in the engineering periodical *Cassier's*

Magazine, could speak only in steady-flow terminology, noting that the crowd masses at the "contracted entrance to the bridge, crowding and struggling to reach the cars and behaving much the same as we may imagine particles of some fluid must do when compelled to pass through a sudden contraction in a channel." Suplee embroiders his analogy by explaining the channeling of steam in a powerhouse, noting the effect of forcing steam from a large pipe "into a contracted pipe of far less cross section."[23] In the typical urban terminal, Suplee and other engineers found a perfect demonstration of "artificial congestion," and they argued that only engineers could unravel the tangled streams of vehicular and pedestrian traffic, "providing every means possible for the continuous flow of the human elements of which the crowds are composed."[24] In the mind of the systems engineer, people are only the human elements of a complicated equation involving space and structure.

Scurrying passengers, reformers, and engineers agreed on one definition of *terminal*. The word denoted three intimately related but distinct places: the railroad yard and approach to the station, the train shed under which people entered and left stopped trains, and the head house or "terminal building," containing waiting and baggage rooms, shops and shoeshine parlors, offices and newspaper vendors. Solving the congestion problem—speeding the scurry—necessitated systematizing all three places.

Railroad yards entranced turn-of-the-century Americans, particularly those able to watch their operation from hillsides or bridges. Popular railroad fiction emphasized their layout and function, as well as their romantic appearance. "The way freight, like a snail, dragged past him, opening, as it were, a panorama of the scene in the yard," wrote Frank Packard in *The Wire Devils*, a 1918 novel. "The low switch lights, red, green, purple, and white, like myriad and variegated fireflies hovering everywhere over the ground; the bobbing lantern of a yardman here and there; the dancing gleam of a headlight, as the little yard engine shot fussily away from a string of lighted coaches—the Eastern Express—which it had evidently just made up and backed down on the main line beside the station."[25] A small yard, far from a large city, easily prompted such impressionistic rendering in railroad fiction, but urban terminal yards evoked similar lines from authors only slightly intrigued by railroading. William Dean Howells, for example, described the spectacle of the Grand Central Terminal yards; the characters in his 1890 novel, *A Hazard of New Fortunes*, look over the yards from a stopped elevated train and wonder at "the flare and tremor of the innumerable lights" and "the coming and going of the trains."[26] The spectacle of the terminal yard, especially at night, entranced almost all but the most jaded onlookers. In her 1912 autobiography of her immigration to America and life in the Jewish ghetto of Boston, for example, Mary Antin recalled evening walks to a street bridging the South Station yards and approaches. "I liked to stand leaning on the bridge railing, and look down on the dim tangle of railroad

Railroad yard, Louisville, ca. 1920. (Caufield and Shook Collection, University of Louisville Photographic Archives)

Yardman, semaphore signals, and yard, 1907. (From Oakley, "In the Railway Yard," collection of the author)

Mary Antin's South Station terminal yards at dusk. (Courtesy of Harvard College Library)

tracks below," she writes of her girlhood quest for a place free of tenement-house confusion and foul air. "I was fascinated by the dotted lights, the significant red and green of signal lamps." For Antin, the terminal yard represented the complexities of American life and the range of options open to a young woman of determination. She likened herself to a locomotive departing the terminal yard: "So would I be, swift on my rightful business, picking out my proper track from the million that cross it, pausing for no obstacles, sure of my goal."[27] From above at least, the terminal yard represented the most ordered of scurries.

Only a rare writer attempted to describe completely and explain such yards to lay readers. For most, the task seemed impossible by reason of its very complexity; impressionistic description commonly sufficed. For Olin J. Ross, however, who equated the great terminal yards of Columbus, Ohio, with the grandeur and potential magnificence of his city, honor required encyclopedic description. Ross doubted that an artist could properly paint "a great switchyard after night," although if he could, he would have "a picture of wonderfully thrilling power and beauty." Antin perhaps shared his concept; a crisp nighttime photograph of the South Station yards illustrates her autobiography. But Ross tried painting with prose, describing in minutest detail the "acres and acres, hundreds and hundreds of acres of steel rails" guarded by signal lights and crossed by scores of locomotives and trains. "As seen from the passenger station at Columbus," the rail yards present "a veritable panorama of color" accessible to anyone willing to walk along the balcony of the terminal building or across the bridges carrying city streets over the rails.[28] While his long description includes mention of many constituents of the terminal yard, Ross knew that most American travelers understood the general layout of such places, and his *Sky Blue* devotes scant space to elementary definition.

A typical terminal yard and approach acted as an hourglass-shaped machine. Passengers boarding stopped trains beneath the huge arched train sheds saw ten or even twenty passenger trains, each on its own track, awaiting or discharging passengers. When their train left the platform it crossed seemingly innumerable switches to the "throat" of the yard, the "approach" of two or three mainline tracks guarded by switchmen peering out from a two-story control tower. The switchmen controlled the throat; from their tower they channelled any incoming train onto any platform track and directed any outbound train onto the correct track away from the city. But after the train passed through the throat, attentive passengers found themselves surrounded by hundreds of other tracks, most filled with stopped trains. The tracks comprised the "staging yard," in which empty trains waited before being backed into the train shed, and in which trains just emptied of passengers arrived for servicing. At rush hour, the typical throat exemplified the congestion that maddened passengers and challenged engineers. Train

The turn-of-the-century Grand Central
Terminal at which Howells and so many
other observers wondered; by 1915,
everything in this view from tracks to
headhouse to steam locomotives had been
replaced by the "new" Grand Central
Terminal, the model underground, efficient,
all-electric urban station. (Courtesy of New
York Central System, collection of the author)

Otto Kuhler's "Playground for Trains,"
a vision of a remembered terminal yard.
(Courtesy of Museum of New Mexico)

after train, many filled with passengers, many empty, passed over the switches, awing young girls like Antin and seasoned novelists like Howells.[29] Maintaining a steady flow of trains through the constriction required the utmost precision; engineers and switchmen cooperated intimately, but delays became ever more frequent.[30] By 1900, the typical terminal yard represented the site of the most vexing traffic snarls imaginable. Commuter trains "fouled" long-distance luxury limiteds, switching locomotives blundered in front of empty trains backing out of platform tracks, and the constantly delayed steam locomotives filled train sheds and urban air with acrid, cindery coal smoke.[31]

Reformers, urban designers, railroad boards of directors, and systems engineers agreed that improving the flow of trains through terminal yards meant the first vital step toward lessening the congestion of human traffic in the head houses and train sheds. Not only would such improvement speed passenger travel; it would enable smaller terminal buildings to accommodate more passengers, and it would abate the "smoke nuisance." In the first years of the century, engineers and farsighted railroad corporations united in two great public improvement projects in the very heart of New York City. Pennsylvania Station and Grand Central Terminal rose as monuments to steady-flow design and to the wonder-working architectural power of electricity.[32]

Both the Pennsylvania and New York Central companies confronted nearly identical problems in their New York passenger operations. The Jersey City terminal of the Pennsylvania, accessible from New York only by ferry, and the downtown terminal of the Central carried far more train traffic than their designers had intended, and the locomotives of the Central polluted dozens of city blocks with smoke and noise. The two firms intended to alleviate their difficulties by building new structures based on the latest theories of systems engineering and powered by electricity. While other companies erected skyscrapers, the two railroad firms dug far beneath city streets.

Essentially, engineers eliminated the stub-ended terminal tracks. The Pennsylvania engineers designed a great underground station of through tracks; trains inbound from New Jersey through the twin tunnels beneath the Hudson River arrived at the new station, discharged passengers, and passed through more tunnels to a staging yard located on Long Island. While the Central designers retained some stub-ended platform tracks for long-distance trains, they provided an underground two-level boarding area. Long-distance trains used the upper-level stub-ended tracks; commuter trains operated on loop tracks on the lower level.[33] Following the precedent set by the Pennsylvania designers, the engineers employed by the Central located staging yards miles distant from the platform tracks. Underground boarding areas and electrically powered trains eliminated the need of arched train sheds; instead of canopies of glass and steel, the designers retained by both firms placed the terminal buildings over the tracks. The Central board of directors immediately recognized the economic advantages in having a large acreage for sale in downtown

New York, and it quickly sold the "air rights" to developers anxious to build hotels and other large structures over the underlying tracks.[34] Despite the expense involved, the two railroad companies almost totally resolved the problem of terminal-yard congestion and provided prototypical terminals for Cleveland, Cincinnati, St. Louis, Chicago, and other cities.[35]

Electricity made possible both New York terminals, for both depended on trains operating underground in lengthy tunnels, something impossible with coal-burning locomotives.[36] Not only did steam locomotives half-choke passengers riding in the cars behind them; the smoky tunnels leading away from New York City terminals proved accident-prone simply because engineers could see neither signals nor trains ahead.[37] In the last years of the nineteenth century, electrical engineers published scores of articles concerning the propulsion of trains across mountain ranges and through tunnels; gradually they convinced railroad officials that electric locomotives, called "motors" by the engineers and eventually by their crews, provided more horsepower, required fewer repairs, made far less noise, and cost far less to operate than steam locomotives.[38] Reliable, swift, smooth-running electric locomotives created a wholly new sort of place.

Erecting the electrified third rail and overhead power wires cost immense sums, and no railroad company could afford to electrify its entire trackage. Both the New York Central and the New York, New Haven, and Hartford companies, the joint operators of Grand Central Terminal, electrified their lines as far as Harmon, New York, and New Haven, Connecticut; the Pennsylvania company initially electrified its tracks from the Sunnyside staging yard on Long Island through the new Pennsylvania Station and Hudson River tunnels to a spot in the northern New Jersey marshes that had no name.[39] At Harmon, New Haven, and the newly named Manhattan Transfer, the tentacles of twentieth-century technological power reached nineteenth-century steam locomotives.[40] As late as 1901, the *American Architect* had editorialized that "the Hackensack meadows afford a clear field for the designing and development of a system unrivalled by anything of the kind in the world, directly connected with all the railroads centering in New York" and had suggested building a deep-water port facility akin to those of Southampton, Hamburg, and other European cities.[41] When the Pennsylvania opened its terminal, tunnels, and new station-in-the-marsh nine years later, it made obsolete the thinking of the *American Architect* editors and the viewpoint of hundreds of urban reformers. A simple, four-track, open-air station permitted two sorts of transfer. Passengers could change between long-distance trains and the electric trains of the Hudson and Manhattan Railroad Company, which operated through other tunnels to a commuter station at the tip of Manhattan Island; sometimes the change involved a brief waiting period, as Dos Passos describes in *Manhattan Transfer*.[42] More important, all trains changed locomotives; electric motors pulled trains between the terminal and the outdoor

Electric locomotive under catenary, west of New Haven. (Courtesy of Smithsonian Institution)

Pennsylvania Railroad train emerging from Hudson River tunnels en route to Manhattan Transfer. (Courtesy of Smithsonian Institution)

George Bellows painted "Pennsylvania Station Excavation" in 1909.
(Courtesy of The Brooklyn Museum, A. Augustus Healy Fund B)

station, and steam locomotives provided motive power beyond. Manhattan Transfer spelled the doom of the Jersey City and Hoboken terminals still relying on ferry boats; other railroad companies continued to use them, but Pennsylvania service to the south and west, so much more convenient and swift, lessened traffic on the ferries owned by the Baltimore and Ohio, Erie, and other companies.[43] It spelled the doom of vast harbor-improvement schemes, too; the little station epitomizing electric-powered steady flow did the work of much larger, oldfashioned complexes of space and structure. No longer did approaching New York City from the south or west necessarily include a termination characterized by scurry, congestion, and ferries. Instead of crowding vestibules at Newark, passengers remained seated past Manhattan Transfer, into the long tunnels, all the way to the platforms awaiting them.

At Harmon and New Haven, inbound passengers watched silent electric motors replace gigantic steam locomotives. The massive electric machines announced the fringe of the terminal zone, a fringe marked also by the appearance of overhead electric wires strung along the tracks, or the elevated "third rail" also charged with current. *Scientific American* and other popular magazines stressed the electric future of railroading, calling attention to the mountain-line electrification projects of the Virginian and Milwaukee Road companies and forecasting the eventual electrification of most trunk lines.[44] The Lionel Company rushed into production several model electric motors that competed strongly with its toy steam locomotives, and other firms manufacturing toy railroad equipment quickly followed.[45]

More than any other structures built in the years between 1880 and 1930, certainly more than skyscrapers, Pennsylvania Station and Grand Central Terminal epitomized the quest for high-speed, steady-flow efficiency, and more than any other structures they captured the public imagination.[46] The *New York Times* marked the opening of Grand Central Terminal with an entire section of its Sunday issue. Every article stresses the extraordinary efficiency of the terminal complex, "through which the entire population of the United States could pass in a single year without crowding and without confusion."[47] Reporters delighted in describing the specially built "kissing galleries" where lovers could greet or part; they marveled at the dressing rooms provided for businessmen who wanted to change into evening clothes before meeting their wives arriving for nighttime entertainment, at the bathtubs and other amenities offered to long-distance passengers, at the "hair dressing parlor," at the women's bootblack room, at the men's barbershop, at the "handsomely appointed restaurant," at the shops lining the "arcade," and at the marvelously efficient post office building integrated into the station.[48] Prompted by the stream of articles in mass-circulation and professional periodicals, the *Times* reporters knew what features deserved special mention. They focused on the ramps leading from one level to another and concluded that "to all intent and purposes it is stairless," the product of prolonged studies involving the effect

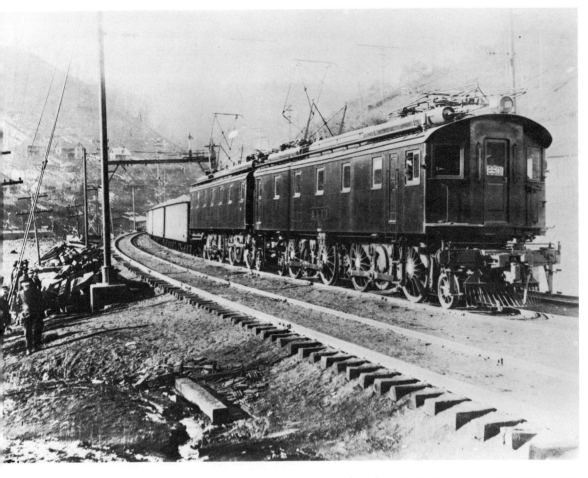

Electric locomotive in the mountains of Virginia, ca. 1917.
(Courtesy of Smithsonian Institution)

of stairs on pedestrian flow.[49] "One of the most conspicuous features of the terminal plans was the obvious effort to systematize every activity with which henceforth it will be astir," noted one reporter, who realized that "every activity" included such seemingly insignificant actions as reading signs.[50] The lettering of Grand Central signs, designed to be intelligible to rapidly striding passengers, represented one tiny element in the attempt "to build a great terminal with the twentieth-century idea of efficiency checking every step."[51] Other reporters fanned out to examine the "yawning train yards," the signal tower—"the central nerve point, the brain of the terminal"—that controlled the throat, and the train loops intended "to save time and friction."[52] Electricity, reported the *Times*, was the key to the entire terminal: "The rock-bottom fact of the entire enterprise is the electric motor, powerful, swift, silent, and clean." The wonder-working marvel of electricity appears frequently in articles describing locomotives, signal systems, and baggage handlers. "All this terminal city," remarked one reporter, "was made possible by the installation of the electric motor."[53] In the view of the *New York Times*, Grand Central existed not only as a gateway to the nation and—for inbound passengers—to the city, but as the model of the future city, not the city beautiful (although its "romanesque" architecture delighted reviewers), but the city efficient.[54]

Magazine writers joined the newspaper reporters in praising Grand Central Terminal and Pennsylvania Station as exemplars of railroad-industry efficiency.[55] Certainly writers for *Railroad Gazette* and other industry journals lavished attention on the monumental projects, as did experts writing for such construction-industry journals as *Engineering Record*.[56] They emphasized such details as the tracks laid on felt packing and creosoted pine blocks to reduce noise, the "special supply of ozonated water for drinking and culinary purposes," the heating and lighting plant and electrical sub-station, and the signal systems. Writers in *Scientific American* presented the same detailed, technical information to the general public, again emphasizing design solutions to traffic congestion. Reporters in Grand Central examined the separation of inbound and outbound passengers, the precise siting of the twelve entrances, the ticket windows, and the waiting rooms, and discovered the importance of segregated functions. The Grand Central engineers segregated inbound from outbound passengers, inbound from outbound baggage, and suburban passengers from long-distance travelers. "Everything, ticket offices, entrances and exits for the express and suburban service, will be entirely distinct and separate, each having its own concourse, its own information bureau, baggage checking places, parcel room, and other facilities for travel," remarked Walter Bernard in a long article subtitled, "How the New Grand Central Station Will Handle, if Need Be, Two Hundred Trains an Hour."[57] And of course the principle of steady flow by segregation extended to the placement of trains on the two levels, in the tunnels, and in the staging yards as well.[58] High-speed efficiency enthralled the *Scientific American* writers; they devoted little atten-

An early 1920s view of Grand Central Terminal. (Collection of the author)

As late as World War II, the great waiting rooms of Grand Central Terminal remained essentially unchanged. (Courtesy of New York Central System, collection of the author)

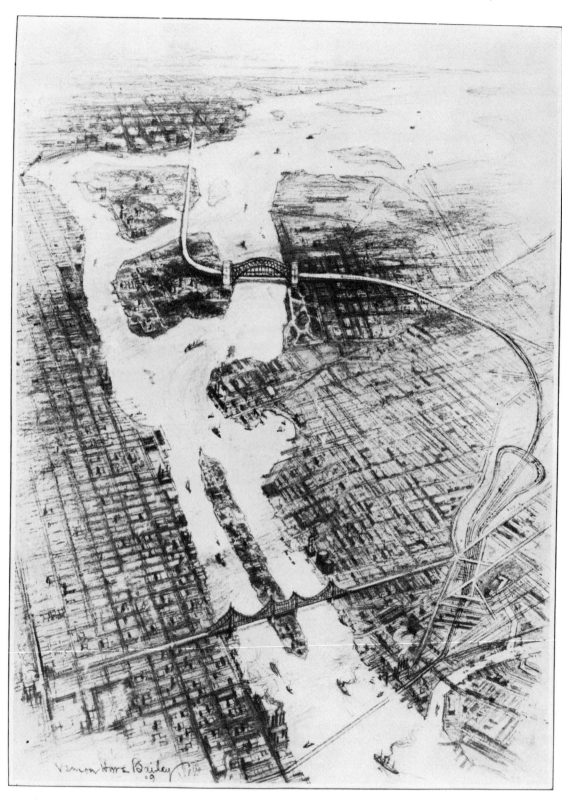

Aerial view of Hell Gate Arch Bridge linking New York City with New England and Canada, 1909.
(From "Linking New England," Harvard College Library)

tion to "architecture." The terminal buildings housing the concourses aroused remarkably little attention in architectural periodicals, perhaps because editors realized how much their architects depended on engineers. In "The Pennsylvania's New York Station," a 1910 *Architectural Record* editorial, the terminal is described as almost gloomy, almost monotonous, and almost too impressive in size.[59] An eerie confusion characterizes the relatively few articles that appeared in architectural publications.[60] Perhaps the writers suspected what journalists employed by railroad, engineering, and technical periodicals implicitly stated. The terminals existed as machines for the efficient moving of people and trains, not as buildings.

At least one city-planning expert perceived the distinction. In a 1911 *Town Planning Review* analysis of Grand Central Terminal, Robert Anderson Pope noted that the heart of the terminal "will never be seen from the street," and that the burying of acres of platform tracks and resultant air-rights development will create "block after block of splendid structures," including "some of the finest apartment houses in the world" along the buried throat under Park Avenue. Unlike the *Architectural Record* editors, Pope knew that the modern terminal represented something more than traditional ideas of structure. "The essence of the idea that runs through all its designing and has been the subject of years of study on the part of the most expert men in America, is this," he concluded. "How to build a station so that John Smith or Mary Jones, who have never been in New York, can arrive at the Grand Central Terminal and pass through it to where he or she is going with the least possible confusion and the utmost tranquility and peace of mind. That is really the ideal that has to be sought after in the construction of a great railway terminal nowadays." In his mind, the terminal existed as an extension of the train, as another sort of people-mover. Passengers "emerge, perhaps, from a highly polished, mahogany-trimmed sleeper," he continued in elaborating his vision. "When they end their journey at the new Grand Central Terminal, they will hardly mark the transition from the elegance of their temporary home on wheels."[61] Implicit in his analysis is a perception of the great urban terminal as an extension of railroad-train engineering, not as a traditional architectural form or even as a modern one like a skyscraper.

Popular writers shared his view. Almost all national magazines carried at least one article describing one or both New York City terminals, and almost invariably the articles emphasized the engineered splendor of the steady-flow machines.[62] Full-page, handsomely illustrated advertisements paid for by railroad companies, electrical equipment manufacturers, and other firms rammed home the engineering viewpoint so clearly expressed by a wide range of authors.[63] Again and again, writers called the terminals "gateways" or "gates" and found in them a wonderfully intricate life.[64]

"The Greatest Railway Terminal in the World," an *Outlook* article of late 1912 describing Grand Central Terminal, exemplifies the popular article stressing

Warren & Wetmore
Architects

THE TERMINAL CITY

THE GREATEST CIVIC DEVELOPMENT EVER UNDERTAKEN—INCIDENT TO THE
NEW GRAND CENTRAL TERMINAL IN NEW YORK CITY, WHICH WILL BE

OPENED FEBRUARY, 1913

This vast undertaking comprehends the erection of a great Terminal City, a city within a city, occupying an area of thirty blocks, in New York City.

It will embrace hotels and modern apartment houses, convention and exhibition halls, clubs and restaurants, and department stores and specialty shops. In short, practically every sort of structure or enterprise incident to the modern city.

These features are all in addition to post office, express buildings and other natural adjuncts of the up-to-date terminal—to expeditiously handle diverse traffic.

All these structures will be erected over the tracks about the terminal itself, while a plaza will surround the Terminal building, reached on the North and South by a new Boulevard, hiding all trace of the railroad yard.

THE NEWLY COMPLETED
GRAND CENTRAL TERMINAL

Will provide every detail essential to the comfort and convenience of its patrons. The Terminal itself is the physical embodiment of the latest and the highest ideal of service. Its adequate description is impossible here. It must be seen to be fully appreciated—or indeed to be completely comprehended.

The Main Terminal alone is 722 feet long and 301 feet wide on the surface, and half again as wide below the street level. It will accommodate comfortably 30,000 people at one time.

Through and suburban service occupy different levels approached by inclines, avoiding stairways, so that each level may be reached without confusion. Incoming and outgoing traffic is segregated and the two currents of travel separated. Every facility is progressively arranged so that no step need be retraced, no time lost.

There are 42 tracks for through travel and 25 tracks for local trains, 33 miles in all, within the Terminal, accommodating over 1000 cars at one time. Dedicated to the Public Service, February, 1913.

New York Central System advertisement for Grand Central Terminal. (Collection of the author)

the engineering of motion. "Out of seeming confusion there was underlying system, the sort of system which moves unseen and accomplishes much," writes Edward Hungerford of the construction operation. "The problem of the new Grand Central was both engineering and architectural," he continues in his careful analysis of the construction decisions. "As in the case of all railway terminals of any real size, it was first necessary to solve the engineering problem." A large part of the design process involved anticipating the growth of passenger traffic until the year 1960, segregating one sort of traffic from another, and employing the latest electrical technology. "There are some pretty big indirect benefits to be charged to the coming of electricity," Hungerford determines; the great Grand Central "civic center," a place of "size, economy, efficiency, beauty—the result in steel and stone and concrete of years of hard thinking by competent engineers and architects," is a creation announcing the engineering marvels of the dawning electrical age. Every movement of traveler, suitcase, mail pouch, locomotive, and employee is somehow channeled, somehow engineered. In the "thirty acres of basement," electricity signals the operation of every train, operation timed to the second. "That precision of the thirteenth second is the precision of the greatest railway station in the world," Hungerford concludes after describing an electric locomotive passing a signal exactly thirteen seconds after leaving its platform. "It is the thing that keeps its operation through the nightly strain of the evening rush hour from being an unmannerly chaos that would be a tangle of hours."[65] The *Outlook* article and many others glory in the engineering marvels everywhere in the terminal, delighting even in new types of electric push-buttons.

Other authors looked more closely at the human element. "The Gates of the City" in *Century Magazine* represents the second sort of article appearing in national mass-circulation magazines after the turn of the century. Jesse Lynch Williams describes the human activity in smallest detail; his illustrator, Orson Lowell, captures it in sketches, not in the photographs so dear to the engineering-smitten observers. Williams catalogues the people passing along the concourses, recording the young woman with two dogs, "the herds of steerage passengers being shunted like cattle into long immigrant trains," "'fresh air' children," athletes, invalids, and commuters. Williams devotes much space to commuters, who "acquire in time a similarity of expression as they pass in and out through the gates," who have "an air of accustomedness to their surroundings, quite as if the station were their familiar club." The commuters use all the terminal services accurately; when they shop at lunchtime, they direct stores to deliver purchases to the parcel room and on their way home pick up the boxes. They eat hurried breakfasts in the restaurants, lease umbrellas on a rainy day or check their raincoats on a suddenly sunny morning, and rendezvous at the telephone booths. So familiar are they with the brilliantly designed terminal pathways that they stride along reading their newspapers, sure that they will flow toward the proper train or proper exit. Others less familiar with the terminal nevertheless usually find their way. Williams describes the late-night theater-going groups taking the last trains home to the suburbs, "the men, with overcoats buttoned up to their chins, striding ahead and fumbling for tickets, the women, holding on to their hats, their high heels clicking on the mosaic floors as they make haste in the interesting feminine way, arousing the sleepy ones waiting for an early morning express." He scrutinizes the impoverished derelicts and the "women adrift, but not yet foundered," who seek warmth on a winter night. He watches the young unmarried couples miss the last trains to the suburbs. "When this thing happens to a solitary couple, unmarried, unchaperoned, and unacquainted in the midnight city," he concludes, "it is a tragic moment as they turn and look at each other, wondering what to do about it."[66] Williams and Lowell wandered about the great terminals, watching, making notes, and sketching. Implicit in their final analysis is a vision of the future American city, a place where all ethnic groups, all social classes, all ages live graciously because of engineering. In a perfectly designed city, so many problems beyond congestion might melt away.

Year after year, authors drifted into the terminals to find "material," to see a new locomotive, to witness the christening of a new train like *The Twentieth Century Limited* or *The Broadway Limited*, or to see humans in organized motion. Franklin Snow's *Christian Science Monitor* article of November 1, 1928, typifies the newspaper filler story; "A Day at Grand Central Terminal" traces the scenes of an ordinary day, recording the telegraph clicking, morning arrivals, departures of limited trains for the Middle West and Canada, the changing train-board signs, flowers arriving for observation cars, the great red carpet being rolled out for passengers boarding *The Twentieth Century Limited*, the evening commuter departure, the illuminating of the lights in the concourse domed ceiling that provides a twinkling representation of the night sky, the appearance of Pullman Company representatives to usher late-night travelers into the proper sleeping cars, the leaving of *The Owl* and other wee-hour expresses, the steady flow of some 100,000 passengers and another 100,000 visitors to the shops, restaurants, and other attractions.[67] Such articles explained to the nation the wonderful ends of the metropolitan corridor, the perfectly engineered terminals of perfect efficiency, structures of movement as elegant as any fast luxury train.

Entering the great terminal buildings meant stepping into the metropolitan corridor away from urban scurry and congestion. It meant experiencing the precise flowing motion of electric propulsion outward to Harmon or New Haven or Manhattan Transfer and of electrically signaled motion to the uttermost reaches of the nation. It meant exposure to what one *Atlantic Monthly* writer of 1900 called "the poetry of the machine age." Gerald Stanley Lee perceived the force of the corridor ordered about the spine of the railroad. "Inspiration shall be looked for more in engine cabs than in pulpits,—the vestibule trains shall say deeper things than sermons say," he grudgingly admitted. "In the rhythm of the anthem of them, singing along the rails, we shall find again the worship we have lost in church."[68] In the terminal, from its doors to its concourse, from platform to throat to yards, precise flowing movement spoke of new forces capable of entrancing the human spirit, of the future, of ages of organized human and mechanical energy rising to the height of poetry.

And the magic of the terminals swept out into the nation, carried by the almost magical trains, *The Twentieth-Century Limited*, *The Wolverine*, *The Lake Shore Limited*, *The Cleveland Limited*, *The Empire State Express*, *The Broadway Limited*, *The Owl*, and scores of others, all announcing the engineered future.[69]

Timetable as advertisement for electric locomotives.
(Collection of the author)

2: ELEGANCE

The Sunset Limited *operating between New Orleans and Los Angeles, ca. 1910. (Collection of the author)*

AT THE HEART OF THE 1929
Lionel *Catalogue* glistened the fabulous *Transcontinental Limited*, pictured in four colors on a fold-out page thirty-four inches long. A jewel-like toy modeled upon the nation's finest express trains, the *Limited* stretched nine feet from the tip of its massive headlight and classification light-equipped locomotive over four Pullman cars to its ornate observation platform. "Viewing this splendid train from the rear end you can easily imagine yourself looking at a real observation platform," begins the paragraph describing the last car. "The observation platform is enclosed in an ornamental polished brass railing, while the electric dome light (in addition to the two interior lights) adds brilliance to the general effect."[1] At $110, "Outfit No. 411E"—the "E" signified extra features—sold for more than many used automobiles, but its splendor made it seem inexpensive, at least in the eyes of boys. Such a toy, rolling gracefully around its long oval of track in a small-town store window or in the Lionel showroom in New York City, spoke to a generation of boys as loudly as it spoke to a generation of grown men.

It spoke of *the* American experience of travel, the experience captured in novels such as *The Great Gatsby*. F. Scott Fitzgerald wrote lovingly of train travel, recalling "the old dim Union Station at six o'clock of a December evening," "the long green tickets clasped tight in our gloved hands," and "the murky yellow cars of the Chicago, Milwaukee & St. Paul railroad looking cheerful as Christmas itself on the tracks beside the gate." In 1925, Fitzgerald's readers understood the powerful significance of train travel. If they had not ridden the fast expresses on which Lionel modeled *The Transcontinental Limited*, they had seen them pass. "That's my Middle West—not the wheat or the prairies or the lost Swede towns, but the thrilling returning trains of my youth," Fitzgerald continued, "and the street lamps and sleigh bells in the frosty dark and shadows of holly wreaths thrown by lighted windows on the snow."[2] American travelers knew two landscapes, the one beyond the train windows and the one comprised only of the train itself; American bystanders knew two landscapes also, one without crack trains and one interrupted intermittently and fleetingly by handsome conveyances racing between cities.[3] Only a rare boy—or rarer girl—awoke on Christmas morning to find *The Transcontinental Limited*, but hundreds of thousands found less expensive electric trains.

And they fell asleep after looking at the lighted locomotives and cars circling and circling in darkened rooms, recreating in miniature the landscape and the vehicle of American traveling romance. All the excitement, all the emotional charge of a real train in a real landscape, all the promise of adventure recalled by Fitzgerald emanates from the gleaming toy whizzing in an oval path laid across the floor, its Pullmans or caboose shining brightly, its headlight gleaming on the polished steel rails ahead. In its enameled paint and buffered brass every child grasped something of the elegance of named equipage.

Named components of named trains, Pullman parlor cars and sleepers trailed baggage, post office, and express cars, gently swaying on the long tangents, heeling slightly on the curves embraced at ninety miles an hour. Nearly ten thousand such cars rode American rails in 1930, almost all in such luxury trains as *The Oriental Limited*, *The Crescent Limited*, *The Orange Blossom Special*, *The Black Diamond*.[4] Above its row of wide windows, each Pullman car displayed the name of its owner, the Pullman Company, and sometimes the name of the railroad company leasing it. Below, in gold-leaf letters less bold, it announced its individual name. By day and by night, *Eventide*, *Nocturne*, *Clover Bluff*, *Shenandoah*, *Brandywine*, and thousands more soothed passengers and awed trackside spectators. Not every Pullman car gleamed dully in "Pullman green" and gold leaf. The firm leased cars painted in a variety of colors designed to suit railroad companies determined to operate extra-fare trains that were instantly recognizable, even from distant vantage points. The Pennsylvania Railroad insisted on tuscan red for all its passenger equipment, and the Milwaukee Road on the pale yellow remembered by Fitzgerald.[5] Only the Southern's crack *Crescent Limited* stood out in a bright Kelley green, however. But Pullman green remained the most common color, chiefly because the Pullman cars moved regularly from one railroad to another according to seasonal traffic fluctuations. After the holiday crush of Thanksgiving and Christmas, a Pullman sleeper would be shifted from the New York Central to handle tourist traffic on the Baltimore and Ohio or Southern Pacific. So the Pullman Company and the railroads agreed that most first-class trains should be painted in a standard color, and, as decades passed, Pullman green came to identify high-speed luxury. First-class passengers expected the absolute best from the sleeping cars, dining cars, club cars, and observation cars carrying the livery of the largest hotel corporation in the world, the Pullman Company.

Fierce competition for first-class passengers forced most companies into a nation-wide race for luxury equipment and service. Speed and ticket prices meant less to many potential riders than the dining car menu, the firmness of the mattress, and the decor of the car interiors. Middle- and upper-class Americans envisioned long-distance, luxury-class train travel as they did ocean passages. "There is leisure here, of body and spirit, leisure and charm and quiet thoughtful comfort, against the beautiful background of those soft gray-green cars," wrote Katherine Woods in 1927 of *The Broadway Limited*, a train that

A 1906 photograph of The Royal Limited *shows the typical positioning of train and camera favored by photographers of the corridor.*
(Collection of the author)

boasted a handsomely appointed bridal compartment, as well as "the sense of the journey's being a delightful personal event, that marks one's departure on any of the most beautiful of the ocean liners."[6] As it had for several decades, the ocean liner of 1927 represented, for its first-class passengers, the epitome of modern design. New materials, electric lights, elevators, communication equipment, air-circulation machinery, and a developing smoothness of corners and surfaces convinced many ocean travelers that the great steamship presaged changes in urban design.[7] The efficiency of the liner, a product of tremendously powerful engines, electrically communicated orders, and strictly disciplined crews, became a model of the perfect urban environment, one as smoothly functioning as anything envisioned in the utopian novels of the early twentieth century.[8] And as Katherine Woods discerned, the great luxury trains shared the public respect. Between 1890 and 1940, boarding a first-class train meant entering into a fantastical world.

First-class passengers encountered several sorts of fantasy, all mixed together and impossible to separate. Certainly luxury created its own fantasy world. Anyone who could afford a ticket stepped into a world filled with servants intent on pampering. In the club car stewards brought drinks to the passengers nestled in revolving chairs set before plate glass windows. In the observation car attendants distributed magazines and books and the latest newspapers, collected postcards and letters written on the engraved stationery supplied gratis, and carried tea to loungers on the observation platform. In the sleeping cars porters shined shoes, made up beds, brought coffee in the morning, and carried luggage. Long-distance trains carried barbers, ladies' maids, and secretaries. The servants, most black and almost all out of their youth (positions on the luxury trains fell only to senior employees of the Pullman Company and of the railroad firms), catered to passenger whims with professional grace.[9] Whatever their true feelings about harried businessmen, demanding widows, children, and splurging honeymooners, their constant care pleased almost everyone, even Europeans accustomed to the great trains of the Continent. Despite the difficulties of hiring "help" in turn-of-the-century American households, despite the growing unrest of so many industrial and agricultural workers, the Pullman Company succeeded in convincing its "guests" that its employees delighted in serving.

Passengers and servants enjoyed a world of fine wood, excellent upholstery, and polished metal. First-class cars exhibited state-of-the-art construction materials and methods. Indirect lighting illuminated the ornately carpeted floors, brass fittings glistened against mahogany tables, and electric fans circulated the air. Each decade provided improvements; electric lights replaced gas illumination, vestibules and elastic diaphragms enclosed the gaps between cars, cooled air replaced circulated air, and eventually showers and bathtubs, gymnasium equipment, radios, and even—on a 1933 Seaboard Air Line deluxe train—a swimming pool appeared to please passengers.[10] On a first-class train, one rode in almost fairytale luxury, or at least in the half-remembered, half-imagined luxury of the antebellum South.

Dining cars exhibited the best mix of lavish decor and perfect service. Woods delighted in the "beautiful dining-car whose gray-green walls are broken by panels of dark green and decorated with a design echoed again in the carpet of the car," but the menu and service pleased her more.[11] The Pullman Company operated few dining cars after its initial experiments; providing delicious food and magnificent service proved absolutely profitless, and individual railroad companies took over the enterprise, happy if they earned fifty cents on every dollar expended. To attract passengers away from competing lines, railroads swallowed their food-service losses and specialized in gastronomical delicacies. Most companies advertised cuisine native to their particular regions. The Northern Pacific featured grouse and salmon, the Union Pacific offered antelope steak, the New York, New Haven, and Hartford specialized in boiled Maine lobster, haddock, and Cotuit oysters, the Baltimore and Ohio emphasized terrapin stew, and the Reading offered scrapple.[12] Long-distance passengers often chose trains according to dining car offerings, and companies like the Chicago and Northwestern, trying to wrest traffic from more established lines, attempted to please the simplest and the most discriminating of palates. The Northwestern luxury train, *The Columbine*, offered an array of delicacies ranging from lyonnaise potatoes to asparagus vinaigrette to ox tongue to sirloin steak while passing through High Plains farm country known for simple, forthright cooking. A Northwestern competitor, the Chicago, Burlington, and Quincy Railroad Company, countered by ordering new cars built by Pullman. "The model for the arrangement and furnishings is the Vienna rooms of high-class German restaurants," reported *Railroad Gazette* in 1906. "A plate rack encircles the car, on which are specimens of ancient ware and steins." Paneled in English oak, fitted with leather-upholstered chairs, and "lighted by electricity from an axle generating system," the new dining cars represented the fierce competition for passengers.[13] A typical dining-car crew numbered thirteen men and included stewards, waiters, chefs, and busboys, none of whom concerned themselves with the serving of alcoholic beverages, aside from table wines. Except for the Prohibition period, luxury trains included club cars outfitted with stand-up bars and cocktail tables.[14] Often coupled next to the dining cars, the club cars allowed passengers to have a before-dinner drink while waiting for the table they had reserved earlier in the day, and after-dinner drinks as well. Men enjoyed the club cars more than did women, but by the 1920s, railroad companies were learning what steamship companies already knew—women wanted to enjoy after-dinner drinks, too.[15] "No man, within twenty-four hours after eating a meal in a Pennsylvania Railroad dining-car, could conceivably write anything worth reading," harrumphed H. L. Mencken in 1920, but most passengers disagreed with the satirist.[16] For the typical first-class passenger aboard a luxury train, lunching

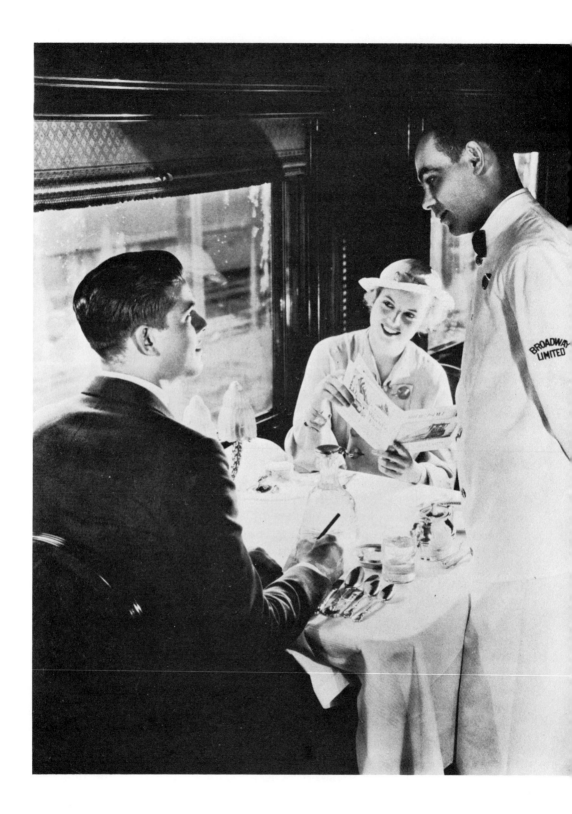

Promotional photograph advertising dinner aboard The Broadway Limited, *ca. 1938.*
(Courtesy of Pennsylvania Railroad Company, collection of the author)

or dining meant savoring luxury comprised of fine surroundings, fine food, and finer service.

Originally, George Pullman called his firm "The Pullman Palace Car Company." To the late-nineteenth-century traveling public, his sleeping cars appeared palatial, and his dining cars, the first of which he named "Delmonico" after the famed New York City restaurant, attracted even greater admiration.[17] His firm prospered and eventually devoured such competitors as the Wagner Car Company, because it made continuous improvements in its cars. After abandoning the operation of dining-cars, the Pullman Company devoted its attention to bettering its fleet of sleeping and observation cars. Not only did it put continuously improved cars into service, but it recalled older cars for refurbishing and even for rebuilding. The Pullman Company advertised its high level of service, but it extolled its "latest" accomplishments. Pressed paper wheels banded with steel for quieter riding, all-steel frames for better safety in collisions (steel-framed first-class cars crushed wood-framed coaches almost every time, and safety-conscious riders could relax more in Pullmans than in second-class cars), and extra-long berths for tall passengers figured in the company's advertisements.[18] Regular riders of luxury trains slowly understood the message in the Pullman Company's improvements. To ride a first-class train was to experience not only the fantasy of luxury, but the fantasy of futurism, too.

Not until the 1930s did corporate rivalry foster extreme strides in industrial design innovation. Late in the decade the New York Central System and the Pennsylvania Railroad Company engaged in a war of streamlining. The Central hired Henry Dreyfuss to redesign *The Twentieth Century Limited*, and the Pennsylvania retained Raymond Loewy to create a new *Broadway Limited*.[19] The spectacular results—all built by Pullman—aroused enormous enthusiasm in general-circulation magazines like *Popular Mechanics* and in specialized periodicals like *Modern Plastics* and *Architectural Forum*.[20] In 1938, *Architectural Forum* published a lavishly illustrated article comparing the two trains and emphasizing the extravagance and newness of their design. The "bar lounge car" on *The Twentieth Century Limited* featured copper-colored cork ceilings, rust-colored carpeting, tables with dark gray Formica tops, and Plexiglas bar shelves. An observation car on *The Broadway Limited* presented riders with blue carpeting, bridge tables covered with dark blue Formica, and light blue drapes.[21] Both trains displayed the latest synthetic color harmonizing, interior decoration, and streamlining, and both prompted industrial designers and architects to redesign home appliances and buildings.[22] Passengers weary of Depression-era scruffiness could take either train between New York City and Chicago and escape into a fantasy world of time-to-come streamlined chrome, plastic, synthetic fiber, and coordinated color schemes.[23] They *expected* to find such futuristic fantasy, and they had since George Pullman's earliest successes.

A late 1930s view of the streamlined Twentieth Century Limited. *(Courtesy of New York Central System, collection of the author)*

Fantasies of luxury and futurism enticed Americans long before the 1930s experiments. Not every crack express displayed the same level of equipment and service, of course, and very few matched that of *The Broadway Limited* and *The Twentieth Century Limited*. Most remained at the level attained by *The Overland Limited* and other western trains. But the *Century* and the *Overland* struck millions of Americans, including millions who only read of them in magazine articles, newspaper columns, and travel books, as the environment of the future.[24]

On June 15, 1902, the New York Central System inaugurated twenty-hour through service between New York City and Chicago with the maiden run of an all-new train, advertised as "a century ahead of its time."[25] *The Twentieth Century Limited* had evolved from other New York Central expresses, most notably the experimental *Exposition Flyer* of 1893 and the subsequent *Lake Shore Limited*. The *Flyer* carried thousands of New Yorkers to the Columbian Exposition and seemed to many passengers as magnificent as the fair itself. Its successor, the *Lake Shore*, carried larger, more luxurious cars but remained more or less a transition-era train. Illuminated by both gas and electric lights, for example, its cars represented the Central's hesitation in adopting wholly modern features.[26] By 1902, however, all hesitation had vanished, and the new train made explicit in its very name its owners' faith in a new century. Representatives of the public and professional press gathered at Grand Central Terminal in New York and at La Salle Street Station in Chicago to watch the departure of the two trains. Each *Century* carried identical equipment. "These trains express the latest art in carbuilding. No effort nor expense has been spared to provide the traveling public with all the comforts and conveniences that are afforded by the highest grade hotels, the furnishings and fittings being complete in every detail," reported one journalist. "The exterior of the cars is painted Pullman standard green color, the ornamentation in gold being simple, but very artistic; gothic lights and oval windows of stained glass set in metal frames lend additional beauty to the exterior elevation."[27] The twin expresses were short. Each locomotive pulled approximately five cars: a buffet car that carried a baggage compartment and a smoking-library section, two Pullman sleeping cars, and one Pullman sleeping-observation car. Within a year, wholly new equipment replaced the "old," and the consist of the trains became well known to the reading public throughout the nation. The dining cars were "attractively finished in Santiago mahogany," and linen, silverware, and crockery were custom designed and manufactured; wall niches carried potted ferns.[28] Other cars arrived in service fitted with barbershops, sections for card playing, and small libraries. Competition with *The Broadway Limited* of the Pennsylvania Railroad prompted New York Central management to continuously improve the *Century*, and within eight years the newly purchased cars were replaced by all-steel cars. "This magnificent train is equipped with Pullman cars of the very latest design and has all the special features which have made the New York Central service so deservedly popular," noted one Central advertisement. "Barber, Fresh and Salt Water Baths, Valet, Ladies' Maid, Manicurist, Stock and Market Reports, Telephone at terminals, and Stenographer."[29] Such handbills not only announced the luxury of the trains, but by 1910 noted reduced schedule times—only eighteen hours between the two cities. Not all passengers favored the company's devotion to futurist design. The new steel cars of the 1910–12 period featured sides grooved to resemble wood; too many riders had feared that lightning would strike an all-steel train and electrocute them as they slept, bathed, or dined.[30] But almost every rider agreed that the ten-dollar surcharge for *Century* speed and service purchased far more than the Central advertised.

"There are trains, and trains, but no train has ever received such adulation as does the Twentieth Century Limited from all New York Central men," noted Franklin Snow in a 1928 *Christian Science Monitor* article. "It is their pet and pride. To them it symbolizes their railroad."[31] By 1928 the *Century* symbolized more than the New York Central System; it represented high-speed, first-class, futurist luxury. The advertising department of the railroad distributed thousands of free calendars to businesses, adults, and—perhaps especially—to boys; many years the calendars depicted the *Century* with superimposed titles such as "A National Institution" or "As the Centuries Pass in the Night."[32] The calendars with their full-color illustrations above the date-pads reinforced year round the visual image of the *Century* racing through storm and fair weather, carrying the most luxurious of equipment and a mail car filled only with priority mail.[33] In time, the railroad learned that its best train had become a national institution, and it published a book aimed at answering the questions of its passengers and other interested persons.

In *The Run of the Twentieth Century*, Edward Hungerford traced not only a trip of the train between New York and Chicago, but also all of the effort necessary to its safe, swift passage. He explained the system that accepted reservations up to two years in advance, and, with the permission of the passenger, grouped professionals of one field or another in individual cars or sections of the train—theater and cinema stars on one car, financiers on another.[34] He explained the decision to replace mahogany interiors with walnut, and the absolute requirement of sending out every *Century* with cars having the same interior wood fittings, so that no passenger might have the shock of walking from a walnut-paneled car into one paneled in some other wood.[35] In great detail, he explicated the meaning of the names of the Pullman sleepers, noting that names incorporating the word *star*—*Stars, Starlight, Starucca*, for example—identify the "stag" sleepers preferred by single men traveling light, and that names like *East Rochester, East Grove*, and *East Albany* identify Pullman sleepers comprised wholly of drawing rooms.[36] Hungerford's book is an advertising device to be sure, but it makes clear the care lavished on the *Century* by a devoted management and staff. Dining cars always traveled with their kitchen ends facing the rear of the train, so that cooking odors might not drift into the restaurant section. Menus changed regularly, at minimum once a week, and the same meals could not be served at both ends of the run on a single day, lest a businessman spending only one day in either terminal city and then returning find the same menu placed before him.[37] Among the details of vacuuming the cars, replacing worn linen, and operating a silver-plating shop for dining-car tableware, Hungerford noted even microscopic details: "It is a rule in the daily makeup of the Century that all drawing-rooms and compartments, whenever possible, must face the Hudson River side of the railroad both coming in and going out of New York," a practice that pleased hundreds of thousands of riders.[38] *The Twentieth Century Limited* attracted the same public interest as did liners like the *Lusitania*, and Hungerford's book addressed it with the intention of stimulating it to ever greater heights.

Speed, service, and equipment combined to make the *Century* special, but the key to understanding its popularity lies in its existence as a unit. No matter how many cars it comprised on any trip—and on at least one 1929 afternoon the eastbound *Century* left Chicago as seven separate trains consisting of about ten cars each—its exterior and interior appearance remained uniform.[39] To the trackside spectator, the *Century* was a speeding unit, uniform in form and color; to the passenger strolling from library car through sleepers and dining car to the observation car, the *Century* was an impeccable, uniformly decorated whole. Not suprisingly, trackside spectators often photographed it, for it represented the promise of industrial development—an efficient, electrically lit, uniformly shaped and colored unit. And not surprisingly, the promotional department repeatedly photographed its interior for advertising purposes, for the interior represented a perfection of manufactured design.[40]

If the *Century*, and its ever-present competitor *The Broadway Limited*, represented the epitome in express-train design, perhaps *The Overland Limited* best represented the typical first-class train. Operating between Chicago and San Francisco, it long remained the train favored by gold-mine millionaires and other well-to-do Californians. Unlike the *Century*, however, it traveled the rails of several railroad companies and never displayed the uniformity of appearance that characterized better-known trains. Its rise to fame began years after its establishment in the late nineteenth century.[41] The Southern Pacific Company announced the refurbished train in an 1899 issue of the company periodical, *Sunset Magazine*. As a result of "the phenomenal tourist travel to California during the coming winter, which now seems assured," the company noted, new trains would be added.[42] A month later, *Sunset Magazine* proclaimed the success of *The Overland Limited*: "It's an Aladdin's Carpet—three days and nights between San Francisco and Chicago; all the comforts that a comfortable mind can suggest; and all the traveling luxuries a luxurious imagination knows."[43] While the railroad emphasized the "ne plus ultra of service," it also advertised a running time reduced by about twelve hours.[44] Although not a remarkably fast train—the Rocky Mountains prevented speeds common in the East and on the Plains—it gradually captured the attention of the region through which it passed.

The *Overland* maintained its reputation as a luxury or "candy train." It carried a barber and a ladies' maid, a smoking compartment separated from the central passage corridor (so that no women might detect the odor of cigars), and, of course, an open-platform observation car.[45] Perhaps the latter amenity acquired the most favor, because the train crossed spectacular wildernesses. In pleasant weather, the platform provided a balcony on the Great West, and on the delectable state of California in particular. "It is truly the unfolding of Nature's Wonderbook to pass through California—that land where glorious climate and rare scenic beauty hold every visitor under a spell of enchantment," read one *Overland* promotional flyer.[46] Adults, of course, enjoyed the fresh air and exquisite views provided by the open rear-end platform, but the vantage point appealed even more strongly to children, especially those traveling to and from eastern preparatory schools.[47] Not every stretch of gorgeous scenery enticed passengers onto the platform, however; in summer, for example, the long run across Humboldt Sink forced even the hardiest passengers away from the wicker chairs. Sand and heat irked women passengers most, and the *Overland* eventually carried a shower-bath so that grit might be regularly washed from skin and hair.[48]

The observation balcony excited onlookers, too. The *Overland* carried a lighted signboard on its observation-car railing. By day and by night, such signs announced the names of trains.[49] Indeed, luxury trains carried many exterior signs: not only the names of their owners but also their services. Such signs existed chiefly for spectators—the housewife, the farm boy, the rancher, the schoolgirl—and only secondarily for the passengers who rushed by them as they boarded or left the trains. From a distance a cowboy might identify the *Overland* by its special cars and by its speed: up close, the small-town storekeeper identified it by its unique signboard.

Not every trip of *The Overland Limited*, *The Orange Blossom Special*, and other limiteds was punctuated by an observation-car signboard. Most luxury trains regularly carried private cars, and such extraordinary vehicles usually traveled at the end of the trains, unless management dictated that they follow baggage cars at the front so that regular first-class passengers might enjoy uninterrupted views from observation platforms. A luxury limited proclaimed its luxury; a private car whispered of mysterious elegance beyond imagination.

Millionaires delighted in their privately owned, ostentatiously equipped cars built by the Pullman Company. About such cars the public knew a great deal, even if it rarely rode in them; magazines repeatedly published descriptions of special double beds, mahogany dining tables, and other custom-made magnificences.[50] The Busch family of St. Louis, for example, piped beer under pressure into each of the bedrooms in its private car. August Belmont ordered the very best of everything for his *Oriental*, a private car he equipped with solid silver hat-racks, Carrara marble washbasins, and other extravagances in addition to such standard amenities as stained glass over-windows and brass beds.[51] Wealthy families doted on their private cars, thinking of them as homes away from mansions; one railroad magnate every year dispatched his car to New Haven so that his sons at college might eat Thanksgiving dinner under their own roof, in the company of lucky guests.[52] Now and then, when luxury trains paused briefly at rural depots or stood waiting at great terminals, ordinary Americans glimpsed through the plate glass windows something of the mysterious splendor of the private chariots of millionaires.

All the nation's car-building companies provided a few deluxe rental cars for the use of Americans too poor to purchase cars like the *Oriental*. The Wagner Company, a firm acquired by Pullman in 1899, rented an entire seven-car private train decorated in the most expensive woods, metals, and stone. The Pullman Company operated an even grander five-car train, which it exhibited to public view at the Columbian Exposition; first-class passengers on *The Exposition Limited* thought that they had experienced the ultimate in luxury until they reached the fairgrounds and saw vehicles beyond opulence— but not beyond the purses of George Gould and the elder J. P. Morgan, both of whom rented the cars to transport friends who could not be comfortably accommodated in the millionaires' own cars.[53] In particular, the Pullman private dining car *La Rabida* awed Exposition visitors and provided a window on the world of the very rich.[54]

Friends of the very rich ate in *La Rabida* and other rental cars, as did personages of great importance—theater and opera stars especially. One reporter noted in an 1898 *Metropolitan Magazine* article that "the modern luxury of railway travel is nowhere more clearly exemplified than in the private palace car of the 'star' actress of today." When another actress visited San Francisco, a *Call* reporter described her rental car in the most complete terms imaginable. "The hand-carved piano of natural wood corresponded with the rest of the woodwork in the room," he marveled. "The paneling was of satin-wood, inlaid with ebony, gold and amaranth."[55] In the 1900s, *The Theater Magazine* not only carried articles about the rented palaces of actors and actresses; it also carried advertisements from the car-rental and railroad companies anxious to transport the public figures in whom the nation evidenced a pronounced and growing fascination that blossomed with the cinema industry.[56]

Rental cars existed for roughing it, too. "Hunting Cars" sheltered wealthy parties intent on exploring—in comfort—the Rocky Mountains and other places lacking fine hotels. The Worcester Excursion Car Company of Worcester,

A typical private car, ca. 1910.
(Courtesy of Smithsonian Institution)

Smoker lounge car on The Merchant's Limited,
ca. 1924. (Collection of Charles Gunn)

Part of the interior of the private car "Kathryne," ca. 1912. (Courtesy of Smithsonian Institution)

Massachusetts, began building and leasing extravagant cars suitable for political campaigning, theatrical tours, and hunting trips. Its *City of Worcester* featured gun racks, ammunition closets, ice-cooled storage chests for game, and, of perhaps more importance to well-to-do young men, a bathtub and a safe. Another of its cars, *The Yellowstone*, carried a specially buffered wine rack that protected valuable vintages from the shocks of rough logging- and mining-company rails and roadbeds.[57] Such cars proved ideal for the exploratory thrusts made by mining and logging investors, who ventured westward intent on examining firsthand their real estate of interest, and who hoped to enjoy a little fishing or hunting, too. Now and then a novelist scrutinized life aboard such rented palaces; Frank Spearman's 1904 tale of western adventure concerns a millionaire party sojourning in a long rented car. *The Daughter of a Magnate* succeeds in part because a rented private car is the only plausible explanation of the presence of several Pittsburgh debutantes high in the western mining country.[58] Such cars made something of the splendor of New York, Philadelphia, and Newport mansions real to the most isolated small-town Americans. And because the cars could be rented, people might dream of traveling in them.

Riding a crack express like those that inspired the Lionel *Transcontinental Limited* meant encountering the fantasy of luxury and of futuristic design, and at least having the chance of glimpsing a private car. But the express offered something more. It exemplified *urban* delight. A crack flyer comprised several first-class hotels, all with room service and conveniences like clothes-pressing. In its consist swayed an absolutely first-class restaurant offering the finest of delicacies cooked to order, a club car providing nightclub atmosphere, perhaps a library car supplied with the latest novels, periodicals, and big-city newspapers, and at its end an observation car with the amenities of a private club. On its open-air platform blazed the signboard that often emphasized the urbanity of the train: *The City of San Francisco* or *The City of Denver* or some similar title. Wherever such a train sped, across western Nebraska, through northern Wisconsin, central Mississippi, or western Alabama, it remained urban in its comforts and lifestyle. "The swift-gliding scenery on the El Paso short line; the invigorating climate of the Southwest country, enjoyed on the observation platform," promised the Rock Island Company in a 1907 *Country Life* advertisement for its prized *Golden State Limited*. "The manifold attractions of the palatial club-on-wheels, with its library, sun-parlor, buffet, barber, electric lights and fans, new Garland ventilators, mission style dining car, drawing-room and compartment accommodations, to be occupied singly or ensuite. What, indeed, is left to desire?"[59] Boarding *The City of Denver* or *The Golden State Limited* in Chicago meant never leaving the city; boarding a luxury train at some smaller city or town meant entering at once into "big-time" metropolitan life, the life of urban dreams where, in the words of the Rock Island advertisement, "every desire is gratified and every moment a pleasure."

Sunset Limited

California Train de Luxe

This world famous train represents the highest standard in luxurious passenger equipment.

Library, barber, ladies' maid, buffet, bath, manicure, observation car, valet, stenographer. Oil burning locomotives, eliminating smoke and cinders. Rock ballast, dust-free roadbed. Automatic electric block signals.

Genial climate permitting open windows all the way. These advantages afford a delightfulness and comfort in travel unexcelled.

The crowning enjoyment is the beauty and fascination of the picturesque and romantic country traversed.

Southern Pacific Sunset Route

New Orleans to Los Angeles and San Francisco

Choice of Rail or Steamship Lines to New Orleans

Write for Southern Pacific literature full of fascinating information c. ' illustrations

L. H. NUTTING, General Eastern Passenger Agent

Room 7, 366 Broadway
(Franklin Street)

1158 Broadway
(27th Street)

1 Broadway
(Bowling Green)

New York

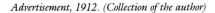

Advertisement, 1912. (Collection of the author)

American novelists understood the urban significance of the fast express, the almost electric charge of boarding a city, of encountering city-wise "traveling men," of being shamed by one's provincial clothes. "And coming out he stepped into the narrow precincts of that modern mystery, the 'sleeper,'" wrote James Oppenheim in his 1912 novel about a young man leaving his small town to seek fame in New York City. "Kirby was overwhelmed by the approach of the Negro porter, who stepped like the master of these mysteries, the wand-waving genie of this passing realm." Oppenheim's *The Olympian* is one of many novels that begin on a fast express.[60] Perhaps the finest is Thomas Wolfe's *Of Time and the River*, published in 1935, which emphasizes the encapsulated world of the luxury train as the proving ground of small-town manhood. "As the boy entered the smoking compartment, the men who were talking together paused, and looked up at him briefly with the intent, curious, momentary stare of men interrupted in a conversation."[61] Slowly, as the night wears on, the men accept young Eugene Gant, offering him a drink from a pocket flask, and speaking of the beautiful women asleep in the Pullmans ahead. Much later in the novel, an experienced, successful Eugene Gant displays his acquired urbanity by embracing express-train travel.[62] Long-distance, high-speed train travel fascinated Wolfe, and from that fascination evolved the magnificent scenes in *Of Time and the River* and *You Can't Go Home Again*, scenes of expresses racing on parallel tracks, long trains roaring downgrade around curves, and great trains stopping at small-town stations.[63] But Wolfe saw more than majesty, speed, and the outward thrust of the urban industrial zone—he saw the essentially urban relationship among passsengers ensconced in luxury.

"One looks at all the pretty girls with a sharpened eye and an awakened pulse. One observes all the other passengers with lively interest, and feels that he has known them forever," he writes in *You Can't Go Home Again*. "In the morning most of them will be gone out of his life; some will drop out silently at night through the dark, drugged snoring of the sleepers; but now all are caught upon the wing and held for a moment in the peculiar intimacy of this Pullman car which has become their common home for a night."[64] Riding the *Limited* meant enjoying basically anonymous relationships with the men of the club car, the women across the dining table or sleeping in the next berth or drawing room, the genies of the Pullman Company. It meant wearing one's best clothes in sumptuous surroundings, dining on food not available in small towns, drinking with strangers and flirting with others. It meant encountering sophisticated men like the traveling man Oppenheim describes as seated next to a fortune-seeking young man: "There was about him an air of success, a suavity and ease of manner, a flow of talk, a well-fed, well-kept exterior, all of which seemed to belong distinctly to a city of theaters, restaurants, and hotels."[65] Riding the express meant riding a long, sinuous, racing city, a city of luxury racing into the future.

So disconcerted were many small-town and rural Americans at the thought

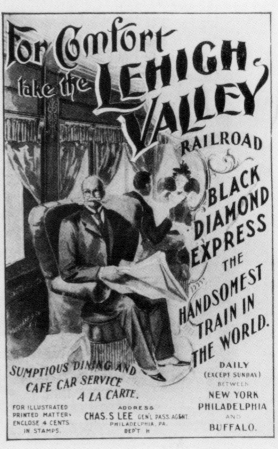

Advertisements, 1906. (Courtesy of Harvard College Library)

of entering such rarified urban space that they either traveled in all-coach trains or consulted etiquette books. Advisors on manners began counseling the uninitiated as early as the 1880s, and some advice changed little over the decades. "A man may, if he choose, make acquaintances on a journey, and a woman also, though with less frequency and freedom," cautioned Virginia Van De Water in her 1924 *Present Day Etiquette*, before warning that "as a usual thing, it is best for a young girl traveling alone, to avoid all communication with strangers, as she cannot know into what complications it may lead her."[66] Such admonition resulted in part from the impression made by novels like Theodore Dreiser's *Sister Carrie* of 1907, in which a traveling man seduces a young woman making her first long-distance journey. But chiefly, such warnings evolved from the anonymous, overnight character of luxury train travel—a young woman, and even a young man, might be snared by urban evil. Of course the etiquette books suggested what sorts of clothes to wear, what types of cosmetics to bring, how to direct the Pullman porter, and how a man and woman must arrange themselves at a dining car table.[67] For the vast majority of Americans, riding a fast express raised them above their accustomed social level, where they encountered the complexities about which William Dean Howells wrote two one-act plays, *The Parlor Car* and *The Sleeping Car*.[68]

Not every American had reason to travel on the luxury limiteds, and many Americans could not afford the surcharges that increased ticket prices on the *Century* and other first-class trains. Hundreds of thousands of travelers made do with slower, unnamed trains equipped only with day coaches simply because they lived in towns in which the expresses did not stop. "No. 7, the way train, grumbling through Minnesota, imperceptibly climbing the giant tableland that slopes in a thousand-mile rise from hot Mississippi bottoms to the Rockies. It is September, hot, very dusty," writes Sinclair Lewis of a 1920s train trip across the High Plains. "There is no smug Pullman attached to the train, and the day coaches of the East are replaced by free chair cars, with each seat cut into two adjustable plush chairs, the head-rests covered with doubtful linen towels."[69] *Main Street* emphasizes the wearisome train journey as the prelude to the wearisome life in Gopher Prairie, a dreary little town through which the great expresses flash without slowing. Gopher Prairie is indeed one of the "lost Swede towns" about which Fitzgerald writes, a town of desperate people who gaze longingly at the limiteds roaring through.

Gazing at first-class trains occupied much of the nation's leisure time in the decades between 1880 and 1930. A luxury express brought a touch of urban glamor to the smallest of hamlets, even if it did not stop. So magnificent was the Illinois Central crack express—*The Panama Limited*—that every day for twelve years the Sixth Mississippi District Court at Vaiden recessed so that everyone could watch it come through the station.[70] Passengers on the *Panama*, a train almost as luxurious as the *Century*, paid a surcharge to ride the all-Pullman train, which was refunded if it arrived more than one hour late, but the citizens of Vaiden paid nothing for their fleeting glimpse of Chicago–New Orleans urbanity. Watching named trains proved a free and enjoyable entertainment, particularly during the Depression, and it endured until the end of the 1930s, and longer in rural areas. The "chief Hyde Park amusement," remarked *Life* magazine in 1940 of a sleepy Hudson River Valley community crossed by the New York Central system's "Water Level Route," "is going down to the station in the evening to watch *The Twentieth Century* whiz by."[71] Until the 1920s, such trains represented prosperity and the promise of greater prosperity, luxury, futuristic design, and urbanity. To some Depression-era watchers, the expresses announced good times returning; to others, they advertised an unequal distribution of wealth. Long before and well into the Depression, however, the fast trains bespoke a peculiarly American *strassenromantik*, one centered on cities flashing across farms and forests, attracting the wondering admiration of children and adults who recognized speed, efficiency, and urban glamor on tracks customarily used by slow freights and unnamed local passenger trains. Every railroad right-of-way shared in the glamor that lingered like the whiff of coal smoke left after the all-Pullman express had passed. In the remotest corners of rural America, in suburbs of broad lawns, in small towns, the luxury express advertised the crackling energy of urban industrial zones.

Inside cover, cigar box, ca. 1925. (Courtesy of S. S. Pierce Company, collection of the author)

3: ZONE

Pittsburgh, ca. 1900. (From Pennell, "Vulcan's Capital," collection of the author)

ZENITH COMPRISES THREE
cities. At the outskirts is Floral Heights, a streetcar suburb of Dutch colonial houses three miles from downtown. Central Zenith, a commercial-retail center of fireproof ten- to thirty-five-story office towers of Indiana limestone or yellow brick and stores selling everything from dictaphones to scarves, hums with speculative prosperity. On suburb and downtown Sinclair Lewis focuses almost all the action of his 1922 novel, *Babbitt*. But between Floral Heights and Babbitt's high-rise real estate office is a third city, an industrial zone Lewis calls South Zenith, although it encircles the city center. South Zenith is "a high-colored, banging, exciting region: new factories of hollow tile with gigantic wire-glass windows, surly old red-brick factories stained with tar, high-perched water tanks, big red trucks like locomotives, and, on a score of hectic side-tracks, far-wandering freight-cars from the New York Central and apple orchards, the Great Northern and wheat-plateaus, the Southern Pacific and orange groves." It is a place of foundries, automobile factories, shops where five thousand men work under one roof, a place threaded with high-speed railroads.[1]

However much reviewers argued about the character of Babbitt and his lifestyle, philosophy, and usefulness as a "type," few questioned the setting of the novel. Indeed, newspapers in five cities, Cincinnati, Kansas City, Milwaukee, Duluth, and Minneapolis, each proclaimed that its municipality was the prototype of Zenith, and Minneapolis actually celebrated a "Babbitt Week."[2] Lewis intended Zenith to represent a type of city; early in the novel, he remarks that "a stranger suddenly dropped into the business-center of Zenith could not have told whether he was in a city of Oregon or Georgia, Ohio or Maine, Oklahoma or Manitoba." His insistence that Zenith is representative explains his sparse description of its industrial zone, "the belt of railroad-tracks, factories with high-perched water-tanks and tall stacks—factories producing condensed milk, paper boxes, lighting-fixtures, motor cars."[3] Within the lean descriptions of the zone Lewis distilled four decades of a peculiar—and now little known—spatial aesthetic, the aesthetic of the factory district, of the industrial zone, of the manufacturing fringe of every great American city east of the Rocky Mountains.

Mystery, and perhaps a willful ignorance, infused the aesthetic from the beginning. Passengers on the trains racing through the industrial zone glimpsed astonishing structural and mechanical forms backlighted against the sky or the glow of open-hearth furnaces. Almost all intercity railroad travel involved intermittent exposure to the industrial zones surrounding commercial down-towns, and by the early 1900s Americans had learned to marvel at their fleet-ing visions of industrial enterprise. The marshes of northern New Jersey, the valleys north of Pittsburgh, the southeast approach to Chicago struck many Pullman passengers as extraordinarily intriguing, beautiful places. Refineries, steel mills, locomotive plants, coal breakers, and mysterious factories com-bined beyond the plate glass windows to make an awesome landscape of built forms. By the late 1900s, essayists and novelists had crafted two decades of unorganized appreciation into a minor but important literary genre.

Adherents of the industrial aesthetic confronted a well-organized, artic-ulate body of reformers who saw only ugliness, danger, sickness, and social decay in the industrial zone. Progressives, and particularly muckraking re-formers working with charitable and religious organizations, produced a powerful literature of their own. *Wage-Earning Pittsburgh*, published by the Russell Sage Foundation in 1914, contained chapters entitled "Factory In-spection in Pittsburgh" and "Sharpsburg: A Typical Waste of Childhood."[4] Magazines such as *The Outlook* and *The Survey* specialized in publishing well-researched denunciations of American industrial conditions, and periodicals such as *Harper's Weekly* and *Collier's* now and then published similar exposés.[5] Such articles eventually helped to prompt legislatures to enact child-labor laws and to mandate factory inspections, but they aroused the wrath and ridicule of factory owners and managers and other upper- and middle-class business-men. Novelists understood the opposition to industrial zone reform; the meat-packing magnate of Robert Herrick's 1905 novel, *Memoirs of an American Citizen*, which appeared first as a *Saturday Evening Post* serial, dismissed Christian Socialism as something that "sounded pretty, but wouldn't work twenty-four hours in Chicago."[6] Only rarely, however, did turn-of-the-century novelists depict the factory owner as a favorable character with a positive political-economic philosophy and a valid environmental aesthetic. In most novels, sensitive, educated men and women see only pain, suffering, and exploitation in the industrial zone. Those who appreciate the manufacturing complexes are like Babbitt, satirizations, unless they are depicted as ignorant or evil. In the novels of Lewis, Herrick, Howells, and other now-respected writers, and in the many articles published in reform-minded magazines, the industrial zone landscape can be appreciated only by those observers ignorant of the problems of factory workers.

Not all Americans subscribed to the reform point of view. Indeed the most casual examination of the popular periodical press reveals the strength of the opposing vision. For those Americans who passed through the indus-trial zone in the comfort of a Pullman car or commanded the great plants

FACTORY

EDITED BY A·W·SHAW

APRIL
1908 PRICE
25 CENTS

THE SYSTEM COMPANY

NEW YORK CHICAGO LONDON

Cover, Factory. *(Courtesy of Baker Library, Harvard University)*

from citadel-like offices, the zone hummed with enterprise. As more and more business executives shifted their headquarters from factories to downtown offices and their homes to distant suburbs, the industrial zone became a belt of throbbing factories crossed twice each day by men engrossed in newspapers, business reports, and trade journals.

Trade journals nurtured the evolving industrial aesthetic. Editorials and articles typically addressed specific issues—foreign competition, improved techniques, and high interest rates. But nearly every issue of *Iron Age, Engineering Record, Cassier's Magazine*, and scores of smaller-circulation periodicals emphasized the glory of American manufacturing, either by running a special feature article describing the industrial zone of a particular city or by extolling the grandeur of a newly built factory. Turn-of-the-century industrialists, plant managers, and other businessmen might claim to be too busy to read novels or poetry, but they usually read the magazine devoted to their particular line of work. Now and then a novelist addressed the power of the trade journal by scorning its effects. Vaughan Kester's 1901 novel, *The Manager of the B & A*, is typical; after meeting an educated young woman and suddenly realizing his ignorance of painting and poetry, the manager returns to his order-books and tables of figures. "They lay on the stand with a pile of trade journals. For the first time in his life he viewed these latter with an unfriendly eye." No longer would they and annual reports of his professional association give him a sense of "intellectual fulness," for that "was a pleasure he had outgrown."[7] The implication is straightforward enough. Trade-journal aesthetics are far inferior to those of high culture. If the content of general-circulation magazines appearing after 1910 is any indication, however, attacks like Kester's made no impact. Indeed, the trade-journal aesthetic acquired more adherents each year, until it rivaled the aesthetic of mountain and forest wilderness.

Representative of the condensed, emotionally charged affirmation of the trade-journal landscape aesthetic in general-circulation prose, Arnold Bennett's 1912 discussion of the industrial zone of Toledo mixed the industrialist's vocabulary with that of the European-educated aesthete. "From a final cat-nap I at last drew up my blind to greet the oncoming day, and was rewarded by one of the finest and most poetical views I have ever seen," he wrote in *Your United States*, "a misty, brown river flanked by a jungle of dark reddish and yellow chimneys and furnaces that covered it with shifting canopies of white steam and of smoke, varying from the delicatest grays to intense black; a beautiful dim gray sky lightening, and on the ground and low, flat roofs a thin crust of snow: Toledo!" Bennett's Pullman-car vision is essentially impressionistic and uninformed; detail is far less important than a careful rendering of the chiaroscuro of stack smoke and steam. About the individual buildings and the peculiar uses of the giant machinery Bennett knew little. But he did know the aesthetic significance of the concatenation of mills, furnaces, factories, and derricks: "A wonderful and inspiring panorama, just as romantic in its own way as any Spanish Toledo."[8] The panorama Bennett admired was new, built within perhaps two decades. Mystery, not age, made it romantic; power, not purpose, made it inspiring.

After 1880 an astonishingly new industrial landscape emerged on the outskirts of most American cities. Innovative manufacturing processes, combinations of previously separate companies into corporate entities, massive increases in the export trade, and new building materials and management practices altered the American factory. A change in scale attracted the most penetrating attention. In 1900, Pennsylvania plants owned by Cambria Steel in Jonestown, Carnegie Steel in Homestead, Jones and Laughlin Steel in Pittsburgh, and Baldwin Locomotive in Philadelphia each employed between eight and ten thousand workers. The General Electric plant in Schenectady, the Deering Harvester plant in Chicago, and the Westinghouse Electric plant in Pittsburgh each employed from six to eight thousand hands, and cities like Yonkers, Chicago, Bethlehem (Pennsylvania), Trenton, Bayonne, Reading, Akron, Worcester, and Youngstown each boasted at least one plant that employed two thousand or more workers.[9] Such giant manufacturing operations required entire complexes of cavernous buildings; steel mill complexes stretched for miles along rivers, their buildings and furnaces linked by conveyors, railroads, and catwalks. The manufacturing operations defied terminology. Words such as *factory* and *mill* made little sense, and gradually the term *works* came to mean all the contiguous structures, cranes, and other equipment operated by a single firm.[10] But areas outside most cities supported dozens of smaller firms employing only several hundred men each and at a distance appeared more amazing than the massive works nearby.

Between 1840 and 1880 American manufacturing evolved from a water-powered, small-scale, rural base to a steam-driven, immense, urban one. Factory buildings evolved from milled wood frame to brick to brick-covered steel frame, and by 1910 exotic materials such as terra cotta tile, poured concrete, and wired glass were being accepted even by tradition-minded company owners.[11] Plant managers, instructed by systems engineers in the most efficient means of channeling worker and material flow, accepted the one-story, sprawling factory or works as vastly more productive than the multi-story, elevator-serviced structures.[12] Companies consequently sold old-fashioned factories and relocated to suburban locations capable of supporting vast horizontal works. Changes in factory design and siting occurred so rapidly that few Americans fully understood the national effect, but mass-circulation magazines attempted to make clear the general trends. Periodicals like the *Atlantic Monthly* and *Harper's Weekly* published technical articles often written by expert engineers.[13] The articles combined with an outpouring of books such as Katherine Coman's *Industrial History of the United States* (1905) and Arthur Shadwell's *Industrial Efficiency* (1909) to explain the changes so evident in the landscape.[14] Simultaneously, they propounded the industrial aesthetic.

Perhaps most discernible in the post-1880 industrial zone was a new sort of factory building, which attracted sustained attention in both trade journals and general-circulation magazines. Edward Atkinson explained the new structures in an 1889 *Century* article entitled "Slow-Burning Construction." After describing the traditional multistory, pitch-roofed factory of the 1860s and 1870s and explaining why so many burned to the ground in fires that killed hundreds of workers, he recounted the efforts of the Factory Mutual Insurance Company to specify a construction that allowed factory employees to extinguish or at least control fires. By illustrating his article with drawings of both unsafe factories and modern, slow-burning factories, he graphically portrayed the extraordinary contribution of the engineers employed by the Factory Mutual Insurance Company and by such other firms as the Boston Manufacturers Mutual Fire Insurance Company. Atkinson knew the intensity with which the general public approached the entire issue of factory safety and included extremely detailed architectural plans among his illustrations. His article represents the intricate connection between the typical trade-journal essay and the popular magazine piece.

Insurance companies shifted operations in the early 1880s. Instead of simply insuring industrial buildings against loss by fire, they began to suggest safety measures, and to insist that manufacturers employ them. If a manufacturer constructed a building with the specified materials and design, he received pronounced decreases in his premiums. Not surprisingly, manufacturers contemplating new buildings obtained the suggested plans and by 1900 followed them closely. The engineering drawings of William H. Whiting reproduced in Atkinson's article typify insurance-company design. The Boston Manufacturers Mutual Fire Insurance Company insisted on the safest possible structures and employed Whiting, a civil engineer, to design a building that could be erected on almost any site anywhere in the United States.[15] Everything in the drawings is specific; window arrangement, flooring and roofing material, placement of fireproof doors. Close examination of the drawings is unnecessary, however, because Atkinson's prose and artist's renderings make explicit the significance of the new thinking.

Most important, Whiting and other designers employed by the insurance companies worked from an engineering, not an architectural, point of view. They eschewed almost all ornament as an unnecessary fire hazard. "In such a factory no cornice is required or permitted, and no sheathing within set off by furrings from the wall can be tolerated," Atkinson noted.[16] Insurance company engineers prohibited all interior wall coverings, forbade any ceiling whatsoever, and often limited the application of paint. They insisted that stairways be placed in the corners of the building, not in some grandiose clock-tower at the center of the building facade. They specified large, standardized windows of wired glass, almost perfectly flat roofs, and one-story

Slow-burning factory, ca. 1900.
(From Atkinson, "Slow-Burning Construction," collection of the author)

Specification drawing for slow-burning roof, ca. 1888.
(From Atkinson, "Slow-Burning Construction," collection of the author)

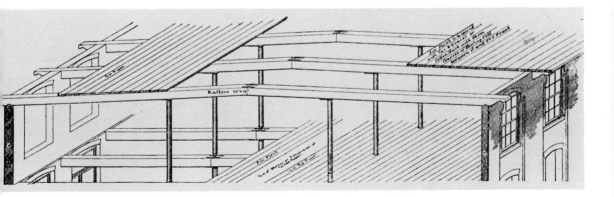

Multistory wooden factory, Braintree, Mass., ca. 1900 (robbed by Sacco and Vanzetti, demolished 1979). (JRS)

heights.[17] Not one of the engineers made apologies for the lack of attention to the dictates of traditional architectural aesthetics.

By insisting on one-story or, at the most, three-story heights, the insurance companies prompted many factory owners to relocate away from the central city. Atkinson understood the traditional attachment to multistory factories and noted that some firms built such structures even in the open country at the edge of cities. "It is not pleasant to witness the mushroom growth of five-story wooden buildings standing often in the middle of a field where land is of little value, in which hundreds of people may be daily exposed to great danger, and hundreds of thousands or even millions of dollars' worth of property are subject to a heavy charge for insurance because the buildings have no right to exist," he asserted in some of the strongest language in his *Century* article.[18] But by 1889, factory owners had begun to learn the financial advantages of insurance-company plans; by locating in open territory where a fire in a neighboring plant would not instantly leap into their own, they could erect a standardized, slow-burning structure of vast proportions and save on insurance fees. Slow-burning construction techniques imperceptibly began the industrial flight from the city. Suburban land was abundant, cheap, accessible by railroads, and lightly taxed; that insurance companies implicitly mandated it as the only safe manufacturing location made it even more attractive.

New factories covered massive amounts of ground. Atkinson casually remarked that many occupied from one-half to three-and-a-half acres of land. A complex of such structures necessarily struck even casual observers as extraordinary, but the stark, instantly recognizable slow-burning design soon connoted more than safety-conscious ownership. It made old-fashioned—and indeed almost decadent—not only small, ornate, wood or stone multistory factories, but all sorts of other buildings, too. "In the evolution of the factory all the faults have been discovered and remedied which now infest nearly all the warehouses, hospitals, dwelling-houses, schoolhouses, college buildings, and other examples of combustible architecture of this country," Atkinson asserted near the beginning of his article. Near its conclusion he returned to the comparison, calling the average hospital or asylum "a picture composed of brick or stone clothing or screening a whited sepulcher well prepared for the cremation of the inmates."[19] The industrial zone of 1910, filled with sprawling, single-story, slow-burning factories, nearly fireproof except for their contents, struck visitors and managerial-level employees as morally admirable, almost beautiful.

Factory owners *expected* the general public to scrutinize their great structures. Not only did manufacturers use engravings, and later photographs, as key elements in magazine advertisements for everything from plumbing fixtures to pianos; they converted their structures into advertising placards. Passengers on commuter trains and crack limiteds noticed the painted slogans

Slow-burning factory with advertising sign. (From Cambridge of Eighteen Hundred and Ninety Six, *collection of the author)*

View from a stopped train, Mansfield, Massachusetts. (JRS)

facing the tracks, but more important in the industrial zone were smokestack signs. Companies directed masons to insert different-colored bricks into chimneys, creating permanent signs visible for miles around. "Court Square Press," "Bay State Taps," "USF Co Silver Refining," "Prov D & B & C Co," "Fells Naptha," and thousands more, spelled in yellow bricks against red-brick backgrounds, led railroad passenger eyes downward from chimney tops to the structures beneath. Smoke pouring from the initialed stacks accented the appearance of permanence and prosperity; like the colored bands of ocean-steamer funnels, the brick letters focused attention on power below while advertising ownership or product. Companies knew how closely the traveling public stared, and they took every advantage.

Trade journals and popular magazines also scrutinized every architectural feature of the zone—windows, smokestacks, water tanks, and roofs. In 1905, for example, *Cassier's Magazine* published a well-illustrated article entitled "Machine Shop Roofs," in which D. F. Nisbet argued that "buildings for manufacturing purpose should be laid out from an engineering viewpoint rather than an architectural one." Nisbet explained how specific roofs might do more than merely shelter the workers and equipment beneath them; his drawings and prose explain the advantages of certain roof configurations in assuring adequate lighting and ventilation and providing room for traveling cranes. His article typifies the turn-of-the-century professional interest in roof design that surfaced in popular periodicals, in both illustrated advertisements for patented roof types and in carefully written, illustrated articles that explained various roof types to interested passersby.[20] By 1920, general-circulation magazines published articles that deciphered the structural confusion of the industrial zone. Lay people approached the industrial zone as they would a puzzle, and by reading the articles they learned how to distinguish an erecting shop from a spinning mill and a foundry from a tool-and-die plant, almost always by correctly interpreting the clues provided by such structural components as roofs.

Other articles explained the placement of factories, works, and entire industrial zones, and again, trade-journal essays closely paralleled ones published in *Harper's Weekly* and similar magazines. "Hunting for a Factory Location," a 1918 *Industrial Management* article, explains the reasons a small industrial zone usually grows larger. "As regards accessibility there is doubtless an advantage in numbers," noted L. W. Schmidt after analyzing the typical history of the isolated factory. "Truckmen will visit more frequently districts where factories abound, railroads will be more ready to extend sidings in the direction of a cluster of factories, while the single manufacturer, be he not a very important customer of the railroad, will find scant consideration."[21] Schmidt devised a system of analyzing industrial sites in which railroad freight, express, and passenger service, daily mail deliveries, highway location, origin points of raw materials, distance to markets, labor market, and power supply are all weighted and evaluated against each other. In the final analysis, an established industrial zone usually provided the best location for a new manufacturing enterprise; at its edge, lower real estate prices combined with preexisting advantages such as electric and railroad service to offer powerful inducements to locate. A successful industrial zone consequently expanded, and Pullman passengers, commuters, and other observers learned from articles like J. A. Wyatt's 1911 *Harper's Weekly* "Building the Factory" why more and more slow-burning–construction buildings surmounted by mysterious roofs, tanks, stacks, and cranes appeared ever further from the commercial downtowns of the nation's cities.[22]

Expansion of industrial zones into suburbs did not escape the eye of trade-journal commentators, and by the early 1920s many experts had perceived the long-term decay of inner-city manufacturing. In a 1924 *Industrial Management* article entitled "Is the Big City Doomed as an Industrial Center?" John A. Piquet analyzed the effect of plant-location theories like that propounded by Schmidt. Small cities like Flint, Lansing, Toledo, Peoria, Troy, and Poughkeepsie were attracting scores of factories. According to Piquet, manufacturers deserted inner cities for well-known reasons—lack of literate workers, poor quality housing, disease, and high real estate prices—along with lesser-known reasons. Firms locating in the suburban edge of the industrial zone, or in new zones in smaller cities in the Far West and the South, found a stimulating lack of railroad and street congestion and room to build one-story, efficient plants. "New Brunswick, N. J., on the Raritan River and Pennsylvania Railroad thirty miles from New York, is an independent manufacturing city of 45,000 population, with a long list of diversified industries, many of which have moved from New York, and which include metal, rubber, textile, wood, automobile, and paper products," Piquet remarked as proof of his assertion that inner-city firms were relocating to the distant fringes of metropolitan areas. Certainly the popularity of the suburban edge of a big-city industrial zone and the attraction of the new zone in a small city originated with the manufacturers, but boosterism sustained interest. Lewis satirized Babbitt's "We zip for Zenith" boosterism, but Piquet understood the power of small-city efforts. "The small city or town displays more interest and will give more cooperation to a striving industry than in a great city, it goes without saying," he asserted near the close of his article.[23] Quite clearly, the years between 1880 and the mid-1920s witnessed not only a new sort of factory being erected in industrial zones, but the spread of such factories across hundreds of hitherto agricultural regions.

"South Philadelphia Works of the Westinghouse Company," a 1918 *Industrial Management* article, typifies the monthly emphasis of trade journals like *Factory*, *Iron Age*, and *Engineering Record*. Anticipation of future expansion prompted the Westinghouse Company to choose a site nine miles from downtown Philadelphia. The same anticipation led thousands of other firms after the early 1880s to locate plants and works on vast parcels of "empty" land in outer suburbs. The South Philadelphia Works objectified the latest in fire-preventive construction, heavy equipment, and concern for congestion-free access. It also typified a changed attitude about history and time. After the 1880s, industrialists began to anticipate the future.[24]

Also representative of the changed attitude toward the future were iron and steel bridges, which entered the national imagination first as engineering marvels, then as constituents of the new industrial zone aesthetic.[25] Bridges like the Brooklyn Bridge attracted the attention of engineers, poets, and the general public, of course, but so also did far smaller spans. Steel construction replaced iron in the decades between 1880 and 1920, and engineers used the new material to construct bridges of markedly different character than those of earlier years. The Pratt truss, the bascule-type drawbridge, the center-pivot swing bridge, all attracted knowledgeable scrutiny in engineering and other trade journals. When James G. Walton published "Some Notable American Railway Bridges" in a 1906 issue of *Cassier's Magazine*, he noted that "massive steel bridges are now so numerous that additions to their number must be of special note before they are considered of sufficient interest for general description."[26] Walton's article consists largely of technical details, but it relies heavily on a series of superbly crisp photographs provided by the American Bridge Company. In each photograph, a bridge is juxtaposed against either an industrial or a river background, and usually against a leaden sky. The photographs hint at the public interest in new, large, and frequently graceful spans.

Industrial zone bridges attracted attention because of their nearness to each other. Travelers in the mountain west, for example, frequently saw nothing of the superb trestles and bridges crossed by their trains; they saw only the dizzying view from the Pullman window. Commuters across the typical industrial zone saw at least several bridges at some distance from the trains in which they rode. Since so much turn-of-the-century manufacturing depended on rivers either for barge access or for water supply and waste removal, most industrial zones stretched along rivers or sprawled across webs of barge and drainage canals. Travelers across two railroad-engineering wonders, the Hell Gate Bridge completed across New York's East River in 1917 and the Newark Bay Bridge between Bayonne and Elizabethport, New Jersey, completed in 1926, saw almost nothing of the spans. But they saw spread out below and around them the myriad of railroad tracks and roads that crossed lesser channels by means of uncountable numbers of smaller bridges.

Having many bridges often meant more to a city than having a single marvel like the Eads Bridge across the Mississippi at St. Louis or the Pittsburgh and Lake Erie Railroad Company bridge over the Ohio at Beaver, Pennsylvania. Pittsburgh citizens gloried in their multiplicity of bridges because the array of spans announced the intense prosperity of their city and the

Sketch of drawbridge, 1904. (From Fuller, "Chicago," collection of the author)

Chicago stockyards, ca. 1900. (From Fuller, "Chicago," collection of the author)

A ca. 1908 view of the Wabash Railroad Company bridge that "freed" Pittsburgh.
(Courtesy of Archives of Industrial Society, University of Pittsburgh)

massiveness of construction advertised the heaviness of rail traffic feeding the iron and steel mills. In Pittsburgh, as in dozens of other cities, many bridges indicated a number of intersecting, competing railroad lines, and therefore better service. Bridges figure largely in John L. Cowan's *World's Work* article of 1905, "Freeing a City from a Railroad's Control," which details the tortuous entry of the Wabash Railroad Company into Pittsburgh. Until 1904, essentially only one railroad company offered service to, from, and around Pittsburgh; the Pennsylvania Railroad Company exercised all the powers of monopoly until the business boom of 1901–02, when its lines became literally blocked by traffic. "The freight service in and around Pittsburg collapsed utterly," according to Cowan. "Freight yards and side tracks were packed and jammed with cars that could not be moved; train-crews were worked to the limit, powerless to bring order out of chaos." The confusion had threatened for some years, at least long enough to convince some manufacturers to locate away from the Pittsburgh industrial zone and to convince the Wabash Railroad Company to find a route into the city. At enormous cost, the company built its line into the downtown commercial center, and into the industrial zone, snaking its tracks through tunnels, along steep hillsides, and across all sorts of the latest bridges. Cowan, along with many other observers, stood awed by the engineering feats. "Where the viaduct ends, the most notable cantilever bridge in the Western Hemisphere is built across the Monongahela River," he wrote. "This bridge is the greatest engineering feature of the whole new line." Cowan paid similar tribute to the line's lesser spans, concluding that the railroad "consists of the most remarkable series of viaducts, bridges, tunnels, cuts, fills, arches, trestles, and culverts ever put together by human ingenuity." Certainly the complexity of the bridges, and the techniques of their construction, enthralled him, but ultimately Cowan saw in the bridges and other wonders the end of "inefficiency and monopoly" and the reestablishment of prosperity. "Great manufacturing establishments are being enlarged, and small ones are springing into existence daily," he concluded in a crescendo of industrial optimism.[27]

An outpouring of articles in mass-circulation magazines reflected and stimulated the admiration for industrial zone bridges that spanned rivers, canals, and railroads. Photography aided the writers by capturing the effect of sunsets behind trusses and magnifying details of construction activities. The literature whetted the public appetite for more and even better illustrated articles.

One type of article analyzed some of the most complex industrial zone works, the steel plants in which bridge components and other parts were fabricated. Waldon Fawcett's 1901 *Century* essay, "The Center of the World of Steel," represents the popular magazine article that nourished the public appreciation of the industrial activity so mysterious beyond the train window. "A first faint conception of the tremendous, almost inconceivable magnitude of this giant industrial exposition, where above all other places a realization of the majesty of manual labor burns itself into the brain, is gained from a glimpse of the tremendous latent energy that is cast aside in the smoke and steam that hang in a heavy black canopy close above the roofs of the city," Fawcett noted, accepting without question the turn-of-the-century admiration of factory smoke as indicative of prosperity. His article explains the workings of converters, hot-steel trains, and furnaces, likening them to "a gigantic fireworks display" and the "multi-colored balls" that burst from Roman candles. Fawcett discovered true romance in the steel mills. "The rail-mill presents many pictures that appeal strongly to lovers of the picturesque," he remarked after describing in technical terms the appearance of half-molten steel rails writhing through presses and choppers. Not everything seemed to him picturesque, however, although his curiously structured vision is not immediately apparent.

Fawcett, along with so many other lovers of the industrial zone picturesque, ignored the workers. Yet Fawcett does describe the hideous effect of gases that strike down a half-dozen steelworkers at a time, the "tiny meteors" that rain down upon the workmen, the continuous peril of overflowing vats of liquid metal. "It is not an unusual sight, at good-sized blast furnace plants of long establishment, to see half a dozen dazed men stretched side by side upon the grass, the ghastly pallor which the gas has wrought intensified by the blotches of grime which partly obscure it," he noted after recounting the deaths of men who toppled forward into the vats. But Fawcett scarcely *sees* the workmen. "It is only when some stray bit of burning iron slips down inside a worker's collar that one realizes that these figures silhouetted against the glare are human."[28] In the "wonderland" surrounding him, in the hard glare of the converter or the rail mill or the furnace, Fawcett, and writers like him, saw only silhouettes.

Fawcett's vision typifies the turn-of-the-century perception—or lack of it—expounded in so many novels, magazine articles, guidebooks, photographic essays, and trade journals. In such publications, workmen exist either as silhouettes or types, if they exist at all.[29] What matters is the physical fabric of the zone, not its inhabitants. "A vision shone and passed, swallowed in night; the sublime spectacle of window-lit mills at the riverside girdling with darkness the fierce flaming of the Bessemer converter, whose several swelling tongues of fire licked at the flaring clouds and crumbled in showers of golden snow."[30] The opening scene of James Oppenheim's 1911 novel, *The Olympian*, displays the same narrowness of focus and romantic aesthetic as Fawcett's decidedly nonfiction essay. In the smoking compartment of the Pullman, Oppenheim's young hero stares at the brilliantly illuminated mills and machinery of the industrial zone and sees not a single workman.

Travel and verbal description shaped the popular acceptance of the industrial zone aesthetic, but photography confirmed it. While Lewis Hine and

A 1900 view of Pittsburgh steel mills made from beneath a bridge.
(Courtesy of Archives of Industrial Society, University of Pittsburgh)

other reforming artists photographed the desperately poor and the laboring children, while James Ames Mitchell published *The Silent War* (1906), which contained William Balfour Ker's drawing of the exploited working class thrusting up a dance floor crowded with the idle rich, the nation's master photographers rejoiced in depicting the industrial zone.[31]

Alfred Stieglitz, Alvin Langdon Coburn, and other masters worked in the established genre of industrial illustration. After the 1870s, however, artists no longer sought out rural mills for meticulous study in oil. More and more firms hired illustrators, particularly advertising illustrators, to depict their factories and plants. Centennial celebrations prompted the first works of the new sort, stark line drawings suitable for reproduction in catalogues, in trade journal advertisements, and on packing crates. No longer did the one-of-a-kind oil painting please advertising managers and plant superintendents, let alone managing directors. Line drawings and halftone prints captured the imagination of factory owners already convinced that black smoke, red brick, and miles of bridges, rail lines, canals, and muddy roads symbolized sublime wonder.

Asher and Adams Company published its *Pictorial Album of American Industry* in 1876, two years after marketing an earlier version. A kind of vanity publication in which a firm paid to have its prose and graphic description appear, *Pictorial Album* sold largely to industrialists. Only a few of the engravings depict rural factories surrounded by trees and farms; most reveal works comprised of several buildings, almost always in an urban industrial zone.[32] Most emphasize smoking stacks, webs of railroads, bridges, and canals, and multistory, very combustible architecture. The book set the tone for hundreds of similar publications aimed at upper- and middle-class audiences, and its engravings shaped advertising copy for decades.

Guidebooks, for example, gloried in detailing the industrial wonderlands of every city. Willard Glazier's *Peculiarities of American Cities* of 1884 urged travelers to approach Pittsburgh by night, and to "behold a spectacle which has not a parallel on this continent. Darkness gives the city and its surroundings a picturesqueness which they wholly lack by daylight." Glazier admitted that a traveler reaching "the Iron City on a dismal day in autumn, when the air is heavy with moisture, and the very atmosphere looks dark" would find that "all romance has disappeared," but he nevertheless exulted in the vast iron and glass works, the excellent working conditions of the workmen, and the prosperity betokened by the cloud of smoke, which Pittsburgh doctors claimed to be beneficial to healthy and diseased lungs alike and to be the "sure death of malaria and its attendant fevers."[33] Of Newark, Providence, and other cities, Glazier made similar if briefer comments. "From an early hour in the morning the eastern bank of the Schuylkill rings out the discordant music of numberless factories, betokening the enterprise of her productive industries," he remarked of Reading. "With the great coal and iron regions of the State at its back, their products brought to it by river, railroad and canal, its manufacturing enterprises are multiplied in numbers, and are almost Cyclopean in their proportions."[34] Authors of guidebooks to specific cities expanded such comments into lengthy catalogues of industrial products and chronicles of manufacturing growth, often illustrating their prose with sharp, clear photographs of the industrial zone. Some of the guidebooks were vanity publications in which firms paid to appear prominently, but authors sometimes played the role of real estate developer by presenting their particular industrial zones as extensive and capable of accommodating many more great works.

Turn-of-the-century urban histories also emphasize industrial zone aesthetics. *The Cambridge of Eighteen Hundred and Ninety-Six*, compiled by a number of writers overseen by "a committee of the city government and citizens," stressed "the city and its industries." A mixture of engravings and photographs depicted the heavy industry of East Cambridge, Massachusetts, almost invariably in the style of *Pictorial Album*.[35] Several token figures stand in the engravings, but few of the photographs reveal a single workman. Stack smoke and heavy clouds form a dramatic background in many of the illustrations, but neighboring plants are deemphasized by artist and photographer alike. A close look at the illustrations reveals that the plants are located in a crowded industrial zone linked by railroads and canals. Aside from a few trees, little remains of the natural environment.

Engravings and photographs of factories appeared in all sorts of advertisements. Firms like the Detroit Photographic Company specialized in photographing factories and works from angles that made the manufacturing enterprise seem almost sublime. But the industrial zone increasingly attracted artists interested in its metallic, distinctly modern beauty. Alfred Stieglitz entitled one 1902 photograph of a railroad yard "The Hand of Man," and indeed everything in the photograph is artificial—the railroad tracks, switches, and signals, the telegraph poles, the small frame and large brick structures half-hidden in the murk of overcast and smoke, the gigantic mill or powerhouse in the distant background.[36] Alvin Langdon Coburn found a similar beauty in Pittsburgh. His 1910 photograph "Chimneys" depicts worker houses nestled at the base of gigantic steel-mill smokestacks; another photograph shows a great steam tug pushing barges past a steel mill during a snowstorm enlivened by billows of escaped steam. At least one of Coburn's industrial zone photographs, showing a twilit steam shovel loading a train, depicts two human figures, but most of his work, and that of Stieglitz, does not.[37]

Such photographs attracted as much critical attention as the paintings of the Ashcan school. Seeing the photographs in galleries convinced many remaining doubters that the industrial zone was beautiful. Certainly the Photo-Secessionist exhibitions altered the viewpoint of many landscape observers. "In the morning I could hardly trust of my eyes when I beheld one 'Hand of Man' after another coming toward me down the track," wrote a *Camera Work*

Alvin Langdon Coburn photographs of Pittsburgh, 1910.
(Courtesy of International Museum of Photography at George Eastman House)

critic of his train journey to the Pittsburgh Photo-Secessionist show in 1904. "The audacity of the Pennsylvania Railroad to plagiarize this idea!"[38] Once accepted as "high art," a process speeded by the publication of such carefully conceived and beautifully illustrated articles as William S. Davis's 1916 *Photo-Era* piece entitled "Bridges as Pictorial Subjects," the new paintings and photographs became powerful prisms through which many educated Americans—not only the readers of *Factory*—examined the industrial zone.[39]

Now and then an observer tried to see through the prism without obscuring his vision by considering the political associations increasingly apparent in the national press. Theodore Dreiser, for example, struggled to understand the industrial zone and its peculiar aesthetic. "Then we came to a grimy section of factories on a canal or pond, so black and rancidly stale that it interested us," he wrote in 1916 in *A Hoosier Holiday*. "Factory sections have this in common with other purely individual and utilitarian things,—they can be interesting beyond any intention of those who plan them. This canal or pond was so slimy or oily, or both, that it constantly emitted bubbles of gas which gave the neighborhood an acrid odor." The scene attracted the notice of the artist traveling with Dreiser, Franklin Booth, and the men stopped to observe more carefully.[40] Several of Booth's sketches of industrial zones illustrate Dreiser's travelogue. By no means are they unrepresentative of the sketches made by other American artists in the first two decades of the century. Hugh Ferriss's 1919 *Harper's* portfolio entitled "American Capitals of Industry" displays the same fascination with angular forms, a middle distance of water or unoccupied land, and towering structures wreathed in a haze, half-smoke, half-steam.[41] The etchings by Charles Henry White in his 1908 *Harper's* piece, "Pittsburg," reveal a markedly similar fondness for bridges, smokestacks, and haze. White's prose explanation makes clearer the implicit assumptions of Booth, Ferriss, and other artists who presented only sketches to the public, and of such photographers as Stieglitz and Coburn.

A peculiar luminosity suffused the industrial zone, one that changed intensity at twilight and other times. It enthralled discriminating observers before and after the perfection of electric light, and artists and photographers sought to represent it in sketches, paintings, and on film. "A shimmering silver river, spanned by many bridges, threads its way between two great rocky promontories and loses itself in an exquisite distance of gray mist faintly flushed with an opalescent pink, where the forest of mammoth stacks is belching clouds of smoke and iron-ore dust, sending great banks of rose-colored smoke soaring, tumbling, and rolling upward in phantasmagoric shapes," wrote White at the beginning of his article. "Through the shroud of smoke loom gigantic shadows of the mighty promontories; a long shaft of fine golden sunlight sifts across the valley where a galaxy of lights flicker and die away like will-o'-the-wisps in the envelopment of the night; the pinnacles of the hill glow with an amber phosphorescence, and Pittsburg begins her night."[42] The haze of stack

Franklin Booth drawings of industrial zones, 1913. (From Dreiser, A Hoosier Holiday, *courtesy of John Lane Company)*

smoke mixed with steam, the glow of furnaces and fireboxes, the remarkable "snow" comprised of fly-ash and condensing steam vapor combined to subtly, and sometimes dramatically, transform the character of light.[43] "The line of the buildings stood clear-cut and black against the sky; here and there out of the mass rose the great chimneys, with the river of smoke streaming away to the end of the world," said Upton Sinclair of the Chicago industrial zone he meticulously defines in his 1906 muckraking novel, *The Jungle*. "It was a study in colors now, this smoke; in the sunset light it was black and brown and gray and purple. All the sordid suggestions of the place were gone—in the twilight it was a vision of power."[44]

After the turn of the century, electric arc and incandescent lights added to the twilight and nighttime glow, almost stunning observers like Dreiser, who recorded the effect of encountering a gigantic illuminated advertisement on the edge of an industrial zone: "A considerable distance off to the north, over a seeming waste of marshy land, was an immense fire sign which read, 'Edison General Electric Company, Erie.'" Intense, artificial light rendered night into something as mysteriously wonderful as the day turned opalescent by stack-smoke haze. A steel plant at night in full operation "is a spectacle never to be forgotten, but to attempt to describe the full glory of these thundering, flaming infernos is to feel the limitations of the language and to grope about for some new vehicle of expression," concluded White in describing the "golden splendor of some gigantic conflagration."[45] In 1927, the Pennsylvania Railroad Company advertised its premier train by distributing thousands of free calendars illustrated with an eighteen by twenty-four inch color reproduction of Harold Brett's commissioned painting, "The Broadway Limited Operating through the Steel District."[46] Of all the scenic delights along its route, the company chose the nighttime scenery of Pittsburgh steel mills to entice travelers onto its crack express. Until 1929, the development of the industrial zone aesthetic was indeed essentially a groping toward new language and new visual representation to capture the forms and light of the new built environments sprawling along the railroad rights-of-way. Old scenery values and land-classification systems proved inadequate.[47]

Avant-garde art critics gradually recognized the industrial zone aesthetic as something portentous for the world of painters and sculptors, but few made determined efforts at explication. In "The Necco Factory," a 1928 *Arts* piece, however, Alfred H. Barr scrutinized the massive new home of the New England Confectionery Company in the industrial zone of Cambridge, Massachusetts. The factory, a C-shaped structure flanking a powerhouse topped by a gigantic chimney, resulted from design by engineers, not architects. "At the risk of offending machine idolators we must pass over, a little regretfully, the interior filled with an amazing complex of dynamos, boilers, automatic sprinklers, miles of process pipes, filters, refrigerators, pulverizers, dehumidifiers, and pumps," wrote Barr, but he knew that the machinery was the "utilitarian necessity" that guided the designing of the immense concrete, lime-stone, and yellow brick building. Barr delighted in describing the twenty different varieties of windows, the Philadelphia Smoke Tower fire escape, and the great rooftop ventilators. The illustrations, photographs by F. L. Fales and Jere Abbott, reveal a similar love of crisply engineered form; most are angular, abstract photographs showing details of the building massing or roof-line or the chimney emblazoned "NECCO." Barr drew only one lesson from the Necco factory; in his opinion, the most beautiful structures were those designed by engineers for essentially utilitarian purposes and ornamented slightly if at all. Railway terminals and garages—and the Necco factory—struck Barr as structures that artists ought to examine, because they pointed toward a wholly new aesthetic, one applicable to factories and to sculpture.[48] In 1928, his view seemed possible, even plausible.

After 1929, when the widespread factory closings prompted by the financial crash created at the same moment a fierce hatred of the industrial system and a fervent hope that it might prosper again, popular magazines avoided the cheerful depictions of industrial zone scenery. But serious artists attracted to the mysteriousness of its light and forms persevered. "I had observed and admired the two bridges for many years—a wonderful structure of blackness even on the sunniest day, but on a gray day the epitome of sinister darkness," wrote Charles Burchfield of a piece of Chicago steelwork that found expression in a 1935 watercolor. "Even the stream below, polluted as it was with various chemicals and oily substances, seemed to be made of liquid black iron."[49] Other artists also worked in the zones; Reginald Marsh painted the same bridge complex in 1930, and John Kane worked in the railroad yards of Pittsburgh.[50] Trade journals now and then encouraged their efforts, and the newest and perhaps most graphically aware, *Fortune*, commissioned Burchfield and others to paint and photograph industrial scenery. *Fortune* editorial writers remarked now and then on the beauties of supposedly ugly industrial places, but by 1930, as thousands of idled factory hands hopped freight trains in a desperate search for employment, Americans began to doubt the magnificence, hopefulness, and fascinating grandeur once obvious in industrial zone scenery.[51] Out of the Depression evolved a new, different industrial zone aesthetic, one alien to that of *Babbitt*. Only the electricity-generating station continued to entrance a public desperate to believe in a bountiful future enlivened by "white coal," by "juice."

4: GENERATOR

A riverfront coal hoist, ca. 1898. (Courtesy of Archives of Industrial Society, University of Pittsburgh)

WHIRRING, HUMMING, SOFT-
ly purring, flanked by coal piles and crowned by plumes of drifting smoke
and steam, the power station thrust its way into the turn-of-the-century
American imagination. In the great industrial zones ringing the nation's cities,
no structure loomed more majestically or thrust its smokestacks higher. As a
symbol of efficient power, the station knew no equal. As the energizer of the
silent, massive, electric locomotives purring through urban terminals and hiss-
ing over mountain grades, it aroused the enthusiasm of all railroad admirers.
As the very generator of the nation's emerging electric vision, the power station attracted the scrutiny of technical and popular writers, artists, and the
general public it ceaselessly and mysteriously served. In the power station,
Americans glimpsed the electric future.

As late as the 1890s, industrialists and small boys knew chiefly the
"powerhouse." Until well into the twentieth century, the term survived to
muddle discussion of the electricity-generating stations that replaced the oldfashioned powerhouses. Nevertheless, the powerhouse remained a significant
structure, for twentieth-century observers saw it as the birthplace of something futuristic.

Originally, mills and factories drew power from water- or steam-driven
wheels, usually located in cellars beneath the manufacturing floors. Hydro-
power technology evolved with the nineteenth century, causing entire buildings to be built over canals whose water drove turbines housed in specially
designed basements. At Lowell in Massachusetts and in other industrial locations, entire complexes of factories stood surrounded and interlaced with canals of rushing water.[1] As steam power replaced falling water as a source of
continuous power, however, the difficulties and dangers of installing steam
engines in each building of every factory complex caused owners and insurance companies to seek ways to isolate the furnaces, boilers, and engines from
the buildings they powered.[2] The "works engine house" evolved as a small,
usually brick structure set near the center of the several buildings owned by
one manufacturer. Within its walls worked at least one coal-fired steam engine
coupled by immense pulleys and belts to the manufacturing machinery in
adjacent buildings.[3] Such powerhouses, often built later than the manufacturing buildings, dispatched power through a seemingly confused web of leather

Electric locomotive passing power substation, 1932.
(Courtesy of Smithsonian Institution)

belts and drive shafts, cogged wheels carrying chain drives, and massive gears. Belts left the powerhouse at almost every imaginable angle, making access to the building difficult and movement within the structure very dangerous. Such constriction necessitated the employment of many men, most needed to shovel coal and ashes, and others to oil the assemblage of flying parts. No structure better represents the pace of nineteenth-century American industrialization, for the powerhouses that supplied energy to the complexes of factories that Americans eventually called "works" evolved in hasty, spur-of-the-moment ways, growing ever more powerful but ever more complicated.

A works powerhouse, therefore, smacked of old and new simultaneously. The word *house* implies an association with an earlier, essentially agrarian time that ordered American language until the early twentieth century.[4] Words like *firehouse*, *gatehouse*, and *waterhouse* indicated a pre–railroad era understanding of industrial structure. By 1920, particularly in the Midwest, the word *house* no longer held sway; new terms, particularly the railroad-derived *station* and the industrial-zone–created *works*, had reshaped old words. Such terms as *roundhouse* and *engine house* reveal the reluctance with which even railroaders departed from the agrarian vocabulary, but terms like *fire station, waterworks*, and, especially, *power station* reflect the environment that changed the language.

Americans understood powerhouses. The coal piled on one side of a powerhouse signified potential energy; the ashes heaped on the opposite side announced energy spent. Within, the fire raging in the firebox quite clearly heated water in the boiler, making the steam that in turn powered the reciprocating engine or engines. Reciprocating steam-powered engines seemed to most Americans perfectly familiar; after all, a railroad locomotive is a "steam engine," with its great wheels and rods driven by reciprocating pistons.[5] Inside a typical powerhouse, visitors encountered something remarkably like a railroad locomotive, something they understood. With pistons flying, balance wheels spinning, and drive shafts revolving, the powerhouse machinery seemed almost as magnificent as a speeding locomotive, and in time it modified American ways of speaking. The colloquialism "pull out all the stops" derives from the safety governor that spun atop most stationary engines; removing one or more of the weighted metal stops caused the engine to work faster and faster—removing all meant running the risk of a runaway engine, broken belts, and catastrophe. Thus even large powerhouses proved understandable as simple shelters for well-known types of machinery, and mass-circulation periodicals gave them little attention.

On the other hand, powerhouses exemplified the urban confusion of movement that alienated Henry James and so many other Americans dismayed by scurrying streetcars, drays, bicycles, and trains.[6] The "buzzing, blooming confusion" described by William James as the world of the newborn infant existed in every powerhouse for any adult brave enough to encounter the maze of belts, drives, and other machinery.[7] No machine better represents the accretionary process of urban development; just as cities grew, adding more and more levels, avenues of traffic, types of vehicles, so evolved typical powerhouse machinery. Each new factory building, every new press or gin or grinder, somehow required more belts or thicker driveshafts or even entire new steam engines. No wonder that the sight of powerhouses in full operation staggered visitors.[8] So much of the created energy seemed wasted in utter confusion; firemen scrambling beneath wheels to feed fires, oilers clambering over madly speeding belts, chief engineers pulling reverse levers and bellowing over the din—power indeed, immense power, power that required the careful bolting of machines to floors and walls, but not power well harnessed.[9]

While the works powerhouse objectified the rapid growth of nineteenth-century American industry, a growth based on seat-of-the-pants engineering, cheap labor, and a willingness to endure mechanical danger, the "power station"—by 1920 and perhaps as early as 1910—represented the promise of twentieth-century change. A power station produced electrical energy for many consumers.[10] It represented a changed attitude toward engineering and building, an affirmation of centralized power generation, and a faith in efficiency. Urged on by a natural curiosity and by magazine articles, the American public began to study and appreciate the structures rising in the industrial zone of every city.

At first, electricity-generating companies followed powerhouse precedent and sited their structures at the geographical centers of the districts they hoped to supply. In the late 1880s, residential electric lighting seemed the greatest potential market; most factories had their own powerhouses that were beginning to generate electricity, and the electrically powered trolley car had not been perfected. Electricity meant "direct current," simple to generate and manipulate, but difficult to transmit over long distances, indeed over a limit of perhaps ten miles. So small plants sprouted in the centers of upper-class urban neighborhoods anxious for incandescent illumination.[11] But quite clearly, locating electricity stations in residential neighborhoods meant encountering difficulties ranging from smoke pollution to coal storage.

Alternating current solved the essential problem. While more difficult to produce and modulate, alternating current moves well over extremely long distances, with only a slight drop in efficiency. Once engineers understood its generation, electricity firms moved quickly to better locations.

Engineering magazines devoted much attention to the proper siting of electric stations. Writers emphasized that the stations ought to be reasonably near their markets, simply to reduce the expense of wire and cable. They stressed also the factors important in siting any business—cheapness of real estate, for example—and perhaps earlier than other industrial writers drove home the need for acquiring enough land to permit expansion of the original station.[12] But station-siting proved a vexing issue for other, more complex reasons.

Almost every station burned coal to produce steam. Water consequently acquired a two-fold importance: siting a power station adjacent to a navigable body of water meant having access to cheaply freighted coal, and proximity to a large body of water meant having the ability to make vast quantities of steam. The evolution of the power station is intimately connected with the development of the nation's waterfronts and riverfronts and lakefronts. Indeed, by 1930, almost every great body of water, including such wild rivers as the Colorado and the Tennessee, struck power-industry representatives as sites for new power stations.

Alternating current created locational difficulties, too. Electrical engineers discovered that only very high voltage alternating current can be transmitted efficiently.[13] For the voltage to be useful in residences and in retail establishments, it had to be "dropped" at small buildings called "substations." Since substations contained only switching equipment, not fireboxes and boilers, and required very little space, they could be located in residential neighborhoods with little objection.[14] Selecting a location for the main station, or "central station" as the industry called it by 1905, meant the corollary locating of substations, however, for the secondary buildings proliferated in areas distant from the generating source. Locating the central station on the waterfront almost invariably meant siting substations in neighborhoods far inland, often in long-established neighborhoods with high property values and no desire for industrial buildings.

With the perfection of the electric streetcar in 1888, locating power stations became even more complicated. The trolleys operated on direct current, and as the lines reached into suburbs and carried increasing numbers of cars, power demands taxed the original stations. For decades, many street railway companies insisted on generating their own electricity and refused to purchase it from "electric-light companies." The independence provided insurance against rate increases but led to the multiplication of generating stations and substations, because the trolley companies required low-voltage direct current. Every extension of trolley lines into suburbs required one or more new generating stations.[15] Only rarely did the trolley companies have the financial resources to acquire waterfront land for their stations. Except for the giant consolidated "rapid transit" companies, electric railway companies built small stations that relied on uncertain streams, municipal water lines, or steam condensers to provide water for steam generation.[16] Their small generating stations punctuated urban and suburban space and aroused the attention of people unfamiliar with the far-off, industrial-zone central stations of the electric company. In the wee hours of the morning, long after the last trolley trip, electric locomotives pulling coal cars to power stations disturbed the slumber of suburbanites.[17]

One group of experts argued that central stations ought to be located in suburbs. "As to the water supply, considerable latitude is allowable, owing to the possibility of piping water from a distance," noted A. E. Dixon in a 1906 *Engineering Magazine* series on power station design. Coal would have to arrive at such suburban sites by rail, but the additional freight cost would be offset by the willingness of quality workers to live in an attractive location. Beyond that, Dixon remarked, "suburban locations, slightly out of the large centers of population, are desirable owing to the fact that labor troubles are not so liable to occur, and should they arise they can be handled better when located outside the lime light." One way of handling such difficulties involved the hiring of strikebreakers, and Dixon understood that "when considerable space is available around the industry on which temporary shelters can be erected," the usefulness of strikebreakers becomes even greater.[18] According to Dixon and other writers of the 1900s, suburban locations might be more useful in the long run than waterfront or industrial-zone sites.

Locating a central station or street railway power station consequently involved analyzing many separate and yet interrelated factors ranging from the efficiency of fuel delivery to the efficiency of the work force. Of all the factors, however, that of material handling attracted the most penetrating scrutiny. By 1930, the electricity-generating industry had evolved an entire technology only tangentially related to the fine art of manufacturing electric power.

Coal and ash piles flanked almost every central station. For as long as oil remained an untested fuel, urban electricity depended on the burning of anthracite or bituminous coal. Burning coal produced the desired heat, of course, but it produced smoke and ash, too. In order to produce the "cleanest" of fuels, electricity, the central station consumed the dirtiest.

At stations adjacent to tidewater, rivers, and canals, coal regularly arrived by collier or barge. Only a few central stations enjoyed the luxury of deep-water docks; such stations received coal very cheaply, because it arrived by coaster from the coal ports of Virginia. Most stations took delivery from barges pushed into position by tugboats.[19] While cheaper than rail transport, water carriage suffered seasonal disturbances. Many rivers freeze during the coldest winter months, and floe ice sometimes chokes tidal estuaries.[20] Companies located on uncooperative waterways found it necessary to employ icebreakers or stockpile coal for the winter months or take some delivery of coal by rail.[21]

Railroads charged slightly more for delivering the same tonnage of coal, and weather interrupted the service only rarely. But "railroads are subject to interruptions from wrecks, storms, and floods, and on several occasions, in the United States during the last few years, have been so badly clogged up with freight that it has been impossible to tell how long a car or train would be on the road," Dixon noted in a passage akin to the theme of Cowan's 1905 article, "Freeing a City from a Railroad's Control." Beyond the blockage prob-

Central station coal-handling equipment with clamshell cranes. (Collection of the author)

Waterfront cenral station. (Collection of the author)

Concealed coal hoist attached to station. (Collection of the author)

lem lay the likelihood of miners' strikes, and, according to Dixon, "it is the practice of the railroads to seize all the coal they dare, which is on their tracks, for their own use; and while such coal is ultimately paid for, coal at such a time is the most precious jewel of the power plant."[22] Wise electricity companies followed the lead of the Commonwealth Electric Company of Chicago. A 1901 *Western Electrician* article notes that the Company intended to build a new generating station on "a large piece of ground west of the tracks of the Monon, Chicago and Eastern Illinois and other railroads."[23] The lack of a waterfront site caused Commonwealth Electric to seek the best possible secondary location—one with a multiplicity of railroads immediately adjacent to its industrial-zone site.

Stockpiling proved the answer to transportation uncertainties. All but the smallest stations stood flanked by enormous coal piles, the reserve supply. Systems engineers agreed that the reserve pile, like the working pile, ought to be placed on the firebox side of the station, not the side of the building housing the actual generators.[24] Keeping coal near the furnaces meant reduced movement costs and also expedited the removal of ashes, which could be conveyed away from the coal piles. Great heaps of coal created management difficulties, however. Not only did the companies lose money in purchasing quantities of coal beyond their immediate needs, but they sustained additional losses due to the deterioration of the coal itself. "Coal stored outside," according to "The Storage and Handling of Coal and Ashes in Power Plants," a 1908 *Cassier's Magazine* article by Werner Boecklin, "exposed to the usual climatic conditions, shows a tendency to 'slack,'" resulting in heat value losses of from 2 to 10 percent.[25] Outdoor storage led to other difficulties, too, among them the freezing of entire piles when cold weather followed long periods of rain and, perhaps the most frightening, the threat of spontaneous combustion.[26]

Maintaining a huge reserve supply of coal naturally caused many companies to acquire sites far larger than the space required for the actual power station. But the working piles consumed acreage, too. One working pile consisted of the coal immediately off-loaded from barges or railroad hopper cars; another, usually indoors, consisted of several hundred or several thousand tons adjacent to the furnaces. Unlike the reserve pile awaiting winter freezes or summer strikes, the working piles represented coal in motion.

By 1927, American central stations consumed forty million tons of soft bituminous coal each year.[27] L. W. Morrow's *Electric Power Stations* makes clear the need to keep coal moving efficiently and cheaply under all circumstances. The appetites of central station furnaces caused electricity companies to pioneer in coal-handling technology and to support equipment manufacturers like the Brownhoist Company of Toledo. So gargantuan was most of the machinery that the public stood in awe of it, much as Theodore Dreiser reported in *A Hoosier Holiday* when he saw entire railroad cars being overturned by a great rotary coal-dumper.[28] At some central stations, locomotives pushed hopper cars onto trestles, where workmen tripped levers that caused the coal to fall from the car bottoms onto piles beneath the rails. At others, conveyors made of endless chains of buckets carried coal horizontally or vertically, never varying speed. But of all the machinery, the one that attracted most attention was the clamshell crane.

Clamshell cranes unloaded barges and railroad cars by dropping clawlike buckets into the coal loads, snapping shut the claws, and elevating the snatched coal; then, slowly and almost gracefully, the booms swung the buckets over working piles and the buckets opened, sending earthward immense showers of coal.[29] Cranes came in all sizes, but those serving central stations in such cities as New York towered several stories, dwarfing everything but the central stations behind them.

By 1910 the quest for efficiency had led engineers to the realization that some coal, perhaps five thousand tons, ought to be stored in the upper stories of each central station. The coal would fall in chutes past the generator rooms and engine rooms to the ground-floor furnaces, where it could be efficiently shoveled or augured into the flames. Ashes would fall from the bottom of the grates into gondola cars waiting in the basement.[30] Central station designers contended with two problems in realizing gravity-flow coal feeding. They had to design very strong buildings to support the coal, and they had to figure out some way to get the coal to the top of the ten- or twelve-story-tall building.

Coal hoists answered the second problem as soon as reinforced steel and concrete construction solved the first. At the Richmond station of the Philadelphia Electric Company, two hoists moved 325 tons of coal every hour to the upper level of the building.[31] The hoists operated like clamshell cranes magnified in size. Their buckets crashed crazily into the working piles, dropping almost like lightning bolts from dizzying heights. Then slowly, the closed buckets rose on steel cables to the top of the station, moved inside, and emptied beyond the public gaze. No urban machine, not even the rotary car dumpers at the Cahokia station of the Union Electric Light and Power Company and other stations, attracted as much attention.[32]

Hoists dominated central stations. "The majority of these plants are located on the water front and arranged to receive their fuel from boats, and from this fact the coal tower is the most conspicuous element," Dixon lamented in a discussion of station aesthetics, "in some cases to such an extent that it entirely overpowers the main building and conveys the impression that there is a coal-handling plant with a power-house annex."[33] But hoists mesmerized casual observers who watched their day-long rhythmic rise and fall from across rivers and harbors. Indeed, the coal hoist clamshell bucket that slammed up and down at so many waterfront central stations eventually appeared at Coney Island and other waterfront amusement parks. The toy clamshell crane, worked by wheels and levers outside its glass box, sought after rings and other treasures in dozens of penny arcades. For the beachgoer, the clamshell crane represented a moment's diversion; for the electric companies, it remained a crucial machine.

Electric stations brought city dwellers into direct contact with mining-camp families. Every municipality from the largest to the smallest enjoyed—or endured—intimate connections with "coal patch," with the hollows of Pennsylvania, West Virginia, and Tennessee.[34] Throughout the first two decades of the twentieth century, when miners struck frequently for better wages and working conditions, the electric station coal piles shrunk, and consumers of electricity worried about shortages. So glaringly obvious were coal piles and hoisting equipment that passenger-train and trolley-car riders noticed them in times of shortage and scrutinized their shrinkage in times of labor unrest. Low-riding barges, long trains of dusty black hopper cars, and even single electrically propelled suburban trolley coal cars spoke eloquently of the dependence of metropolitan America on far-off coal towns.[35] Central station coal piles spoke loudest, however.

Ashes spoke more softly, but only slightly less insistently. Boecklin warned that "the ashes-handling problem needs fully as much consideration as that of the coal," but for decades engineers treated ash-handling as a secondary interest.[36] Essentially, electric company engineers worried chiefly about removing ashes from the ash pits beneath the stations; the remainder of the problem they only half-heartedly attacked, for good reasons.[37]

A typical large electricity-generating station produced anywhere between ten and twenty tons of ash every hour. When the ash fell from the grates its temperature hovered around 1800 degrees Fahrenheit; in consistency it seemed a cross between rock and slag, a form called *clinker* in ash pit terms. As soon as ash handlers sprayed it with water to cool it for handling, the clinker produced what one author called "corrosive and offensive acids and gases."[38] When the sulfur and phosphorus combined with water, the resulting acids could eat through iron and steel. Engineers striving to economize at first attempted to remove ash with the same conveying equipment that charged furnaces with coal.[39] In about ten years they proved that ash acids would destroy the complicated hoists and conveyors, and they finally settled on the simple technique of dropping live ash into specially built hopper cars. The tiny cars, "moved by men, animals, tractors or locomotives," according to Morrow's *Electric Power Stations*, could be unloaded by dumping directly into a waiting barge or into railroad cars.[40] While a few companies acquired water-sluicing machines to flush ashes from under grates, most attempted to perfect the gondola-hauling technique. Once safely away from machinery, coal piles, and the station itself, ashes had little interest for the central station chief engineer.

Consequently, the typical central station site appeared reasonably neat, if somewhat unbalanced. Reserve and working coal piles covered much of the site; on the remainder of the area stood the immense central station and coal-

An electric-powered ash dumping crane at work in the New York City ash heaps, ca. 1899.
(Courtesy of Loeb Library, Harvard University)

hoisting towers, and a small railroad yard for the ash cars. Careless passersby might think that coal moved in one side of the structure and electricity flowed out the other. More perceptive onlookers noticed the ash-handling equipment, the dust and steam from the ash heaps, and the billowing smoke. The conversion of coal to electricity fell short of perfect efficiency.

Electricity crackled across cities, running in the underground conduits and along steel and wooden poles. It crackled into the sprawling streetcar suburbs, powering the trolley cars that carried businessmen to electrically lit houses. And ashes followed, rarely to the finest suburbs, but more frequently to those lying on the outer edges of industrial zones, as in the High Bridge section of New York City, where land sold very cheaply.[41] "This is a valley of ashes—a fantastic farm where ashes grow like wheat into ridges and hills and grotesque gardens; where ashes take the forms of houses and chimneys and rising smoke and, finally, with a transcendent effort, of men who move dimly and already crumbling through the powdery air," wrote F. Scott Fitzgerald in *The Great Gatsby*. "Occasionally a line of gray cars crawls along an invisible track, gives out a ghastly creak, and comes to rest, and immediately the ash-gray men swarm up with leaden spades and stir up an impenetrable cloud, which screens their obscure operations from your sight."[42] Fitzgerald's 1925 novel emphasized the wonders of electricity; the gaily illuminated mansions, the electric orange-juice maker, the blinking beacon on a dock, all products of central-station electricity. Not all observers saw valleys of ashes, but many railroad passengers did, particularly commuters who raced twice each day across industrial zones. Every zone had at least one ash dump receiving clinker ash from central stations, lighter ashes from factories, and gritty, half-burned ashes from domestic furnaces. The electricity of the light bulb, the clothes iron, the humming trolley car seemed clean only at first glance.

Ash pits, conveyors, and cars might be half hidden, but smokestacks and smoke were constantly apparent. Central station managers disposed of ashes continuously, sending out one or more trains each day to distant dumping grounds. They disposed of smoke, waste steam, and stack gas, too, even more continuously and expeditiously. By 1907, however, such disposal required increasing care. "Plumes of black smoke wreathing the tops of the stacks were badges of industry, and more smoke meant more work," remarked C. H. Benjamin in a *Cassier's Magazine* article entitled "Smoke Prevention in the Power House." Benjamin accurately understood the industrial zone aesthetic: "Even the advertising pictures in catalogues and periodicals were incomplete without this inky foliage, the natural accompaniment of factory chimneys."[43] But increasing use of bituminous coal made ever darker clouds, and reformers took up the cause of smoke abatement.[44] Not until engineers learned that decreasing smoke saved money, however, did the nation's smokestacks begin to clear. Dark smoke signals incomplete combustion; railroad smoke inspectors issued demerits to locomotive firemen when engines poured forth sooty smoke—not so much because the public disliked it and complained loudly, but because such smoke announced waste of fuel.[45] Central stations, partly because they burned enormous amounts of soft coal and also because changing weather conditions required starting and stopping some boilers while running others full tilt, early displayed mechanical stoking equipment. Such equipment saved money in several ways, one of them being a marked reduction in the tonnage of coal needed to supply a given amount of heat. In the process, Benjamin gloated, engineers discovered a dramatic reduction in smoke. "It may as well be understood first as last that smoke abatement becomes a commercial reality when it saves fuel, and not till then."[46] Once central station engineers knew for a certainty that mechanical stokers would decrease coal consumption by ten to fifteen percent, however, they quickly embraced smoke-abatement movements.

Smokestacks proclaimed not only the number of great furnaces blazing far beneath the station roof—some large plants thrust more than four great chimneys into the sky—but they advertised the efficiency of the electricity-making operation.[47] Very tall stacks created efficient drafts and elevated smoke and noxious fumes far over city streets; by the early 1930s, central station stacks usually emitted only steam and nearly transparent hot air. Unlike the stubby chimneys of industrial-zone factories that spewed forth inky smoke and ashes, the jutting red-brick power station chimneys, like the great steel funnels of Atlantic liners, advertised the white-hot efficiency of the works inside the superstructure.

Only a rare nineteenth-century powerhouse received the attentions of architects, but by the late 1920s, electric companies regularly employed such designers to help engineers make new power stations beautiful. "There is nothing that has even remotely paralleled these structures in use or design," mused Donald Des Granges in "The Designing of Power Stations," a 1929 *Architectural Forum* article. "These modern buildings are intended to house huge machines and few people, to protect from the elements forces that are stupendous and superhuman." By the 1920s, central stations often stood 100 to 150 feet tall, exclusive of stacks and coal hoists, and stretched 1,000 feet long. "There is a feeling of grandeur and of poetry and of beauty in the orderly assembly of this modern, efficient and economical equipment," he continued after describing the spatial needs of cranes and other machines, "and it acts as a stimulant and an inspiration to the designer of the structure which houses it." Other forces combined to convince electric companies to build magnificent stations, however, the most important being the need to advertise the industry's concern for the public it served. "Like great railroad terminals," Des Granges concluded, the central stations "are being looked upon as institutions of public service" and require "a certain architectural dignity."[48] Most architects concerned themselves only with facades, however; the real design work remained the province of engineers.

A. E. Dixon, while he agreed with the editors of *Street Railway Journal* that many power stations resembled a "shoe box crowned with a piece of stove pipe," avoided discussing poetry and beauty.[49] Instead he clarified the guiding principles of power station design and enumerated construction features that characterized most stations built after 1910. Two great principles guided power station designers. The first emphasized the primacy of machinery in ordering building form; as Des Granges intimated, the structural form can be created only after all of the machinery, particularly boilers, has been chosen by the mechanical and electrical engineers. Unlike the awe-inspiring New York City railroad terminals, unlike even the great steel mills of Pittsburgh, East Chicago, and other manufacturing cities, the great central stations existed almost entirely for sheltering furnaces, boilers, generators, and switching equipment. Grand Central Terminal and the Homestead Mill Works, gigantic as they were, evolved from a need to shelter hordes of railroad passengers and steel workers; their scale is a scale suited to human crowds. Boston Edison's Edgar Station in North Weymouth, Massachusetts, and Gulf States Utilities' Neches Station in Beaumont, Texas, evolved from a requirement that immense machinery must be protected.[50] The second design principle evolved from the first. By 1910, central stations exhibited faith in the future; engineers designed them to be easily expanded. The "unit system" of making each firebox, boiler, and generator a single, nearly autonomous unit meant that power stations stretched in a series of bays, each bay housing one or more mechanical units.[51] As electricity consumption increased, companies could add new bays at one end of the station, expanding generating capacity quickly and cheaply. Boston Edison's Edgar Station, for example, anticipated an increase in consumption. The "proposed ultimate development" drawings created by the engineering-architectural firms show the coal-fueled station topped by four pairs of stacks and stretching along the waterfront more than a thousand feet.[52] No wonder the old word *house* fell into disuse. A central station existed for machines, not workmen, and, most unlike a house, it anticipated orderly expansion.

The principles dismayed architects. Des Granges ended his article in near confusion, knowing that "the design of the building must not interfere with the perfect coordination of turbine with condenser, of economizers and preheaters with the boilers," and with other machinery relationships. He hoped that "an attempt should be made to express strength,—that is power—and where the limitations of the mechanical and structural designs are not too great, at times real beauty can be secured." He perhaps envisioned a structural aesthetic approximating that found by Barr in the concrete-and-brick Necco factory. But the engineering principles muted his optimism. "Yet one of the deterring factors in obtaining beauty is the piecemeal fashion in which these stations must often be built," he noted, "for the building must be chopped off at any point which will satisfactorily house the equipment then being in-

Edgar Station with covered coal conveyor. (JRS)

Power plant with decorative arched windows. (Collection of the author)

stalled." The meteoric pace of power station machinery redesign and the ceaseless trials of new grates, hoists, and ash conveyors mocked the architects' attempts to achieve effects based on "mass, beauty of proportion, and relations of voids and solids together with texture and color."[53] Engineers insisted on doorways larger than the largest known machinery, on areas for cranes not yet invented, on a thousand and one details that defeated architectural principles. In the years between 1890 and 1930, architectural magazines published only a handful of articles commenting on central station design.[54] Magazines like *Electrical Age*, *Cassier's*, *Electrical Review*, and *Western Electrician* published scores.

Dixon summed up the role of architects. "In power-house design, however, it is the results attained from the completed machine which must be considered, and while a good architectural effect is to be desired, the efficiency of the plant cannot be sacrificed to gain it." His lengthy analysis of the details of central station construction revealed a forward-looking attitude that belies his use of the old term "powerhouse."[55] He commented on slow-burning materials, on caulking chimney ports, and on the arrangement of boiler-room walks. By 1907, central station design hinged on intimate knowledge of the constituent equipment that made up the power station machine. In their enthusiasm to design structures wholly new, engineers sometimes surpassed even innovative architects.

Cement and reinforced concrete began to replace brick as the dominant material of central stations in the first decade of the twentieth century. Central station engineers accepted the new materials faster than those employed to build factories, and by 1920 power stations announced modernity in both color and texture. "It has been well said that a concrete structure, whether built of blocks or by the more common wooden-form method, soon becomes a part of the geology of the landscape," asserted H. S. Knowlton in a 1907 article, "Reinforced Concrete in Power Station Construction," "and there is no doubt that the effect of strength and permanence which well-designed structures of this kind exhibit is one of the most important architectural advantages."[56] Beauty attracted only slight attention, however. As Knowlton and other experts pointed out in the pages of engineering magazines, concrete is nearly fireproof. Properly constructed concrete floors, according to a 1905 *Electrical Age* article, withstand "the test of fire and water better than any other kinds of floors." A "fireproof" concrete wall two inches thick could replace a four-inch-thick brick wall and would last longer; moreover, high-voltage cables laid in concrete conduits or buried in cement floors proved safe from fire.[57] Another advantage of reinforced concrete construction, one especially boasted of by Knowlton, was "its ability to resist the strains imposed by reciprocating or revolving machinery."[58] Engines and generators needed absolutely solid mountings, and concrete provided bases positively stable. Indeed, only ashes defeated concrete; the strong acids ate through concrete flooring and bins almost as rapidly as they corroded steel. While Dixon remained skeptical of the long-term uses of concrete block, the electric company engineers soon adopted reinforced concrete as the best possible material for power stations.[59] By 1930, most stations exhibited a mixture of red brick and gray concrete; the newer the station, the greater the proportion of gray.

As early as 1905, however, engineers had contrived their own aesthetic theory. From "the engineering point of view, the plant is 'beautiful,' and if external appearance adds to the effect, it has only been furnished as a suitable housing for a thoroughly up-to-date installation," asserted Keppele Hall in "A Model Power Station," an optimistic, forceful *Electrical Age* article.[60] In the eyes of the mechanical and electrical engineers who designed and operated the central stations, beauty derived from efficiency.

In coal-handling difficulties originated the quest for efficient operation that eventually shaped all aspects of central station design and management.[61] Again and again, experts and editors mentioned the advantages of efficient coal handling. "Efficiency in Power Plants," a 1906 *Cassier's Magazine* editorial, emphasized that "the attainment of the highest degree of efficiency in the conduct of a commercial business based upon the conversion of fuel into power" would undoubtedly challenge engineers in subsequent years.[62] The editor stressed coal and ash handling as the operations most in need of help and casually introduced the subject of labor force reduction.

Central stations objectified the industrial interest in efficiency and heightened productivity that preoccupied American businessmen in the first decades of the twentieth century. The "unit system" of linking machinery, for example, enabled operating engineers to immediately isolate defective equipment without interrupting the workings of other units. Clamshell cranes and coal hoists systematized the movement of coal from barge to coal pile to upper-story holding chambers. Chain grates and coal injectors reduced coal consumption and dramatically reduced stack smoke. Every invention, every new arrangement of machinery reduced the labor force.[63]

Smoke-abatement reformers inadvertently destroyed the livelihood of thousands of men. "The cost of an extra helper or two in the boiler room does not look very formidable at $1.50 per day each, but the matter appears different when these wages are capitalized," Knowlton argued as early as 1905. He concluded that "it pays to spend almost $9000 to eliminate such a man." Other engineers supported his view. "If there were no question of saving fuel or stopping smoke, the labor question alone would justify the introduction of mechanical handling in any large or medium-sized plant," Benjamin asserted two years later.[64] Clamshell cranes and automatic stokers reduced one station's force of firemen and coal passers from forty to four.

In 1905, W. P. Hancock, an engineer employed by the Boston Edison Electric Illuminating Company, explained labor force efficiency to the readers of *Electrical Age*. "The Organization of Working Forces in Large Power Houses" is a lengthy, comprehensive article analyzing the role of every employee within the walls and coal yard of a great central station. Hancock's guiding directive, "pay the man for what he can deliver to you in brains or manual labor equivalent," orders the entire essay. Hancock emphasizes that good wages and good working conditions attract and retain the best workers, and he devotes as much attention to manual workers as to assistant engineers. "We want men who, when occasion requires, will hand-fire 2000 pounds of coal an hour, and do so for several hours, if necessary," he remarks of firemen. "We want men who will burn coal, and not simply dispose of it; men who will use judgment in both firing and cleaning fires." Implicit in the essay is a strong faith in employing intelligent men, because only such men work efficiently. Supervisors and foremen must be "of sterling worth in the handling and judging of men" and must "realize that a fireman is a man, and, as such, is entitled to proper treatment at all times."[65] Much, much more explains Hancock's argument than moral enlightenment. An efficient, precision-operated central station employed very few men, but those men had the capacity to cripple the production of electricity by simply walking away from the complex machinery that had replaced unskilled laborers. Replacing the strikers with new hands might be possible, but not at short notice, and no electric company could afford even a momentary failure of production.

In the late 1920s, the central station epitomized the high profits and contented work force promised by such efficiency experts as Frederick Winslow Taylor and Frank Gilbreth.[66] A few men, hand-picked for intelligence and reliability, operated the massive machines that replaced the work gangs of three decades before. One controller in the clamshell crane did the work of a hundred men; two or three firemen tending stokers and chain grates did the work of forty husky young men; one gray-headed oiler tended a half-dozen self-oiling generators. And someplace far above the generator room sat the system operator at his panel of meters and switches, monitoring machines that seemed to run themselves.

Central stations fascinated the general public, and electric companies encouraged the fascination. Rate-setting disputes caused the companies to engage in sophisticated public relations maneuvers, among them invitations to the public to tour stations. Hancock, for example, worried about visitors spying coal dust and other filth and insisted that cleaners played a part more important than companies recognized. Some companies tried hard to beautify station sites with trees and other plants, and most made some effort to improve structural facades.[67] The electricity industry published booklets explaining the operation of stations and the transmission of electricity and cooperated with journalists intent on deciphering stations.[68]

Two mass-circulation periodical articles are typical of the explanatory genre. Arthur Howden Smith's "The 'Peak of the Load': What It Means to Light New York City and Transport Her Crowds" appeared in the August, 1909, issue of *Putnam's Magazine*. Four years later, Alan Sullivan's "The Power That

Serves" appeared in *Harper's Monthly*. Both articles focus on the role of the operating engineer. "As a type of human efficiency consider the system operator—this modern and impassive Jove, distributing benignant thunderbolts," wrote Sullivan of the man who "manipulates his hundreds of thousands of horse-power with a touch of delicate finger-tips," and who has orders "to wreck any appliance up to the largest turbine rather than permit an interruption to the service."[69] Smith also honored the man who "can throw off the current from any particular station by a mere twist of the wrist or a nod to a subordinate."[70] Like so much turn-of-the-century explication of railroad operations, which focused on the locomotive engineer, the articles emphasized the role of one man, perhaps because only his role was intelligible. Smith and Sullivan attempted to see the central station through the eyes of the system operator, but they failed. Both journalists shifted their gaze to the activities of the station itself, almost as though the station had its own intelligence.

Both writers used the same device to order their articles. A change in weather from clear skies to fog or thunderstorm gloom causes millions of people to reach for light switches. "No matter how impatiently the consumer asks, the light is there," Smith noted, "flashing up to his pressure on a switch." At the central station, however, "whistles blow shrilly, signalling to engineers scattered throughout the immense building, the telephone rings continuously; men are toying with the switches that control the untold kilowatts of power," he continued. As a single machine, as one intelligence, the equipment responds to the cloud drifting over the city. "Great fires are stoked up; boilers strain under the additional pressure placed upon them; furnace doors swing back, revealing the ravenous maws within; the whirr and thunder of machinery, the power of which is estimated in hundreds of thousands of horse-power, drowns out the rest of the world in a void of bewildering sound." A quick change in weather prompts undreamed-of mechanical complexity.

Smith concluded his article by noting that "it is not difficult to discern in 'the peak of the load' a final confirmation of the absolute triumph of civilization."[71] While few other observers shared his sentiment, at least one, Arnold Bennett, understood the central station as a triumph of American civilization.

In his 1912 *Your United States*, Bennett described a nighttime visit to a New York City central station. His hosts led him along "deserted, narrow galleries, lined with thousands of small, caged 'transformers,'" up to an observation platform facing "an enormous white hall, sparsely peopled by a few colossal machines that seemed to be revolving and oscillating about their business with the fatalism of conquered and resigned leviathans." Bennett related a variety of emotions, perhaps chiefly wonder, and noted the eeriness of it all. "Immaculately clean, inconceivably tidy, shimmering with brilliant light under its lofty and beautiful ceiling, shaking and roaring with the terrific thunder of its own vitality, this hall in which no common voice could make itself heard produced nevertheless an effect of magical stillness, silence, and solitude. We were alone in it, save that now and then in the far-distant spaces a figure might flit and disappear between the huge glinting columns of metal." Everywhere, the station seemed bereft of workers, in the generating room, even in the stokehold where coal moved "scarcely touched by the hand-wielded shovel." The "solitude of machinery, attending most conscientiously and effectively to itself" made "a singularly disconcerting spectacle."[72] Bennett had wandered into the new industrial world, the throne room of the engineer.

As early as 1881, when Charles Barnard published his collection of engineer-glorifying short stories entitled *Knights of Today, or Love and Science*, every sort of engineer, including the railroad locomotive engineer, had received increasing artistic attention.[73] The electrical engineer epitomized the earth-moving, precedent-shattering role of the young American engineer, however. The rapid expansion of urban central stations forced the electrical engineer into public view as the master of the nation's most complex, most mysterious, and most labor-efficient manufacturing operation. By 1929, dozens of companies produced toys that taught something of the wonders of electricity. The Lionel Company produced not only electric trains, but miniature power stations and operating switchboards and transformers, too; other companies manufactured electric motor kits, wet-cell battery components, and "electrical novelties."[74] A career as an electrical engineer might not begin too early, thought many parents, mystified by electric current but aware of its promise. Directing a central station meant directing the very essence of twentieth-century urban life; it meant controlling the metropolitan future.

Young electrical engineers brought the metropolitan electric vision to suburban and rural America. As they directed the stringing of trolley line catenary and electric wires, they promised changed lifestyles. Electric companies advertised all the glories of the electric-powered lifestyle. To encourage businessmen to erect illuminated signs, they placed signs on the facades and chimneys of central stations and sold retail-store signs on installment plans.[75] To encourage housewives to consume more electricity in daytime hours, they distributed nearly free clothes irons on hot summer days, when women sweltered next to the coal stoves warming oldfashioned cast-iron flatirons. To encourage manufacturers to consume more electricity, they leased motors at cut rates.[76] Central station electricity reached only short distances from cities; until the Depression spawned the Rural Electrification Agency, most American farm families did without, or relied on wind-generated power. But where the transmission lines did go, there followed metropolitan lifestyles. Where trolley companies strung wire, people achieved cheap, swift transportation; where utility companies stretched wires and cables, families could suddenly enjoy bright lighting, washing machines, radios, and fans. And always a young "college man," a knight of today, personified the extension of metropolitan power, of "high tension" electricity.

In the long corridors of metropolitan space, the electrical engineer ruled

Suburban all-electric bathroom, ca. 1920. (Courtesy of Harvard University Library)

as a chief expert. It was he who made possible the smooth functioning of the railroad terminals, who illuminated the industrial-zone factories that mesmerized Sinclair Lewis, who conceived the smokestack-top electric signs that transfixed Theodore Dreiser. Central stations objectified his capacity to organize fuel, machinery, and manpower into single entities producing "clean" power, the power of efficiency epitomized. But transmission wires linked the central station—and the young electrical engineers—to the houses and workspaces of less magical Americans.

Electricity flowed along wires suspended on wooden poles or steel towers. It snaked soundlessly along country roads, powering farmhouse lights and trolley cars; it stretched tautly along railroad lines, powering the fastest expresses and the heaviest freights; it crested mountains, bringing power to mining equipment and lighting the deepest shafts and levels.[77]

High-voltage electricity flowed in channels prepared especially for it, channels that typically followed the routes of roads and railroads, and that often crossed such rights-of-way at oblique or right angles. Corridors of high-tension wires followed direct lines through forest, swamps, industrial zones, and suburbs.[78] Hikers came upon them unexpectedly, as Robert Frost noted in a 1916 *Atlantic Monthly* poem, "An Encounter." The narrator of the poem, having wandered far from a country road into a cedar swamp, discovers a telegraph pole "dragging yellow strands / Of wire with something in it from men to men," and asks, "'You here?'" and "'Where aren't you nowadays?'"[79] Electricity, the "something" in the yellow wires, had fascinated poets in Thoreau's time, of course, but by the early twentieth century the power-line corridors stretched away from the central stations into the deepest of forests, not just along railroad tracks.[80]

No such clearly defined channels marked the course of industrial-zone electrical transmission. As early as 1909, observers marveled at the weblike catenary strung along streets between factories. "In the first place notice the wires overhead," remarked Arthur Shadwell in *Industrial Efficiency* of the "outskirts" of Pittsburgh. "There is a network of them—telegraph, telephone and tram wires—and they are put up in a slovenly, makeshift fashion." Shadwell scrutinized the supports, finding "not straight, dressed poles, firmly planted and braced upright, but rough trunks of fir trees leaning in every direction, with the wires between them not drawn taut but sagging heavily."[81] The British industrial expert found no satisfactory explanation for the makeshift poles and catenary, but experts might have provided one. So rapidly mounting was the desire not only for telephone communication but for electricity that power companies found themselves hard pressed to build in a substantial manner. The frantic pace of improvement in transmission techniques made obsolete one sort of wire after another, and companies began throwing up flimsy poles in the firm anticipation that something would replace them. Metal wire supports, used for a time in Germany, proved too permanent and costly; in the

American tradition of flimsy, temporary building, power companies stood foremost.[82]

Not everyone saw in the central station and in the "highways of power" radiating from it the promise of better living through clean energy. By the middle 1920s, more and more astute thinkers had learned that entire regions evolved according to the spread of one firm's power lines, that utility companies could manipulate business development through rate adjustments, that electricity caused as much unemployment as it created jobs.[83] To such critics, the power lines seemed like a great spider web, somehow entrapping old conceptions of municipal political independence, self-reliance, and industrial development.[84] Only in storms, when wires fell crackling to the ground and electricity shot forth uncontrolled and deadly in all its blinding sparks, did many Americans give thought to the physical danger beside which they lived. And indeed not until the Great Depression did they learn what life powered by electricity meant when they had no cash to pay electric bills.

Such concerns interested only a few observers in the late 1920s, however. For most Americans with businesses and houses wired for electricity, the central station provided a convenience of living undreamt of in years before. And for the millions still unconnected to the industrial-zone dynamos, the central station represented the epitome of modern metropolitan life, the life of electric vitality. By 1911, the expression "live wire" denoted a cable filled with the mysterious product of the central station—and it connoted a young person full of the energy of the metropolitan corridor.[85]

No wonder, then, that the Lionel Company manufactured so many toy electric stations, transmission poles, and switchboards to provide scenery for its trains. The whirring, humming central stations made possible the urban terminals served by the mysteriously silent locomotives that swept luxury trains through industrial zones to Manhattan Transfer or New Haven. They made possible all the mysterious, electric "remote-controlled" machinery of the railroad right-of-way beyond the range of electric-powered locomotives. And they made possible the toy electric train and its toy right-of-way, the diminutive replication of the great trains and magical tracks of the metropolitan corridor.

5: HIGH IRON

Jasper Cropsey, "Starrucca Viaduct," 1865. (Courtesy of Toledo Museum of Art, gift of Florence Scott Libbey)

𝒜LONG WITH *THE TRANSCON-*
tinental Limited and dozens of other passenger and freight trains, steam- and electric-type locomotives, and all sorts of cars from cattle cars to refrigerator cars to cabooses, the 1929 Lionel *Catalogue* advertised the makings of a toy "high iron," the slightly elevated steel rail backbone of the metropolitan corridor. In its pages children found signal towers, bridges, crossing gates, semaphore signals, and, of course, sections of curved and straight track and switches. What Lionel called "electrically controlled accessories" came equipped with multicolored lightbulbs or color-changing lenses, moving cross arms, or even nickeled steel bells. "Gongs ring while train passes over track section to which it is connected," announces the prose description of a railroad crossing warning device. "Bell automatically stops when grade crossing is clear." The accessories, all built of steel made colorful with "beautiful enamels baked at high temperature," converted the Christmas-morning oval of track into something resembling—at least in the child's eyes—the high iron of real railroad companies.[1]

By 1929, railroad rights-of-way represented pronounced extensions of the urban industrial zone, and particularly of the electric stations. Even along rails unfitted for electric locomotives, the wonder of electricity sped telegraph and voice messages, moved a hundred sorts of safety signals, and illuminated junctions, yards, and other places of potential collision. The right-of-way advertised urban technology almost as explicitly as the crack flyers emphasized urban luxury. Lionel accurately perceived the public fascination with the habitat of the fast express; it manufactured and advertised miniature replicas of mysterious, electric, seemingly automatic trackside equipment. Of its "Semaphore-Train-Control (Electrically Illuminated)" signal, "our latest marvel," which automatically stopped and started toy trains, the company could write almost entirely in exclamations. "It is startlingly real! It operates as if by magic!" The complicated mechanism of the toy duplicated the seemingly random operations of real signals. "You will be absolutely thrilled as you watch the unique action of this almost-human railroad device."[2] The semaphore signal and other electric accessories produced the same kind, if not the same degree, of mystification created by the constituents of the

Thomas P. Rossiter, "Opening of the Wilderness." (Courtesy of Museum of Fine Arts, Boston, M. and M. Karolik Collection)

trackside ecosystem that snaked everywhere through the nation, comprising one of the most studied, most respected types of American scenery.

Turn-of-the-century professional photographers understood *railroad scenery* to define everything associated with the right-of-way.[3] When H. T. Williams published *The Pacific Tourist* in 1879, he understood the public fascination with long-range vistas of mountain ranges, deserts, and rock formations, and his guidebook emphasized such features as they appeared from express trains. But Williams knew that the public enjoyed seeing engineering marvels like snowsheds, truss bridges, and deep cuts, and *The Pacific Tourist* called attention to such built wonders, too.[4] Pullman tourists traveled west to wonder at natural magnificence, but also to view what William M. Thayer called "marvels of enterprise." Thayer's massive 1890 guidebook, *Marvels of the New West*, emphasized built marvels and enticed many tourists into long, comfortable Pullman-car journeys.[5] Railroad companies built most of the marvels in the West, and a large number of those elsewhere in the nation, and the companies employed painters, engravers, and photographers to depict not only the natural scenery visible from the trains, but also the infrastructure created *for* the trains—the viaducts, tracks, roadbed, and signals.

Artists born just before the railroad era viewed trains and tracks with mixed emotions. George Inness, whose 1854 railroad-company commission resulted a year later in "The Lackawanna Valley," reconciled railroad with rural landscape by placing roundhouse, station, and other railroad structures in a luminous distance and by depicting an almost trackless train moving through newly made fields.[6] By de-emphasizing railroad scenery, especially the roadbed and tracks beneath the train, Inness stressed the ephemeral nature of the vision. When the train passes out of sight, everything—in the foreground and middle distance, at least—is again traditionally rural. Other painters embraced the Inness technique of painting trains, not tracks. Only a few found anything of interest in the right-of-way; Thomas P. Rossiter's "Opening of the Wilderness" (ca. 1846–50) depicts a roundhouse surrounded by locomotives, and in the foreground a small but solid wooden trestle.[7] The painting stresses detail—no luminosity conceals rails and abutments—and represents a dawning fascination with the train and railroad as marvels deserving artistic scrutiny. Jasper Cropsey and other painters arrived in wilderness Pennsylvania in the 1860s to study the great Starrucca Viaduct with and without trains.[8] Awed by its massiveness and dwarfed by its scale, the many artists perceived its untrainlike permanence and delighted in depicting its setting, texture, and form. Starrucca Viaduct was the first marvel of railroad scenery to attract voluntary artistic expression, and the first depicted separately from the trains for which it existed. Painters who could not reconcile traditional visions of rural landscape with trains and railroads found it possible to reconcile trains and railroads with wilderness. In wilderness areas, trains and railroads represented not a disturbance of a spatial order favored by most American painters, but rather they symbolized industrious-ness and the promise of agricultural land emerging from forest. Gradually, even observers steeped in romanticism and Transcendentalism—and in tra-ditional rural landscapes—appreciated the railroad right-of-way as a space having its own character.

Long observation caused Thoreau, for example, to distinguish carefully between the train and the railroad. The Fitchburg Railroad curved around Walden Pond about a hundred rods south of his tiny house; the "whizzing sound" of its trains caused him to look up from his reading and wonder at the invention newly established in Concord. *Walden* sometimes presents the train as a glorious, cometlike conveyance, its bell announcing "that the cars *are coming*, without long delay, notwithstanding the veto of a New England snow-storm." But *Walden* emphasizes the anti-image, too. "We have con-structed a fate, an *Atropos*, that never turns aside."[9] Thoreau sometimes longed for pre-locomotive days. "That devilish Iron Horse, whose ear-rending neigh is heard throughout the town, has muddied the Boiling Spring with his foot," he complains in a chapter devoted to the beauty of local ponds, "and he it is that has browsed off all the woods on Walden shore."[10] Of the train, and particularly of the locomotive, Thoreau held conflicting views, and much of *Walden* records his attempts at reconciliation. About the actual rail-road itself, however, Thoreau wrote cheerfully and knowledgeably.

When he walked from Walden Pond to Concord Center, Thoreau usu-ally followed the railroad "causeway." So often did the train crews spot him along the same stretch of line that they took him for an employee. "I cross it like a cart-path in the woods," he wrote, although he knew that the right-of-way was different:

> What's the railroad to me?
> I never go to see
> Where it ends.
> It fills a few hollows,
> And makes banks for the swallows,
> It sets the sand a-blowing,
> And the blackberries a-growing.[11]

Essentially, the railroad as depicted in *Walden* is a new sort of ecosystem, one born in the disruption of an older one and offering the naturalist an intriguing place for investigation. "Few phenomena gave me more delight than to ob-serve the forms which thawing sand and clay assume in flowing down the sides of a deep cut on the railroad through which I passed on my way to the village," he recorded in the chapter called "Spring," "a phenomenon not very common on so large a scale, though the number of freshly exposed banks of the right material must have been greatly multiplied since railroads were in-vented."[12] Thoreau studied the sand formations on the sides of the cut, and in the drainage ditch that lined each side of the roadbed, and fancied that the shapes represented some grotesque, hitherto unknown vegetation. Such cuts are absent in mid-nineteenth-century paintings of landscapes crossed by railroads, perhaps because painters like Inness devoted little time to actually observing the railroads. As the season lengthened, Thoreau studied the weeds flourishing in the disturbed environment, cataloguing life-everlasting, goldenrod, pinweeds, johnswort, meadow-sweet, and many other species typically eradicated by farmers anxious for weed-free fields.[13] Prolonged exposure to one railroad cut only a half-mile long prompted Thoreau to create an aesthetic different from the traditional one to which most painters of rural landscape ascribed.

Trackside ecosystems intrigued generations of Americans who lived near them, farmed next to them, or walked among them. Particularly in the grid country west of the Appalachians, railroad rights-of-way provided convenient if unsafe shortcuts for boys going fishing and farmers hiking to neighbors' fields. Almost everywhere in rural areas, and later in suburban and village districts, too, railroad companies fenced their rights-of-way to prevent collisions between livestock and trains. Such collisions frequently derailed locomotives and all too often involved companies in protracted lawsuits. When companies failed to fence their boundaries, farmers did so out of self-interest; sometimes companies combined fencing efforts with those of abutters. Barbed wire and woven wire fencing eventually replaced the stone walls and rail fences erected in the 1850s and 1860s, but any fence created an artificially protected ecosystem between it and the rails. Within the protected zone on either side of the track flourished the very wildflowers and weeds farmers sought to eradicate. Ragweed, dewberry brier, and sankfield prospered along southern railroads, and everywhere west of Illinois, the fenced-in railroad property preserved the wild prairie grasses plowed under by sod-busting farmers. Elsewhere in the country, railroad rights-of-way protected yarrow, purple horsemint, loosestrife, Queen Anne's lace, mullein, and the brilliant orange butterfly weed.[14] Wandering livestock grazed roadsides everywhere in the nation and devoured weeds along with grass; only railroad tracks remained edged with tall, flourishing weeds and even small trees like scrub oaks and pines.

Cuts and fills, as Thoreau noted, created even more complex mini-ecosystems. A nation accustomed to uneven, almost contorted roads looked with admiration on the very gentle gradients of the railroads. By its tracks did men know the fierce directed energy of the iron horse. Unlike lesser creatures that stumbled through gullies and struggled up steep hills, the iron horse molded topography to suit its peculiar demands. A hill cut through or a ravine filled over—or a mountain tunneled—objectified the immense power of the absent locomotive and its train of Pullmans or freight cars. Photographers understood the significance of such topographical shape-shifting; just after the Civil War, men like A. J. Russell began photographing the illusion of converging rails that still delights people gazing down railroad tracks.[15] Russell traveled the newly completed transcontinental railroad and photographed such marvels of enterprise as Malloy's Cut near Sherman, Wyoming, and a long fill across Granite Canyon in the same territory.[16] Cuts attracted more attention than fills because they revealed unsuspected and often beautiful rock formations. *The Pacific Tourist* directed its readers' attention at Bloomer Cut, just west of Auburn, California, "where the train passes through an interesting conglomerate, showing a well-exposed strata of boulders, sand and coarse gravel."[17] Gold and silver discoveries caused most late-nineteenth-century Americans to scrutinize all rock formations with more than passing care, and photographers discovered that a sharp photograph of a railroad cut spoke not only to the strong public interest in geology, but also to the national love of enterprise and the still unsatiated love of pictorial illusion. Freelance and railroad-company–employed photographers and guidebook writers educated the Pullman and day-coach public to the "message" of enterprise implicit in the cuts and fills.[18]

Writers of fiction addressed the issue, too. Dozens of *Railroad Magazine* short stories involved the building and maintaining of railroad lines in the face of such environmental opposition as mountains, quicksand, deserts, and blizzards.[19] Two novels represent the genre. Samuel Merwin's 1905 novel, *The Road Builders*, traced the construction of a railroad across a murderous desert; Frank H. Spearman's *The Daughter of a Magnate* appeared a year earlier and traced the maintaining of a mountain line in the face of floods and snowstorms. While both novels involve subplots, they share a similar hero, the college-educated engineer. In Merwin's novel, the young engineer graduates from his first job wiser not only in the ways of engineering, but also in the ways of handling laborers. Spearman's engineer completes his work in the mountains, marries the daughter of the road's president, and moves east to an executive position. In both novels, the railroad right-of-way, well built and impeccably maintained, represents civilization triumphant and the mastery of the expert engineer.

Merwin focused the action of *The Road Builders* on the "instrument and stake men" who sing college songs aboard the work train hastening to end-of-track and who listen most carefully to the tales of the senior engineers. The novel resembles campaign fiction, and indeed Merwin often drew military allusions. "It rested with these two lean men whether an S&W train should enter Red Hills before October," he wrote of the senior engineers. "They both felt it, standing there at the track-end, their backs to civilization, their faces to the desert."[20] Military organization orders the novel; the senior engineers give orders to the young ones, who in turn "boss" the thousand laborers. "The dead plain—alive only with scorpions, horned frogs, tarantulas, striped lizards, centipedes, and the stunted sage-brush—stretched silently away to the dim mountains on the horizon," he wrote of the enemy. The sounds of track-

Bloomer Cut.
(Courtesy of Harvard College Library)

Advertising photograph, ca. 1900.
(Collection of the author)

laying are like the sounds of battle, "deep, significant, nineteenth-century music," in the mind of one engineer who later realizes that the men have "fought like soldiers." The young hero slowly realizes the vision of his senior fellows. "When not engrossed by the actual work, his thoughts were ranging beyond, far into the deeper significance of it." The tracks would bring civilization, an essentially urban civilization. "Timber, bricks, stone would be rushed into these new lands, to be converted into hotels, shops, banks, dwellings."[21] All the asides of the novel are essentially secondary; what mattered to Merwin was the cultural importance of laying track across desert wilderness, an importance he considered so great that he published a key chapter of the novel in an issue of the *Saturday Evening Post*.[22] In the march of rural civilization, the pioneer rancher and farmer took the lead; in 1905, as urban civilization reached along the railroads, the professional engineer attained heroic leadership, and human work became mechanized. "The work was not going to stop, he knew that, yet this complicated mechanism, the job, seemed to be running on without any mainspring," thinks the young engineer at a moment of confusion. A few days later, his mentor tells him that "we must work together as prettily as a well-oiled engine."[23] The siting, building, maintaining, and operating of a railroad right-of-way by the turn of the century represented the efficient use of geographical, mechanical, and human resources to advance not the traditional civilization of agriculture, but the electrically charged, efficient civilization of cities.

Midway in the novel, a private car carrying the vice-president of the road and his party rumbles into the construction camp. The easterners clearly do not belong; Merwin described the ladies of the group "picking their way daintily" toward the private car "where savory odors and a white-clad chef awaited them" even as the engineers and laborers slaved on under the punishing sun.[24]

Private cars and eastern gentry figure prominently in Spearman's novel, but *The Daughter of a Magnate* concerns the maintaining of a mountain line open to luxury trains. Sumptuous cars and bonbon-eating debutantes belong on the mountain rails only as long as the maintenance engineers keep trestles, snowsheds, and track absolutely safe. Spearman's long tale of freshets, landslides, and blizzards traces the awakening of the easterners to the awesome responsibility of the thirty-two-year-old engineer in charge of their safety. The novel opens with a technically detailed account of defending a three-span bridge against a rampaging river and closes after a harrowing narration of mountain-pass snow clearing.[25] Between the two scenes, the millionaire daughter falls in love with the "new man" of the twentieth century, the engineer.

Implicit in these and other novels is the dual meaning of *engineer*. The Lionel Company understood boys' fascination with driving the locomotive, but it knew too their parents' hope for meaningful careers. Running the train opened one world, particularly to younger boys. Building the "layout," which involved figuring track locations, curve radii, and junction positions along with gradients and wiring patterns, might lead—as the Lionel Company claimed it often did—to a career as a civil, mechanical, or electrical engineer.[26] A railroad engineer might be the man holding the throttle; he might also be the man who understood the building and maintaining of the right-of-way.

Americans consequently cast more than a passing glance at the essential components of the right-of-way. Not only did waiting for trains frequently cause them to scrutinize it as the path along which their train must come, but it indeed represented the spatial manifestation of the engineering mysteries hidden in the horizontal factory, the steel mill, the electric station, and in the sprawling urban terminals.

Even the roadbed received scrutiny. Beneath the creosote-treated wooden ties which scented the air on sultry days lay the ballast of cinders, sand, or crushed stone. As the decades passed, prosperous companies endeavoring to increase passenger traffic ballasted their lines with broken granite laid several feet thick. Such ballast prevented passing trains from raising the dust that annoyed summertime Pullman passengers in pre-air-conditioning days and kept weeds from obscuring the rails. More important, thick, clean ballast elevated ties and rails above standing water and provided an absolutely firm foundation on which to bed the track necessary to high-speed operation and very heavy luxury passenger cars.[27] Only high-speed, heavily used routes received such ballast; spur lines and sidetracks warranted lighter rail, thinner ties, and a skimpy ballast of sand or cinders. Throughout the nineteenth century, indeed until about 1930, railroad tracks, and especially the well ballasted tracks Americans called "the high iron," provided about the only dry pathways in rainy weather. Schoolchildren, farmers, and hoboes risked death rather than slop through the muddy roads that paralleled tracks.

Railroad bridges, particularly tall viaducts and towering wooden trestles, entranced observers lucky enough to spot a train pass over them, and attracted trespassers. More than cuts and fills, such structures impressed everyone with the power and enterprise of the railroad companies.[28] Monumental works like the Starrucca Viaduct and the Eads Bridge across the Mississippi River attracted continuous interest during building and long afterward. But even small, culvertlike trestles in the rolling plains states impressed farmers. Tiny wooden bridges, meticulously sited, footed, and constructed, withstood freshets and floods that devoured the amateur structures erected by local road-building committees still building in the common way. Railroad companies publicized bridge-building efforts not only to assure passengers of their concern for high-speed safety, but to justify ticket and tariff price increases. Bridges exemplified the growing respect for mathematical building, for the work of mechanical engineers.[29] Schoolboys learned that mathematical skill alone created such structures, and the father buying his son a Lionel toy bascule bridge perhaps hoped to inspire a technical career.

By 1900 no one crossed a mainline railroad track as Thoreau crossed a cartpath in a woods. First the trespasser climbed over or wriggled through a fence, then walked several yards through weeds before encountering a drainage ditch often filled with standing water, cardinal flowers, and loosestrife. Next he jumped the ditch and scrambled up the gravel sub-ballast onto the even higher crushed granite ballast on which lay ties and rails. To continue in a straight line meant encountering the same obstacles in reverse order. To proceed was to walk over a dry, almost level surface paved with wooden ties nine inches wide placed nine inches apart—exactly the wrong distance for comfortable adult walking.[30] And so, from Thoreau's time through the 1940s, walked Americans, listening for the frantic warning whistle of the fast express, watching for the railroad policemen, and gazing dully or intelligently at the bounded ecosystem of weeds and manmade components. Railroad space lay beyond the everyday landscape and beyond the popular understanding of privately owned land. It belonged to a faceless corporation and had no inhabitants, except hoboes.

Wanderlust and repeated financial panics sent thousands of American men adrift on the railroads, some in search of adventure, most in search of work or escape from responsibility. Railroad hoboing began at the end of the Civil War, but not until the panic of 1893 forced thousands of job seekers onto freight trains did the public learn to fear the ragged drifters it identified as tramps or hoboes.[31] Respectable folk saw hoboes staring from empty boxcars, crouching on express train baggage cars, and trudging along railroad tracks. More than warning signs and the rare railroad policeman, hoboes and the fear of hoboes kept women and young children from walking on or near rights-of-way. Many, perhaps most, of the drifters were honest if conniving beggars, as Jack London noted in his 1907 account of his own hobo adventures, *The Road*. According to London, all but a few engaged in backdoor begging and occasional chicken theft. The remainder, particularly the young teenaged gangs who preyed on adult itinerants and, in urban areas near railroad yards, on the inebriated walking home after dark, usually stopped just short of murder.[32] Turn-of-the-century magazines railed at the "tramp menace," raising the specter of bolshevism evolving from Wobblism and depicting the reality of sabotage. Despite the efforts of London and other sympathetic writers, the public favored the view of the railroad companies.[33] Every hobo arrested by a railroad policeman or ordered off a freight car by a brakeman harbored grudges that might one day prompt him to derail the midnight express carrying honest, hard-working people.

Social reformers and some artists fastened on the hobo as the personification of economic injustice. They juxtaposed the Pullman passenger, the "lounge lizard," with the hungry, ill-clothed man huddled against a fire in a hobo jungle. In the jungle a transient leaping from a slowing freight usually found some cans upended on bushes or the same cans being used by other

Jack London demonstrating the proper method of sneaking onto a box car roof. (From London, The Road, *courtesy of Harvard College Library)*

Youthful vagrants in a jungle. (From London, The Road, *courtesy of Harvard College Library)*

Tramps waiting at a water tank. (From Flynt, "The Tramp and the Railroad," collection of the author)

Turn-of-the-century advertisements frequently depict tramps as subhuman aliens. (From World Today, January 1906, courtesy of Harvard College Library)

hoboes in preparing "mulligan stew," the concoction shared among everyone who contributed some vegetable or shred of stolen meat to the common pot.[34] In 1850 the public viewed such communal activity as a proper corporate enterprise by which explorers and settlers of the West shared resources and information. A half century later such activities drew only scorn and attracted squads of policemen or Pinkerton Company detectives. The continuous attention paid to the tramp menace familiarized magazine and newspaper readers with the peculiar landscape of the right-of-way.[35] The phrase "hobo jungle" connoted overgrown vegetation governed by a more brutal law than that of the wild—the law of the jungle.[36] In the jungle of sumac, scrub oak, and chokecherry trees—Tree of Heaven had not yet escaped from parks to overrun indigenous tree species—a wandering child might encounter savages, placeless drifters acknowledging no law but that of the International Workers of the World, of socialism, of brutality.

In what was perhaps the last gasp of the pioneer spirit of communal land use, the brotherhood of hoboes—like the Brotherhood of Locomotive Engineers—considered the railroad right-of-way as their own. Cryptic chalk marks, the expression of a code-language of hoboes, appeared on fences, signals, stations, and other railroad property. Hoboes loved writing their nicknames, "monikers" in hobo-argot, on railroad property and writing coded information concerning police locations, ease of begging, and other vital matters wherever they liked. The graffiti, if it did not somehow convey the sense of proprietorship, certainly magnified the tramp population in the eyes of the public.[37] Magazine writers determined to decipher the chalk marks now and then visited the jungles and recorded ballads, rhymes, and other oral material.

> I went down to the water tank.
>   It was all marked up with chalk.
> There was stiffs from every State
>   From 'Frisco to New Yawk.
> Your attention for a while
>   One and all I'll thank
> And I'll mention some monikas
>   Seen on that water tank.

The list of monikers seemed endless, for the hobo songs stretched for dozens of stanzas, but the names—Hypo Gann, Lefty Moran, Little Punk Klein, K. C. Jack, Mobile Mac, Spokane Slim, Chi Red, and hundreds more—emphasize the essential rootlessness of the drifters. While many claimed a city of origin, most knew only the right-of-way as home, and the jungle as a sort of city:

> We gathered round the jungle fire
>   The night was passing fast;

> We'd all done time for every crime,
> And talk was of the past.[38]

Hobo fires publicized the existence of jungles, and small-town newspapers and national magazines directed attention to the fires, the chalk marks, and the likelihood of the miniature urban skid rows appearing like spores everywhere.[39] By 1910, the public viewed the typical right-of-way, especially if it seemed overgrown with weeds and scrub bushes, as somewhat sinister, probably the habitat of the feared derelicts. American boys certainly feared the hoboes, but the responsibility-free life of adventure lured them, too. "Hoboland is overrun with youngsters who have got there on the railroads, and very few of them ever wander back to their parents," wrote undercover investigator Josiah Flynt in an 1899 *Century Magazine* article entitled "The Tramp and the Railroad." "Once started 'railroading,' they go on and on, and its attractions seem to increase as the years go by."[40] The railroad right-of-way beckoned the poor boy to an adventure as thrilling as that offered by Pullman cars and luxury express trains to the wealthy. Like boarding a named train by oneself, wandering down a railroad on foot meant eventual contact with the hundreds of thousands of hoboes. Like the flask of liquor passed to Eugene Gant in the Pullman smoking compartment, the cigarette bummed by a hobo from a farmboy in Thomas Wolfe's short story "The Bums at Sunset" marks the farmboy's entry into the traveling life. "Far off, half heard, and half suspected, there was a faint dynamic throbbing on the rails," the story concludes. "The boy sat there quietly, listening, and said nothing."[41] No wonder parents kept their sons away from the rights-of-way, or at least tried. At sunset the wandering youth might discover urban evil right at the edge of the farm or small town.

Juxtaposition of Pullman express and hobo influences much American poetry, perhaps because many poets at one time rode the "side door Pullman," the hobo-named boxcar, and heard such ballads as "The Gila Monster Route." The song tells of the experiences of a "dingbat," the lowest in the hierarchy of trampdom, ordered from a train in the midst of a desert like that described in Merwin's novel.

> The lingering sunset across the plain
> Kissed the rear-end of an east-bound train,
> And shone on a passing track close by
> Where a dingbat sat on a rotten tie.

With "nothing in sight but sand and space," the hobo declares himself "in the ditch / With two switch stands and a rusty switch."[42] Hoboing proved an education to many American poets. Hart Crane, for example, knew something of the right-of-way, as he notes in *The Bridge*:

> So the 20th Century—so
> whizzed the Limited—roared by and left

three men, still hungry on the tracks, ploddingly
watching the tail lights wizen and converge, slip-
ping gimleted and neatly out of sight.[43]

Other writers caught the experience, too. "The rails go westward in the dark,"
wrote Thomas Wolfe in the 1930s. "Say brother, have you seen the starlight
on the rail, have you heard the thunder of the fast express?"[44] But in popular
literature, in *Railroad Stories* and *Saturday Evening Post* alike, and in advertising, hoboes received no kindness. Publishers of sheet music, and later the
recording industry, purged hobo ballads of anything anarchistic and socialis-
tic; in 1929, the first disc recording of a decades-old ballad called "The Wabash Cannonball" replaced the line "While she's traveling through the jungle
on the Wabash Cannonball" with "As we ride the rods and brake-beams of
the Wabash Cannonball." Railroad companies, under continuous pressure to
eradicate the tramp menace, cleared the vegetation that masked jungles. And
the Lionel Company manufactured nothing that smacked of hoboing, not
even a boxcar fitted with a toy tramp or two.[45]

By 1920, the railroad right-of-way away from station areas had acquired
mysterious, slightly sinister qualities. In *Main Street*, Lewis marks the edge of
Gopher Prairie, and the edge of marital fidelity, at the railroad where Mrs.
Kennicott encounters Erik Valborg. "They sat on a heap of discarded railroad
ties, oak logs spotted with cinnamon-colored dry-rot and marked with metallic brown streaks where iron plates had rested," wrote Lewis of the erring
housewife and would-be lover. "The telegraph wires thrummed, thrummed,
thrummed above them; the rails were glaring hard lines; the goldenrod smelled
dusty."[46] Away from the restrictions of the small town of Gopher Prairie and
not yet in the purity of farmland, the two stumble into a different zone, a
zone beyond traditional understandings of moral and physical safety.

Of course railroad companies sought to give an opposite interpretation,
emphasizing that walking on tracks was dangerous because of the trains but
insisting that the passenger was absolutely safe from harm. Throughout the
1880s and 1890s such efforts bore little fruit; too many hideous derailments
and collisions claimed too many lives, sparked too many muck-raking exposés,
and prompted too many government inquiries. Better regulations and track-
work dramatically improved the safety of train travel, but signals marked the
improvement best.[47] Signals punctuated railroad scenery in the 1880s, but
not until the first decades of the twentieth century did they seem everywhere
along railroad lines. Their aspects still intrigue any observer, including the
one with no interest in trains; the lights suddenly changing color, the semaphore silently moving from a horizontal to a vertical position mystify onlookers now as they did decades ago.[48] By the early 1920s, novelists found them
familiar enough but still intriguing, and at night even romantic. "Below the
bridge curved a railroad, a maze of green and crimson light," wrote Lewis in

Babbitt in 1921. "The New York Flyer boomed past, and twenty lines of polished steel leaped into the glare."[49] Colored lenses brightly illuminated, marker lights swinging on the observation car racing into the night, even the red, yellow, and green kerosene lanterns swung by crewmen hanging from caboose steps or standing by switches appear repeatedly in travelogues written after 1880, but about them travelers knew little.[50]

Some ten thousand people died in railroad accidents each year in the years between 1900 and 1905. About four times that number were injured. Train collisions accounted for only three thousand deaths each year; the remainder perished in grade-crossing accidents—like that depicted on a *Harper's Weekly* cover, in which a fast train bears down on a buggy pulled by a panicked, rearing horse—or in other "train-related" accidents.[51] Public clamor combined with directives from the Railway Mail Service and labor union demands resulted in the installation of all sorts of signal systems, most manually controlled from stations or towers, and a few nearly automatic. Electricity aided both systems, along with pneumatic and mechanical forces; companies strung additional wires from the telegraph poles already lining most tracks and hoped that the lines would withstand sleet and wind storms and permit the signals to function perfectly. By 1900 the more prosperous, heavily traveled eastern routes displayed many kinds of signals, most of which figured in the company photographs printed on timetables and calendars and dominating magazine advertisements.[52] Such signals towered over the tracks, making the right-of-way visible from long distances and puzzling observers. Popular periodicals explained the workings of the systems to the interested public; even children's magazines carried articles.[53] Of all the systems, the one most noticed by the public and most frequently explained was the interlocking system.

Interlocking signal systems linked signals and track switches to control positions manned by operators charged with the safe routing of trains. Operators and the supposedly fail-safe machinery shared two-story watch towers placed at junctions and other points of danger.[54] Companies named the towers to insure accurate identification by train crews; near great cities and on lonely prairies, the towers gave identity to points along the metropolitan corridor. Indeed, they created nodes beyond the imagination, and outside the vocabulary, of traditional political philosophy. Trains flashed by the towers emblazoned with curious, sometimes bizarre names. Just north of Providence in Rhode Island, *The Merchants Limited* slowed for a junction guarded by a tower called "Fern"; south of the city, it accelerated past another tower, "Lawn." Some of the towers, "Oak" near the Hell Gate Arch Bridge approach, for example, watched over bridges and trestles; others, like "Harold" just north of Pennsylvania Station in New York City, safeguarded the convergence of hundreds of trains. Hudson Tower adrift in a sea of salt marshes north of Newark, Mayfair just north of Milwaukee, Sheff in Indiana cornfields existed separately from houses, stores, and post offices; signalmen reached them by

The Overland Limited *passing semaphore signals.*
(Courtesy of Wyoming State Archives Museums and Historical Department)

Interlocking signals and tower. (Courtesy of New York Central System, collection of the author)

A distinctly modern built environment: an interlocked junction and a power station, ca. 1930. (Collection of the author)

Signalman's shack with semaphore indicating "stop." (Courtesy of Colorado Historical Society)

pumping handcars along the tracks, for the towers often lacked road access.[55] But they served as ganglia of telegraph and electric wires; poles supported mazes of lines leading to signal masts or stretching off into the distance. Unlike the railroad station, or even the grade-crossing tender's shanty, the interlocking towers had not the slightest connection with the world beyond the edge of the right-of-way. Despite their oftentimes bucolic names, they existed as nodes along the line of tracks and telegraph wires. Now and then one spawned traditional commercial and residential development—Enola Tower near Harrisburg, now the site of a town and a large railroad yard, began as a tower named for its lonely operator ("alone" spelled backwards)—but most existed as part of the interlocking system, the marvel of a safety-conscious age.

Interlocking systems, at first mechanical, by the early 1920s electrical, epitomized the futuristic technology of the metropolitan corridor. Basically, an interlocking system consisted of bars and levers (in later decades, of electric relays) that prevented a signal operator from opening convergent routes for two or more trains, or from displaying signals indicating clear track when such track was "fouled" by another train or an open track switch. The interlocking system linked signals, track switches, and tower operators in a supposedly fool-proof alliance. The actual machines, housed in the lower story of each tower, were the nation's first large-scale computers, essentially "thinking" to solve the problem of routing one or more trains over a single track or complex junction in perfect safety. Although operated by humans, the machines existed to eliminate human error, to prevent derailments and collisions caused by human confusion, inattention, sleep.

Interpreting the signals taxed the ingenuity of humans not trained by railroad experts. Young boys and girls struggled to master the meaning of red over red lights, green above yellow, or three horizontal yellow lamps.[56] Only prolonged observation of the relation of signal-lamp aspects to train movements produced any pattern of cause and effect, and even then patterns misled. Slow-moving freight trains crept past the same red signal that halted a luxury express; a diagonal row of yellow lights slowed a commuter train that might pass an angled semaphore at speed. Along the signless spine of the metropolitan corridor flourished a visual language mysteriously intricate and continuously connoting ever-present electricity and technical care.

The array of signals, wires, and towers soothed passengers traveling smoothly enough, in luxury, but nevertheless at more than one hundred miles an hour. "Looking back, we see that every semaphore behind us drops to horizontal as we pass. On the other tracks we see signal arms moving to horizontal, to vertical, to the half-angle between," mused Katherine Woods in *The Broadway Limited*. "Sometimes there are two arms above each track, and they are moved—by some unseen force—in different directions. Every minute or two we pass a signal bridge across the tracks, every five or six or seven minutes a switch-and-signal tower."[57] Along with thousands of other passengers on the high-speed limiteds, Woods walked to the rear of the observation car, opened the door, and sat on the open-air platform for a better look at railroad scenery. "I go out on the platform, sitting on a folding arm-chair within the shelter of the glassed side, to watch them better, and when the brakeman comes out to do something to his lanterns at the rear of the train I draw him into talk about the signals' meaning."[58] Woods and other passengers concerned with safety used the observation platform not only to gaze at industrial-zone steel mills and electricity-generating stations, but to examine roadbeds, trestles, vegetation, hobo jungles, and—particularly—signals. The expert passenger glanced or stared at the mountains or plains beyond the corridor but reserved some attention for the railroad scenery that spoke volumes about safety.

Passengers waiting for trains and observers relaxing on a summer evening watched the signals that until the 1940s dignified almost every American station. Before *The Panama Limited* or *The Black Diamond Limited* raced through, the semaphore blades shifted position and the lights changed color. Almost every station agent operated one or more signaling devices, and adults and children learned how to interpret the changing aspects that indicated caution or full speed or stop. In so doing they learned a little about the complex engineering operation of the railroad company; in particular, they learned something of the latest in electro-mechanical technology, of the essentially urban technology that by 1920 began to transform small-town and farm life.

Railroad-company–funded artistry simultaneously stimulated and reflected the ever-growing public interest in the high iron, the spine of the metropolitan corridor. Hundreds of thousands of calendars distributed each year, magazine advertisements, and full-color posters nailed up in railroad station waiting rooms, hotel lobbies, and ticket-exchange halls graphically portrayed the intricacy and up-to-date modernism of the railroad right-of-way. By the first decade of the twentieth century, however, such advertising illustration existed alongside a wealth of graphics paid for by no railroad but instead offered by illustrators genuinely smitten with the right-of-way as a line of beautiful images. A full-color *Scientific American* cover announced on June 17, 1911 what Thayer had asserted years earlier, that a railroad through mountains represented *the* marvel of modern industrial progress.[59] The railroad right-of-way attracted dozens of photographers and other illustrators employed by railroads, and hundreds of freelance artists who knew that any magazine might purchase a well-crafted railroad picture. It enticed thousands of amateur photographers, too, many eager to capture a speeding limited, and others hoping to make a fine photograph of the converging rails or line of telegraph poles. Family photograph albums of the 1900–30 period frequently include one or two pictures of a speeding locomotive made by a young boy experimenting with a new box camera or by a couple courting far along the high iron.[60]

Professional and amateur photography magazines explained the best ways to capture the high iron, just as they described effective methods of capturing industrial-zone images. Most amateur photographers attempted imitations of the images made by professionals employed by railroad companies. When Charles C. Smith won second prize in a 1916 *Photo-Era* speed-picture photography contest for his image of *The Empire State Express* shooting past a sextuple semaphore signal guarding an interlocked junction, he was perhaps following the advice given in the magazine only three months earlier.[61]

"How I Photograph Railroad-Scenery," a lengthy article by William H. Rau, emphasized specific cameras and films for specific problems of space, scale, and lighting, but implicit in the well-illustrated essay is not only a definition of "railroad scenery," but an explanation of its author's successful work for the Pennsylvania Railroad Company and, subsequently, for the Lehigh Valley Railroad Company. Rau understood that railroad companies hoped to place enlargements of his photographs "in many fine hotels," as advertising, and so created a genre of illustrations that used the railroad right-of-way as its central feature but included such natural scenic wonders as river valleys or mountains.[62] Rau favored junctions as pictorial subjects, not only because the additional trackage provided many different angles crossing the foreground, but because junctions displayed many signals.[63] His photographs of Penn Haven Junction and Black Creek Junction reveal impeccable ballast, ties, rails, and safety signals, while his photograph of the marvelous Musconetany Tunnel shows an engineering wonder placed in the midst of superb rural scenery and a signal tower with interlocked signals. The hundreds of Rau photographs focus on railroad scenery but integrate it into the wider metropolitan corridor. In time his work became the standard for both amateur and professional photographers determined to portray the railroad as elegantly and as vividly as any illustrator hired by mass-circulation magazines—or by the railroad companies.

Certainly the outpouring of sketches, full-color drawings and paintings, and particularly photographs directed ever-increasing attention at the spine of the metropolitan corridor. Cuts, fills, signals, interlocking towers, and all other constituents of the high iron became by 1930 something deserving of respect, of serious attention. Despite the unnerving presence of socialist-minded tramps and the frequent incidents of derailments, the high iron strengthened its grip on the popular imagination. As the path of the crack luxury expresses, as the proving ground for the latest technological devices, as a place of steady-flow, fail-safe efficiency, as a favored location of future-minded photographers, the spine of the corridor received continuous, penetrating scrutiny. Almost no one crossed it as they would a cart path in a forest.

Rau photographs of the Lehigh Valley right-of-way.
(Courtesy of Frederick A. Kramer)

6: CROSSING

Oval crossing sign and "level" crossing. (JRS)

TWO SHORT, ONE LONG, AND
one extended blast of the chime whistle, and the luxury limited, the midnight
flyer from St. Louis, New York, San Francisco, or New Orleans boomed over
the grade crossing and vanished. The "road crossing" signal varied slightly
from one railroad company to another, but every rulebook emphasized its
importance.[1] As Thoreau knew many decades before, it warned of Atropos,
the speeding fate unable to swerve aside. Every intersection of railroad and
way represented a crossing of two kinds of space, one metropolitan and futurist in character, one essentially rural and traditional. At every grade crossing evolved a microenvironment shaped by the confusion of metropolitan
space and landscape.

And the confusion killed, when it did not maim. In 1902, the Interstate
Commerce Commission recorded that nearly 4,000 people "struck by trains,
locomotives, or cars" died instantly or within twenty-four hours of the collisions; another 3,563 suffered injuries.[2] Federal statistics under-reported fatalities and injuries, however, because the commission never adequately defined
such terms as *persons*, *persons not trespassing*, and *trespassers*.[3] In fact, the commission struggled unsuccessfully with defining terms relating to the locations
of collisions, and early-twentieth-century journalists investigating the emerging scandal of grade-crossing catastrophe learned to distrust both government
and private industry statistics. Despite warped or incomplete statistics, however, expert observers eventually understood the magnitude of the problem.
"Two hundred thousand trespassers have been killed or injured by the railroads of the United States in the past twenty years," wrote one journalist in
1921. "Thirty thousand of them were children, and more than 125,000 of
them wage-earners."[4] Railroad travel became increasingly safer for the passenger, but it grew increasingly dangerous for those Americans termed *crossing
maniacs* or trespassers. Each year of the new century saw more fatalities; in
1919 alone, nearly 14,000 persons died after being struck by trains.[5] Railroad
officials and government officials agreed with journalists that a new disease
had struck the nation, but no one clearly understood its underlying cause.

High-speed trains accounted for many collisions, particularly on tracks
most commonly used by slow freights. "A big, fast passenger engine and tender fully loaded with coal and water weighs well over three hundred tons, not

to mention the weight of the train, and will often be hitting eighty, with modern fast schedules," wrote one *Saturday Evening Post* writer. "It is obviously chewing up the track at a lively rate, but there is no swooping acceleration about the picture."[6] A number of magazine writers tried to explain express-train speed in terms more precise than "a lively rate," but they discovered the difficulty of relating words to visual concepts. "A train running at a speed of 60 miles per hour covers 88 feet in a second; a man walking three miles per hour covers a trifle less than 4½ feet in a second," explained Frank V. Whiting in "Stop, Look, and Listen," a 1913 *Outlook* article on grade-crossing carnage.[7] Unfortunately, the general public consistently misjudged distances and misunderstood such explanations as Whiting's. When other writers explicated train braking distances, therefore, readers totally misunderstood. "On a level track with dry rails it is impossible to stop a train running at the rate of 60 miles an hour within 1200 feet," asserted Day Allen Willey, a railroad safety expert writing in *Cassier's Magazine* in 1905. Effecting such a stop meant using the full force of air brakes and risking serious injury to the passengers; using the brakes more gently added another eight hundred feet to the stopping distance. Higher speeds proportionately increased braking distances; at ninety miles an hour, an engineer needed three thousand feet for emergency brakes to stop a heavy train under the same conditions.[8] On downhill tracks, or in icy or snowy weather, stopping distances grew frighteningly longer. People walking or driving over railroad tracks simply misunderstood the speed of oncoming trains; they mistook laboring freight locomotives for express flyers and crossed the tracks with time to spare—and they judged express locomotives to be freight haulers and died.

Grade-crossing form caused thousands of accidents, too. An early-twentieth-century grade crossing zone consisted of a large, roughly circular space, with a radius of about 1,320 feet. The distance of the radius depended on the length of track from either side of the actual railroad/road intersection to the white-painted whistle posts erected by railroad companies.[9] By the early 1930s, many railroad companies had accepted 1,320 feet as the standard distance, although many placed posts according to specific traffic and topographical conditions. A roughly similar distance marked the pedestrian part of the zone, for within that length of road the whistle usually sounded clearly. Nearer the tracks, about 300 feet from the rails, walkers on busy roads sometimes encountered round white signs emblazoned with two capital *R*s.[10] The signs marked the edge of the danger zone; signs placed next to the tracks marked the center of peril. Within the grade-crossing zones evolved spaces and structures peculiar to them, but the actual intersection of track and way remained the focus.

Topography complicated most grade crossings, and railroad engineering compounded complexities imposed by nature. In the High Plains and Southwest, rails and roads often intersected on vast, nearly level surfaces free of tall vegetation. Such crossings gave engineers, pedestrians, buggy drivers, and horseback riders clear views of the intersection; wayfarers could detect trains at long range and halt with time to spare. Elsewhere, however, rails crossed roads in cuts like that beloved by Thoreau. Right-angle crossings meant that wayfarers had to stop dangerously near the tracks in order to peer up and down the cut; where roads crossed curving tracks in cuts, looking for oncoming trains from the inner side of the curve proved nearly impossible.[11] Since many railroads operated along rights-of-way cut into hillsides to avoid steep gradients, wayfarers often approached crossings while ascending or descending steep, often curving and rutted roads. Approaching such crossings from the downslope side meant peering up at the railroad; if the tracks lay in a curving cut, it meant peering up and around, a feat possible only at trackside.[12] High, well-drained ballast elevated rails above the height of most roads, and banking curves to provide superelevation safety for speeding trains further raised the track. From the downhill side, a typical American grade crossing mocked its very name; rails and road intersected at dramatically different levels, except for the actual space between the rails.

Vegetation and structures also obstructed views. Thousands of the nation's quarter-million grade crossings stood camouflaged by coniferous trees, by such scrub undergrowth as sumac, or by densely growing shrubs. In rural locations farmers planted corn and other tall-growing crops almost to the trackside, sometimes renting railroad land to increase arable acreage.[13] In industrial zones and inner residential suburbs, factories and other structures often lined rights-of-way, blocking wayfarers' views of the tracks stretching away from the crossings, and terrifying engineers condemned to operate high-speed trains down boxlike channels intersected by grade crossings.[14] The peculiar grade-crossing zone economy prompted many businessmen to locate structures at rural crossings, too, adding to the other obstructions. The hand of man aided natural conditions in creating zones perfect for collision.

From federal statistics, newspaper accounts, period photographs, and magazine articles emerges a picture of several sorts of train/wayfarer collision.

Trespassers died by the thousands in the first decades of the twentieth century. By "trespasser," railroad companies understood two kinds of people. The vast number of trespassers wandered along rights-of-way far from public- or private-way grade crossings. Among the thousands killed, tramps comprised a large percentage, although no definite statistics exist concerning deaths of vagrants. Homeless drifters struck dead while walking along tracks received little attention from railroad detectives or county coroners. Many corpses simply decayed unnoticed in the thick vegetation that abutted ballast, and some, buried by humanitarian-minded gandy dancers, received neither death certificate nor headstone for their trackside graves.[15] County and municipal officials buried the dead transients in paupers' graves but rarely inquired into the exact circumstances of death. Sometimes engine crews watched tramps flung from locomotive pilot-beams, but often the accidents happened unseen, perhaps when a hobo fell from a boxcar or missed his grip when boarding a moving freight. Industry and government officials paid much more attention to "respectable" trespassers, although statistics never distinguished among the subgroups.

The Hudson River Valley "water level route" of the New York Central System separated farm children from river swimming holes. In a 1921 *American Magazine* article, "People Act as if They *Wanted* to be Killed," R. Stuart relates his experiences as an observer in the locomotive cab of *The Empire State Express*. "A few miles beyond," he writes of the stretch north of Poughkeepsie, "another boy, hurrying to join a throng swimming in the river, turned to glance backward, saw the engine looming close, leaped aside, and waved to us, laughing at his narrow escape." Children, particularly boys, made light of such incidents, and, falsely secure in their own fleetness of foot, often played "chicken" in front of trains, jumping away at the last possible instant—or being caught and mangled by the madly shrieking locomotive. "Kids, especially, like to pretend that they don't hear; and then, when you are almost on them, they leap aside and laugh as if it were a good joke," commented one veteran express-train engineer. "I've seen them get onto the track and dare each other to stay there as long as possible."[16] Passengers in day-coaches and Pullmans rarely saw such heart-stopping incidents, for the great plate glass windows provided no forward vision.

Rollo Walter Brown investigated one child fatality a moment after "wild shrieks of the whistle" and a violent application of airbrakes that threw dining car tableware to the floor announced its occurrence. "Since I had finished eating, anyhow, I went to the nearest open vestibule to lean out and see what had happened," he wrote in *I Travel By Train*. Brown swung down, walked to the locomotive, and found the corpse of a fourteen-year-old boy, "almost completely nude from having been dragged and rolled over the rough limestone ballast," entangled in the front wheels of the baggage car. The trainmen confronted the dozens of Italian immigrant children who ran down the hillside to the right-of-way, asked for the family of the dead boy, and heard one boy complain that "'The train was running on the wrong track.'" Indeed it was, as Brown recorded; track repairs had put the westbound limited on the eastbound track. Brown walked back along the cars, noting the dining car "crowded with people who were obliviously enjoying their breakfasts and the bright morning," and finally seated himself in the observation car to regain the sideways view so reassuring.[17] Some fifteen hundred children died that way each year.

Adults, too, crossed tracks away from proper crossings. Industrial zones became death-traps at quitting time, when thousands of factory workers took shortcuts across railroad yards and high-speed tracks.[18] Even in rural areas, wildflower pickers and women like *Main Street*'s Carol Kennicott, musing about small-town life and unable to catch the city-bound express, trespassed in metropolitan space—and died.

Now and then, information gatherers separated such trespassers from another group of people wrongfully on the tracks. Several thousand people died in the 1900–20 period because they climbed over gates, fences, and other barriers erected by railroads as safety devices.[19] Such accidents attracted extraordinary public attention because they revealed the seeming uselessness of so many of the safety devices patented in the frenzy to decrease grade-crossing accidents. According to many railroad officials, a pedestrian or other wayfarer had a perfect right to cross railroad tracks at any grade crossing; but crossing in spite of signs and gates when a train loomed near made the person into a trespasser. Such fine distinctions became important during damage suits and liability settlements, and attorneys, judges, and juries worked diligently to ascertain how grade-crossing accidents occurred. Discovering negligence proved complicated indeed.

In the early years of the century, horses caused some thirteen percent of the grade-crossing collisions.[20] While many horses, particularly industrial-zone dray horses accustomed to machinery, proved perfectly capable of waiting at a crossing while locomotives whistled past, others did not. The cover of a 1911 *Harper's Weekly* issue depicts an all-too-common incident. A buggy horse, rearing on the tracks, spotlighted by a wildly whistling locomotive about to crush it and its carriage represents an image of crossing-zone experience.[21] Harnessed horses stood almost ten feet in front of the typical farm wagon; four-horse teams stretched almost twenty feet beyond the front wheels and reins-holding driver. Approaching a crossing of undulating topography or otherwise constricted view with a harnessed horse meant either climbing down and leading the horse to the point of observation or else risking destruction by driving close to the tracks. The second alternative, of course, was to stop horse or team almost at the rails, perhaps the worst possible point. Even a distant locomotive making its first whistle signal might frighten the horse; a panicking driver might first urge the horse to back, a difficult maneuver in any situation; then, if backing failed, urge the horse forward, *up and over* the elevated tracks. A sixty-mile-an-hour limited moved from whistle post to crossing center in about fifteen seconds, too little time to quiet a rearing or balky horse, or even to urge a steady dray team to haul clear a loaded wagon. Some horses, once frightened by a locomotive whistle, remained skittish at any railroad crossing, train or not.[22] One 1913 article pointed out the problem caused by horses of the opposite temperament; some exceptionally docile animals pulling vehicles over established routes learned routines so well that their drivers fell asleep. Such horses pulled wagons directly into the paths of speeding, whistling locomotives.[23]

Horse-driving problems exacerbated difficulties caused by crossings in cuts and on hillsides. Farmers, teamsters, and delivery drivers often whipped

Magazine cover. (Courtesy of Harvard College Library)

up horses pulling wagons downgrade, secure in the belief that the equipage would clear the locomotives. Often such driving resulted from necessity. In winter, for example, sleighs and sledges could not be stopped on snowy or icy hills, and a driver could only whip on his team, or jump. Heavily loaded wagons moving slowly uphill toward crossings presented other difficulties. Hot, tired horses could not always be counted on to start the wagon after its driver stopped before the additional obstacle of the raised ballast and rail; kindhearted farmers trying to spare their animals by not stopping and starting on hills consequently died when trains surprised them at crossings.

Suburbanites and rural dwellers collided with trains also because they accepted schedules as inviolable. Residents within whistle range of the tracks frequently drove thoughtlessly through crossings because they knew that no trains were due. "Experience has shown that the majority of those killed on grade crossings are not tourists traveling over strange routes but residents of the immediate vicinity familiar with every train on the line," argued Russell Holt Peters in a 1934 *Forum* article that bemoaned the ever-increasing grade-crossing carnage.[24] As railroad companies struggled to maintain perfect running times, therefore, they increased the chances of grade-crossing accidents. The schedule-certainty collision points up the extraordinary distinction between the rural landscape, where many farmers had no need of watches and so owned none, and the railroad right-of-way, where urban clock-time ruled every train. Every rural crossing zone created a very real time-warp. As the popular song said, "Folks around these parts get the time of day, / From the Atchison, Topeka, and the Santa Fe."[25] What it did not say, however, was that fluctuations in schedule-keeping killed unwary rural folk who believed absolutely in railroad time-keeping accuracy.

At night, even the safest crossing zones became peculiarly sinister. Strangers, totally unaware, wandered into many zones; until the 1930s, in fact, most zones had no warning signs at their edges, but only next to the tracks, where wayfarers noticed them too late. Darkness made estimating train speed doubly difficult, especially since many railroads operated locomotives with markedly different headlight types. On a foggy night, when moisture-laden air disguised whistle-tone intensity, unwary wayfarers mistook close oil-burning headlights for much more distant electric headlights and crossed rails to their deaths.

Henry James scrutinized rural crossings and signs in the first years of the century. At the beginning of *The American Scene*, he notes of a sleepy New England rural village that "the present, the positive, was mainly represented, ever, by the level railway-crossing," the "localization of possible death and destruction." For James, the ubiquitous signs lettered LOOK OUT reflect "a kind of monotony of acquiescence" to the railroad trains, an unnerving intrusion of industrial power into bucolic scenery.[26] For less contemplative Americans, the signs announced danger, pure and simple.

Crossing signs, usually painted white with black letters, evolved slowly. On some western railroads, small rectangles painted with lengthy legends sufficed to warn wayfarers who could see for miles in any direction; on plateaus, for example, both the Denver and Rio Grande Western and the Santa Fe contented themselves with rectangular signs perhaps four feet long and two feet high, nailed to posts about six feet above the ground. Eastern railroads, often hidden by vegetation and carrying faster, more frequent trains, relied first on thick white posts, painted with warnings lettered vertically down the shafts. Oval, often mass-produced signs, usually lettered RAILROAD CROSSING: STOP, LOOK, AND LISTEN, replaced the shafts in the Middle Atlantic States and much of the Midwest east of the Mississippi River.[27] In New England and in the South endured the triangular, very tall sign made of linked boards; lettered LOOK OUT FOR THE CARS—DANGER, it avoided the use of the more modern term *train*.[28] While many of the triangular signs lasted until the 1960s in rural areas, by the 1920s the "sawbuck" sign marked most mainline crossings in the northeastern and midwestern sections, and in California. Two crossed white-painted boards, one lettered RAILROAD CROSSING and the other lettered with the familiar litany, STOP, LOOK, AND LISTEN, placed atop a ten- or twelve-foot-high post advertised by their form the existence of a crossing. Many companies nailed additional signs on the posts, particularly one labeled TWO TRACKS.

Multiple-track crossings required the accessory signs because wayfarers died beneath the wheels of the trains that arrived just after trains in the opposite direction had passed. Pedestrians and drivers stopped for a train approaching from their right, for example, watched it pass, and crossed directly into a train coming from the left, and hidden by the first.[29] Crossings of three or four main-line tracks vastly increased the likelihood of such accidents. Railroad and municipal officials concerned with crossing safety learned, however, that the accessory signs attracted little notice even from wayfarers standing several feet from them.

By the 1920s, crossing-safety experts agreed that only an understanding of psychology would enable them to solve the grade-crossing problem and shed some light on the seeming uselessness of every sort of warning sign. The New York Central System safety department assigned agents to observe every wayfarer crossing busy grade crossings in Syracuse, Detroit, and Indianapolis during a twelve-hour period. The 1920 study revealed that "out of 7,779 persons only 359 looked both ways to see whether or not a train was coming, and not *one in five hundred* stopped and looked and listened."[30] Grade-crossing safety united railroad management and unions with police departments and public-spirited reformers, but no one clearly understood the significance of the statistics gathered to explain the psychology of the crossing-zone.

In all the published literature, only one experienced locomotive engineer hit on the psychological crux of the grade-crossing carnage. "Some people are always cussing the railroads and saying we are careless and risking the lives of people," he remarked when questioned by a magazine writer. "But they certainly don't *act* as if they thought we were careless."[31] All the safety equipment installed in the last decades of the nineteenth century, and the massive publicity campaigns of the 1900–15 era aimed at convincing the public that semaphores, interlocking plants, and automatic train stop devices made collisions between trains and derailments of trains almost impossible, backfired at every crossing. By the 1930s, analysis of train/automobile collisions began to bear out the opinion of the single locomotive engineer. So convinced was the public of the alertness of enginemen and the efficacy of air brakes and signals that it assumed every crossing to be safe. Automobiling sharpened the perception of railroad safety officials even as it increased the number of grade-crossing fatalities.

Railroad companies warred long and hard against streetcar companies, not only out of a fierce hatred of low-fare competition, but out of a genuine dread of trolley/train collisions at grade crossings. Street railways operated without the complicated mechanical and electrical signaling systems that characterized dense-traffic railroads, and from time to time, careless motormen whisked trolley cars directly into oncoming trains.[32] Whenever possible, railroad companies insisted that trolley lines cross over their rights-of-way on high trestles; such expensive bridging sometimes broke the resolve of trolley lines to enter a railroad company's territory, but it did spare the lives of countless passengers.[33] Automobiling proved less possible to control.

Early motorists quickly acquired the habit of racing trains to grade crossings, perhaps to test the mettle of their new machines, perhaps to prove their driving skills to passengers. Magazine advertisements encouraged the pastime; a full-color, full-page advertisement in a 1910 issue of *Collier's* champions Oldsmobiles by illustrating one outdistancing a speeding express. Unfortunately for so many daring motorists and their riders, roads often curved unexpectedly across the rails, forcing the speeders to choose between narrowly missing the locomotive or ditching into the adjacent fields or woods, a choice that sometimes devolved into no choice at all. Sometimes the racket of the automobile engines drowned out the locomotive whistle, sometimes engines failed in the effort to drag cars up and over high-ballasted rails. Primitive automobile braking systems often failed on long downgrades crossed by bottom-of-the-hill railroad alignments, and more than one engineer watched motorists roar directly into his path.[34] In the early years of the new century, many neophyte motorists panicked when confronted by unusual situations, and the popular tale of the farmer yanking back on his flivver steering wheel and yelling "whoa" as his car careened down Main Street or into the barn perhaps explains the accidents in which motorists struck not the fronts of locomotives but coal tenders or even cars of the trains. As the death toll increased, railroad companies and municipal authorities set about making grade crossings safe

Magazine advertisement. (Courtesy of Oldsmobile Company, collection of the author)

for motorists, and they ignored the perception of the lone engineer who mused about public perceptions of railroad safety equipment.

At busy crossings, particularly in cities and inner suburbs, railroad companies employed flagmen to wave flags or red lanterns at the approach of every train. When pedestrians and many motorists ignored the watchmen—and in some cases knocked them down in their haste to cross the tracks—companies installed wooden gates to be lowered by the men when trains approached.[35] Lowering the white or white-and-black striped gates activated alarm bells at many crossings; at night, gatemen hung red lanterns from the gates to make them even more visible. At urban and suburban grade crossings, gate-tending meant continuous, hard work spinning wheels or cranks. "In greater New York alone there are 477 grade-crossings which are designated as dangerous," observed a 1913 *Scientific American* article entitled "The Grade-Crossing Scandal." "It is noted that in Brooklyn between Norwood Avenue and Jamaica there are from 210 to 322 train movements, daily, over the crossings at each street, and that at one of these an average of 423 school children cross the tracks four times each day." Flagmen and gate-tenders found it almost impossible to keep sidewalk and road traffic from backing up in such locations, because the frequent trains meant lowering the gates constantly. "An investigation of Railroad Avenue in Brooklyn showed that in an hour and a half 453 persons went over a crossing, over which 11 local trains and 25 express trains passed during the same period," the article continued.[36] Even assuming that some of the trains passed the crossing simultaneously, such heavy rail traffic suggests that the gateman lowered his barriers about every two minutes; typically, gates remained down for about one minute during the approach, passing, and leaving of the train.[37] Often they remained down if another train approached on a different track, and they remained down for several minutes while protecting long, slow freight trains. By the early 1920s, some freight trains reached nearly a mile in length; such a train, struggling uphill perhaps, might take ten minutes to cross a road. Crossings like those in Brooklyn constantly enraged wayfarers and encouraged people to race trains; watchmen frequently rescued children and groups of children from almost certain death. And when trains stalled on crossings, perhaps because of switching activities, pedestrians often crawled under cars or, even worse, clambered over the couplings between cars; when stopped trains suddenly started, people died.

Adding gates, bells, and electric flashing lights at some crossings at first seemed to help, especially if the gates overlapped each other to prevent motorists from snaking past them onto the tracks. But by 1913, experts knew that "numerically as well as comparatively more persons are killed at protected crossings," at crossings defended by watchmen, gates, bells, lights, and signs.[38] What accounted for "comparatively"? Certainly protected crossings usually passed many more wayfarers than unprotected rural crossings far from towns, but why did proportionately more people collide with trains there? Did carelessness born of some mad scurrying haste account for the deaths, or was it the old "familiarity with the timetable" syndrome? If anything, a sort of early-twentieth-century highway hypnosis might explain the accidents at protected crossings. "How many of you readers heard your clock strike the most recent hour?" asks Whiting in his 1913 article.[39] People intimately familiar with their route to work, to shopping, to school simply did not *realize* the protected crossings. Lost in some sort of waking trance, they walked past the lights or drove directly into and through the gates. "Disgusted railroad men will some-times tell you that the more you protect a crossing, the worse people behave," Furnas noted in 1937. "They seem to figure that if the company has taken all that trouble, the driver is absolved of responsibility for himself."[40] So con-cerned were California authorities that as early as 1917 they began designing speed bumps into paved highways approaching crossings, hoping that a vio-lent jarring would knock motorists out of their trances and apprise them that they "should cut down speed and be on the lookout for warning signals."[41] By 1937, after the speed bumps had increased in height to two or three feet, one magazine writer concluded that they did nothing to alert motorists. Driv-ers simply breezed over them, crashed through gates, and struck trains.[42] When reformers suggested that railroad companies install gates so solid that motor-ists could not break through them, companies replied that such gates could not be designed. The flimsy gates, they explained, existed to permit motorists to crash through both pairs and escape death, or through the far pair if they entered the crossing as the gates lowered.[43] By the early 1930s, the protected grade crossing displayed the gadgets of mechanical, electrical, and efficiency engineers—and all of the engineers had failed.

As early as 1911, the backfire effect of protecting crossings with flagmen and machines attracted attention. In "Speed: The Price We Pay in Lives for a Thing We Do Not Get," a lengthy *Hampton's Magazine* piece, Charles Edward Russell declared that "out in the country the only safeguard is a ridiculous little sign-board, undiscoverable at night, reading 'Railroad Crossing' or 'Look Out for the Cars,'" often located "where it cannot be seen until one is upon the tracks." Denouncing such typical signs as "deadly snares," Russell ex-plained the consequence: "As he drives or motors along the country road he knows not what moment he may see too late the maddening little sign 'Rail-road Crossing,' and a flying express be upon him."[44] Buried in Russell's fiery piece is the germ of a concept that occurred to safety experts in the 1920s. Protecting dangerous crossings with gatemen, gates, lights, signs, and bells implies that crossings not so protected are essentially safe. In actuality, the reverse often proved true. Heavily protected crossings, usually in urban or suburban locations having very heavy wayfarer traffic, often stood at places where trains ran reasonably slowly. In rural areas, where few wayfarers crossed a particular crossing, express trains might be hurtling along at a hundred miles an hour. Farm families might know about such scheduled juggernauts, but

Patent warning signal, ca. 1915. (Collection of the author)

tourists like Henry James, motoring in a heavily wooded, hilly countryside in search of charming vistas and traditional landscape, did not.

Keeping the motoring public aware that any turn in the road might lead into a crossing zone aroused the efforts of safety educators and of at least one manufacturing corporation. In the 1930s, the Burma-Shave Company lettered many of its well-known sequential advertising signs with warnings of grade-crossing danger. Motorists driving along country roads passed groups of seven signs, each lettered with one or two words of a jingle that advertised the company product. Usually humorous, the signs delighted the automobile drivers, but about one subject the company never joked, although puns barbed its serious messages. "Remember This / If You'd / Be Spared / Trains Don't Whistle / Because They're Scared / Burma-Shave," announced one seven-sign sequence. "Train Approaching / Whistle Squealing / Pause! / Avoid That / Run-Down Feeling! / Burma-Shave," warned another. The signs certainly boosted sales of the firm's toilet products; perhaps they also boosted public awareness of the deadly crossing zone into which motorists sped at ever-increasing speeds. But rising death and injury tolls indicate that many drivers disregarded the company's advice: "Drive Like / A Railroad Engineer / Take It Easy / When the Road's / Not Clear."[45] Any railroad official knew all too well that most motorists drove with only a fraction of the care and skill demanded of locomotive engineers.

Cows derailed trains, despite the pilots called "cow-catchers" by the public, but only rarely; in train/wagon collisions, locomotives usually remained on the rails. But motor cars, and motor trucks, represented vastly more serious threats, if not to the train passengers, certainly to the engine crews. "I've seen this cab so full of busted glass when we hit a bus that you couldn't walk for it," reported one engineer frightened of encounters with steel-frame vehicles. "And last year, well, we hit a light truck doing over seventy and the back end of it came off and ripped the whole side off the engine cab."[46] Such reports, increasingly common in the 1920s and 1930s, often included eyewitness accounts of pieces of motor cars flying up and raining down on baggage car roofs far behind locomotives. Trucks carrying sand, coal, and other very heavy materials often derailed locomotives and trains, but the nightmare of every engine crew after 1920 involved gasoline-carrying trucks. Burgeoning automobile use caused gasoline stations to sprout everywhere and large tank trucks to trundle gasoline from industrial-zone refineries to them. When such a truck stalled on a grade crossing, or lost its trailer while jolting over the rails, an engine crew knew that braking was impossible. To stop the locomotive, or worse, the passenger cars, in the midst of a sea of flames ignited by sparks from the locomotive ash box and grinding steel meant incinerating crew and passengers. At such instants, engine crews did not check speed but hurtled on, praying that locomotive and cars would stay on the rails and stop away from the inferno.[47] Despite such incidents, despite the appearance of such a disaster in an early 1930s Hollywood film, despite the fierce orders from their supervisors, drivers of the wheeled bombs lettered "This Vehicle Stops at all Railroad Crossings" persisted in rumbling in front of trains.[48] As early as 1918, railroad crews, management, and passengers had had enough; by 1925, when the protected grade crossing struck so many observers as a joke, railroad companies and a large portion of the public embraced the cause of grade separation.

Operating multisection express passenger trains caused many railroad companies to advocate the separation of rails from roads. While the typical grade-crossing collision usually did little damage to Pullman-passenger quietude, stopping a leading section of a multisection train meant risking a rear-end collision of the sort that occurred on December 9, 1923, just outside the tiny hamlet of Forsyth, New York. The second section of *The Twentieth Century Limited* collided with an automobile at a rural grade crossing and screeched to a halt. The third section, following at high speed only several minutes behind, lurched to a stop as its engineer noticed the red signal light glowing murkily through rain and fog. As the rear-end observation car passengers tarried over nightcaps, the fourth section rammed into the third, killing and injuring scores of people and awakening the sleeping farm families with a midnight crash that boomed for miles.[49] Subsequent investigation faulted the engineer of the last section for overrunning signals, but the cause of the accident, as editorials and politicians claimed, lay at the grade crossing.

Eradicating grade crossings, like abating power-station smoke, produced unanticipated results. Two groups of reformers offered ways to decrease the crossing-zone carnage, and both learned the vexations of simple, physical environment solutions applied to problems of environmental behavior.

One group urged the dead-ending of roads. "Apparently it has never occurred to many who campaign against grade crossings that much of the trouble would disappear by the simple expedient of eliminating a number of the roads that now cross the tracks," concluded one 1934 *Forum* writer. Russell Holt Peters argued that vast numbers of "section roads," especially in the High Plains, could be terminated at trackside, for "after all, if their users are forced to travel three miles to [another] railroad crossing they will have consumed only five or six minutes, at the most, in their automobiles." Peters insisted that the Union Pacific could abolish nearly three-fourths of the crossings along its Omaha to Cheyenne main line if little-used dirt section roads could be dead-ended. He claimed that "the selfishness of various individuals" worked against his clear-minded plan, but dead-ending created other difficulties.[50] When a road ended in a permanently fixed fence, some railroad companies learned, many motorists for reasons not clearly understood simply drove into them, through them, and onto tracks, "by a kind of unpremeditated breaking and entering," in the words of another journalist.[51] But self interest,

Separated crossing, Ohio. (JRS)

From grade crossing to grade separation in Memphis; two views from the late 1920s. (Courtesy of Loeb Library, Harvard University)

as Peters admits, caused most dead-ending attempts to terminate in controversy and open crossings, not fences.

Self-interest hampered the alternative, too. Separating track and road meant remarkable feats of elevation, often involving the lowering of track and the raising of road, or vice versa. Such engineering feats produced secondary environmental changes, too, of course, often totally unanticipated. Replacing a four-track grade crossing with a highway underpass meant directing pedestrians and motorists through a fifty-foot-long tunnel; building an overpass meant elevating the road for some distance, often five or six hundred feet if the road carried trolley cars, on either side of the railroad right-of-way. Most public observers denounced highway underpasses for creating "Chinese walls" that divided towns. "Cutting through the center of town, spoiling the view from salable houses and lots, and intruding itself" on the public notice, elevated railroads quickly acquired evil names for what they did to such downtowns as Philadelphia and Providence, for suburbs like Forest Hills Gardens and Forest Hills outside of New York and Boston, and for damage to countless small towns like Winchester, Massachusetts.[52] Abutters of the newly safe railroad perched high on its embankment learned of its fierce wall-like effect.

Dead-ending city and village streets struck many reformers as unwise in an era of growing automobile congestion and dangerous from a political point of view. Elevating main lines meant the automatic dead-ending of some streets immediately adjacent to the one crossed by a new railroad bridge, because the regrading of the railroad right-of-way created hills on either side of the bridge, which cut across formerly level grade crossings. "The proprietor of the snubbed gas station, the owner of the abutting land, the local politician spurred into action by these gentlemen, will all get up on their hind legs and protest bitterly about having their thoroughfare dead-ended," complained one safety-conscious writer. Offering such aroused citizens a highway overpass did little to quiet them, because the elevated pavement loomed above their businesses. From time to time, grade separation succeeded, but often only when grade-crossing danger overpowered such strong opposition, or, as in South Pasadena, when the city and railroad companies installed overpasses before abutting land was developed.[53] In more settled locations, such efforts usually backfired.

Railroad companies learned quickly that even if state, county, and municipal governments shared half the cost of elevating or lowering railroad tracks, tax assessors treated the entire finished structure as a wholly taxable improvement. Consequently, despite their anxiety concerning grade-crossing collisions, many companies moved slowly, and when they did, they encountered political whirlwinds like that aroused in Winchester, a Boston suburb, in the first twenty years of the century.

A typical grade-separation controversy occurred at Winchester, but one better documented than most. So fierce was the dissension to one plan after another that the town meeting appointed a special committee to inquire into each of the submitted plans, choose one, and defend it publicly. Since the committee could not arrive at a joint decision, debate continued. Not for several years, and then only by compromise, did Winchester resolve its safety problem.

The Boston & Maine tracks split Winchester's small commercial district, delayed pedestrian, streetcar, and carriage traffic, and proved a place of death and "many a narrow escape." At the grade crossing, Main Street encountered a force more powerful than anything local businessmen could muster, something that literally divided the town. Designers proposed several solutions; the Boston & Maine Company, by then wise in the ways of local politics, told the town that it had no plan but would build anything the town wanted. Once certain of the railroad company's cooperation, designers proposed three solutions: depressing the tracks in a trench and raising Main Street a little; elevating Main Street on great ramps over undisturbed railroad tracks; or lowering Main Street a little while elevating the tracks a little. Of course, local topography and local business conditions created additional problems. Chief among them, according to the *Report of Special Committee on Grade Crossing*, stood the necessity of maintaining smooth streetcar circulation along Main Street; the street railway companies did not want any grades over the railroad track.[54] Elevating Main Street on bridges not only meant taxing the climbing ability of the trolley cars, but the taking of some buildings. Depressing the tracks in a trench meant interfering with roads paralleling Main Street, either by dead-ending them or by building additional bridges. One citizen proposed building two bridges rather than dead-ending one road, but the committee, aware of the expense implicit in such a compromise, continued examining single-bridge plans.

As in so many other municipalities, the town fathers determined to select "the simplest plan all other things being equal," constantly remembering that the best plan must also be the cheapest and must cause "the least divergence of travel from its customary and most convenient routes" as well as "the least disturbance to private property by the taking of or changes in the same." Juggling such conflicting standards meant in Winchester, as in so many other business districts, adopting the plan that called for partially lowering Main Street and partially elevating the railroad.

The committee members agreed on the scheme for a number of reasons, each of which it carefully explained. Aside from keeping lines of travel in their former directions, not changing the location of "the present business center," the railroad station, and the village green, and causing the least damage to private property and the least interruption of travel during construction, the "Stone Arch Bridge Plan" provided other benefits, at least at the beginning— and middle—of the debate. "Less work is necessitated for man and beast in dropping seven feet and going up again than in climbing sixteen feet and going down again as is necessitated by all of the other plans," the *Report*

Today the elevated right-of-way still bisects the commercial district of Winchester. (JRS)

1930s crossing-zone commercialism, Ohio. (Courtesy of Library of Congress)

determined. Streetcar traffic would not be deflected, nor hampered by dangerous turns and grades. Raising the railroad right-of-way would even the route of trains over the depression in which the commercial center stood, and "on account of this feature the plan will probably receive the support of the railroad." And finally, and most important, the plan "automatically abolishes the grade crossing at the foot of Walnut Street, at the present railroad station."[55] By elevating the railroad tracks, therefore, Main Street businessmen channeled more and more traffic to Main Street, away from Walnut Street. Since almost everyone—with the possible exception of Walnut Street businessmen—agreed that a second bridge would be prohibitively expensive, Walnut Street would be dead-ended.

As built, the grade separation reveals the channeling effect never explicitly addressed in the *Report*. Walnut Street crossed under the right-of-way, but only in a pedestrian tunnel, not in a tunnel big enough for vehicles larger than bicycles. Winchester achieved safety, but at a clearly visible cost. The railroad embankment divides the Main Street commercial center at right angles to the chief shopping street, passing over Main Street on a heavy bridge that makes street traffic pass through a dark, almost tunnel-like hole. Walnut Street businesses, suddenly cut from regular traffic flow, remain distinctly secondary.

Not surprisingly then, many businessmen chose to fight grade-separation schemes. They knew that real estate adjacent to a crossing proved valuable in many ways. Pedestrians and motorists delayed by trains looked in shop windows, bought ice cream, or purchased gasoline. By 1930, crossing zones included more than tracks and ways intersecting at a spot marked by signs and often protected by gates, bells, lights, and watchmen. Businesses jammed against the tracks, and their jumble of lighted signs and other attention-getting devices frequently deflected motorist attention from the warnings of collision danger.

Crossing-zone commercialism remained starkly simple at most crossings, especially in rural areas. Not every rural crossing boasted a general store or a gasoline station; most did not. But at many evolved a commercial environment like that described by Ellen Glasgow in her 1925 novel, *Broomsedge*. The "bare station," "the crude frame buildings," the "gleaming track which ran north and south," "the telegraph poles and the hitching rail by the store," and "the sunken road winding in scallops through interminable acres of broomsedge" represented some trace of urban commercialism that remained after the passenger and freight trains had passed. For the heroine of the novel, "the passing trains had been a part of that expected miracle, the something different in the future," the something that led away from the crossing-zone general store. "There was glamour for her in the receding smoke," Glasgow continued in her description of the girl imprisoned in the crossing zone. "Some day, so ran the bright thread of her dream, the moving train would stop," and a handsome stranger would whisk her aboard. "And the train would rush on with them into the something different beyond the misty edge of the horizon."[56] Across rural America, landscape indeed intersected something different at every grade-crossing zone. It intersected the essentially urban, advanced technology, high-speed track of Atropos.

Closer to cities, where industrial zones and residential suburbs existed along the spines of railroad rights-of-way, crossing zones focused public awareness on the importance of rail traffic—and its difference from road traffic. The separated rail/road crossing epitomized the early-twentieth-century reluctance of town and suburb to merge with the metropolitan space of the right-of-way, to not only adjoin it, but to become one with it. "Danger," warned the grade crossing sign—danger not only of collision, but of the melding of traditional landscape into something new.

7. DEPOT

Main Street running almost at a right angle to depot and tracks. (Courtesy of Colorado Historical Society)

ALL THE WONDERS OF THE
metropolitan corridor, the elegance, the speed, the precision, and, above all, the energy sapped the traditional strength of small-town America, making Main Street into an extension of Depot Street or Railroad Avenue. In the years after 1880, railroad depots became the hubs of small-town life; around them developed businesses dependent on train transportation, and in them converged people anxious to learn the latest telegraphic news, to greet travelers from the corridor, and to depart from traditional life to the mysteries of Pullman sleepers and underground terminals. No longer did the general store, barber shop, and post office focus small-town life; instead the depot, the gateway to the corridor, attracted everyone interested in metropolitan excitement.

Not every small town boasted a depot. The hill towns of northern New England, the crossroads villages of the Tidewater South, the smallest villages of the Midwest and High Plains often languished miles from the nearest high iron. At the end of the nineteenth century, such communities existed as shadows of their once-prosperous selves; their "best" citizens deserted them for places with "get-up-and-go," and American slang identified them as "wide places in the road."[1] No metropolitan-corridor vitality quickened business in their streets or prompted storekeepers and householders to paint their structures.[2] After 1890 the national periodical press simply ignored them.

In countless other places, the depot stood a mile or more from Main Street, located by civil engineers at a location convenient to railroad operations, not townspeople. Railroads skirted towns built in hollows or on hilltops, and turn-of-the-century small-town businessmen slowly learned the dangers of having depots located so far from stores, hotel, and offices. Shabbiness stalked such towns, and residents shivered.

American novelists understood the striking significance of the depot separated from the town it served. "The lonely station of Manzanita stood out, sharp and unsightly, in the keen February sunlight," begins Samuel Hopkins Adams's 1921 retrospective novel, *Success*. "A mile away in the dip of the desert, lay the town, a sorry sprawl of frame buildings, patternless save for the one main street, which promptly lost itself at either end in a maze of cholla, prickly pear, and the lovely, golden-glowing roseo." Sited on the railroad, "a line as harshly uncompromising as the cold mathematics of the engineers who had mapped it," the station is home to the only "wide-awake" citizen of Manzanita, its young agent, who takes "a special and almost personal interest" in the operations of the railroad, and particularly in the passage of *The Transcontinental Limited*. "Past the gaunt station she roared, only seven minutes late, giving the imaginative young official a glimpse and flash of the uttermost luxury of travel: rich woods, gleaming metal, elegance of finish, and on the rear of the observation-car a group so lily-clad that Sears-Roebuck at its most glorious was not like unto them."[3] Of course, the *Limited* never stopped at Manzanita, but Banneker, the young station master, delights in assisting its flight over the line.

Banneker is tied more directly to the metropolitan life of the *Limited* than he is to the dusty street of Manzanita. Adams deftly portrays the daily existence of a small-town station agent, describing Banneker's brush with hoboes, occasional selling of a ticket, and ever-present attendance upon the clicking telegraph sounder. Indeed the telegraph wire acquires more significance than the luxury express, for it links the agent with his dispatcher in the city, and with unofficial urban business. Banneker devotes his days to sitting on the sunny station platform—always within earshot of the telegraph sounder—browsing through "the great Sears-Roebuck Semiannual Mail-Order Catalogue," not actually shopping, but rather "seeking oracles in those teeming pages."[4] Banneker delights in ordering practical and whimsical items from the mail-order firm, and his freedom from telegraph and express fees enables him to purchase more frequently than less fortunate readers of the catalogue. Adams makes clear Banneker's independence from Manzanita main-street stores—the agent even orders canned goods sent out from the city. What, then, is the frame station a mile from Manzanita? And what is its agent?

Writers of popular railroad fiction assumed readers knew the answers to such questions. "The local racketed its way past—the red tail-lights winked, and vanished—and there fell a silence, a drowsy night silence, broken only by the chirp of insects and the far-distant mutter of the receding train," wrote Frank L. Packard in his 1918 novel, *The Wire Devils*. "A few hundred yards away glinted the station semaphore and window lights; the siding switch light, nearer, showed green like a huge glowing emerald in the black; there was nothing else. There was no sign of habitation—nothing—the little hamlet lay hidden in a hollow a mile away on the station side of the track."[5] Readers understood that the isolated railroad station existed chiefly for the operation of the railroad. Its agent manned signals, received telegraph messages which he scrawled on flimsy sheets of paper and held aloft on bamboo sticks to train crews rushing past, assisted in the switching of cars, and provided countless other services helpful to *The Transcontinental Limited* tearing east or the coal train chugging west. Such stations provided important elements in the cinemalike view from speeding trains, particularly from night expresses. Their multicolored signal lights and dimly illuminated, bay-window operator's offices, set against backdrops of solid blackness, momentarily flashed upon the Pullman-car windows and vanished.

Isolated stations appealed to Adams, Packard, and other writers devoted to the metropolitan corridor because they straddled both modern and traditional space. In the view of the railroad employee—and in the vision of the passenger—they existed as markers along the corridor, places passed on time, or seven minutes late.[6] For the townspeople a mile or more distant, however, they served as portals, both to the corridor and to home, and so enjoyed something of the status accorded the "town" depot at the foot of Main Street, surrounded by grain elevator, freight house, stores, and shanties.

Town-depot architecture objectifies the curious double nature of the American small-town railroad station operation. While the depot belonged legally to the railroad company, it belonged emotionally to the townspeople it served. In the last decade of the nineteenth century, small-town Americans learned to view the structure with love and distrust.

While Pennsylvania Station, Grand Central Terminal, and other urban terminals represented large-scale architecture-by-efficiency, even the smallest wayside depot built after 1880 represented the railroad-company search for efficient structures. The typical small-town depot existed to serve several purposes, each clearly defined by its builders. It provided accommodation for passengers waiting to board and alighting from trains, sheltered people waiting for arriving friends and family and seeing off others, and received people having business with the telegraph office. Most Americans clearly understood such functions. Of secondary interest to the public, but because of its high profits, of chief importance to the railroad company, the freight business required adequate accommodation, too. Finally, the station sheltered a wide variety of activities vital to the safe operation of trains. In order to house these at times mutually contradictory activities in the most efficient manner possible, the companies turned to efficiency experts to guide architects and engineers. In the typical turn-of-the-century small town, only the depot objectified the metropolitan quest for crisp, almost crackling efficiency.

Passenger-handling operations involved a number of complex issues. A station had to accommodate people waiting for trains, of course, but it had to recognize that women might prefer separate waiting rooms, that in southern states all blacks had to be separated from whites, and that many would-be passengers might wish to smoke. Restrooms had to accommodate the often large numbers of people waiting for delayed trains, and coal-burning stoves had to be properly located in each of a station's waiting rooms. In the interest of efficiency, a single ticket window had to serve all waiting rooms, and all parts of each room, and the entrances to restrooms had to be visible from it, so that the agent might detect unruly individuals, tramps hoping to warm themselves by the stoves, and would-be passengers asleep in corners. Doors to the waiting rooms had to communicate directly to the station platform and

Small-town depots, ca. 1910. (Courtesy of Smithsonian Institution)

to the street side of the structure. In even the smallest of stations, passengers in the waiting rooms needed easy access to baggage-check windows.

Included in passenger service, to the bane of railroad company presidents and station agents, baggage checking and handling consumed uncountable man-hours of labor and vexation. Since so many passengers arrived just before train-time, the most efficient depot provided easy access to both ticket and baggage windows. At the same time, however, the baggage room required unobstructed access to the station platform wagons on which valises, trunks, and other objects, including pets, could be trundled to baggage cars. Corpses— "remains" in polite railroad language—traveled partly as passengers, partly as baggage, as one lugubrious turn-of-the-century song, "In the Baggage Coach Ahead," makes clear. Bereaved family members wanted coffins treated with utmost respect and insisted on their traveling in passenger train baggage cars. The typical depot baggage room, therefore, had to accommodate not only the hastily checked luggage of the dashing passenger, but coffins, snarling dogs, and steamer trunks, and it had to do so as efficiently as any in Grand Central Terminal.

Freight handling required a freight shed at all but the tiniest stations. As company instruction books make clear, freight included everything from small parcels sent express to mail to boxcars half-filled with boxes of sewing machines to hopper cars loaded with coal. Carload shipments required individual attention; consignees backed wagons against car doors and off-loaded the goods. All lesser shipments involved the station agent, who carried small parcels from the express cars of passenger trains, dragged mail sacks, and lugged bundles of newspapers. In a pre-truck era in which almost every long-distance shipment involved rail transport, the small-time depot received and shipped everything from raw milk in great cans to crates of strawberries to barrels of nails. Larger towns provided enough freight traffic to support separate freight stations; in smaller places, however, one structure sheltered both passenger and freight operations.

Operating the trains placed further demands on the structure. At almost every depot, train crews watched the signal called the "order board"; when it showed yellow or red, they slowed or stopped and received directives from the train dispatcher relayed through the station agent. Every station agent telegraphed the progress of trains passing his platform, so that the dispatchers knew the exact location of every train. Beyond such ever-present demands on his time, the agent looked after tools and equipment belonging to the company and used by repair crews. Consequently, almost every station thrust out a bay window toward the station platform; from his desk in the window, the agent could look both ways along the track, signal trains, and attend to his voluminous paperwork.[7]

At the majority of turn-of-the-century depots, one or two men carried out all the passenger, freight, and operating responsibilities. Heavy train traffic sometimes justified a round-the-clock operator to man signals and tele-graph key, just as heavy freight shipments required a warehouseman. While the relaxed pace of the agent in *Success* is an accurate reflection of life in a western, out-of-town station, few town stations enjoyed such relative peace. *Railway Station Service*, an extraordinarily detailed handbook of 1911 by Ben-jamin Chapman Burt, an executive of the Northwestern Railroad Company, focuses on the design and use of the small-town depot; it makes clear how little time most agents had for relaxation.

Burt surveyed the intricate responsibilities of the small-town depot-master, touching on such matters as the difficulty of selling tickets to rural folk unsure of their destinations, the federal postal regulations governing the carriage of mail, the sealing of refrigerator cars, and the washing of station floors and windows. Out of his long, detailed book emerges a picture of the agent as the ultra-efficient man of the century at work in a structure designed to encourage efficiency. He wrote of the "quasi-military nature of railway organization" and explained the nature of the railroad system. By *system*, Burt meant not only the entire railroad industry, but a mechanical and an organic entity. The me-chanical system is the quasi-military one, in which the agent and station are cogs in a vast machine operated according to well-conceived principles em-phasizing hierarchy, precision, and obedience.[8] Linked with it is the organic system of the railroad in its larger environment, and in the second system the station agent and depot are more than cogs.

Burt emphasized that every agent acts as an ambassador for his employer. Certainly, a good agent knows the condition of the track in front of his station, and in the process of selling tickets "may have to familiarize him-self with a territory twenty thousand miles, more or less, in extent." But the same agent must understand "the geographical, climatic, agricultural, miner-alogical, industrial," and other "physical and economic conditions" of his lo-cation, and he must report on such matters to the traffic department in the home office. "He will, if in an agricultural vicinity, for example, naturally seek to obtain complete and accurate information regarding crop conditions,—the kinds of crops, the acreage of each, progress in growth, the actual or probable yield, etc.," wrote Burt. "The agent desires to be, and is recognized to be, a real and beneficent force in the territory. While fully loyal to the company, he 'runs' his station in the interest of the community as well as of the company." If he does his job well, the station "comes to stand in truly organic relation to its surrounding territory, its environment."[9] Implicit in his handbook is a vi-sion of the station as a bridge between right-of-way and small town, a bridge guarded by an agent loyal, in the end, to the railroad company, not to the town.

Small-town depot architecture makes clear the role of the agent and helps define not only the metropolitan corridor but the public perception of it. The corridor edge lay at the street side of the station; within the doors a casual stroller encountered a structure designed for efficiency. The typical depot, a long, narrow rectangle parallel with the track, pivoted on the bay window in which the agent sat to operate signals and telegraph. On one or both sides of the operator's room were the waiting rooms, and beyond, at one end of the station, a freight room. A baggage room extending from the operator's office separated the two waiting rooms; often an extension of the baggage space provided rooms for toilets.[10] In such a structure, one or at most two men could carry out all the complexities of passenger, freight, and operating duties. In smaller stations, one man could sell tickets, check baggage, and give schedule information, all the while monitoring the telegraph key clicking in the bay; between passenger trains he could attend to the paperwork on his desk opposite the ticket-baggage window, or else walk to the freight room through a connecting door. In larger depots, one man handled everything but the responsibilities involving baggage and freight.[11] The central electricity-generating station, with its few workmen tending the most modern equipment in an engineered structure, did nothing less remarkable than a good agent in a busy, well-designed, small-town depot. Hardware and dry-goods stores, ice-cream parlors and livery stables exhibited little of the "live wire" scurry that characterized turn-of-the-century urban America. Only in the depot at train time did townspeople glimpse something of the scurrying efficiency that ruled the metropolitan corridor.

Company engineers consequently devoted much attention to creating "perfect" depots capable of one- or two-man operation. Once they discovered perfect form, the engineers proved remarkably reluctant to innovate.

Most western railroad companies, particularly the Union Pacific, the Santa Fe, the Great Northern, and the Chicago and Northwestern, evolved standard station types late in the nineteenth century. The last firm, for example, distinguished between its "No. 1" and "No. 2" station types; the first measured ninety by twenty feet and included a women's waiting room, while the second, intended for smaller towns, measured seventy-two by twenty feet and had only a combined waiting room.[12] When the Northwestern opened a new line across the High Plains, it bestowed one or the other on existing towns, according to the amount of passenger and freight traffic each municipality seemed likely to produce.

Other railroads made finer distinctions in the gradation of towns—and complementary depots. The Minneapolis, St. Paul, and Sault Ste. Marie Company, known throughout the nation as "the Soo Line," built three types of depots in North Dakota, calling them "standard" first-, second-, and third-class stations. "Some roads, often when constructing new lines, have had their engineering departments design a cheap, wooden, standard station," remarked a Chicago, Burlington, and Quincy Railroad Company booklet, *Farms in Iowa*, in 1907. "If business justifies, they improve it."[13] The Soo, following typical western practice, first erected temporary stations, tiny, twelve-foot-wide structures built in varying lengths. Once business improved, however,

"Standard No. 2" depot, Dike, Iowa, ca. 1906. (Courtesy of Division of the State Historical Society, Iowa State Historical Department)

RIGHT: *In the first years of the twentieth century, Coleraine, Minnesota, had only a tar-papered station. (Courtesy of Minnesota Historical Society)*

Temporary station, Bennett, Nebraska, 1872. (Courtesy of Nebraska State Historical Society)

In 1911, the Great Northern Railway Company provided the tiniest of stations for Enfield, Minnesota. (Courtesy of Minnesota Historical Society)

the firm replaced the first structures, usually with "standard second-class" depots. Built after an 1891 design, the second-class depot stood two stories tall; waiting rooms, ticket office, and operator's bay occupied the first floor, while the second floor provided housing for the agent and his family. The main structure, a rectangle of twenty-four by thirty-two feet, adjoined a single-story freight house, usually twenty-four or forty-eight feet in length, depending on the amount of freight traffic. Unlike the symmetrical stations favored by many companies, the Soo second-class depot had its ticket office and operator's bay at the end nearest the freight shed; the arrangement provided staircase space for the entrance to the upper-story living quarters and allowed the agent to enter the freight area without wholly abandoning his view of the waiting room and platform, and without passing out of earshot of the telegraph sounder. Between 1891 and 1920, the Soo built more than two hundred such depots in North Dakota alone, each characterized by shape, clapboard walls and cedar shingle roof, and function. A few large towns received the "first-class" depot, symmetrical structures organized about central ticket-operator offices and crowned by hip roofs, and thirteen others received "third-class" stations, one-story structures containing passenger waiting room, freight room, and agent office under a hipped roof, all in a rectangle twenty-four by fifty-six feet.[14] The standardization of depot design saved the firm money not only by dramatically reducing design and building costs, but also by heightening the efficiency of its agents, who worked in carefully planned spaces intended to reduce waste motion. Certainly, the standardization policy prevented disputes among towns and railroads concerning the quality of stations; no medium-sized town could complain that its depot looked less imposing than that in another town of similar population. The policy also anticipated structural changes resulting from traffic increases; just as the central electricity-generating station expanded by adding bays, so most standardized small-town depots expanded quickly and cheaply by the addition of bays—usually twenty-four-feet long—attached to freight rooms. Finally, the policy provided the Soo with an extraordinarily effective advertising device; the compact, well-built second-class station became a visual emblem of the firm and objectified the standardized service provided by its trains and employees.

Railroads depending heavily on tourist traffic expanded the concept of the standardized station to help create advertising images of the regions through which they passed. The Santa Fe Company, for example, devoted much attention to the "mission revival" or "mediterranean revival" type of station in an attempt to lure passengers to sunny southern California. While other railroads also erected a handful of such depots, the Santa Fe embarked on a substantial building program. In the first two decades of the twentieth century, it replaced many frame stations with stucco-covered or cement buildings characterized by red tile roofs and arcaded platforms.[15] While "Spanish" architecture meshed well in such New Mexico towns as Santa Fe, the curved windows, arches, and stucco proved far more noticeable in such railroad towns as Tucumcari, New Mexico, and in Illinois towns like Homewood. In full-page magazine advertisements, however, the distinctive depots leaped out as a powerful company trademark. For a time, the company considered replacing many of its small-town frame depots with a mass-produced cement structure in the "traditional" Spanish style.[16]

Almost all railroads continued to build frame structures much less flamboyant than the Spanish-style stations erected by the Santa Fe. Few boards of directors missed the advertising potential of depots, and by 1910 most firms had developed paint schemes instantly recognized by the general public. From a mile away, farmers could identify a Minneapolis & St. Louis Railroad Company station by its bright Kelley green color, or spot a Chicago Great Western one by its maroon sides and cream trim. Even eastern companies whose stations predated the era of standardized architecture adopted standardized "liveries." The Reading, for example, became famous for its "chocolate and vanilla" paint scheme.[17] Standardizing shape and color proved marvelously effective in boosting public recognition of a railroad company. "We have simple structures along our route that serve the public's needs," commented a Burlington & Missouri River Railroad Company superintendent of his firm's identical stations. "By having them shaped alike and painted the same color, they beome heralds. Since the public recognizes them as ours, we do not need to trouble ourselves by placing the railroad name on these depots."[18] Manipulating paint schemes for advertising purposes preoccupied railroad officials, who learned to paint freight and passenger cars distinctive colors, too. By 1911 they had hit upon a wonderfully useful way of magnifying the importance of their companies in small towns. Many firms leased property adjacent to small-town stations; operators of grain elevators, coal dealerships, lumber yards, and other businesses often found a leased location adjacent to a rail spur the most profitable spot to site their buildings. The businessmen quickly learned, however, that their leases required them to paint all their structures in the paint scheme of their railroad-company landlord.[19] The simple legal clause created great blocks of color near many small-town depots; the cluster of identically painted buildings, particularly the grain elevator thrusting far above adjacent roofs and trees, signified the importance of the railroad company in a way far more dramatic than a mission-revival station.

Standardized timekeeping aided the advertising effort, too. By instituting "standard time," the railroad industry made itself timekeeper to the nation. Over many stations loomed clock towers facing Main Street and other populated places; while the public enjoyed the chiming of church-steeple clocks, it looked to station clocks for perfect accuracy. Once a week, for decades at noon on Thursday, the Western Union time signal flashed across telegraph wires everywhere. Railroad officials used it to verify the correct time so essential to safe operation, but agents used it to adjust station clocks. The general public,

In 1913, La Bolt, South Dakota, boasted a new station adjacent to its earlier one; the windmill pumped water into the tank that served locomotives. (Courtesy of South Dakota State Historical Society)

After completion of the new depot, the railroad company removed the previous "temporary" one to another fledgling community. (Courtesy of South Dakota State Historical Society)

increasingly anxious about the accuracy of its timepieces, checked pocket watches and clocks against the time displayed on the station tower or, in most stations, on an inside wall. Incessant magazine advertising emphasized precision time-keeping in the hope of selling more watches; gradually the full-page notices proved effective, and farmers and other people accustomed to life without second-hands acquired the devices.[20] Small-town businessmen, with only slightly more need for watches—unless they needed to catch a train—acquired fine timepieces in an attempt to ally themselves with urban businessmen. In many towns gradually evolved the weekly custom of businessmen and boys drifting over to the depot around noon on Thursday to assess the accuracy of their watches. The electric time signal and the station clock governed small-town time almost everywhere in the nation.[21] The clock in the drug store or on the church steeple told time, but only the station clock provided the "standard" time of the metropolitan corridor.

Not only time signals flashed along the telegraph wires. By 1900, the typical small-town depot had become the entrepôt of nearly all news. The mail sacks handed down from local trains—and flung from high-speed ex-presses—contained letters, newspapers, magazines, and catalogues, all windows on the larger world. Many isolated depots and some small-town stations housed post offices in waiting-room corners, and in the years before the estab-lishing of Rural Free Delivery and, subsequently, Parcel Post, farmers and townspeople picked up and dispatched mail just inside the edge of the metro-politan corridor.[22] On many railroads, special "railway post office" cars, car-ried regularly on fast passenger limiteds, offered townspeople at selected stops the luxury of dropping letters directly into rolling post offices; inside the "RPOs," postal workers sorted mail and delivered it down the line. Small towns received no such service; as *The Fast Mail* or *The Eastbound Mail* roared through, a mail clerk flung out a sack of mail to the station agent, and in a whir that delighted adults and children alike, grabbed a waiting sack of letters from its hook at one end of the platform.[23] Other messages arrived in town by the company-owned telegraph lines—"the self-consciousness of the rail-way system," according to Burt—or by Western Union, which advertised its public wires by uniform blue-and-white signs nailed to depots across the na-tion. "The night telegraph operator at the railroad station was the most mel-odramatic figure in town: awake at three in the morning, alone in a room hectic with clatter of the telegraph key," noted Sinclair Lewis in 1920. "All night he 'talked' to operators twenty, fifty, a hundred miles away." In small-town fiction like Anderson's *Winesburg, Ohio* and in railroad fiction like Frank Packard's *The Night Operator*, the depot agent–telegraphist does far more than receive reports of weather changes, election results, family emergencies, and prizefights. He alone fluently speaks and understands the audio-visual lan-guage of the corridor; only he interprets the multicolored signals, and only he makes sense of the staccato Morse code.[24] In turn-of-the-century small

B. & M. Station, Woburn, Mass.

Small-town station with clock tower. (Collection of the author)

Using a rolling post office, ca. 1900.
(From James, "The Railway Mail Service," collection of the author)

A rolling post office, brand new in 1898. (Courtesy of Delaware State Archives)

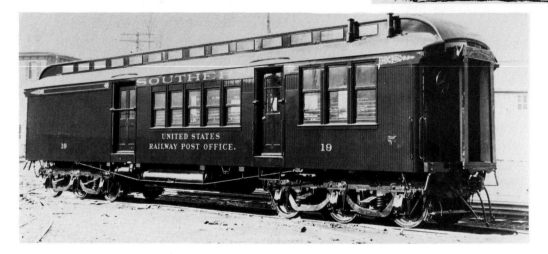

Railroad station and post office, telegraph office and freight house, on the Delaware & Hudson Railroad. (Courtesy of Delaware & Hudson Railroad, collection of the author)

Depot agent Harry Ellis, surrounded by the mysteries of telegraph equipment in the Solway, Minnesota, station, ca. 1910. (Courtesy of Minnesota Historical Society)

Illustration from "The Men Who Miss the Train." (Collection of the author)

In 1914, at Mountain Lake, Minnesota, and hundreds of other small-town stations, train time meant metropolitan bustle. (Courtesy of Minnesota Historical Society)

towns, the depot served not only as the information funnel, but as a prism through which Main Street folk peered at metropolitan life.

As early as the mid-nineteenth century, Thoreau had grumbled that the arrivals and departures of trains at the Concord depot regulated the village day, but not for fifty years did the small town become dependent on the depot for its daily existence. So gradual was the change that it passed essentially unnoticed, except by occasional poets and other seers into the future. In an 1892 poem, "The Men Who Miss the Train," Sam Walter Foss remarked on the small-town men whose time-keeping proved less than precise:

> I loaf aroun' the depo' jest to see the Pullman scoot,
> An' to see the people scamper w'en they hear the engine toot;
> But w'at makes the most impression on my som'w'at active brain,
> Is the careless men who get there jest in time to miss the train.

The first stanza, part of the long-established genre of rural humor, gives little hint of the overall message of the didactic poem: "The Grand Trunk Railroad of Success, it runs through every clime, / But the Cars of Oppertunity they go on schedule time."[25] In his insistence on "success" as something found only in metropolitan ways, Foss mirrors the theme of Adams's novel, *Success*. Success in turn-of-the-century small-town America involved a clear understanding of the metropolitan energy that flowed along the high iron and spilled out the depot door.

Once poets and novelists began advertising the fact, small-town Americans awoke to their absolute dependence on depot activities. One magazine story after another begins in the way Frances Weston Carruth introduces her 1898 *Four O'Clock Magazine* short story, "In Grafton": "The railroad station was Grafton's one connecting link with the outside world. There one train rumbled in daily, depositing a scanty mail-bag and newspapers—but rarely any passengers." Such tales of small-town peacefulness become less frequent in the periodical press after 1890, however; more and more often appear stories scrutinizing the town as something other than self-sufficient. "Blizzard at Imogene," a 1900 *McClure's* short story by Frank B. Tracy, describes a meningitis epidemic in a town on the Dakota prairies. As one child after another dies, as the general practitioner proves unsuccessful in treating the disease, the townspeople learn the real horror of the blizzard raging about them: "They could not summon help from a distance, or go for it themselves, because telegraph wires were mute, and railway tracks and prairie roads were choked and absolutely impassable. The village seemed doomed." Only after a brave mother sledges her way to the next town and the railroad president learns of the crisis does the tone become optimistic. The railroad rotary snowplows smash open the drifts, a team of urban physicians and nurses is directed by the station agent to the houses of the critically ill, and the defeatism vanishes: "The epidemic was now soon conquered. The arrival of the train gave to the people courage and hope." Implicit in the story, however, is something other than the shallow "all's well that ends well" optimism of its conclusion. Tracy depicts a town not only demoralized by sudden disease, but somehow lacking in the oldfashioned pioneer spirit. Its men refuse to make the sledge journey, and finally only a determined mother sets out, together with her ill child and hired boy. "Fat, self-satisfied, and vain," Tracy calls the townspeople at the beginning of the story.[26] So dependent are they on the railroad that when the blizzard cuts the umbilical cord they simply wither. The mother saves her infant, but the railroad president, a master of the corridor, saves the other stricken children and in so doing rescues the town as well.

By 1920, when one literary critic labeled it "the revolt from the village" genre, the outpouring of poetry, novels, and short fiction analyzing the decline of small-town life offered an explanation for the complacency and defeatism Tracy describes in his short story. In the minds of dozens of writers, all of the "live wires" had deserted American small towns and fled to cities.

Small-town depots figure prominently in the genre, particularly in concluding scenes of novels. "After George counted his money he looked out of the window and was surprised to see that the train was still in Winesburg," wrote Sherwood Anderson in his 1919 collection of short stories concerning a boy growing up in a sterile midwestern town. "The young man, going out of his town to meet the adventure of life, began to think but he did not think of anything very big or dramatic."[27] *Winesburg, Ohio* makes clear why the preacher father of Waldo's *Magic Midland* forbids his son to while away hours at the small-town depot. Anderson, Waldo, and other contemporaneous novelists understood that boyhood fascination with city life began at the depot. When *The City of San Francisco* or *The Empire State Express* flashed by in all its urban splendor, the thoughts of a boy might all too easily follow the brass observation platform as it vanished down the high iron.

Railroad companies encouraged travel urges by providing not only free, handsomely illustrated calendars, but maps, posters, and timetables.[28] Novelists knew the imaginative power of such free, colorful literature. "He stopped at the railway station, and found that there was no train at this hour which stopped at the village," wrote Floyd Dell in the last paragraphs of his 1920 novel *Moon-Calf*. "Then he would walk. He turned to go, and his eye was caught by a map on the wall, a map in which a dozen iron roads were shown crossing the Middle West and centering in a dark blotch up in the corner."[29] The map offers an escape to the young hero, and he decides to flee along the iron roads. But as Dell made clear in a subsequent novel, the hero experiences a failure of nerve; the opening paragraphs of *Briary Bush* find him working on the town newspaper, in "his mind's eye the map on the wall of the railroad station."[30] Unlike the authors of so many stories and novels, the hero is "stuck" on Main Street, unable to experience the elevating mystery of boarding a Pullman—or even of hopping a freight, the poor man's way out of town.

Poor people understood characteristics of the depot missed by most other Americans. To the poorest, the hoboes hiking along the high iron or perched atop freight cars, every station represented a checkpoint on the right-of-way. Every bay window housed an agent or telegraph operator charged with apprehending or warning off such drifters.[31] Hoboes saw small-town depots as places to steal some warmth on a winter night or to "lift" the lunch basket of an unwary passenger. In the view of Jack London and railroad policemen, criminal tramps often preyed on baggage and freight shipments momentarily unguarded on the depot platform. Adams accurately portrays the role of the small-town station agent; when Banneker tells two tramps that "the hoose-gow is old and the sheriff is new," he says nothing different from the brusque line repeated at so many depots.[32] Every station agent accepted the responsibility of evicting trespassers from the right-of-way, and homeless people learned to avoid depots and remain crouched in the jungles.

"Deserving poor" found depots somewhat more accommodating. Immigrants arriving in agricultural regions, particularly the northern High Plains, encountered small-town stations as temporary refuges from travel and as sources of vital information. Out-of-work men found the depot agent a master of odd jobs; depending on the amount of traffic, an agent might hire one or more laborers to help load or unload freight cars, shovel coal, or perform other heavy labor. "Live-wire" boys learned that lesser jobs awaited them, particularly if the agent knew them to be of excellent character.[33] Boys delivered messages from the agent to townspeople, washed windows, and swept platforms; sometimes the agent paid his young helpers, sometimes he offered them the incomparable privilege of entering the bay-window office and sitting at the telegraph desk.

Akin to the boys anxious to watch the excitement of railroading and willing to do a little work in exchange for opportunities to experience inside matters like the telegraphing of train orders, "depot loungers" spent hours at small-town stations, particularly in summer.[34] Such men, often retired, did no work, except to give an occasional hand to an agent struggling with a heavy mailbag or trunk. "On the station platforms there are always two or three wooden packing-boxes, apparently marked for travel, but they are sacred from disturbance and remain on the platform forever; possibly the right train never comes along," observed Booth Tarkington in his 1899 novel about midwestern small-town life, *The Gentleman from Indiana*. "They serve to enthrone a few station loafers, who look out from under their hat-brims at the faces in the car-windows with the languid scorn a permanent fixture always has for a transient, and the pity an American feels for a fellow-being who does not live in his town."[35] Tarkington unwittingly identifies the crucial difference between the lounger and the tramp. The first is a citizen of the town and uses the station waiting room or platform as an extension of the hardware or general store, focused about a pot-bellied stove, or the courthouse-square bench;

in his mind, the station is his, because he is a citizen of the town to which the station "belongs." But the tramp is a citizen of the right-of-way, and an illicit citizen at that; as a trespasser on railroad property, he has no rights whatsoever to the depot, and his shabbiness of dress makes proper townspeople, especially women, identify him at once as a creature of the corridor.

Near the station, in a limbo between honest and dishonest poverty, lived the residents of shantytown. Almost every American small town, despite the boasts of its local newspaper, possessed one or more flimsy dwellings identified by proper townspeople, when such upstanding residents admitted to their existence, as part of the corridor, not part of the town.

Many shanties belonged to railroad companies and housed employees. Station agents deserved proper housing for their families, but lesser employees received much more flimsy dwellings. The lowliest dwelling, the car-body type, consisted of an old boxcar or passenger coach minus its trucks and propped on railroad ties. Car-body stations served only the tiniest, most insignificant towns; more frequently they existed as isolated stations useful for passing train orders but not passengers or freight. The Soo Line used car bodies for tool houses, offices, and for bunk houses; in the years between 1914 and 1916, company property officials recorded dozens of such structures in North Dakota alone.[36] In the age when railroad companies frequently housed their workers, particularly in isolated locations, such dwellings appeared at drawbridges, signal towers, and junctions, often inhabited by employees injured in the train service and reassigned by patriarchal companies to less active work. Loneliness often made such employees friendly, and glad of visits from anyone—except tramps. "The abandoned car upon the grass-grown siding had a light in the lower end and the door was open," writes Waldo of a particularly magic place in *The Magic Midland*. "The Welchman's quarters were cozy indeed. When the oil lamp was lighted on the red table cover, and maps spread out, when nights glistened blue-black in the car window-panes and trains went whistling by, it was easy to fancy you were traveling in your private cabin or special car—and that strange coasts were drifting past."[37] These dwellings proved enticing to adolescents not merely because they stood adjacent to *The Sunset Limited* and housed talkative, friendly masters of the right-of-way; they were physically one with moving trains. As curious hybrids between vehicle and structure, the cast-off car bodies struck many boys as extraordinarily wonderful places in which to live. Again and again in popular railroad fiction, they appear as the homes of corridor folk.

Slightly above the car-body in status, the shanty or shack, a flimsy frame structure covered with tar paper, housed employees with families. Most often, such dwellings sheltered maintenance laborers responsible for the condition of a section of track perhaps ten miles long. Charged with tamping spikes, filling gullies, and reporting dangerous damage, "track walkers" or "section men"—known as "gandy dancers" to the general public, a nickname resulting

Car-body housing, Colorado. (JRS)

Trackside shabbiness, 1931.
(Courtesy of Library of Congress)

from their rhythmic motions in swinging sledgehammers, picks, and other tools manufactured by the Gandy Tool Company of Chicago—not only worked along the spine of the corridor but lived in company shanties located on company property, sometimes in an isolated spot, but more often near a station.[38] Sometimes several railroad-company–owned shanties stood adjacent to a station, perhaps near the edge of the town, where land values remained cheap. Often shantytowns grew slowly, at towns' edges, when a retired gandy dancer or his widow bought a fragment of land and built a shanty freehold. Thoreau wondered at such shacks as early as the 1850s, noting in *Walden* that he found "the shanties which everywhere border our railroads" to house the "degraded poor," the Irish laborers on the right-of-way.[39] Decade after decade, railroad companies hired immigrants to work as section men, and shanty towns remained ethnically different from the residential streets abutting Main Street. The nickname gandy dancer is doubly important, for it not only identifies the distinct work of the section men, but hints at "foreign" dances and other after-hours entertainment that enlivened shanties and aroused the wrath of small-town clergymen like the father described by Waldo. Railroad fiction unwittingly reveals the changing ethnic character of shantytown; by the 1890s, trainmen have Yankee or Irish names, while section men have Italian names; one or two decades later, Italian-Americans work in roundhouses and scorn the "foreign" Hungarian immigrants pounding spikes and living "down by the tracks."[40]

Once a shantytown grew beyond two or three dwellings and spread away from railroad-company land, it might grow into a larger community, like that described in the opening scene of *Our Town*, Thornton Wilder's popular play of 1938: "Up here is Main Street," says the narrator with a wave of his hand toward backstage. "Way back there is the railway station; tracks go that way. Polish Town's across the tracks, and some Canuck families." Shantytown, chiefly Polish-American, is consequently "beyond" Main Street, but in the zone of the depot. A few lines further on, the narrator explains that the depot agent "is gettin' ready to flag the 5:45 for Boston," and that nearby "in a cottage over by the tracks" a Polish-American woman has just given birth to twins.[41] In the years before 1938, *cottage* had acquired new meanings.

Traditionally, a cottage had no land around it, not even a yard, and in the eyes of the law it existed as a movable domicile, by definition a dwelling, a place of temporary residence.[42] While a few mid-nineteenth-century architects tried to popularize the word as the designation for a two- to four-room suburban house, *cottage* dropped from American usage, simply because almost all Americans owned houses, usually on farms, or rented domiciles with yards.[43] Dwellings without yards originated in factory towns—where some residents called them *cottages*—but first entered the national scene along railroad rights-of-way. So flimsy were the dwellings that Thoreau and other observers called them *shacks* or *shanties*; they seemed much less solid than the worker housing of mill villages. As Thoreau made clear in *Walden*, one man could quickly dismantle and move a railroad-worker shanty; such structures lacked cellars, fireplaces, masonry chimneys, and other features that give permanence to a structure.[44] The nickname "gandy dancer" has here still another connotation: a dancer is not rooted to any particular spot; he needs only a dwelling for shelter, since he is likely to move on. Between 1900 and 1930, however, as small-town Americans learned that residents of shanties would not move on but would have children requiring added rooms, *cottage* became a euphemism for *shanty*.[45] In so many small towns, the shanties had become permanent fixtures of shabbiness.

In cities, the preoccupation with shabbiness evolved largely from the aging of temporary structures and from the concerted efforts of a few reformers smitten with the beautiful city centers of Europe. As Frederick L. Allen pointedly remarked in a 1915 *House Beautiful* article entitled "Our National Shabbiness," Americans "build for the moment only," confidently expecting to replace new structures with better, bigger ones within two or three decades.[46] Of course, such structures when not replaced often aged terribly, exhibiting not the charm of an English brick or stone architectural gem, but a hideousness compounded of wood construction, poor-quality painting, and initial flimsiness of design. A few reformers emphasized the necessity of building exquisite structures every time—in 1905, Mary Bronson Hartt argued in a *World's Work* article that every shopping street ought to have blocks of stores in English half-timber or Queen Anne style—and others, including Frederick Law Olmsted, Jr., advised concerned Americans to find in pre-industrial New England towns the models for small-town beautification.[47] Almost none of the partisans of the City Beautiful and Village Improvement movements addressed the economics of small-town shabbiness, and their injunctions to plant street trees, clear away litter, and paint fences in the end produced little genuine improvement.[48] Camouflage could not conceal such powerful shabbiness.

On the one hand, shantytown shabbiness crept outward from the right-of-way. More shacks and perhaps a tiny grocery store or bar often appeared on the land adjacent to that owned by the railroad company. In towns with a factory or two, such extensions of tar-paper hovels often linked right-of-way with the minute small-town industrial zone.[49] Pullman passengers might momentarily grimace at the shacks, and "respectable" townspeople might fear the spread of shabbiness, but in the end, another, more terrifying shabbiness aroused small-town emotions.

In the years when Hartt, Olmsted, and other beauty-minded reformers published their condemnations and improvement-guides, another group of observers recorded the demise of small-town existence—and indirectly explained the shabbiness.

Perhaps the most perceptive of the observers was Charles Moreau Harger, who published "The Country Store" in a 1905 *Atlantic Monthly* issue.

Harger analyzed the effect of "the catalogues" on the crossroads and Main Street merchant and concluded that the great urban mail-order businesses might well destroy oldfashioned mercantile prosperity.[50] Massive advertising first threatened the Main Street businessman; when farm families and townspeople read advertisements in magazines and newspapers they wanted to compare the advertised products with those already in local stores.[51] Every bundle of magazines, every stack of circulars trundled from railroad mail car to depot to post office required storekeepers to stock new items. Then followed price wars, as the mail-order firms began offering cheaper prices on identical goods. Not surprisingly, Richard Warren Sears began his business career as depot agent in Redwood, Minnesota; in 1886, by selling watches from an unclaimed shipment, he suddenly realized the vast potential of mail-ordered, railroad-shipped merchandising; in a few years, the firm of Sears & Roebuck struck riches beyond imagination.[52] "Immense shipments of catalogs from Sears and Sawbuck, Monkey Ward and other mail-order houses—known by these names rather than by their formal titles—came two or three times a year," remembered one autobiographer of depot activity in a Missouri small town.[53] Harger pointed out the effect of such shipments, the price wars, and the willingness of the mail-order firms to entertain visitors at their urban locations.

"Instead of streets of brick blocks where thriving business houses bring the attendant features of modern town life, there would be only a railway station, post office, blacksmith shop, doctor's office, and grain elevator," he wrote of the long-term spatial change. "The county newspaper, which would contain no advertising except mail-order house announcements printed on its 'patent inside,' could probably occupy one end of the commodious freight depot which would be necessary to care for the many shipments of goods."[54] Harger quoted the "dark prediction" of a storekeeper in western Nebraska to the effect that such a catastrophe was imminent, and while his article did explain the strengths of the local stores—among them the willingness to extend credit—it clearly expressed deep concern, one voiced by hundreds of observers who watched small towns grow shabbier as luxury express trains grew ever more elegant.[55]

In the years between 1880 and 1930, Main Street storekeepers fought a losing battle with the mail-order firms. Novelists understood the power of urban advertising and the delights of urban goods; in *Main Street*, a 1920 bestseller, Sinclair Lewis depicted the worrisome problem of buying urban goods and alienating storekeeper neighbors, or purchasing locally available items and getting something other than one's true desire. The droughts, crop failures, and produce-price fluctuations of the 1920s caused financial chaos in many western small towns, of course, but the continuing effort to stay the power of the mail-order firms helps to explain the shabbiness of small-town America.[56]

Redwood, Minnesota, depot. (Collection of Donovan L. Hofsommer)

National advertising, national "brand-name" items, and mail-order buying combined to make the edges of small-town Main Streets seem shabby, as this 1920s view suggests. (Courtesy of Loeb Library, Harvard University)

Main Street businessmen had little capital and less energy to spend on beautification. Everywhere in the nation, they repainted their stores less frequently, put off projects like planting street trees or installing fountains, and—most important—chose not to replace the structures they once thought of as temporary. The buildings, never intended to last, required ever larger sums to maintain them, or to improve them, and the sums decreased the capital available for rebuilding. In the absence of economic studies, conclusions like those of Harger seem correct; the mail-order business drained money from Main Street and slowly made the once-glamorous stores seem shabby.

Again, nicknames suggest something of the importance of the mail-ordered, railroad-delivered trade. While a nickname like "gandy dancer" is essentially humorous but tinged with scorn, names like "Sears and Sawbuck" and "Monkey Ward" reveal the small-town and rural uncertainty concerning the city. "Monkey Ward" makes the great firm of Montgomery Ward more knowable, more manageable, more like a small-town neighbor. Small-town and rural Americans first applied such nicknames to political figures—"Andy" Jackson being perhaps the first—and eventually to railroad companies.[57] Calling the Chicago, Burlington, and Quincy the "Q" or the Missouri, Kansas, and Texas the "Katy" made the corporate entities somehow more familiar, and advertising agents now and then used the nicknames on boxcars as an attention-getting device.[58] More critical than the small boys and loungers, down to the "Katy" or "Frisco" depot at train-time went small-town capital, passing through the station doors en route to cities.

Adams's novel *Success* brilliantly captures the power of the station and mail-order catalogue by combining the two elements. Small-town America entered the metropolitan corridor in three stages: first, by receiving magazines, advertising circulars, and other urban literature delivered through the depot; second, by ordering and receiving mail-order goods ranging from canned food to bagged sugar to summer hats to kitchen stoves, all shipped through the station; and finally, by entering the depot, buying a ticket, and boarding the local way train or *The City of New Orleans*.

Not surprisingly, then, the small-town depot appears again and again in American literature as a liminal zone through which young people pass into adulthood, into adventure, and into real or seeming wisdom, and through which they sometimes return to find the towns of their youth, rarely beautiful but more often tawdry, "run-down" in the American expression that connotes a town hit by a train.[59] The depot exerted its fascination on children, and particularly on teenaged boys, because it was the threshold opening on metropolitan glamor and technological excitement.[60] It opened away from the restrictions of childhood and the smothering effect of conformist shabbiness. No wonder the Lionel Corporation sold so many different types of toy stations.[61]

And no wonder so many townspeople worried about the impression made

Station as threshold, seen from a grain elevator. (Collection of Donovan L. Hofsommer)

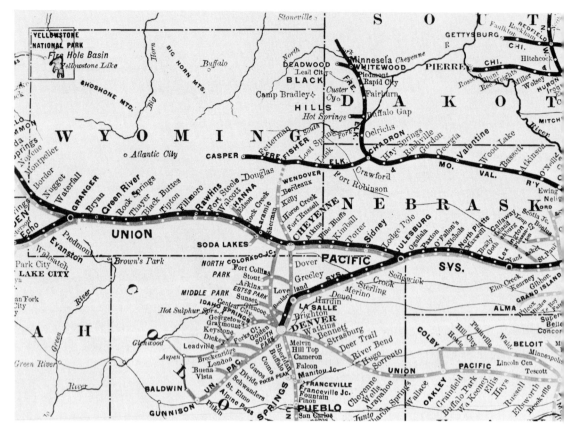

A 1902 Chicago & Northwestern Company system map represents small towns as appendages to the corridor. (Courtesy of Harvard College Library)

Perhaps taken from a grain elevator, this panoramic view of Roseau, Minnesota, in 1909 shows Main Street intimately connected to the corridor. (Courtesy of Minnesota Historical Society)

by "their" depot on express-train passengers. They worried that "their" Main Street would appear like so many others, a straight street running at right angles away from the corridor, as railroad companies printed the names of towns on system maps.[62] Standardized depot architecture and paint schemes did indeed make small towns seem remarkably alike, and urban American slang gradually reflected a Pullman-car viewpoint. Derogatory terms like *tank town* and *jerk-water town* refer to communities at which express trains stopped only to take on water; firemen jerked down the great spout of the elevated water tank and filled locomotive tenders while conductors worried about losing time and passengers gazed uninterested at a standardized station painted a standardized color, a few shanties, perhaps a lumber yard and grain elevator, nothing more—except one more Main Street. Afraid that a "No. 2"—or worse, "No. 3"—station might prompt Pullman riders to dismiss their town as one more in an endless blur of anonymous, insignificant "whistle stops," all flashing past like frenzied cinemagraph frames, Main Streeters fought against standardized architecture and painting. When the "Q" positively refused to repaint its depot in a color satisfactory to the citizens of Stanton, Iowa, the townspeople trespassed en masse and painted it white.[63] When Lewis's *Main Street* heroine embarks on a scheme to improve life in Gopher Prairie, however, she sets out "plants in the tiny triangular park at the railroad station." Unlike the people of Stanton, Carol Kennicott, believing in the "public-spiritedness of fuchsias and cannas," joins the great movement against shabbiness and fights to beautify not only the portal to the metropolitan corridor, but the corridor itself.[64]

8: GARDEN

Chestnut Hill station on the Boston & Albany nestled in immaculately kept grounds; even on a rainy day, structure and space remained attractive. (Courtesy of Loeb Library, Harvard University)

RAILROAD COMPANY
does not beautify its station grounds for philanthropic reasons," remarked
Paul Huebner of the Reading Railroad System in a 1906 issue of *Horticulture*.
"The basic idea is to increase traffic, and to do this, surroundings are made as
attractive as possible. Another point we have aimed at is hedging for the
purpose of preventing snow-drifts, as well as for ornament."[1] In the end,
however, even railroad-company employees admitted that everyone benefit-
ted from the massive plantings of trees, roses, privet hedges, and flowers.
Only vestiges endure of the magnificent gardens that won the admiration of
passengers and heartened civic improvement societies from coast to coast. The
railroad gardening craze convinced the public that corporations cared for beauty,
and that landscape architects could do more than create handsome cemeteries,
urban parks, and home grounds. Indeed, the gardens that delighted luxury-
train riders and refreshed weary commuters represent an innovative and highly
successful attempt by landscape architects to synthesize the diverse needs of
corporations, municipalities, civic betterment groups, and outspoken individuals.

Several forward-looking European and American landscape architects realized the potential for railroad gardens just after the post-1860 popularization of railroad travel. Europeans soon noted the haphazard plantings surrounding so many railroad-owned buildings. Many of the gardens resulted
from the European practice of building stations, switch towers, and signal
shanties with living quarters for employee families. Wives lavished attention
on the flower and vegetable gardens laid out by their husbands along the
station platforms and tracks. In France, railroad companies made token efforts
to beautify their structures, setting out, in the words of one critic, "the same
plants in the most different sorts of soil" at station after station, "finally creating an assemblage of irrational combinations." Edouard André scorned both
the company-sponsored efforts and the vernacular ornamentation he found in
England. "I have often seen the names of stations spelled out in small white
stones or in flowers on an embankment and other childishnesses of the sort,"
he remarked in 1879 in *L'Art des jardins*. Only in the plains of northern and
central Prussia did he find properly planted stands of trees adjacent to many
stations. The shade trees and flowers refreshed travelers stretching their legs

Station with garden, Greencastle, Pennsylvania, ca. 1905.
(Courtesy of Loeb Library, Harvard University)

during long stops and prompted André to develop the "principal traits" every station garden ought to display. He insisted that station grounds should have pleasant walks; trees planted to please the eye, provide shade, and not interfere with the walker's ability to see arriving and departing trains; perhaps a refreshment stand open in the summer; and "an extreme simplicity in the overall design and in the plant materials."[2] European railroads adopted several of André's suggestions, although many trackside gardens remained the work of station agents and gate-tenders, and of their families. In later decades, the mature railroad gardens of Europe exerted a powerful influence on American designers.

As early as 1867, a Connecticut agricultural reformer and landscape architect had already learned the lesson of European railroad gardens. Using the "charming wayside stations upon the Continent—in France, Germany, and Switzerland—where the station-master is also manager of a blooming garden" as examples for Americans, Donald G. Mitchell introduced readers of *Rural Studies* to the necessity of beautifying the railroad right-of-way.[3] Mitchell insisted that such gardens not only pleased the eye, but provided railroad employees with cash from the sale of bouquets of such flowers as roses, heliotropes, and marguerites. He doubted that American station-masters would be "capable of making themselves good florists at a bound," but he expressed confidence in their ability to garden under competent direction.

Mitchell's two chapters, "Railway Gardening" and "Landscape Treatment of Railways," include a wealth of far-sighted detail based on an intimate knowledge of soils and plant types. If municipal and corporate authorities could cooperate, he argued, the vicinity of railroad stations might be converted from muddy, garbage- and equipment-strewn wastes into "greens that should give piquant welcome to every stranger, and grow to be an object of town pride." He suggested that a custodian be appointed by either town or company, charged with the maintenance of the planting. Not only would such a well-designed, well-maintained site advertise the wisdom of both town and railroad company, but it would be a powerful advertisement for landscape architecture, since it would be visible to thousands. "It is in the way of being seen," Mitchell concluded, "of those who are not immediately engrossed with other care than the easy care of travel; it gives suggestions to them in their most accessible moods."[4] Mitchell's argument is extremely significant, for it is one of the first to imply that landscape architects should begin to "beautify" heavily used places within the metropolitan corridor, rather than building only parks and other retreats from scurry.

Mitchell argued for more than station "greens" and flower gardens. He addressed the complex issue of the railroad in the rural and suburban landscape and introduced the concept of planting for the benefit of passengers and for the stationary observer gazing at the passing train. He specified the sort of ground covers to use on south- and north-facing slopes of railroad cuts, commented on the usefulness of rhododendron, kalmia, English ivy, and grasses, and noted the possibility of planting columbine in the crevices of rocky cuttings. Such planting would bind soil and please the traveler gazing outward, but, as Mitchell admitted, it would be nearly invisible from any vantage point above the cut. About fills Mitchell was even more articulate. He suggested planting conifers to screen passing trains and explained the necessity of irregular alignments: "All right lines—whether of annual crops, hedge-rows, or avenues—will, of a surety, lose effect by being established parallel to the line of road." Mitchell's sensitivity to alignment resulted partly from his scrutiny of the gently curving railroad right-of-way, and also from his understanding of the peculiar landscape perception enjoyed by a train passenger. Above all, however, it originated in his assessment of a train as a pleasant object in a rural or suburban setting. He argued that a screen of conifers "should have its open bays upon the embankment itself, disclosing at intervals a glimpse of the passing trains."[5] A suburbanite assisted by a landscape architect might so plant a railroad embankment that the trains would provide a distinctive kinetic beauty as they flashed from one opening in the planting to another.

A suburbanite in a republican country ought to have some concern for the traveling public, he insisted, and therefore have an obligation to beautify any portion of his property abutting a railroad line. The same openings in the conifers that please the suburbanite sitting on his porch allow the passengers to glimpse the suburbanite's handsomely arranged lawns and flower beds. Mitchell consequently formulated the guiding principle of railroad gardening: the garden exists for both the observer of the station and the train, and for the observer in the station and the train. "The finest and highest triumphs in landscape art are wrought out in dealing with portentous features of ugliness," he concluded, "and so enleashing them with the harmonies of a given plan as to extort admiration."[6] Nothing of the nascent industrial-zone aesthetic informs his thinking. For Mitchell, the landscape architect had a duty to conceal or ameliorate anything non-rural.

Such thinking struck home in the newly created railroad suburbs evolving along the metropolitan corridor. Beautifying railroad station grounds and rights-of-way became to passenger agents nearly as important as erecting imposing stone and brick station structures to entice commuters—and wives of commuters—onto trains. Architect-designed suburban stations and landscape architect-designed station grounds reflected the railroad company attempt to understand and please the psyche of the commuter. By building fine stations sited among shrubs, trees, and flowers, railroad companies hoped to make new, half-developed suburban towns attractive to prospective residents and make the daily commute reasonably pleasant, at least pleasant enough that the commuter would not move back into the city. Good stations and grounds attracted passengers, and so made good business sense.

As early as 1881, Samuel Parsons noted the increasing emphasis on beautifying suburban stations and rights-of-way. In a *Scribner's Monthly* article entitled "Railway, Church-Yard, and Cemetery Lawn-Planting," he directed attention at the aesthetics uniting several seemingly different sorts of landscape design. His description of the station-grounds at Demarest, New Jersey included a careful cataloguing of the trees (linden, oak, weeping beech, maple), dwarf evergreens (Nordman's fir, glaucous juniper, conical spruce), shrubs (rhododendron, azalea), vines (moneywort, Virginia creeper, periwinkles), and grass and flowers, along with an analysis of the imported soil, use of local rocks, and general design. "A little of everything that properly pertained to a lawn was here, for variety had been one of the main objects sought, in order that the tedium of the waiting passenger might be alleviated as much as possible," he remarked of the site crossed by an oval carriage drive and a meandering path. The anonymous landscape architect had designed a compact but charming place where commuters might wait for the morning train, and where wives and children might gather to wait for the evening trains from New York and Newark. The low-maintenance planting pleased the railroad company, and the overall design pleased everyone else, including Parsons. "It was surprising how large the place seemed, as one rambled over this undulating path," he asserted. "The matter-of-fact visitor was even betrayed into the expression that it was as good in its way as anything in Central Park."[7]

A few such successes in eastern suburbs prompted other towns to request similar treatment. Railroad companies did not invariably comply, however, perhaps out of fear that such a rapidly spreading movement would eventually cost them a great deal of money. In the face of corporate disinterest, commuters sometimes formed groups similar to the one that retained Charles Eliot in 1890 to improve the grounds of the Boston and Maine station in Beverly, Massachusetts. Eliot created a simple plan, and the "improvement society" paid for its implementation, the railroad company refusing to do anything beyond the donation of some material and labor.[8] By 1900, however, prompted by public emotion and the desire to counter the public rage against high tariffs and hideous wrecks and emboldened by the example of the Boston and Albany Railroad, the nation's railroad companies began improving station grounds in dramatic ways.

According to a 1902 *House and Garden* article by Charles Mulford Robinson, the B&A involved itself in station-ground improvement through the publicity aroused by the success of a suburban station-master in planting a strictly vernacular sort of garden around his structure. He was soon assigned to study at the Arnold Arboretum and became the company's superintendent of station gardens. In the early 1880s, the B&A was just opening its "Newton Circuit," a commuter line through most of Boston's wealthiest suburbs. It had retained the architect H. H. Richardson to design the stations, and in an attempt to make commuting even more pleasant, hired Frederick Law Olmsted, Sr., to design the station grounds. Olmsted worked on a small budget; he

ABOVE: *Demarest depot, 1881. (From Parsons, "Railway, Church-Yard, and Cemetery Planting," collection of the author)*

BELOW: *Demarest depot, ca. 1950. (Courtesy of Smithsonian Institution)*

Newton Circuit stations and grounds.
(Courtesy of Loeb Library, Harvard University)

dispensed with lawns and annuals at the beginning and planted the grounds with perennials such as wild roses, bridal wreath, and Japanese ivy, along with such shade trees as white willow, American beech, and white pine. The rugged plants withstood the harsh winters well and cost little for maintenance; since most were low-growing, they accented rather than hid Richardson's low-level stone stations. Along the right-of-way on either side of the stations, Olmsted planted hardy shrubs, particularly wild roses, so that passengers looking out from stopped trains might have a pleasant view. Not everything turned out well in the collaboration; Robinson remarked that the lighting apparatus seemed remarkably ugly when juxtaposed with such fine buildings and grounds and noted that some manufacturer would one day make a magnificent profit by marketing a lamp-post different from "an electric globe on the end of a long curved arm of iron which is fastened to a wooden post." But the whole design struck Robinson as remarkably effective, with the exception of the lack of platform trees.[9] Again and again, observers of railroad gardens lamented the lack of planting on the track side of the stations; their laments derive from their ignorance of the safety hazard implicit in any arrangement of objects that obstructed the engineer's view of the station platform.[10]

Aside from such cavils, Robinson discovered the newly laid out grounds to be superbly attractive. "One can imagine a business man choosing Chestnut Hill for his place of residence for no other reason than the soothing charm with which its little station would daily wait his return and the lingering caress of beauty with which it would send him forth," he remarked of a typical Richardson-Olmsted project.[11] Two years later, in another *House and Garden* article, Robinson analyzed other stations on the B&A suburban routes. "To the commuter using a suburban railway the erection of pretty stations and the beautifying of their grounds is a matter of great concern," his article began. "It means the extension of the home atmosphere quite to the railroad track." By "home atmosphere" Robinson perhaps meant what might be termed "suburban atmosphere," because he analyzed very closely the new values of the quiet, curvilinear suburb. Among those values was a new concept of "home," as a continuum stretching from house to street to station park.[12] The success of Richardson and Olmsted brought many well-to-do commuters to the B&A-served suburbs and brought the company immense favorable publicity. It reprinted both of Robinson's articles as pamphlets and sought to extend the Olmsted-designed beauties to stations beyond suburban limits.

By 1905, learning to design station grounds had become an accepted part of landscape architectural education. "Rural Railway Station Grounds," an *American City* article of that year, explained an assignment given by Frank A. Waugh, a Massachusetts Agricultural College professor of landscape architecture, to his students. The studio project required students to return from Thanksgiving vacation with sketches of station grounds, classifying the sketches according to such component parts as platforms, foot approaches, and traffic space and analyzing the ornamental treatment of the sites. "The railroad station, being the front door to the neighborhood, should have the same artistic qualities as the front door of a public building or private residence," Waugh taught his students. But Waugh departed from the planting favored by Olmsted. He insisted that herbaceous plants required more expert care than shade trees and lawns and suggested to his students that a wide lawn in the end required less outlay of funds.[13] Waugh's article represents a turning point in railway-gardening literature. After 1905, the public expected suburban station grounds to be at least attractively maintained and hoped for some elements of beauty.

One landscape architect, Annetta E. McCrea, chaired the Railroad Improvement Committee of the American Civic Association, and in 1905 she issued a comprehensive report on the status of railroad station gardens. She discovered that many lines had employed landscape architects to redesign station grounds totally and to instruct company employees in the care of the plantings. The Michigan Central Railroad Company had built greenhouses to supply flowers for dining car tables and station-ground garden beds, the Norfolk and Western was emphasizing shrubbery, the Union Pacific was trying to grow deciduous trees at its desert stations in order to refresh weary passengers, the Central Railroad of New Jersey "park department" was setting out fifteen thousand plants each year, and the Boston and Maine, the same company that had refused to improve the Beverly station, had given each station agent ten dollars with which to purchase plants and had established a prize system that rewarded the best station gardens.[14] McCrea noted the difficulties of achieving color harmony in the lush climate of California, the success of the Pennsylvania Railroad in planting sod, and other details, but her chief discovery concerned the quality of planting. Railroad companies were gradually abandoning their former allegiance to beds planted with annual flowers. Instead they had begun to emphasize perennials, and especially local plants such as bittersweet, sweet fern, bayberry, and sumac. While some companies tried to grow plants unsuited to soils and climates—the Union Pacific's attempt at growing shade trees in Wyoming was an example—most had discovered the financial rewards of massed groupings of low-maintenance perennials.[15] But in 1905, many companies still ignored local plant materials in favor of imported varieties.

As late as 1913, the president of the American Civic Association pleaded for an end to the "hydrangea stage" of railway gardening, and a commitment to "naturalistic treatment." "I remember going through a town in central Texas some years ago, and being both aggravated and amused by the decrepit geranium beds in the Bermuda grass lawn which was the only bright feature visible," he remarked of a typical High Plains station garden. "For the fifty miles preceding the arrival at this station, and for one hundred miles beyond it, the train passed through the wealth of wild flowers at some seasons particularly characteristic of eastern Texas. All the passengers were on the jump to note

Scarsdale, New York, station and grounds. (From Baxter, "The Railway Beautiful," collection of the author)

Union Pacific station gardens in Wyoming. (Courtesy of Wyoming State Archives Museums and Historical Department)

Jefferson City, Missouri, station and grounds. (Courtesy of Loeb Library, Harvard University)

Union Pacific station gardens in Wyoming. (Courtesy of Wyoming State Archives Museums and Historical Department)

these flowers, which the speed of the train made it impossible to see with satisfaction." J. Horace McFarland concluded that if the railroad company had planted wildflowers around its station "the ten minutes while the train waited there would have been keenly enjoyable to the passengers on the train."[16] McFarland unwittingly embraced one side of a complex argument that eventually splintered the railway gardening movement.

Despite the growing public and corporate acceptance of railway beautification and the enthusiasm generated by illustrated magazine articles depicting European successes, the mid-1900s witnessed a division in the American effort. A single question divided proponents into two camps. For whom did the gardens exist? According to McFarland and others, the station and right-of-way plantings existed almost entirely for passengers on the trains, but for James Sturgis Pray, a Harvard University professor of landscape architecture, and for a number of other teachers, practitioners, and magazine commentators, they existed for the delight of townspeople and other non-train viewers.[17] McCrea and several other landscape architects tried to unite the two camps, but with little success. The two-part thinking foreseen by Mitchell in the late 1860s became the norm by 1915.

Articles in *Park and Cemetery* and other periodicals emphasized the potential of station grounds as public parks. At least one railroad company, the Canadian Pacific, did lay out station gardens that covered entire city blocks; at Red Deer and Macleod in Alberta, its station gardens were primarily for the enjoyment of non-train observers, and its bandstands and fountains inspired proponents of the station-garden-as-park.[18] As the station grounds at Demarest had proved decades earlier, and as the Olmsted-designed grounds that merged with a public park at Wellesley, Massachusetts, continued to show, the Canadian Pacific examples were far from unique. James Sturgis Pray, in the pages of *Parks and Recreation* and in a booklet called *Railroad Grounds*, emphasized the station-garden-as-park argument. He noted that at Red Deer and other Alberta locations, the railroad owned the land, but the municipality paid for its upkeep, and he insisted that until other cities and towns recognized the need for assisting the railroad companies the likelihood of station gardens serving as public parks remained slim. Nevertheless, Pray asserted that since the siting and building of stations and station grounds were "among the most difficult and vitally important problems in the field of city planning," the companies ought to take care to design grounds capable of "intensive utilization" by people other than those waiting for trains.[19] But the railroad companies faced serious difficulties in creating such parks, as J. H. Phillips remarked in an *Architectural Record* article of 1914. Aside from very obvious problems posed by the narrowness of land available at most sites (only rarely did railroad companies own much land on the street side of stations) and by the location of stations away from town centers, especially in the commuter suburbs, the problems of use perplexed railway superintendents. Should the park extend to both sides of the tracks, for example? The typical suburban station was often two structures, a large, heated building with ticket office next to the track leading into the city, and a mere shelter adjacent to the outbound track; most patrons spent at least several minutes every morning either inside the heated structure or enjoying its grounds, but almost no one spent more than several seconds at the shelter as they detrained in the evening. As railroad traffic increased, the pedestrian grade crossings over the track became safety hazards, and, as Phillips noted, companies replaced them with overhead footbridges and stairs. "The plain, large plate girders spanning the tracks may be economical and practical, but they certainly are not graceful, and one feels that one would like to see a bridge more in harmony with the station building and the tower which it connects," he remarked.[20] Implicit in his articles and in those of others was a growing opposition on the part of the railroads to creating grounds enticing to children and to casual pedestrians; no railroad company wanted to attract the public onto its property, to lure them near to speeding trains, or to risk serious legal liability. In the corporate mind, station grounds ought to be ornamented in order to please people waiting to board trains, people leaving trains, and people waiting for friends and family arriving by train. Beyond that, station gardens displayed the "neighborliness" of the railroad companies; nothing better proved a railroad's devotion to civic beauty than the central Texas garden of green lawn and annual flowers. Planting a garden of wildflowers meant nothing to the citizens of the town who saw them every day, but the sight of the station agent watering the Bermuda grass impressed everyone with the company's allegiance to the keep-off-the-grass front-lawn ideal.[21]

On the other hand, railroad companies delighted in pleasing their passengers, and by 1920 they spent more and more money not on station grounds, but on improving their rights-of-way. Pray recognized the insistence on pleasing passengers and understood that many railroad companies, forced into planting conifers to stop snowdrifts and vines and other covers to stop soil erosion, intended to plant such "useful" vegetation in ornamental ways. Other purely utilitarian needs prompted the companies; several firms set out tamarack seedlings in order that they might one day harvest timber suitable for ties, and other companies planted dense, high-growing trees to limit the blowing of smoke and cinders from locomotives.[22] Pray suggested setting out "dwarf hardy native shrubs and small trees—such as sweet fern, bayberry, sumachs, wild roses, red dogwood, woodbine, bittersweet, low-bush blackberry, shrubby cinquefoil, Dyer's greenweed, dwarf willows, grape-vines, honeysuckles, and other such tough and hardy natives" appropriate to binding soil and providing beauty. But Pray understood the safety hazard implicit in tall-growing vegetation, and he admitted that oaks, spruces, and other dense trees would have to be planted with meticulous care for view lines.[23] Trackside fires started by coal-burning locomotives prompted companies to ban any shrubbery likely

Trackside planting, Wellesley, Massachusetts. (Courtesy of Loeb Library, Harvard University)

Maintenance crew, Boston & Albany Railroad. (Courtesy of Loeb Library, Harvard University)

to explode in flames during droughts and prompted designers to experiment with sodding entire rights-of-way. As early as 1905, the Pennsylvania Railroad Company had begun sodding its right-of-way between Philadelphia and Pittsburgh. The blue-grass lawn lining the inside slopes of cuts along a fifteen-mile teststrip cost an enormous sum, but maintenance engineers quickly discovered that during downpours very little vegetation washed down the slopes into drains.[24] Within ten years, however, the experiment proved less than satisfactory; drought caused the grass to lose its hold on steep slopes, and wet weather necessitated endless mowings.[25] Lawn-planting did please suburbanites and long-distance travelers smitten with the new suburban fashion of making and maintaining home lawns, though, and several companies continued efforts to create linear lawns. Other firms abandoned greensward; the Boston & Albany directed Olmsted to plant clumps of wild roses along its tracks one-quarter mile on either side of its suburban stations, so that commuters on slowing and accelerating trains might be refreshed by the sight.[26] But right-of-way planting—greensward or roses—existed only for train passengers and almost never for the stationary public.

One experiment in ornamental right-of-way planting owed almost nothing to railroad companies or to landscape architects. The editor of *Ladies' Home Journal*, impressed with the station gardens lining the tracks between Paris and Fontainebleau returned home to Pennsylvania determined to beautify the suburban main line running west from Philadelphia and traveled by thousands of commuters. At the station at Merion, Edward Bok planted 250 flowering fruit trees, "running the gamut of the cherry, the plum, the crabapple and the white and pink peach, so that I should have a succession of bloom lasting some two or three weeks." Emboldened by his dramatic success, Bok convinced the president of the Pennsylvania Railroad Company that long-distance passengers could enjoy trackside plantings if the plantings were massive in scale. Bok asked only permission to plant and tend several thousand rose bushes on either side of a massive cut. "Now, after six years—and the roses have done superlatively well—it is a customary sight to see men busy talking on the rear platform of the observation car on a western express suddenly stop, point to the rose banks, and comment on the bloom," remarked Bok in 1927. "For it is roughly estimated that the thousands of roseplants have a bloom each summer of over half a million roses at one time and present a veritable blanket of pink bloom." The massed planting prompted officials of the New York, New Haven, and Hartford Railroad Company to plant the same types of roses along the approaches to stations at Rye and New Rochelle, New York, and at Providence, Rhode Island. And Bok learned a lesson he later shared with interested company officials: "plant a few flowers and the public is tempted" to pick them; "plant a mass and the public desire is lost." The Bok rose planting made an extraordinary impact on the traveling public, but the expense involved in it brought only a few imitators.[27]

In time, the Railway Gardening Association formalized the division between the proponents of station-grounds-as-parks and the champions of railway-beautification-for-passengers-only. The association, founded in 1906 and very powerful by 1914, comprised almost entirely executive employees of railroad companies; only a few representatives of nurseries and lawn-mower manufacturers belonged.[28] The association effectively talked only to itself and vanquished suggestions by the American Civic Association and other groups convinced that railroad gardens existed for other than railroad reasons. Its annual reports display an intense concern with utilitarian planting for snowbreaks and other purposes and an interest in simple but attractive station gardens. Reports on soils followed reports on the duties of railroad gardeners, and reports on expenses followed reports on public interests. Almost never do the reports mention past or present contributions by landscape architects. Implicit in all the reports is a view of beauty as something easily created by engineers taking a minute from designing drainage ditches and roadbeds. The companies claimed, perhaps with reason, that magnificently beautiful gardens, even those planted largely with perennials, proved too expensive to build and maintain. They forgot that landscape architects like Olmsted had created the finest examples on minimal budgets.

In 1929 the Lionel Company manufactured a "station platform" complete with "a terrace which contains beautifully landscaped flower beds," a stairway, and a retaining wall that "represents ornamental masonry." The platform could hold any of the firm's toy stations and made a beautiful setting at which to halt a toy electric train.[29] Until the 1950s, when increasing automobile traffic prompted most railroad companies to bulldoze station gardens in order to increase parking areas, the Lionel toy train station grounds accurately represented the typical ornamentation of American railroad stations. Simple, symmetrical, and planted with a mix of annual flowers and perennial grasses and shrubs, the Lionel toy grounds epitomized *typical* station landscapes, not the finest, not the worst, and not the work of landscape architects.

Why did landscape architects ignore the Railway Gardening Association and abandon the railroad beautification movement? Part of the answer lies in business conditions; in the 1920s, landscape architects found prosperity in designing for municipalities and for families—it was an era of park- and playground-making, and for the laying-out of suburban house sites.[30] Part of the answer lies in the grudging support of the railroad companies, many of which disdained landscape architects as expensive consultants likely to suggest extravagant planting ideas. But the crux of the answer perhaps lies in a new cast of mind. After the 1900s, landscape architects often sought out government and domestic clients rather than corporate industrial ones.[31] Reformist politics urged many younger landscape architects to build public parks before they laid out gardens intended to attract railroad passengers, to lay out school lawns before they confronted the planting of windbreaks and snowbreaks.

Railroad companies seemed peculiarly well fixed to dismiss landscape architects; the firms employed all sorts of engineers and great gangs of laborers, and they found it convenient to exclude landscape architects first from maintenance and renewal decisions, and then from design discussions.[32] Nevertheless, the landscape architects made not only a clear, public statement about their ability to improve space frequently dismissed by aesthetes but convinced the general public that corporations could—with assistance—beautify privately owned, essentially industrial space.

"The actual roadbeds, and the wonderful trains moving over them are all objects of the highest sort of organic beauty," Pray concluded near the close of his booklet, "the beauty which comes from the perfection of form to use."[33] Not all Americans agreed wholeheartedly with him, however. Despite the romantic attachment to railroading, despite the glamor and mystery of railroad scenery and of the industrial structures that bordered the rights-of-way leading from cities, passengers, and particularly commuters, insisted on beautifying what Pray admitted was already beautiful. The railroad gardening movement derived from—and helped to strengthen—a new spatial aesthetic neither rural nor urban. The shrubbery, ornamental trees, and particularly the depot and right-of-way lawns represent the first fruits of a spatial aesthetic peculiar to suburbs and dear to the hearts of commuters torn between rural and urban aesthetic values.

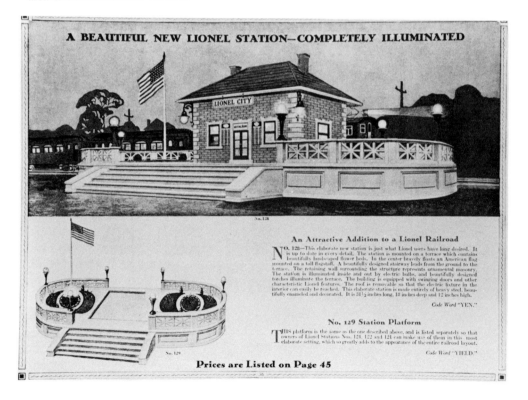

Lionel station and grounds. (Courtesy of Lionel Company, collection of the author)

9. CINEMA

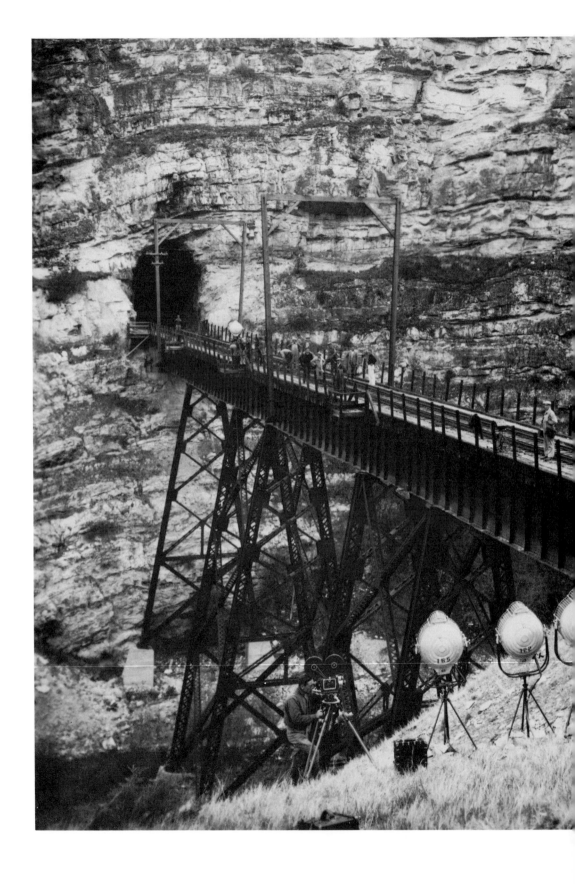

Part of the set of Danger Lights. *(Courtesy of Museum of Modern Art, Film Stills Archive)*

NOT EVERY PASSENGER ON
The Blue Comet and other express trains appreciated railroad scenery. Most
appreciated only the comforts of the Pullman, the scenery supplied by uphol-
sterers, woodcarvers, and other craftsmen. Luxury trains fostered a peculiar
distancing of passengers from landscape. "So we hum along easily, in a train
built for our security, our farthest detail of comfort, the pleasant reposefulness
which comes from pleasant surroundings," Woods noted near the end of her
book on *The Broadway Limited*.[1] For her, and for most other luxury train
passengers, "pleasant surroundings" connoted the interior of the train, not
the landscape beyond the plate glass windows. Henry James understood
something of the distancing effect. "We had travelled indeed all day, but the
process seemed simple when there was nothing of it, nothing to speak of, to
remember, nothing that succeeded in getting over the foot-lights, as the phrase
goes, of the great moving proscenium of the Pullman," he commented in *The
American Scene*. Despite his attentiveness, the great plate glass window in his
Pullman separated him in some obscure way from the landscape beyond. "So,
as if the chair in the Pullman had been my stall, my sense had been all day but
of intervening heads and tuning fiddles, of queer refreshments, such as only
the theatre and the Pullman know, offered, with vociferation, straight through
the performance." James worried about his suddenly skewed vision. Trains
had changed since he had visited the United States a quarter century before;
in 1907 the Pullman glided too quickly, too smoothly. "I was a little uncertain, afterwards, as to when I had become distinctively aware of Florida; but
the scenery of the State, up to the point of my first pause for the night, had
not got over the foot-lights."[2] What James finally failed to comprehend, what
Katherine Woods two decades later simply accepted, was the encapsulating
power of the de luxe express train. For its occupants it became the world, and
the world beyond it became a series of snapshots flashed by a cinemagraph
performance.

People educated before the railroad era wondered at the railroad view of
the landscape. "One has dim foresight of hitherto uncomputed mechanical
advantages who rides on the rail-road and moreover a practical confirmation
of the ideal philosophy that Matter is phenomenal whilst men and trees and
barns whiz by you as fast as the leaves of a dictionary," wrote Emerson in

1834. "The very permanence of matter seems compromised and trees, fields, hills, hitherto esteemed symbols of stability, do absolutely dance by you."[3] In 1834, Emerson thought carefully about the view from the train and compared his vision of landscape with that of a darting swallow. Nine years later, however, novelty had vanished, along with critical appraisal. "Dreamlike travelling on the railroad," he recorded in his journal. "The towns through which I pass between Phila. and New York, make no distinct impression. They are like pictures on a wall. The more, that you can read all the way in the car a French novel."[4] In less than a decade, Emerson moved from novelty to acceptance; only occasionally did he later remark on such visual effects as the blurring of fences and other features: "the snow-banks swam past like fishes; the near trees and bushes wove themselves into colored ribbons; the rocks, walls, the fields themselves, streaming like a mill-tail."[5] Despite his extensive railroad traveling, his journals are almost silent about visual effects. Emerson, and his successors, chose to read, not look from the window.

As a train gathers speed, passengers viewing the landscape at right angles discover that the spatial details nearest the window are the first to blur. At five miles an hour, an intent observer can discern flowers and other elements of the scene immediately adjacent to the rails, but at ten miles an hour he must look at objects fifteen feet from the side of the car. At thirty miles an hour, everything within the thirty- or forty-foot mark appears blurred, unless the observer is willing to swivel his head as the train passes. Increases in speed force the observer to look ever further from the car, and particularly east of the Mississippi River, such long views are rare. Even in farming country, trees and high bushes growing in the protected right-of-way make vistas few. At ninety miles an hour, the railroad passenger intrigued by the passing scene must fix his attention only on very distant objects; doing otherwise creates eyestrain and headache.

More irritating than the blurring effect is the ephemeral quality of the view. As William James noted in his 1890 *The Principles of Psychology*, objects at the edge of the blurring zone seem unduly near; in focus for only an instant, the passenger is unable to scrutinize them.[6] In "A Passing Glimpse," a poem of the 1920s, Robert Frost displayed his vexation with the distorted view:

> I often see flowers from a passing car
> That are gone before I can tell what they are.
> I want to get out of the train and go back
> To see what they were beside the track.[7]

Other poets tried to awaken their readers to the perceptual trap of the high-speed train. The narrator of Hart Crane's *The Bridge*, directing notice at the "Hobo-trekkers that forever search / An empire wilderness of freight and rails," pleads:

Oh, lean from the window, if the train slows down,
As though you touched hands with some ancient clown,
————A little while gaze absently below
And hum Deep River with them while they go.[8]

Such advice had little effect. Not only did leaning from open windows create the danger of lethal accidents, but by the mid-1930s, air-conditioning required sealed windows. Most passengers found prolonged window-gazing absolutely exhausting, and, like Emerson almost a century earlier, directed their attention inward, toward novels or newspapers.

Passengers did see things, however, and their visions of the landscape deserve notice, for they are remarkably similar in form and content. Almost invariably, the visions involved aloneness, twilight, and a peculiar intimacy.

Robert Frost catches the essence of the experience in the first lines of "On the Heart's Beginning to Cloud the Mind," a poem of 1936:

Something I saw or thought I saw
In the desert at midnight in Utah,
Looking out of my lower berth
At moonlit sky and moonlit earth.

The poet wonders about a flickering light in a house visible far off and quickly composes two stories about the meaning of the light. But then the train races further on, and the poet loses sight of the lamplight:

This I saw when waking late,
Going by at a railroad rate,
Looking through wreaths of engine smoke
Far into the lives of other folk.[9]

While not unique, the vision in Frost's poem is rare, because it involves a broad vista and time for reflection. The typical vision of the Pullman era involved different characteristics.

Thomas Wolfe devoted much attention to deciphering the Pullman-car vision of the landscape. He presented his findings in *Of Time and the River*, in a long passage that outlines the "typical" experience. At first, the passenger felt that only the express train was stationary; everything else was moving, sweeping past the car window. "And under the spell of this lonely processional of white field, dark wood and wild driven sky, he fell into a state of strange waking-sleepfulness, a kind of comatose perceptiveness that the motion of the train at night had always induced in him," wrote Wolfe of the young man snug in the Pullman berth. "In this strange state of comatose perceptiveness he was conscious first of the vast level snowclad fields of the Canadian boundaries, the lights of farms, the whipping past of darkened little stations" and other features of the moonlit, snow-covered landscape.[10] Neither asleep nor awake, lulled by the sway of the train into the half-alert mental state Frost calls "clouded," the passenger watched indiscriminately, simply recording images, not analyzing them. Travel writers like Katherine Woods knew the curious drowsiness produced by prolonged gazing at twilit landscapes and delighted in it, for it produced a deep, relaxing sleep.[11]

If the passenger did not sleep, or woke from sleep and pulled up the window shade beside his berth, he experienced the critical moment of the vision. "And now the train had slowed to a full halt; he found himself looking at a wall of old red brick at one of the station's corners. It was one of the old brick buildings that one sees in the station section of almost any town," Wolfe continued, describing small-town shabbiness. "And at the corner, in the first floor of the old brick building, he could see a disreputable old barroom, and this, too, had this dreamlike, stage-like immediacy, it was so near to him that he could almost have touched the building with his hand, a kind of gigantic theatrical setting, overpowering in its immediacy, as strange and as familiar as a dream. Without moving in his berth he could look through the windows of the bar, which were glazed or painted half way up, and see everything that was going on inside."[12] In a few sentences, Wolfe captured the critical essence of the Pullman vision—the passenger, suddenly alert, alone, scrutinizing some feature of the trackside environment illuminated by poor light. Frost saw a farmhouse, Arnold Bennett saw the Toledo industrial zone, Wolfe's central character saw a red-brick station and barroom-brothel, not a well-planted railroad-company garden. All see, all take in the immediacy of color, shape, light, and all watch the objects vanish.

Wolfe strengthened his equation of Pullman vision and theatrical performance by introducing early in *Of Time and the River* a scene in which an express-train passenger saw beyond his window a "moving-picture theater" and felt a sudden oneness with its patrons, who were themselves glimpsing fast-moving images.[13] Ever faster trains produced a better analogy than the proscenium described by James; the cinema struck observers as a close parallel to the view through the car window. In the cinema theater the viewer sat alone among others, in twilight sharpened by flashes of bright illumination, and watched images flashed past his eyes. Like Frost, who could not stop the train to examine trackside flowers, the cinema viewer could not halt the images. The rapidly, almost jerkily passing cinema images struck many authors as the perfect twin to the Pullman-car image of a landscape seemingly flashing past in a series of frames separated one from another by telegraph poles. In any speeding passenger car, coach or Pullman, but especially at dusk or dawn, the gazing passenger entered a theaterlike, cinemalike, dreamlike state. In Pullman and cinema-house, now and then one became instantly alert to a fleeting image, then lost it.

Novelists and poets pondered the express-train vision. Only rarely did they comprehend the distancing effect. Willa Cather's *My Antonia* is a case in point. The novel begins aboard a fast express racing across Iowa. "While the train flashed through never-ending miles of ripe wheat, by country towns and bright-flowered pastures and oak groves wilting in the sun, we sat in the observation car, where the woodwork was hot to the touch and red dust lay deep over everything." In the observation car, the characters talked "about what it is like to spend one's childhood in little towns like these, buried in wheat and corn."[14] What was beyond the window was essentially a stage-set, peopled with remembered characters. Cather never resolved the distance between the observation-car riders and the characters of their far-off childhood; the novel—of the *rahmenerzählung* or framework genre—lacks a concluding "frame," deliberately leaving its reader aboard a speeding train. Booth Tarkington grappled more successfully with the distancing effect. His 1899 novel, *The Gentleman from Indiana*, begins with a much more frank appraisal of the effects of the Pullman-car vision.

"There is a fertile stretch of flat lands in Indiana where unagrarian Eastern travellers, glancing from car-windows, shudder and return their eyes to interior upholstery, preferring even the swaying caparisons of a Pullman to the monotony without," the novel begins before describing a level, bleak landscape. "The persistent tourist who seeks for signs of man in this sad expanse perceives a reckless amount of rail fence; at intervals a large barn; and, here and there, man himself, uncurious, patient, slow, looking up from the fields apathetically as the Limited flies by."[15] Tarkington understood what Wolfe described four decades later, that to an observer of the train the express is "a wall of movement and of noise," but to the observer on the train everything beyond the window is so much spectacle.[16] Tarkington followed the argument further than even Wolfe dared, however, by suggesting that farmers beyond the right-of-way struck passengers not as individuals but as a type, or even worse, as quasi-human stereotypes like those described by Edwin Markham in "The Man with the Hoe." Real people, in Tarkington's introduction, were only those sitting among the sumptuous Pullman fittings. As in Cather's *My Antonia*, they talked among themselves, or perhaps they read; never did they lean from the window if the train slowed down. Never did they examine the landscape or human figures beyond, except during a cinemalike, snapshot moment.

Tarkington spun an intriguing novel out of the local color of Indiana, beginning it in a classic turn-of-the-century way as the chief character alights at the railroad station. Other novelists dealt with the distancing effect of high-speed rail travel more directly. Instead of writing local-color novels to be read by Pullman passengers speeding through the regions of the novels, they addressed the issue in essays.

Robert Herrick's *Yale Review* essay of 1914 confronted the problem squarely by analyzing the role of landscape in American fiction. "When an American entertains a vision of his country as a totality," he argued in explanation of the widespread ignorance of regional landscape peculiarities, "it is a confusing panorama of plain and mountain and seacoast, or else the picture of his own small community hidden in the vast territory." Herrick wondered why such ignorance continued in a time of swift trains and implied that somehow the Pullman insulated its passengers. "A New Englander, emerging from his Pullman in Louisiana or Arizona or Montana, to take a few scattered instances, cannot recognize anything in these strange landscapes in common with his own rocky pastures and thin meadows," he asserted before concluding that much of the perceptual difficulty arising from "seven-league strides across the continent" in search of "scenic wonders" involved not only high-speed trains but seemingly undistinguished landscapes: "From Cheyenne to Chicago, from Chicago to New Orleans or Pittsburgh, there are thousand-mile stretches of undistinguished, commonplace landscape."[17] Herrick suggested that authors devote far more detailed attention to accurately seeing and describing the commonplace landscape. Only then, he argued, would readers sharpen their own sensibilities and understand the built forms that link regional landscapes. William James, Tarkington, Crane, and Wolfe—and Herrick—all understood the significance of changing environmental observation, and all knew the special difficulties of seeing space from the high-speed, luxurious Pullman. Despite their best efforts, however, vast stretches of the American landscape became increasingly less visible to the well-fed, drowsy passengers whizzing through them.

Perhaps the passengers had good reason for perusing menus or French novels. Railroad companies, travel agencies, and the Department of the Interior had begun extolling the grandeur of some American scenery as early as 1900. Within ten years the efforts had attracted thousands of Americans to the new national parks and to other places of "magnificent natural scenery." Package tours, like that described at length by Francis Lynde in 1897 in *A Romance in Transit*, dramatically reduced fares; by 1917, clerks and secretaries found it surprisingly cheap and easy to take long-distance vacations in trains equipped not with Pullmans but with modest "tourist sleepers." "The all-providing agency not only attends to these details," remarked a railroad company executive of the agencies that cared for baggage handling and hotel accommodations, "but also furnishes lecturers and literature descriptive of the places visited. It tells the traveler what to see and what he should know about the places seen, and sets him free to devote his full attention to undisturbed enjoyment of the trip."[18] Unfortunately, for travelers anticipating the glories of the Grand Canyon or Yellowstone, or returning from visiting such wonders, the vast majority of their trip did indeed seem exactly what Herrick called it—undistinguished and commonplace. The bombardment of photographs, line drawings, and verbal descriptions of scenic wilderness made pale, and often shabby, the landscape through which most trains passed. Despite the efforts of rare observers like Rollo Walter Brown, whose 1939 *I Travel By*

Train catalogues and savors such "isolated impressions" of ordinary landscape as "a low unpainted but weather-boarded house with a porch extending out from the slope of the house roof, and with slender rickety-looking posts reaching down to flat foundation stones" and "rows of corn fodder that had been left standing in a small field sown to timothy," many train travelers looked up from their reading only when conductors announced scenic wonders, or when their trains flashed through trackside plantings as stunning as Edward Bok's half-mile rose garden.[19] For most riders, even for those paying an extra one cent a mile to ride the fastest, most luxurious expresses, railroad scenery and snapshot-clear visions of station platforms, main streets, mown fields, silos, farmhouses, and shanties passing, in the words of one 1901 writer, "like the films of a cinematograph," meant far less than the scenery dignified in print and published photographs.[20] Nothing compared with the parlor table folio of scenic views or the stereographs of mountains. When the passengers in the mahogany-appointed Pullman observation car yawned at commonplace landscape and anticipated only the views among the Appalachians and the Rockies, the open-air observation platform hosted only fresh-air fiends, children, and passengers intrigued by the high iron and semaphores.

Not every luxury limited traversed the Rocky Mountains. Most swept along metropolitan corridors offering little to delight the passenger searching for folio-worthy scenic wonders. Even on such trains, however, first-class passengers nevertheless enjoyed the absolutely kinetic perspective of the observation-car platform.

Europeans delighted in the perspective. "Capable of holding four chairs, and enclosed by an iron railing," the private-car platform entranced H. Hussey Vivian during an 1878 cross-country trip. "As we are always at the end of the train, we sit on the platform for hours in this fine climate, and have an unbroken view of the scenery," he remarked in *A Tour in North America*, an experience that most first-class riders enjoyed within two decades.[21] While the platform offered an open-air vantage point from which to view such wonders as the Mississippi River, most passengers learned that it gave the best view of railroad scenery. As Woods discovered, for example, it provided an excellent observation post from which to scrutinize semaphores. Moreover, it enabled a passenger to look down on the blur of railroad ties streaking away from the train. Nothing, not even the brass-cased speedometer frequently mounted at the rear of observation cars, more clearly announced the speed of the train along the corridor. Certainly no other place provided a better view of the high iron.

The ties blurring away, the shining rails converging in the distance, the telegraph poles and signals flashing past indeed provided a cinemalike vision to the passenger sitting on the wicker chairs or leaning against the rail. Being outdoors at high speed vanquished the boredom that sometimes overcame passengers forever gazing sideways, the boredom that in one instance prompted

Observation platform and wicker chairs. (Courtesy of Smithsonian Institution)

a cowboy to fire his revolver at telegraph poles.[22] The incident, described in detail by Richard Harding Davis in his 1892 travel narrative, *The West from a Car-Window*, badly unnerved a traveling salesman from Chicago, but the conductor dismissed it as the result of a law officer needing target practice. For Davis, it epitomized the culture of Texas and also hinted at the vexing distancing effect of coach windows. Davis apparently found few trains that carried observation-car platforms; he admitted that he could "only give impressions from a car-window point of view."[23] Vivian relays sharper impressions, because his was largely an outdoor trip enlivened by looking up, not sideways, at the mountains looming on both sides of "cuts" and by firing at herds of antelope.[24] As railroads replaced open-platform cars with vestibule cars and as passengers learned that each car fit snugly against its mates, the observation-car platform at the very end of the train became the only place in which people could ride outdoors and have a nearly 360-degree view.

No wonder the Lionel Company emphasized the observation platforms of its finest trains. Riding the platforms gave both child and adult nearly the same thrill as riding in the locomotive. "Came the hoarse scream of the whistle, the clattering crash as they shattered the yard switches, a blurred vision of dark outlines dotted with tiny scintillating points, and a little town with its station, yard, lights, switches, and all were behind him," wrote Frank Packard in 1925 of the nighttime passage of a luxury express.[25] For the child who never rode on the platform, the Lionel Company toy train brought the dream somewhat closer. Hollywood movie makers brought it closer still.

Between 1921 and 1930, some 100 "railroad films" played in the nation's movie theaters.[26] Closely paralleling the themes already well known in popular railroad fiction, the feature-length films detailed life along the railroad spine of the metropolitan corridor. Thousands of other films depicted a speeding locomotive or great terminal in a sequence or two, of course, but the railroad films did more.

Many of the films emphasized the new sort of man, and sometimes woman, needed to operate the trains and other corridor machinery. Films like *The Black Diamond Express* and *The Midnight Flyer* of the mid-1920s revolved around love affairs, but love was tempered with technological necessity.[27] In a 1928 film, *The Night Flyer*, Walter Woods and Walter Lang adapted Frank Spearman's 1901 anthology, *Held for Orders*, into a movie with a love affair as plot but technological mastery as the key to the heroine's heart.[28] The hero wins his love, and a contract for his company, by delivering a shipment of mail in record time. In other films of the genre, elements of the railroad become the chief stars, and plots involve daily life on the rails. Public fascination with signals produced a number of films depicting in detail the workings and malfunctions of signals. *The Signal Tower*, a 1924 adaptation of Wadsworth Camp's short story of the same name published four years earlier in *The Metropolitan*, displayed the workings of an interlocking tower, its signals, and track switches, and climaxed in a sequence involving a runaway train; two years later appeared *The Block Signal*, another film in which human frailties, particularly jealousy and color-blindness, combined in a love-affair plot.[29] Other films emphasized such mainstays of popular railroad fiction as private cars and grade crossings. *The Danger Signal* of 1925 depicted a mail robbery and the near wreck of a private car; *The Black Diamond Express* began with a crossing accident. A 1925 film, *The Overland Limited*, traced the building of a great railroad bridge, and a 1923 film, *Kindled Courage*, involved tramps.[30] *The Midnight Express* of 1924 focused on the tension within an isolated mountain station and a subsequent wreck, and *The Midnight Special*, released six years later, involved sequences of train dispatching, a wreck, and robbery.[31] Certainly such films stressed excitement, and they often detailed robberies of private cars or railway post offices in order to justify collisions, mistaken signals, and other unusual happenings. But even such exciting love stories as the 1926 film *The Warning Signal* contained lengthy footage describing life at a remote signal tower and explained the complex and fragile technology of the railroad right-of-way.[32]

Such films present visions within visions, perspectives rotating about perspectives.[33] Film crews often photographed the landscape as seen from Pullman car windows or else set up cameras on observation platforms. Directors and cinematographers struggled to capture the vision peculiar to riders of high-speed trains, shifting sequences rapidly from frames showing passengers on observation platforms as seen from trackside to frames showing the trackside as seen through the passengers' eyes. As the titles of so many films make clear, directors gloried in the mystery of the railroad at night, and cinematographers filmed the uncanny illumination of the headlight flashing from one structure to another, the eerie beam of the signal light, the gyrations of the hand-held kerosene lantern. In a movie theater, the viewer of such films ensnared himself in a concatenation of visions in which the railroad train seemed the only bridging element.

A 1930 RKO Radio Pictures Company film typifies the rotating visions of the popular railroad motion picture. *Danger Lights* ostensibly involves a love triangle; two railroad men struggle to win the heart of a young heroine, herself the daughter of a retired locomotive engineer. But the real star of the film is the railroad and its trains: the Chicago, Milwaukee, St. Paul & Pacific Railroad Company. The company names appear on locomotives, passenger cars, and structures, and the characters speak of actual company trains, including the luxury express, *The Olympian*. Love intrigues play a strictly secondary role. The film begins with a landslide blocking an electrified segment of mountain track, and the appearance of Dan Thorn, the division superintendent, to repair the rails. He drafts hoboes to help the repair crew, discovers a former locomotive engineer among them and offers the out-of-work man employment, and opens the line. The newly employed locomotive engineer falls

A scene from The Black Diamond Express *showing a typical cinematographic view of the blurred landscape beyond the observation platform. (Courtesy of Museum of Modern Art, Film Stills Archive)*

An industrial zone setting from The Midnight Express. *(Courtesy of Museum of Modern Art, Film Stills Archive)*

A boy's introduction to railroad glamor; a scene from The Signal Tower. *(Courtesy of Museum of Modern Art, Film Stills Archive)*

in love with Thorn's girl, but a series of exciting adventures involving railroad trains, tunnels, trestles, and other Milwaukee Road property provides the action. Eventually Dan Thorn rescues his opponent from certain death by dragging him from an electrically operated, remote-controlled switch, but Thorn himself is struck by the speeding train. The chastened engineer, with the permission of railroad officials, volunteers to rush Thorn to Milwaukee for surgery, providing the audience with lengthy scenes of a madly speeding train, the approaches to a great terminal station, and the terminal building itself. Thorn lives, gives his blessing to his former adversary marrying his girlfriend, and returns to his true mistress, his railroad line.

Despite the syrupy plot, *Danger Lights* offered extraordinary cinematography. Karl Struss and John Boyle stationed cameras at places crucial to understanding the operation of the railroad, if not the plot. Aerial views of a great freight yard, interior shots of a locomotive roundhouse, and, especially, views from speeding trains inject immense energy into an otherwise slow-paced film. In filming locomotives rushing down upon cameras, and in showing railroad ties vanishing in a blur of motion, the cinematographers captured something of the view from the high-speed train.

Such cinematography complemented the technical dialogue of the film. While lovers converse in rather uninspired fashion, employees speak in terminology with which the director of the film clearly expected the audience to be familiar. Railroad men direct attention to the meaning of white flags atop a locomotive, to the significance of whistle signals, and to semaphore indications. Even Mary Ryan, the heroine, casually talks about "the dynometer car going back to the yard." As the film advances, however, Dan Thorn abandons the vocabulary of love and uses technical jargon to explain his love of railroading. "We're railroad men. We gotta keep the schedule," he tells one engineer distraught at the death of his wife. "We gotta pull the throttle. That's our religion. That's our life." As Thorn begins such philosophizing, the film focuses on life in the metropolitan corridor, extolling the respect of one man for another, the devotion to duty shown by responsible railroad men (Thorn leaves his engagement party to direct the repair of a washed-out section of track), and the cooperation of men expert in the intricacies of modern machinery. By the end of the film, when a convalescent Thorn returns to direct his segment of the main line, the audience knew that only the most virtuous, energetic of men could build and operate a railroad. The men say so themselves, explicitly.

In *Danger Lights* and so many other films, cinematography and dialogue combine to overshadow the simple plots on which the action hinges. Railroad scenery is almost the only scenery in such films, and actors speak of its details, sure of the audiences' familiarity with and devotion to it. Not surprisingly, firms like the Milwaukee Road willingly volunteered their rights-of-way and trains as properties for the filmmakers to arrange. The dominant tone of the films, and the rarity of wrecks injuring passengers, reassured moviegoers that railroad companies strove valiantly to provide safe, fast service to the traveling public. With men like Dan Thorn in charge of its track, what *Olympian* rider need worry?

Popular railroad films of the 1920s and early 1930s resembled contemporaneous westerns, and some—*The Great K&A Train Robbery* of 1926, for example—involved posses, cowboys, and holdups. Other traits of the western characterize the popular railroad film. The brave railroad-employee hero is at home in an environment that overpowers lesser men; he is master of complex machinery, other men, and of his own emotions; and he is frequently a loner, married to the railroad and unable to be a loving husband. By fitting industrial zones and railroad scenery, locomotives and signals, and sunsets over converging rails into a well-known framework of desert and cow towns, horses and six-guns, and sunsets over lone riders vanishing across prairies, the directors of many railroad films advertised the metropolitan corridor as a new place of adventure, a place in which rugged Americans rediscovered the worth of old virtues and new skills.

In the railroad film, as in the paperback railroad novel or the short fiction published in *Railroad Stories* and other magazines, Americans came ever closer to the complex vision created by the high-speed train racing along the metropolitan corridor. The view from the window that perplexed Emerson, James, Cather, and Wolfe—but not Woods—and the view of the train that transfixed so many observers combined to create a new aesthetic of environmental appreciation, one that continued to puzzle Herrick and other critics.[34] No longer did the traveling American move slowly enough to savor details. Instead he adapted himself to glancing at one thing after another, to reveling in the stream of structures and spaces sweeping past his window, to classifying buildings and arrangements of buildings according to type. In the cinema view, one fireproof factory seemed very like another, one Main Street remarkably like the next.

By 1930, however, only one sort of American had fully accepted the new view of space. The commuting suburbanite knew both the view from the train and the view of the train and no longer thought much about either.

10. VILLA

The Owned Home is Necessary to the Welfare of the Child.

The owned home, and the family stability and permanency that it helps to create, does more than any other thing to promote the physical, mental, and moral well-being of children.

It lessens the dangers from sickness and accident.

It shelters youthful innocence against moral dangers.

It creates a right attitude toward life in the growing mind.

It provides wholesome interests and lessens the attraction of outside excitements.

It makes childhood happier.

Every Child Has the *Right* to a Home of Its Own

The rearing of a child is a serious and difficult matter. It is the busines of the home—*the chief business of life.*

Few parents succeed in meeting the responsibilities of child training t their own complete satisfaction. No parent, therefore, can afford to ove look a means that will greatly lighten this responsibility and aid him i mastering many of its most important and delicate details.

The permanent family home is such a means. It is the greatest of all aids in the rearing of children. A large part of the failures in after life can be traced directly to its absence.

It establishes a permanent condition and influence in their lives that averts many of the worst dangers, both physical and moral, to childhood; molds their ideas and ideals of life and creates a powerful influence for success throughout their lives.

The child's danger from sickness is far less in the owned home than in the rented house in which many families of unknown habits have lived.

In old houses and neighborhoods, hidde sources of infection are many and a difficult to locate until too late. The is less of sunshine in the closely built-u sections and in the vicinity of the high buildings. The circulation of fresh a is poorer and the summer radiation heat from buildings and pavements f greater than in the more open outer di tricts. Infant mortality increases you approach the center of any city.

In the more central localities, which a the chief rental areas, the conditions a all against the safety of life and limb The traffic dangers from playing in th streets, and in going to and from schoo are constant. Each day takes its tol

Every child has the RIGHT to a home of its own. The child raised in a rented house or apartment is CHEATED.

he Owned Home Provides dditional Sources of Income

he family that is permanent- located on its own plot of ound has in its back yard a luable resource that can be sily made to earn a very sub- antial addition to its income.

A good home garden will earn from $50 to $150 a year.

The home poultry yard solves the problem of a family meat supply.

Together they make a family largely independent of high food prices.

They ensure more wholesome food and better health.

They provide a dependable food reserve in times of emergency.

They enable you to live better.

Your Own Garden

The back yard of your home is the most profitable Food Factory on earth.

It enables you to cash in on every hour of your spare time that you care to devote to it, and to convert that time into valuable food products. By thus saving a large part of your living expense the garden adds that much to your income.

The average sized back-yard vegetable garden, with ordinary care, may be made to produce from $50 to $150 worth of vegetables each season, with an hour's work a day, by some member of the family, and a nominal outlay for seeds. The addition of fruit trees, grapes and berries will increase this amount, after they are in bearing, by another $50 to $100.

By special attention and expert care, the the amount that can be realized even from this small area is surprising.

There are many instances throughout the United States of families that make their *entire living* from their back yards, not only raising all the vegetables, fruit and poultry products needed for their own

use, the year around, but surplus enough for sale to provide for all the other living expenses.

In many cases they carry on outside work as well, thus earning a double income. There are instances where the back yard has been made to pay for the home itself.

The results from a home garden are practically all profit. The time you put into it is time that would otherwise have been wasted—and in any case is more than balanced by the valuable exercise and mental relaxation.

On this basis the profits from a garden, above all money expense for seeds and other costs, are often 1000% to 2000% or over.

It has been found that, considering your garden returns as *wages*, every hour of intelligent work that you put into your garden earns you at least $1.00, and often more.

Why not increase your earnings by adding an hour or two of garden work daily at $1.00 an hour?

Pages from A Home of Your Own. *(Courtesy of Loeb Library, Harvard University)*

ONLY THE COMMUTER AC-
cepted the cinemalike view from the train. As his train raced or crawled toward the city in the morning, he only glanced from his newspaper at the impeccably planted privet hedges and wild roses, at the immense power plants, at entire industrial zones, at semaphores and other constituents of railroad scenery. In the evening, snug in his accustomed seat, he read the evening paper until he alighted at his accustomed station. "To live in the country, the real country, yet be able to attend to one's business in the city, is a dream which modern methods of rapid transit are fast making come true," asserted Winthrop Packard in a 1905 *Suburban Life* article.[1] But not everyone agreed. In the first years of the new century, a few perceptive observers discovered that life in the railroad suburbs meant life in the metropolitan corridor.

In a 1907 *Century* article analyzing the many users of the great terminals of New York City, Jesse Lynch Williams pondered the curious nature of the commuting suburbanite, who "is often in a hurry, but is seldom flurried," who "keeps on reading the afternoon paper, as he strides abstractedly through the iron gates, and mounts the steps of the moving train with much the same assured air of ownership as when he ascends his own porch, perhaps an hour later, far away from the hurly-burly." Williams concluded that the true commuter is a man "who takes to routine," who likes "the clock-like regularity," "the pleasant social aspect of the early morning trip to town," the time for reading papers or playing whist. The more he observed the "army" of commuters, the more worried Williams became. "He neither gets all the way into the life of the city nor clean out into the country," he concluded of the typical commuter. "So his view of things has neither the perspective of robust rurality nor the sophistication of a man in the city and of it." And Williams understood the growing power of such men. "Much of our literature, art, and especially criticism shows the taint of the commuter's point of view."[2] Some observers studied suburbanites; Williams studied commuters, and so perceived the peculiar nature of the creatures of the metropolitan corridor.

Commuters supported a wholly new sort of publication, the "country life magazines," of which *Suburban Life* noted in 1905 that none was more than five years old and that each promised bountiful returns to its publisher.[3] *Suburban Life*, *Country Life*, and other new periodicals reoriented the content

Farm Annual *cover. (Courtesy of W. Atlee Burpee Co., collection of the author)*

of older magazines like *Horticulture* and *Ladies' Home Journal* and stimulated changes in journals like *House and Garden*. Urban newspapers learned to report suburban news or risk losing commuter readership. Within a few years of the founding of large railroad suburbs, newspaper editors perceived the necessity of providing columns on gardening and home improvements, matters about which commuters loved to read. By 1915, the typical commuter strode through the great urban terminals convinced that his way of life represented the apogee of civilization. Much of what he read during his morning and evening commutes confirmed his view of himself as someone enjoying the best of city and country by mastering the complex corridor that connected rural villa with downtown terminal.

Certainly Lionel Company engineers and advertising experts knew the force of suburbanization. Among the many advantages enjoyed by children growing up in the railroad suburbs, roomy basements perhaps struck the firm as most important, for they provided space for permanent Lionel layouts. The 1929 *Catalogue* honors suburban living by advertising handsome "villas," diminutive metal houses painted to resemble brick, stucco, and stone, each illuminated by a lightbulb and each "architecturally perfect." Lionel manufactured sets of villas and bungalows, naming the sets "Lionel Manor" and "Lionelville," and even offered "Lionel Terrace," the finest set of all. "A real village in miniature, containing houses and lamp posts, all electrically illuminated," read the description beneath the full-color illustration. "Adds realism to your train outfit, and ideal in connection with sister's doll house. The buildings are in a beautiful landscape setting complete with grass plots, bushes, shrubbery, trees and gravel walks." The "terrace" of three houses and a 22-by-19-inch platform of metal trees may have been intended to attract sister to brother's hobby, but the placement of the villas, bungalows, and terrace sets amid illustrations of grade-crossing signals, catenary poles, and semaphore signals suggests otherwise.[4] The message of the 1929 *Catalogue* endures: suburban houses, lawns, and trees belong next to trains, in the metropolitan corridor.

Railroad suburbs sprouted along the high iron leading away from most major American cities, and commuters firmly believed them to offer the best advantages of rural and urban living. At the heart of their belief lay a continuing respect for agriculture, particularly for small-scale vegetable gardening, and by the early 1890s their respect had begun to change national notions of planting and harvest. In its 1888 *Farm Annual*, for example, the W. Atlee Burpee Company revealed its shifting market. The 129-page mail-order catalogue graced with line drawings and full-color plates offered a profusion of "garden, farm and flower seeds," proven over the years and winners of many state-fair first prizes. But only 8 of the 129 pages advertised field crop seeds; clearly the Burpee Company hoped to sell seeds other than oats and buckwheat. It advertised vegetables of value in ornamental gardens, emphasized

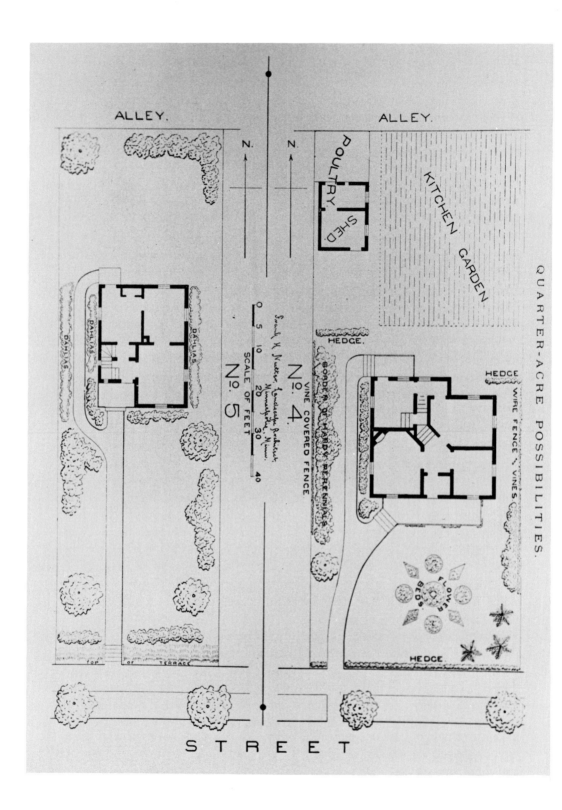

Page from Quarter Acre Possibilities. *(Courtesy of Loeb Library, Harvard University)*

flower seeds, and urged readers to buy vegetable seeds "so unique and valuable that they should be in every garden."[5] No longer did farm families dictate sales techniques and seed offerings; suburbanites ruled the marketplace.

The Burpee Company published a popular booklet, *How and What to Grow in a Kitchen Garden of One Acre*, aimed at suburbanites anxious to enjoy fresh air and sunshine while reducing grocery expenditures. The guidebook passed through edition after edition and helped to answer the increasing need for small-scale agricultural information.[6] Professional designers supplemented *How and What to Grow* with books of their own. Frank H. Nutter's *Quarter Acre Possibilities* of 1898 employs diagrams, site plans, and before-and-after photographs to "illustrate the first principles of landscape art, and show their application even to the most humble homestead." The book reveals Nutter's awareness of the new-found suburban love of such lawn sports as croquet and tennis, and of fads like the raising of dahlias, and his understanding that many suburbanites intended to recapture something of the agricultural lifestyle they remembered with nostalgia. Nutter provided plan after plan of houselots measuring roughly 50 by 125 feet, each with a small house at its center. "Like many householders, our friend desires some of the pleasures of rural life on his suburban lot," remarked Nutter of one plan, "so the rear portion is set apart for a small garden and poultry yard, and a short arborvitae hedge at either side of the lot hides his successes and failures from the public eye." The front lawn, however, is "claimed by the lady of the house as her special realm during the summer season."[7] On such lots, suburban families planted Burpee "Fairmount Park" grass seed, experimented with flower seeds, and rejoiced in "novelty" vegetable seeds perfect for backyard gardens. In the 1888 *Farm Annual*, in Nutter's *Quarter Acre Possibilities*, and in the Lionel Company toy villas and terraces lie keys to interpreting not the streetcar suburb of single- and multi-family houses sprawling away from industrial zones, but the suburb far less densely populated—the railroad suburb of single-family, large-lot houses dependent on commuter trains and wholly integrated into the metropolitan corridor.

Railroad suburbs took two forms, but "the suburban good life" guided the development of both. Speculator suburbs, characterized by quickly erected houses lining new streets across former farmland, blossomed at former village depots within commuting distance of large cities. "Model" suburbs, usually the result of "enlightened" speculators willing to chance long-term profits, were designed and built as whole entities, the schools, churches, shopping districts, and other amenities erected simultaneously with the houses. A typical model suburb displayed uniform architectural styles, carefully blended plantings of street trees and other shrubbery, curving streets, gravel walks, parks, and ponds, all created in the beginning.[8] While some speculator suburbs displayed few such characteristics, many did, and by offering both small and large houses and terraces, the Lionel Company enabled children to mix housing types and landscaping to create suburbs akin to their own. Railroad suburbs, for all their outward differences, evolved from a philosophy expressed again and again in turn-of-the-century periodicals. "A person never gets the most from his contact with the earth unless he owns a bit of it and has the right and privilege to manipulate it," editorialized Liberty Hyde Bailey in a 1915 issue of *Countryside Magazine*, "land in which he may dig, on which he may plant trees and then unplant them if so he shall desire, from which he may gather flowers in spring and nuts in the autumn."[9] Dozens of periodicals embroidered the philosophy until by 1920 it ruled the imagination of all residents of the railroad suburbs—and of many city people as well.

Donald G. Mitchell, advocate of railroad gardening and longtime editor of *Hearth and Home*, emphasized the philosophy behind railroad suburbs and applied it in one example after another. His long life—1822 to 1908—spanned the years of the republic's transformation from a rural to a technological nation, and his many writings display a powerful faith in both the agricultural ideal and in the advantages of railroad commuting. By the late 1860s, however, Mitchell had grown disillusioned with his efforts to improve the efficiency of American farming and the tone of farm life; upset at the narrowmindedness of farm families, at their inability to adopt new machines and techniques, he slowly learned what the Burpee Company learned years later—tradition bound farmers too tightly. In 1863 he published *My Farm of Edgewood*, a guide to renovating half-abandoned New England farms. In the years immediately following its appearance, he published a number of articles in *Horticulturist* and *Hours at Home* and collected them in an 1867 book, *Rural Studies*.[10] Within a few years, however, Mitchell discovered that his audience consisted not of farm families, but of city dwellers anxious to move into the country, and for the rest of his life he spoke to its anxieties, hopes, and ignorances.

When he reissued *Rural Studies* in 1884 as *Out-of-Town Places* he knew his audience intimately. The book counsels the commuter about hiring a gardener, farming a little for fun and profit, and shaping lawns. The fictitious characters called "Mr. Lack-Land" and "Mr. Urban" learn how to commute thirty-five miles from the city to "estates" ranging from two-and-a-half to fifty acres without sacrificing the care of poultry yards, vegetable gardens, and lawns big enough for baseball. In his books, editorials, do-it-yourself columns, and articles in such magazines as *Scribner's*, Mitchell traced the evolving theory of suburban good life and applied it to places adjacent to railroad lines. Along with such other champions as Edward Bok, the editor of *Ladies' Home Journal*, he understood the intimacy of commuter train, corridor, and home.

In their arrangement of houses and yards, railroad suburbs bespoke new understandings of work, family responsibilities, and beauty. Certainly tradition exerted a powerful influence in most suburbs—after all, the suburbanites had deserted cities in order to achieve "rural living"—but life in the railroad suburbs reflected the new vitality so evident elsewhere in the corridor.

Hundreds of thousands of urban families dreamed of raising at least part of their own food, for example, and between 1880 and 1935 their dreams shaped backyards in every railroad suburb. They sought the moral uplift of traditional rural activity, recounted in a spate of backward-looking books that appeared throughout the half century. "It is one of the greatest virtues of farm life that the boy must learn to do disagreeable tasks, and to stick to them to the finish, however irksome they are," wrote Clifton Johnson in *The Farmer's Boy*, one of the 1890s "remember the farm" books that struck chords in the minds of parents remembering rural childhood.[11] Books like Lucy Larcom's *A New England Girlhood* and E. H. Arr's *New England Bygones* sentimentally recalled the joys of agriculture while ignoring the narrowmindedness that repelled Mitchell and other reformers.[12] In cities, thoughtful men and women determined that their children would enjoy something of such uplifting rural work; in the Midwest and High Plains, farmboys slipped down to water tanks to hop freight trains headed for cities.[13] In time, the metropolitan corridor served both groups—the middle and upper classes heading for suburbs and the rural people seeking cities.

Emory O. Hersey sold estates in the new suburbs along the Old Colony Railroad south of Boston, and his advertisements published in Boston newspapers in the first years of the twentieth century showed his understanding of the rural nostalgia shaping mass-circulation magazines. One described a "cosey home" of seven rooms in great detail, but emphasized the lot, "now a garden; can raise vegetables enough to last year round; room for hen yard, shrubs, cherry trees, fine strawberry bed." Another stressed the acquisition of "9 pear trees, 2 cherry, 1 quince, 1 apple, grape arbor, 6 vines, jacque-mint roses, shrubs, and flowers," and another described a "large garden, all planted, apples, pears, grapes, currants, strawberries, blackberries, shrubs and flowers in plenty."[14] Apartment-house residents read such advertisements in the Boston *Transcript* and wondered about the financial potential of such miniature rural locations. Could backyard agriculture help to pay mortgage costs, or at least cover commuting expenses?

Suburban poultry-raising offers a reasonably clear answer. Before it became fashionable in the 1880s, it claimed the attention of every farm family; women and children traditionally cared for fowl. As early as 1850, one of the first proponents of suburban living argued that "to children, especially, fowls are objects of exceeding interest." In *The Architecture of Country Houses*, Andrew Jackson Downing insisted that "he who will educate a boy in the country without a 'chicken' is already a semi-barbarian."[15] As rural nostalgia gathered force in cities, poultry-raising came to represent all livestock husbandry; no suburbanite could expect to keep a herd of cows on his lot, but he could maintain a small flock of hens. Indeed he almost had to, if he wanted the true

Emory O. Hersey established his real estate office just across the road from the Mt. Bowdoin depot on the edge of Boston. Between 1895 and 1916, the area "developed" quickly, as these views reveal. (Collection of the author)

rural experience. "A country place is not a country place without chickens," remarked one *Suburban Life* essayist in 1905.[16] But rising food prices, not nostalgia, created the great suburban poultry-raising fad.

As early as 1871, one author suggested that chicken-raising might help to pay for suburban living. While men might complain that they had too little time at home to care for fowl, wrote William M. Lewis in *The People's Practical Poultry Book*, "this objection is easily overcome by leaving the care of them in the hands of the good housewife, who would esteem it a great pleasure to care for the chicks and teach children how to rear them."[17] On a small scale, suburban poultry-raising efforts did pay, certainly in the eggs and meat consumed at home, and most probably in those sold to local grocers or neighbors. Housewives could offset commuting costs while giving children a chance to experience something of farm-life responsibility.

Many magazines championed the fad, insisting that even a few hens "made sense." Now and then someone published an article recounting financial losses, but the majority of authors emphasized profits and model henhouses. Inventors explained "A-shaped" houses, coops made of logs to blend in with shrubbery, portable coops and runs, and dozens of other structures. "The outside of the building is very attractive, being dark green with white facing under the eaves," asserted one 1913 piece. A 1915 article emphasized that a poultry house should be "consistently in harmony with its surroundings and with the other buildings" adjacent to it. The do-it-yourself movement embraced poultry-raising simply because nerve-wracked commuters needed weekend exercise; building houses and runs offered the jittery executive some physical relaxation.[18] F. W. Hallett's 1919 booklet, *Plans for Poultry Houses*, is something of a carpentry manual, too; Stephen Beale's *Profitable Poultry Keeping* and Harry R. Lewis's *Productive Poultry Husbandry* emphasize innovations in design and building techniques. Behind many traditional-style suburban houses stood a "modernistic" poultry house made by the suburbanite in accordance with plans published in magazines or by poultry-feed companies. Such a structure advertised its builder's facility with woodworking tools and his willingness to accept new architectural styles—at least in backyard areas.[19] It reflected his love of rural ideals coupled with up-to-date efficiency. And just possibly it sheltered the enterprise that produced enough income to offset commuting costs.

Early-twentieth-century suburbanites devoted careful attention to balance sheets, as a number of magazine articles attest. In "The Back Yard Profitable," a 1906 *Suburban Life* piece, Frank A. Gardner explained how to garden "to the limit"; another article of the same year, E. P. Powell's "The Balance Sheet of a Country Home," analyzed bookkeeping as closely as it did fruit-and-vegetable growing. "It is quite fair to say that from an expenditure of $23.05 we received in actual value not less than $65 worth of produce harvested and correctly appraised," remarked one *Countryside Magazine* correspondent in a 1915 article entitled "The Debit and Credit of a Tiny Suburban

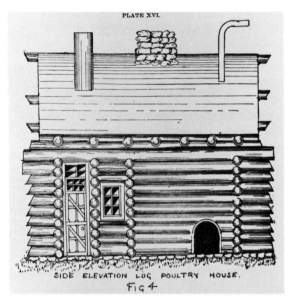

Log poultry house. (From Hallett, Plans for Poultry Houses, *collection of the author)*

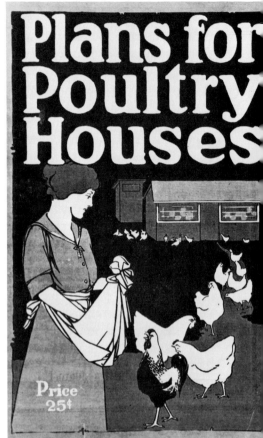

Cover, Plans for Poultry Houses. *(Collection of the author)*

A 1920s chicken house now used for storage. (JRS)

Garden."[20] Raising poultry and growing fruit and vegetables struck hundreds of thousands of Americans as profitable, partly because housewives and children did almost all the work. No magazine author calculated the cost of housewife labor, let alone the labor contribution of children. Such "free" labor, sometimes disguised by the concern for providing character-building chores for children and fears of adulterated food processed in industrial-zone factories, made backyard agriculture profitable.[21] In an era of rising food prices, housewives gloried in their ability to use "leisure time" to add to their family income. The possibility of pure food, and even occasional dreams of fresh strawberries for breakfast, combined with the promise of escape from rising food costs to fuel the powerful pro-suburban movement.

Advertising stoked suburban food-raising enterprises. Readers of *House and Garden, Ladies' Home Journal*, and other magazines encountered advertisements urging them to "keep bees for fun and profit," to buy a knocked-down, easily assembled all-weather greenhouse, a new wheeled cultivator, and the latest seeds.[22] Such advertisements hammer home the message of efficiency; in an age of efficient factories, railroads, power stations, and trolley cars, the backyard agricultural enterprise ought not be the reincarnation of eighteenth-century farms. Instead it ought to be mechanized, systematized, and crisply effective at producing high-quality, inexpensive foodstuffs.

When the National Association of Real Estate Boards published M. V. Folsom's *A Home of Your Own and What it Means to You* in 1922, soaring food prices preoccupied the nation's housewives—and their husbands. Folsom argued that "the back yard of your home is the most profitable Food Factory on earth" because it "enables you to cash in on every hour of your spare time that you care to devote to it, and to convert that time into valuable food products." The full-color pages spoke glowingly of "$50 to $100 each year in effective profit or saving of food expense, from a back yard flock of a dozen or two of carefully selected hens" fed on table waste and garden forage; hens "will pay your taxes," one eight-year-old apple tree will produce a $75 profit, and "there are instances where the back yard has been made to pay for the home itself."[23] *A Home of Your Own* probably speaks too optimistically, but countless city dwellers accepted part of its message. Backyard farming might pay the commuting costs and make practical a family's relocation to a railroad suburb. Always, of course, such agriculture remained tinged with nostalgia, but by the Depression, when owning an efficient, up-to-date, carefully designed food factory helped millions of suburban families endure poverty, suburban farming tingled with metropolitan energy, not the slothfulness increasingly associated with rural life. By the 1920s, many Americans viewed farmers as Mitchell and other reformers had learned to view them—as stubborn, ignorant, blatantly inefficient workers out of touch with high-speed, systematized efficiency. Words like *hayseed, clod-hopper*, and *soddie* hint at the transformation wrought in part by efficient suburban gardening and poultry-raising.

Magazine advertisement, 1911. (From Garden Magazine, *November 1911, Loeb Library, Harvard University)*

A GOOD LIVING FROM POULTRY

HOW I MADE $1500.00 IN TEN MONTHS ON A CITY LOT 40 FEET SQUARE

WHEN I originally made the above statement, it seemed incredible, but now I can prove it by not only my own experience, but by the enthusiastic testimony of thousands of Philo poultry raisers throughout the United States. I will give you their names; show you their letters; prove to you just what they are making and how they are making it.

The Philo System is Unlike All Other Ways of Keeping Poultry

and in many respects just the reverse, accomplishing things in poultry work that have always been considered impossible, and getting unheard of results that are hard to believe without seeing.

The New System Covers All Branches of the Work Necessary for Success

from selecting the breeders to marketing the product. It tells how to get eggs that will hatch, how to hatch nearly every egg and how to raise nearly all the chicks hatched. It gives complete plans in detail how to make everything necessary to run the business and at less than half the cost required to handle the poultry business in any other manner.

Two-Pound Broilers in Eight Weeks

are raised in a space of less than a square foot to the broiler, and the broilers are of the very best quality, bringing here 3 cents a pound above the highest market price.

Our Six-Months-Old Pullets are Laying at the Rate of 24 Eggs Each Per Month

in a space of two square feet for each bird. No green cut bone of any description is fed, and the food used is inexpensive compared with food others are using.

Don't Let the Chicks Die in the Shell

One of the secrets of success is to save all the chickens that are fully developed at hatching time, whether they can crack the shell or not. It is a simple trick and believed to be the secret of the ancient Egyptians and Chinese which enabled them to sell the chicks at 10 cents a dozen

Chicken Feed at 15 Cents a Bushel.

Our book tells how to make the best green food with but little trouble and have a good supply any day in the year, winter and summer. It is just as impossible to get a large egg yield without green food as it is to keep a cow without hay or fodder.

Our New Brooder Saves 2 Cents on Each Chicken

No lamp required. No danger of chilling, over heating or burning up the chickens as with brooders using lamps or any kind of fire. They also keep all the lice off the chickens automatically or kill any that may be on them when placed in the brooder. Our book gives full plans and the right to make and use them. One can easily be made in an hour at a cost of 25 to 50 cents.

Our new book, THE PHILO SYSTEM OF POULTRY KEEPING, gives full particulars regarding these wonderful discoveries, with simple, easy-to-understand directions that are right to the point, and 15 pages of illustrations showing all branches of the work from start to finish.

Testimonial

DENVER, Col., Oct. 30, 1910.

MR. E. W. PHILO, Elmira, N. Y.

DEAR SIR:—No doubt you will be interested to learn of our success in keeping poultry by the Philo System. Our first year's work is now nearly completed. It has given us an income of over $500.00 from six pedigree hens and one cockerel. Had we understood the work as well as we now do after a year's experience, we could have easily made $1,000.00 from the six hens. In addition to the profits from the sale of pedigree chicks, we have cleared over $960.00 running our hatchery plant consisting of 56 Cycle hatchers. We are pleased with the results and expect to do better the coming year. With best wishes, we are

Very truly yours, (MRS.) C. P. GOODRICH

Others are succeeding in every state and Mr. Philo's NEW 96-page book entitled, Making Poultry Pay, gives accounts of their experience and success, and carefully selected matter of permanent value to every poultry raiser. This book will be mailed for 10c in stamps or money, or if ordered with the *New Enlarged Philo System Book* both will be sent for $1.00.

THE POULTRY REVIEW

is a monthly magazine edited by Mr. Philo and a score of other expert and practical poultrymen, and now has over 110,000 subscribers.

SPECIAL OFFER

Our New Book, "MAKING POULTRY PAY," 96 pages,	$ .10
New Enlarged Edition of the "PHILO SYSTEM BOOK"	1.00
If ordered at once will mail the two books for	1.00
"THE POULTRY REVIEW" (one year) - - - -	1.00
"MAKING POULTRY PAY," "PHILO SYSTEM BOOK" and "THE POULTRY REVIEW" one year, postpaid, all for	1.50

E. R. Philo, Pub., 2291 Lake St., Elmira, N. Y.

U. S. DEPARTMENT OF AGRICULTURE
FARMERS' BULLETIN No. 1044

THE CITY HOME GARDEN

Backyard orchard, ca. 1906.
(Collection of the author)

By 1924, even the Department of Agriculture had recognized the force of backyard farming.
(Collection of the author)

Exactly as Jesse Lynch Williams noted in his article on the growing power of suburban prejudices, the success of a suburban agriculture based on expert-designed structures, gadgets, and free labor shaped urban and suburban attitudes. No longer did most Americans respect farmers as intelligent, innovative thinkers; instead the once-honored agriculturist became a hillbilly, the butt of jokes concerning traveling salesmen. He was, after all, a man without a lawn.

By the end of the 1930s, greensward symbolized railroad suburbs, the suburbs miniaturized in Lionel Company terraces. Urban houses had no space for broad lawns, and farmhouses—in the urban and suburban imagination, at least—stood surrounded by weeds, paddocks, and fields of crops. Whatever the suburban family built in the backyard—tiny orchard, large vegetable garden, modernistic hen house—it insisted on a lawn in front, the emblem of large-scale estates, English country homes, and wealth.

In the 1880s, families living in the railroad suburbs possessed much information about lawns, largely through the pages of *The Horticulturist*, *Garden and Forest*, *Atlantic Monthly*, and other magazines. Article after article explained the correct seed, the correct soil, and the correct shrubs and trees needed to create the correct lawn. What explains the fascination with lawn-making? Surely not profit-making, for greensward produced no revenue. Surely not agricultural tradition, for the nation's farm families spent little time making lawns. Perhaps the answer lies in the suburban fascination with ordered efficiency, as much as it lies in the attempt to make a modest house resemble an English manor.

The front lawn reflected the suburban embracing of ordered, manipulated space.[24] Mowing a lawn offered every commuter the chance to restore mind and body while maintaining a beautifully ordered outdoor space.

Turn-of-the-century *Scientific American* articles chronicled the rapid innovation in lawn-mower design. Inventors struggled to produce an easily pushed mower that would create a smooth lawn; the magazine dutifully reported each invention. Attaining perfect smoothness required more than a perfect machine, of course; garden magazines advised suburbanites about the proper mixtures of grass seed, the draining of muddy areas, and the correct use of the mowers.[25] By 1910, the typical suburban lawn announced the invasion of the industrial zone into rural America. In a 1906 *Suburban Life* article, "How to Have a Good Lawn," Samuel T. Maynard emphasized that the lawn mower is of prime importance in creating a smooth lawn. "When nicely adjusted, and in good working order, it may be kept so by a hair's breadth turn of the adjusting screws or bolts, and no one should be allowed to meddle with these parts unless he fully understands them."[26] Before the automobile era, therefore, suburban men owned a complex machine that required skilled maintenance and skilled operation. But the mower provided only one element of industrial-zone technology. Chemistry offered another.

DESIGN FOR A LARGE SUBURBAN LOT.

W. ATLEE BURPEE & CO., PHILADELPHIA.

URPEE'S "FAIRMOUNT PARK" LAWN GRASS SEED.

Nothing adds more to the attractiveness of a rural home than a well-kept, close, velvety lawn. The first requisite is good seed, and for this purpose we can confidently recommend Burpee's "Fairmount Park" Lawn Grass Seed. This is the very best quality of a mixture of the finest varieties of natural grasses, embracing such as are of neat growth, hardy and best adapted to produce a permanent and fine turf. The quantity of seed required per acre is from three to four bushels. For the convenience of many of our customers, who require only a small quantity of seed, we have put it up neatly in **Quart Boxes,** with the illustration and full directions printed on each. Price per quart 30 cts., or 2 boxes (each containing one quart) for 50 cts., **postpaid, by mail.** We offer the seed in bulk at $1.25 per peck; $4.50 per bushel of 14 lbs.

☞ PRINTED INSTRUCTIONS

"How to Prepare a Lawn" will be sent with every order for seed of Burpee's "Fairmount Park Mixture"

A **Cheaper Mixture,** and yet a good one, can be supplied at $3.00 per bushel of 14 lbs.

Maynard recommended "a little nitrate of soda, one hundred to three hundred pounds an acre" to achieve the dark green color characteristic of a proper lawn. While some writers suggested using organic materials like manure and wood ashes, as the century progressed more and more magazine experts counseled a reliance on chemicals. "A small crystal of copper sulfate (blue stone, blue vitriol) applied" to dandelions "will kill them," remarked another *Suburban Life* authority. In his 1910 "The Way to Make a Good Lawn," H. H. Henry explained the uses of such modern materials as strychnine, which poisons lawn-creasing moles.[27] Chemical and mechanical products imported from the industrial zone by rail eventually shaped the typical suburban lawn into a nearly artificial creation.

Shorn to an evenness impossible to achieve without delicately adjusted mowers, colored a green scarcely ever found in the richest of well-manured meadows, the railroad suburb lawn represented the epitome of order. By 1926, when M. E. Bottomley published *The Design of Small Properties*, almost every suburban family understood the aesthetic of smoothness, greenness, and order. Six years later, when Bottomley published *The Art of Home Landscape*, the nation's lawn-mower manufacturers had apparently determined that grass height should be standardized at one and a half inches; most lawn mowers could not be adjusted for greater height. Bottomley argued that lawns ought to be trimmed taller in early spring and early autumn, but the force of mechanical standardization proved too powerful.[28] Suburbanites wanted close-cropped, smooth lawns.

Tennis, croquet, badminton, and other lawn sports became known as suburban sports, played by wives and children in backyards on weekdays and by entire families on weekends. High-paced, dependent on smooth surfaces, and, increasingly, on marked courts, the sports display the characteristics of the metropolitan corridor. The suburban lawn depended on constant maintenance, continuous mechanized care combined with regular infusions of chemical-works products. It provided not only the playing area of modern sports intended to relax and stimulate commuters weary from urban scurry, but a clear indication of the rigidly engineered nature respected in railroad suburbs. Indeed the lawn is engineered nature, as Samuel Merwin hinted in *The Road Builders*, when he portrayed the chief engineer of a railroad-building operation far from suburban Chicago writing home to direct his wife in the proper planting of their home grounds. The letter-writing scene emphasized the similarities between railroad-building and lawn-making, of course, but it revealed the engineer to be a dedicated suburbanite, a true creature of the metropolitan corridor, as true as the commuter gazing at the lawns and backyard henhouses and gardens beyond his train window, thinking about playing croquet or badminton on a summer evening.[29]

Perhaps one book best explicates the particular niche of the railroad suburb in the larger metropolitan corridor. *The Garden of a Commuter's Wife* appeared in 1902, dedicated to "the commuter," meaning both the author's husband and all commuters. Mabel Wright wrote precisely and wittily about the suburban spaces seen from commuter trains, about new suburbs still half treeless, and about the relation of efficient backyards and smooth front lawns. "The commuter's wife should have a hen rampant as her coat of arms, and adopt it as her patron saint," she comments before describing her poultry-raising enterprise. But she is also aware of the need for mowing the lawn and takes pleasure in it, too: "Now among the outdoor sounds, bird music at its height and the babbling notes of the early nestlings, comes a new tone, the voice of the lawn mower." She listens to it sympathetically, describing its sounds when it is "happy, cheerfully talkative, easily garrulous" in low, even grass, and speaking in "thick and choked" accents when struggling with tall grass. Her book, not a guidebook in the usual way, interprets life in the corridor, life revolving around the departure and arrival of her husband, her daily and seasonal activities outdoors, and her growing hatred of occasional visits to the city, the place of congestion, dirt, and noise.[30]

The Garden of a Commuter's Wife essentially concerns residence in the corridor, wholehearted embracing of system, efficiency, regularity, and order. It describes life adjacent to the commuter depot and its railroad-company–owned garden. It describes life within sound of the train whistle, life focused on productive backyard, handsome front lawn, and house. It describes life in Lionelville, in Lionel Terrace.

Croquet, ca. 1883. (Courtesy of Vermont Historical Society)

11: TROLLEY

An emerging trolley corridor, 1908. (Courtesy of Loeb Library, Harvard University)

DETERMINED TO BEGIN

their married life with a "spectacular start," Clinton and Louisa Lucas set off in 1904 on a quirky, almost bizarre wedding trip. "We had been seized with trolley mania so long that it was only natural we should be carried away by it even on our honeymoon," noted Clinton Lucas in the first chapter of *A Trolley Honeymoon*, the record of a five-hundred-mile electric excursion from Delaware to Maine accomplished, with a brief interruption of railroad travel, wholly on trolleys.[1] Armed with luggage and last-minute wedding gifts of a tube of nickels for fares and a Kodak camera for recording the passing scene, the newlyweds embarked on a joy ride. *A Trolley Honeymoon* remains perhaps the finest record of trolley—not streetcar—travel. Its sustained recording of trivial events, curious angles of vision, and attitudes toward "rural trolleying" reveal a landscape laced by rail lines placed in or along country lanes and traveled by wonderfully pleasant vehicles, the "electrics" of a now-forgotten age of rural and suburban transportation.

By 1910, *streetcar* and *trolley* connoted dramatically different vehicles. Implicit in the connotations was a factor only a few authors described at length, because Americans had quickly accepted it. Streetcars provided a distinct sort of ride and a peculiar view of the landscape; trolley cars offered a different quality of ride, and an equally peculiar vision of the countryside. The streetcar objectified turn-of-the-century urban scurry and danger, while the trolley exemplified the promise of technological leisure.

Henry James, for example, hated streetcars. When he returned to New York City after a twenty-five-year absence, he watched "the mob seeking entrance to an up-town or a down-town electric car fight for life at one of the apertures" and stood almost transfixed by the mad scramble. James wondered at skyscrapers, at great bridges, at apartment-house hotels, but he learned that to view such marvels from the street meant risking collision with the streetcars. "The electric cars, with their double track, are everywhere almost as tight a fit in the narrow channel of the roadway as the projectile in the bore of a gun," he determined after watching several cars speed abreast down city streets.[2] The rows of streetcars made the crossing of streets perilous indeed. Foot traffic, he asserted bitterly, "in any fashion consistent with personal decency or dignity, was merely mocked at, when the stony-hearted 'trolleys,' cars of Jug-

Open trolley, ca. 1904. (Courtesy of Smithsonian Institution)

gernaut in their power to squash, triumphed all along the line."[3] Astute though he was, James missed the connotation of *trolley*; his *American Scene* accurately depicts the effects of urban electric cars, but his terminology confuses the shades of meaning implicit in American slang.

Almost as soon as Charles Sprague proved that electricity drawn from overhead wires could power passenger-carrying horsecars converted to electric-motor propulsion, owners of horse-car companies and civic officials arrived in Richmond, Virginia, for first-hand demonstrations. Before the end of the year 1888, Sprague had standing orders from some two hundred "street railway" firms anxious to dispense with horses and acquire electric-driven cars.[4] So rapid was the conversion that cities slightly hesitant found themselves ridiculed. "Electric cars are started on St. Charles Avenue. They create as much excitement as a Rex parade. Yesterday, for the first time, New Orleans rode by wire. The experience proved delightful, safe and successful," reported *The Picayune* on February 2, 1893. "Now that the system is perfected, New Orleans will desire to speedily forget the fact that all over the North and West, even in the smallest towns, the electric cars have for a long time been in popular use."[5] New Orleans embarked on a typical excursion into an electric-powered urban future. Street-railway companies laid track to the fringes of the city, built amusement parks that attracted evening and weekend riders onto the cars, and rewarded the passengers with a brilliantly illuminated vision of the future "electric city." Their tracks frequently reached to a public beach and popularized quick excursions to watch sailboat races, sunsets, and the new water sports. Gradually the companies stretched tracks into undeveloped fringe areas of the city, creating in time the pattern of suburban residential development that Americans soon recognized as "streetcar suburbs."[6] Such success spawned the novel difficulty of traffic congestion, however, especially in downtown retail districts where the radiating lines converged on an area of only several city blocks. In 1902, the *Street Railway Journal* published a photograph depicting the "normal" streetcar traffic operating over the five sets of tracks that made New Orleans' Canal Street into a pedestrian's nightmare, especially at nine o'clock in the morning, when the photograph was made.[7] Within a few years, such congestion plagued most large American cities, and the resulting furor caused by streetcar/pedestrian accidents prompted street railway firms to install automatic safety fenders that leaped out to catch pedestrians brushing the fronts of cars. The furor led also to municipal studies of subway tunnels, and to the opening of the nation's first subway in Boston in 1898.[8] Despite the continuous jams and the brutal accidents, the public love of the electrics endured, although most citizens reserved their affection for trolleys, not juggernaut urban streetcars.

In "The Broomstick Train; or, The Return of the Witches," a poem of 1890, the aged Boston poet Oliver Wendell Holmes likened the mysteriously propelled trolley car to the witchcraft power of seventeenth-century New En-

Canal Street chaos, 1902. (Collection of the author)

gland. His poem argues that the witches' broomsticks are the poles connecting the cars with the overhead electric wire:

> Often you've looked on a rushing train,
> But just what moved it was not so plain.
> It couldn't be those wires above,
> For they could neither pull nor shove;
> Where was the motor that made it go
> You couldn't guess, *but now you know*.[9]

Holmes caught the specific quality of the electric trolley car; it made no noise, had no visible source of propulsion, yet accelerated at an amazing rate. Now and then, of course, it made bright sparks, particularly stunning in the evening, but on the whole it seemed as magical a machine as anything concocted in colonial Salem.

Trolley lines stretched rapidly from downtowns into suburbs, and from rural railroad stations into the backcountry. Farm regions that had never known railroad service suddenly discovered that they might have the advantages of a "car line." The tracks followed public roads on cheaply and quickly constructed roadbeds that followed contorted curves easily and required the lightest of bridges; cars operated without expensive signaling equipment, used stores as stations, and required only one- or two-man crews, not the five-man crews necessary to operate passenger trains.[10] Remarkably little capital sufficed to begin construction, and while many lines passed into receivership before completion or else merged with connecting systems, by 1916 some 1,000 firms owned 60,580 miles of track in city, suburbs, and countryside.[11] The majority of the eleven billion passengers carried that year rode streetcars, not rural trolleys, but the small, silent cars operating far beyond city limits began reshaping rural space and social customs.

Life on a rural car line struck many turn-of-the-century observers as remarkably pleasant. Cars ran regularly, often on twenty- or thirty-minute headways; away from villages, they proved quite speedy, humming along at thirty miles an hour on most lines, and running at up to seventy miles an hour on a few well-patronized, especially well-constructed lines. Cheap fares—often only five cents, less than one-fifth the comparable railroad fare—encouraged frequent use. Children rode trolleys to school, particularly to the high schools being established in so many small towns. Housewives and farmwives rode the cars to visit and to shop, even to the nearest small town to attend movie-theater matinees. Regular service and cheap fares encouraged men to work away from their farms, indeed, to farm part-time. Freight trolleys, called "box motors" from their box-like appearance, collected milk from farms, carried eggs and other poultry products to nearby markets, and brought farm families newspapers and other town goods.[12] Despite strenuous opposition from railroad companies, the trolley firms succeeded in arranging schedules to connect

A rural trolley-car corridor, ca. 1905. (From Rice, "Urbanizing Rural New England," Harvard College Library)

Small-town, battery-powered trolley. (Courtesy of Library of Congress)

OPPOSITE: *By 1904, the trolley-car corridor reached northward along the Connecticut River valley, connecting nearly every major town. (Courtesy of Loeb Library, Harvard University)*

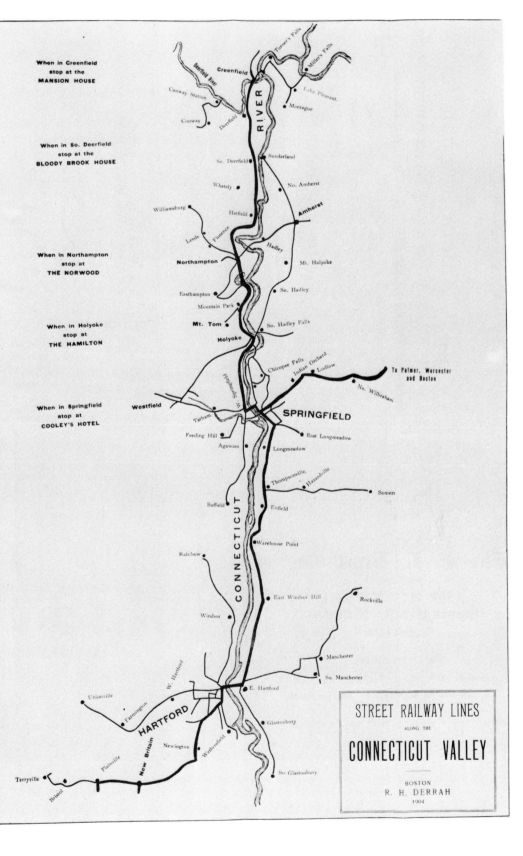

When in Greenfield
stop at the
MANSION HOUSE

When in So. Deerfield
stop at the
BLOODY BROOK HOUSE

When in Northampton
stop at
THE NORWOOD

When in Holyoke
stop at
THE HAMILTON

When in Springfield
stop at
COOLEY'S HOTEL

STREET RAILWAY LINES
ALONG THE
CONNECTICUT VALLEY

BOSTON
R. H. DERRAH
1904

Laying trolley tracks, ca. 1908.
(Photo collection of the
Huntington, New York,
Historical Society)

By 1910, the metropolitan glow of the central station gleamed everywhere along rural
trolley lines. (From Rice, "Urbanizing Rural New England," Harvard College Library)

with passenger trains, and sometimes to compete with them. Trolleys offered fast, regular, cheap, silent—and personalized—transportation to the nation's rural population, and to the rural people of the Northeast and upper Midwest in particular.

"The habits of the trolley-car change very materially in the country," asserted Sylvester Baxter in an 1890 *Harper's Monthly* piece entitled "The Trolley in Rural Parts." Baxter noticed the dramatic change in operating character that occurred as the car rolled beyond built-up districts. "With a zip and a whiz it darts forward, taking the free track with a bound that brings laughter to careworn lips and blood to the cheeks." The change in pace creates "a holiday mood" among the passengers; "the gong ceases its querulous clang, and the car rushes along at a speed that at first seems a bit reckless to those accustomed to the creeping pace of urban transit." One key to understanding Baxter's interpretation of the importance of the trolley in reorienting American attitudes toward countryside travel lies in his verbs. Throughout his article, he uses words like "swish" and "hum" to identify the activity of the trolley; consistently he speaks of the "purring of the motor," the "whiz" of the car. The near-silence of the trolley makes the car's appearance all the more surprising to the rambler in meadows and woods: "Suddenly he notes a faint humming in the air—something strangely familiar. It gradually grows louder, and a steady purring undertone keeps it company. Before he can realize the meaning of it all there dashes across his astonished vision—flying swiftly down the rural highway or darting through the solemn woods—a sight all too common in his eyes: a gay-looking electric car in all its splendor of fresh varnish, bright lettering, and trimmings of nickel and brass."[13] What, then, *was* the rural trolley car?

Baxter's terminology suggests that it appeared to him almost as an insect, and indeed the inference explains not only the words like "humming," but the darting path of the car. The turn-of-the-century rural trolley was the nation's first off-the-road vehicle; if it followed rural highways for miles at a stretch, it was equally likely to suddenly shortcut a curve. "In going through the woods, it bounds aside and plays hide-and-seek through the trees with the farm wagons on the road it has left, for the track makes a new right of way for itself— a way arched by a delightful sylvan tunnel, where the air is sweet with resinous breath of pine-trees."[14] The rural trolley required almost nothing of the complicated right-of-way absolutely necessary to the safe operation of the railroad train. Its sharp turns, thin ballast, and low rails made it seem as without track as any flying insect, and the branches of elms and other trees camouflaged its overhead wire, so that only close scrutiny disclosed its route through fields and woods.

Riding the car seemed like riding a dragonfly. For the first time, Americans rode a power vehicle in which they looked straight ahead, over the motorman's shoulder. Ahead they saw only the rails half-hidden in grass and the

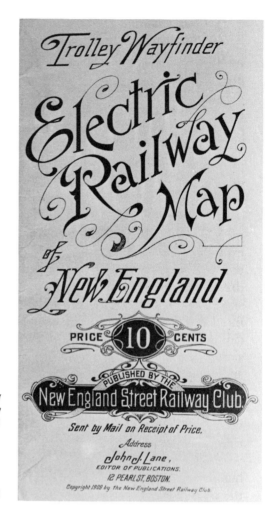

Trolley Wayfinder

Electric Railway Map

of

New England.

PRICE **10** CENTS

PUBLISHED BY THE
New England Street Railway Club

Sent by Mail on Receipt of Price.

Address
John J. Lane,
EDITOR OF PUBLICATIONS.
12 PEARL ST, BOSTON.
Copyright 1909 by the New England Street Railway Club

Vacationers wandered along the trolley-car corridors clutching detailed "wayfinders" filled with route, schedule, and scenery information. (Courtesy of Loeb Library, Harvard University)

Trolley hearse, ca. 1911. (Courtesy of Smithsonian Institution)

line of poles carrying the wire through the landscape. At thirty miles an hour, the silent car thrilled its riders not so much with the sense of speed—express trains easily tripled that speed in the early 1890s—but with an almost overpowering intimacy. No smell, no sound interfered with the passengers' experience of the landscape rushing past; so enamored was the public with its newfound experience that most trolley-car firms purchased two sets of cars, one set equipped with windows for winter use, the other lacking sides altogether. Passengers delighted in the wind whipping across their faces and rejoiced in smelling wildflowers, new-mown hay, and other summertime fragrances. The car darted from one enchantment to another exactly as a honeybee hummed from one flower to the next.

William Dean Howells discovered in the rural trolley car the perfect summertime vehicle. In a 1902 essay, "Confessions of a Summer Colonist," he explained his "love of the trolley line," remarking that it, "by its admirable equipment, and by the terror it inspires in horses, has wellnigh abolished driving; and following the old country roads, as it does, with an occasional short-cut through the deep, green-lighted woods or across the prismatic salt meadows, it is of a picturesque variety entirely satisfying." In Howell's view, riding open trolleys combined "exhilaration" with "an occasional apprehension when the car pitches down a sharp incline, and twists almost at right angles on a sudden curve at the bottom without slacking its speed." Courteous conductors, frequent trips, and low fares combined with the exhilarating ride and "ease and comfort" of the cars to win the favor of farmers and summer visitors alike, and, Howells noted somewhat grumpily, to attract pleasure-riding excursionists.[15]

Open trolleys attracted thousands of pleasure riders, especially on hot, humid evenings when the thirty-mile-an-hour breeze seemed more than worth the five-cent fare. Car companies quickly learned that a mosquito net ought to be hung at the front of the car to shield the riders from flying nuisance, but other amenities took longer to be invented and perfected. By 1915, however, many rural car lines sported specially equipped "party cars" designed for long-distance summer excursions. Such cars were almost entirely open, except for a closed central section containing a gramophone, ice-cream chest, and perhaps a bar; on the front and rear platforms stood chairs for the enjoyment of guests, although the wicker furniture was easily pushed aside if the passengers wanted to dance. The cars, chartered for birthday parties and other festivities, appeared to bystanders almost as fireflies might, for most sported strings of electric Japanese lanterns that swayed as the car swished past.

"Trolley mania," the phrase Lucas used to define the fascination that linked him and his wife even before their honeymoon trip, involved dozens of novel sensations unique to the rural electric cars. "An exhilarating trolley ride is the best sauce," he commented near the beginning of *A Trolley Honeymoon*, a book intended to explain all the subtle flavors of the sauce. Again and again, Lucas described the right-of-way peculiar to the rural trolley car, referring to "a grass track under arching shade trees," "the vista of arched trees" ahead of the car, the grass track beneath shade trees "that banished the plague of dust" common on urban streets.[16] Thin ballast coupled with alignments on roadside shoulders meant that within a year or two most trolley rights-of-way became overgrown with grass and wildflowers, and in an era before Dutch elm disease destroyed the long rows of mature, overarching trees planted in the 1870s to celebrate the national centennial, the greenery surrounded the cars. An open trolley, little more than a platform with a roof supported by a few poles, enabled riders to reach out and grab at leaves or high-growing flowers, and to revel in the natural odors created by the car brushing against plants. "The scent of clover and new mown hay was in the air," Lucas remarked of one stretch through rural Pennsylvania, but equally important was the smell of something turn-of-the-century urban Americans had learned to value—fresh air: "The sun had come out broiling hot, so that we were heartily glad to be seated once more in an open trolley car and to go scudding along in the teeth of the speed-generated breeze."[17] As Lucas and his contemporaries make clear, a great many summertime riders rode to no place in particular, but rode to enjoy the cooling, sometimes bracing breeze. "All the front seats, however, had been pre-empted by a merry trolley party (the first we had met on our trip), a group of women hatless and radiant in white shirtwaists, who chattered vivaciously over a hand-to-hand feast of caramels," he noted. Grabbing the front or "motorman's" bench preoccupied the Lucases, for that seat provided the best view and the best breeze, as well as some insight into the mysteries of electric control. As Baxter said, the humming was odd, and Lucas remarked on it, too, speaking of the car in insectlike terms. "Now we scurried over the main highway, now we darted through the woods and spluttered out again upon the Chester pike," he wrote approvingly. "Up hill and down we tore, zigging and zagging through garden and orchard until crossing the State line we neared the river's edge."[18] Trolley mania derived from the half-mischievous, half-orderly behavior of the mysterious car, and while many riders asked the newlyweds why they had not taken a fast train to the Maine coast, almost all the questioners understood the answer given by Lucas—the thrill of trolleying in July.

A few did not. Open cars carried only canvas awnings for protection against rain, and on a rainy day the cars offered a damp, sometimes drenching, ride, especially during high winds. Of course, rainy mornings prompted most companies to replace open cars with the closed cars normally operated in cold weather, but the closed trolleys trapped humidity and cigar-smoke and made trolley-tripping less than joyful. Not every trolley route rewarded joy riding. Now and then the Lucas excursion traversed industrial zones which made the trolley's intimacy with adjacent landscape a genuine liability. While the Pullman passenger enjoyed a comfortable plate glass, air-cooled separation from such industrial nuisances as noise and venting gases, the trolley passenger embraced them. *A Trolley Honeymoon* ignores the industrial landscape. When the Lucases were lucky, their car skirted factories and works. "The scene shifted quickly to the muddy Schuylkill, of which we had a hurried view from the bridge above. Its banks were lined with coal yards and blackened walls, while from the yellowish haze peered many towering chimney stacks, smudging the sky with inky smoke," wrote Lucas of one lucky miss. When luck failed, the newlyweds plunged into smoke, racket, and noxious fumes. "We followed the turnpike to Jersey City—a jumbled association of marshy flats and inlets; dense jungles of railroad tracks; unspeakable fertilizing plants; and last a dash through unsightly suburbs," he remarked of the great metropolitan industrial zone characterized by "the saturnalia of noise and the odor of escaping gas."[19] On such lines no one understood why newly married people had chosen to ride a trolley. The machine offered too much contact with the environment.

Lucas disliked the industrial zones through which the trolleys passed. In heavy traffic, the free-running trolley became a streetcar, clanging its gong, fighting for a path through jams of pedestrians and drays.[20] Lucas's dislike of the industrial zone is explained by more than the operation of the electric car, however. At Newark, a few miles from Manhattan Transfer, "the character of wayside scenes rapidly changed; and by the time we had trundled into Newark, the transformation was complete," he noted with disdain. "The calm deliberation of rural trolleying now began to give way to the speed and rush mania. We caught at once the infectious spirit."[21] Industrial zones slowed the speed of the trolley but increased the rush of riders to board and exit, and the dense population of such zones frequently overcrowded the cars. Implicit in *A Trolley Honeymoon*, and in many periodical articles of the time, is a developing love for rural privacy. One force fueling the trolley mania was the suburban—and urban—desire for a ride in the country away from crowds, on cars where an individual might laze on an entire bench or walk about the car at will, or eat a picnic lunch in breezy isolation. A Pullman passenger enjoyed such pleasures as a matter of course; the named train racing from rural regions through industrial zones provided a continuous and pleasant degree of privacy and personal space. When a trolley swung into an industrial zone, even a small one composed of a few mills and several streets of workers' housing, the joy rider dreaded not only the slowing of speed and the possibility of odors and noise, but the sudden crowding of the car. In the country and outer suburbs, the humming car seemed to most observers as a free-ranging insect; in industrial zones—and certainly in cities—the shackled car seemed beseiged by masses of insectlike humans. Lucas reserved his most biting comments for the hordes that now and then swept over "his" car despite the shouts of conductors that another car followed just behind. By the time the pair reached southern Connecticut, Louisa had gleaned from guidebooks and maps an al-

Trolley in an industrial zone. (From Pennell, "Vulcan's Capital," collection of the author)

most entirely rural route to Maine, one offering pleasant landscapes and polite privacy.

Trolley guidebooks offer rare insights into the turn-of-the-century landscape, and into the angle of vision unique to trolleying. Lucas notes how much his bride delighted in spotting features of scenic or historic interest and in working out routes, and he records her dismay at losing the guidebooks someplace between Hartford, Connecticut, and Springfield, Massachusetts. "We were freed from their tyranny, I secretly consoled myself," Lucas commented, but clearly both felt the loss of specific "what to see" and "what route to take" information.[22] While Lucas avoids mentioning the titles of the guides, the newlyweds' route suggests that they carried one, or perhaps two, of the best-known New England guides.

Katherine M. Abbott published *Trolley Trips: The Historic New England Coast* in 1899, having already published two others dealing with parts of Massachusetts. *Trolley Trips* is a brief, chiefly historical guide emphasizing such long-ago events as the hiding of the colonial Connecticut charter in an oak tree and deemphasizing routes and equipment.[23] Like most guidebooks of the period, however, *Trolley Trips* made lavish use of photographs, many of which occupied entire pages. For day-trippers, her guide provided much information of topographical-historical nature, the sort desired by joy riders familiar with routes and junctions, anxious to enliven their breezy journeys with the spark of identifying important landscape features. Robert H. Derrah's 1904 guidebooks, *By Trolley through Western New England* and *By Trolley through Eastern New England*, had begun as earlier, briefer guides, and retained regional variations; the western guidebook was known in a "Connecticut Valley Edition," and the Lucases perhaps carried an early version of the 1904 edition.[24] Derrah's books represent the extraordinarily detailed sophistication of the early twentieth-century American guidebook, a sophistication customarily associated with European guides only.

"This booklet is published for the purpose of enabling one to learn what may be seen from the cars of the different lines described, to tell you how to reach a given place, to record the mileage, running time, fare and such additional information as will contribute to one's ease of mind and pleasure," Derrah asserted in his introduction. But a specific conception of landscape appreciation underlies the information, too. According to Derrah, looking forward to the interesting features of the landscape prepares the mind to accurately see and remember them: "Anticipating them, you bestow on each your undivided attention for the moment, thus insuring a memory picture far more vivid than would otherwise be possible."[25] Based on his extensive riding and on information provided by the companies, his western guidebook produced what it promised.

The guidebook presented the stories associated with old inns and houses, described lineside vegetation, and recommended places to dine, all the while noting the best places to transfer, the frequency of cars on single routes and at junctions, and the best "walks" away from the lines. Derrah emphasized the intimacy of the trolley with its landscape; any rider could pull the cord or wave at the conductor, stop the car, and walk around the historic house or village green, and then jump aboard the next car, which, according to the schedules Derrah printed, usually arrived in about thirty minutes.[26] Behind such advice to alight and scrutinize the landscape lay the trolley companies' desire for more business. The joy rider who frequently stepped off to walk paid many more fares than the one who remained aboard; so Derrah and other guidebook writers, especially those employed by trolley companies, emphasized the wisdom of frequent leave-takings.

"Trolley fishing" exemplifies the on-and-off-and-on nature of much joy riding. "Fishermen are always irresponsible, but the trolley fisherman has outdone in irresponsibility anything heretofore recorded," remarked Albert Bigelow Paine in a 1903 *World's Work* article entitled "Short Vacations by Trolley." "With rod and line and bait he simply sits and rides, or exchanges fish tales with the conductor until water is sighted." After trying his luck, the typical fisherman usually waited for another trolley and rode to the next likely spot. "I fished most of the way to Chicago," Paine declared, "and I shall fish all the way to Boston to June." Paine discovered other riders who frequently ordered the car to stop. Antique hunters struck him as travelers who made a great many stops: "the very atmosphere of West Brookfield suggested blue china, brass fire things, and old mahogany."[27] Other magazine writers remarked on the almost annoying propensity of trolley companies to carry riders past one alluring feature after another. The Berkshire Street Railway Company operating north of Pittsfield in western Massachusetts issued its riders brief guidebooks keyed to roadside posts marked with red seals, each of which noted a place of historic interest. "Yet, there were one or two places marked with 'the Red Seal'—of immortality—where I should have liked to have the opportunity of stopping," concluded Richard Le Gallienne in a 1919 *Harper's Monthly* piece, "and, if I may make a suggestion to the Berkshire Street Railway Company, which, so far as it goes, has so wisely conceived of its 'territory' as a historical museum, I would say that even its shareholders would profit by its issuing 'stop-off' transfers at one or two points of its rapid pilgrimage."[28] Of course, the firm understood the profits implicit in having no such transfers; riders like Le Gallienne eventually found something they had to visit, and they told the motorman to stop.

Similar landscape features were mentioned repeatedly in the guides. Old houses, particularly those in which famous poets wrote or heroes braved British perils, received much attention and many photographs, along with Civil War monuments, academies, colleges, and public buildings. Lawns received much attention, too. "The car going up the valley of the Connecticut may be taken anywhere on Main Street or opposite Cooley's Hotel, the stopping place of all trolley tourists," began Derrah's chapter entitled "Springfield to Green-field: Trips to Holyoke, Mount Tom, Northampton, Hatfield, and Deerfield." "The ride up Main Street is between handsome buildings and private residences set upon ample green lawns."[29] Abbott likewise emphasized spacious lawns, and at one point drew her readers' attention to a "Grass Garden" operated by the Connecticut Agricultural Experiment Station. "In the turf laboratory the squares of individual grasses are each from one root, and in absolutely pure cultures," she noted. "The sods are a checkered demonstration in geography. You may here step into Inverary, Kildare, Devon, Denmark, Zurich, Auckland, N.Z., and all the countries of northern Europe."[30] Guide-book authors enjoyed describing lawns, and indeed their books suggest that trolleys frequently operated along lines abutted for miles by rolling lawns. If one believes the books, trolleys scarcely entered industrial zones of any kind, and never the sort endured by the Lucases. But the lines did serve manufacturing communities, and now and then the authors noted them in such phrases as "a car line runs up the valley between the hills to Gilbertsville, a small manufacturing village."[31] The authors simply ignored such industrial places or else mentioned them solely with regard to junctions and schedules. The emphasis on old houses and spacious lawns and the deliberate ignoring of industrial areas through which the trolleys operated hint at the cultural significance of trolley touring and trolley joy riding.

For working people, especially for the hundreds of thousands of factory workers, a trolley ride on a summer evening was a cheap, invigorating excursion, perhaps to an amusement park to hear a brass band, but usually to no place and back. Such joy riders wanted to escape their workplaces and so wanted to ride lines that wandered through forest and rural areas. Not surprisingly, guidebook authors emphasized what the day-trippers and tourists hoped to see. But trolleying effected a dramatic change in the national understanding of the road. Since the 1840s, railroads had specialized in transporting strangers; the typical rural family knew most of the people who walked or rode past its front door. The train, which almost never stopped except at stations, became a city of strangers at which children waved, knowing that further, more personal contact was extremely unlikely. For a half century, strangers proved few on even main-traveled roads, and Americans learned to think of the road beyond the doorstep as an extension of private property.[32] The trolley filled with joy riders, often with joy riders of immigrant origin and employed in factories, not only upset authors like Lucas—he at one point remarks on "the rapid increase of the foreign element in New England"—who disliked the European propensity for crowds and garlic-reeking picnic baskets, but disturbed the families who lived adjacent to trolley lines.[33] For many such families, and particularly for families building new houses along rural and outer-suburban trolley lines, lawns became defenses against trolley-borne strangers.

Trolley on small-town residential street. (Courtesy of Loeb Library, Harvard University)

Such lawns are only one component of the built environment that evolved along trolley routes. Baxter, in the final analysis, proved wrong. The rural trolley did indeed "bring other city sights and sounds in its wake," as Ernest Ingersoll noted in 1896. His *Harper's Weekly* article emphasized the new accessibility of the countryside to families desperately needing a day's vacation from urban scurry. "The result is that many suburban lines are taxed to their utmost in summer, especially on Sundays and holidays, to provide for this pleasure-excursion traffic," he concluded. "One sees the dear old roads and lanes along the Bronx, up the Hackensack, out on Orange Mountain, down on the heights of Castleton, filled on pleasant Sunday afternoons with sauntering groups, happy and healthy in this new-found enjoyment." In his opinion, the low fares and frequent schedules allowed vast numbers of New York City residents a chance to enjoy the countryside partly by electric car, partly on foot. "The mere fact that he can feel the soft earth under his feet and can bathe in the quiet of the country means a great deal to the man who paces all the week the city pavements and is half stunned by the roar of the town."[34] Baxter, Ingersoll, and other writers implied that suburbs existed as empty recreational areas; they ignored the residents of the countryside intermittently inundated by strangers alighting everywhere along trolley lines, and they ignored the message in the ever larger lawns and the new houses set ever further back from the roads.

Trolley cars caused spatial change, especially in rural areas. According to the many writers who commented on their effects, they brought urban life to hitherto isolated places. Frederick Rice, Jr., remarked as early as 1906 that trolley cars would end the age-old division between country people and urban dwellers; his *New England Magazine* piece, "Urbanizing Rural New England," is part of a larger literature of the period devoted to deciphering cultural shock. While he worried that progress meant the coming of urban problems into the country, he concluded that electric transportation outweighed such urban vices as consumerism. "The farmer's wife, who used to drive perhaps once a fortnight into town, now runs in several times a week," he noted in a long listing of lifestyle changes. "The older children go back and forth to the city schools."[35] Of course, he bemoaned the alterations of traditional landscapes, commenting that trolley junctions meant that "the ancient village greens have come to look like city squares," but on the whole he determined that electric cars would reverse the long decline of New England agriculture and the consequent afforestation of meadows and fields.[36] "A capital example is to be noted in the thinly populated and heavily wooded country of western Rhode Island, a land of abandoned farms of many years' standing," he remarked by way of example. "Into this district, overgrown with scrub oak, the freight-bearing trolley has penetrated, quickening communities that not long ago seemed moribund."[37] Such remarks are typical. In "The Trolley Car as a Social Factor," Karl Edwin Harriman told readers of the February 1906 issue of *World Today* that midwestern farm families embraced the trolley as the provider of urban recreation, education, and business opportunities. His article also used examples, particularly of the region around Detroit, where he found dozens of farm families riding the electrics home from evening entertainments. Schoolchildren found opportunities to attend high school in county seats or in larger cities, and farmers found inexpensive transportation for dairy products and other farm produce.[38] But more happened to the rural landscape than the erection of poles to carry the overhead wire, the refurbishing of several stores around those New England village greens that served as trolley junctions, and the placement of small milk-can platforms at the end of farm lanes in western Rhode Island or central Iowa or southern Wisconsin.

One minor change resulted from the immediate obsolescence of horse-cars. The oldfashioned vehicles, junked by those companies that did not try to electrify them, became the constituent units of the nation's first modular housing. "At Avon Park Heights, Bridgeport, Connecticut, there are a score or more old Broadway cars, transformed into homes," reported *House Beautiful* in 1905. "A cottage of two rooms," made by fitting two cars together, "sheltered a family of eight through the preceding winter." In upstate New York, twenty cast-off horse-cars provided vacation lodging for factory girls. Outside San Francisco evolved the beach community of "Ozonia" or "Carville," a "village of cars" acquired by a speculator for ten dollars each and sold to willing buyers. A 1907 *Country Life* article, printed on the same page as a large *Overland Limited* advertisement stressing "the best of everything," noted that some "houses" consisted of several cars joined together. The communities struck most reporters as vaguely like hobo jungles, or shantytowns, in short, as something slightly sinister.[39] Already the suburban view, especially of privacy and lawns, had begun to warp periodical reports. Suburban Americans spurned the experimental housing in favor of the housing evolving along trolley lines everywhere in the nation, already common in railroad suburbs, with productive back yards and well-kept greensward.

Trolley lines prompted dozens of town families to move a few miles into the country. Such moves are important, although the suburbanization occurring around the nation's major cities masked them from all but a few observers. Certainly, the establishment of the streetcar suburbs covering hundreds of square miles represents a chapter in the urban history of the United States. But equally significant is the mass movement of small-town families, particularly the families of businessmen, away from streets adjacent to Main Street. "The trolley passing the door of his little country holding, delivers him, at a minimum of cost, at the door of his factory or office in ample time to begin the day's work," wrote Harriman of the changes occurring in the Middle West. "And the same trolley car puts him down in his country dooryard for the evening meal with his family, which, in the meantime, has concerned itself with its garden, its sunshine, and its pure air."[40] The move away from small-town residential streets stemmed in part, perhaps, from the businessman's nostalgia for his rural boyhood, and from his desire to provide his children with a taste of country living and country virtue. But it often proceeded from vexations accompanying the growth of many small towns, which changed from wholly commercial centers to centers of light manufacturing. Even small industrial plants brought immigrants—and problems of housing and behavior—and as families learned that houses on Main Street stood perilously close to new and disturbing noises and events, many moved outward, along the one or two trolley lines entering town.

Sometimes the families purchased farmhouses, converted some of the meadow into lawn, and rented the remaining fields. Often they built new structures. Within ten or fifteen years, certainly by the beginning of the Great War, many rural roads had become trolley streets. The original houses often stood quite near the roadway, but the houses built by the newcomers stood further back, separated by lawns and fences. High Street, in Norwell, Massachusetts, is a classic example of such a street. Originally a twisting farm lane laid out in the mid-eighteenth century, by 1905 it had become an extension of the manufacturing village in the adjacent township. Poles carried the overhead wire that powered the trolley cars whisking mill owners and successful retailers the four or five miles to Rockland center. Time has scarcely mellowed what must have been a jarring clash of architectural styles; close to the road stand small Cape Cod farmhouses, but interspersed among them are houses built in turn-of-the-century styles. The Queen Anne and Second Empire houses were defended from trolley-borne strangers by lawns and fences that survive as shadows of a changed perception of the road.

The High Street trolley line meandered along country roads, sometimes in the roadway itself and often paralleling the road on its own right-of-way, carefully grassed to keep down dust and noise. In Hingham, it paralleled Main Street and eventually intersected a railroad line; to the west, beyond Rockland, it wandered as far as the great shoe-manufacturing city of Brockton. Eventually the shoe-factory workers brought their families on pleasant Sunday trolley excursions to the ocean at Hingham and Nantasket Beach. The weekend crowds found little to tempt them to alight in Norwell or western Hingham; until the track neared the railroad station it lay between defensive lawns.[41]

Hundreds of American trolley lines followed similar routes, as the trolley guides make clear. Rural towns so underpopulated and poor that no railroad company would risk building discovered themselves linked to manufacturing centers and railroads. Farm families learned to walk or "borrow a ride" to the nearest trolley line, take the electric car to the railroad town, and either shop there or take the train for larger towns and cities. By 1905, a few futurists had begun to talk of a transportation system or network, and one, Frederick W. Coburn, argued that "a city five hundred miles long and one hundred miles wide, extending over a strip of the Atlantic coast from Portland, Maine, to Washington, D. C., is actually in the making." Coburn argued that the strip—he called it "greatest New York"—depended on railroad and trolley line interaction for its future development. "Between New York and New Haven, though revolutionary and colonial relics described in guidebooks and cherished for the delectation of trolley-trippers still abound, and though elm-shaded streets preserve a little of pristine tranquillity, yet the omni-present suburban villas, improved residential parks, beach properties, trolley car stations and clanging trolleys, telephone pay stations, newsboys hawking late editions of the metropolitan 'yellows'—these assure the traveler that he has not left the city universal behind him."[42] Coburn remarked on the closeness of rural townships and manufacturing villages, the large numbers of newly arrived immigrants, rural areas serving as suddenly discovered recreation areas for entire regions, and the rapid conversion of summer cottages to year-round homes. "Suburbia is still crude, too often a hodge-podge of jerrybuilt atrocities," he determined after riding about in "rural" trolleys. "But it is the city of the future."[43] Others shared his sentiment. In *A Student's History of the United States*, a 1917 high school text, Edward Channing directed his young readers' attention to the electric trolley car, the extender of metropolitan corridors.[44] And in a 1926 short story, "The Young Gentlemen," Edith Wharton explained the corridor-extending effect of a seashore trolley line like that described by Howells two decades earlier. "How we resisted modern improvements, ridiculed fashionable 'summer resorts,' fought trolley lines, overhead wires and telephones" and other elements of the corridor snaking toward the nearly forgotten village, she wrote of a time lost to modern inventions.[45] Coburn, Channing, and Wharton understood that the trolley line created a metropolitan corridor only slightly less complex than that created by railroads. The overhead line that powered the "broomstick train" connected hitherto isolated places with the electricity-generating station, with big-city newspapers, with urban scurry.

Despite his prescient article, Coburn never defined *city*. Implicit in his article is a definition compounded of lifestyle haste and electric power. He glimpsed the covert metamorphosis of the brass-trimmed, brightly colored, insectlike rural trolley car into the shabby, dirty, slow-moving city streetcar, but he could not fathom how urban space would follow along trolley lines. Channing and Wharton did understand, for they had the benefit of observing environmental change firsthand. The rural trolleys that whizzed away from railroad stations into the isolated hinterland created suburbs out of rural communities. They charged sleepy places with electric jolts, reoriented residential patterns and real estate values, and struck an urban tempo along back roads and village streets. *City* is the wrong word for the spaces created by the curious vehicles that were half train, half automobile. The proper word is *metropolitan*, for the trolleys carried much of the form and lifestyle of the metropolitan corridor into regions remote from railroads.

12. BEYOND

W. L. Taylor, "The Passing of the Farm." (Courtesy of Harvard College Library)

IN 1901 *THE LADIES' HOME Journal* honored the new century by glancing backward at the nation's progress. On the whole, the magazine concluded, the nineteenth century indicated a steady progression toward an ever more prosperous future. Indeed, only one feature cast a somber note. In June appeared "The Passing of the Farm," a picture showing an aged woman gazing at a decrepit farmhouse before entering a waiting stagecoach. "The farm stock was sold, the barns stood empty, and brakes and bushes grew in the once well-kept fields," remarked W. L. Taylor in his caption. "The family dwindled to one; it may have been the old wife and mother left alone." The meaning of the illustration? "One long farewell look; the coach door slammed and the farm was abandoned." Taylor perhaps acquired the idea for the illustration from a similar one that appeared seven years earlier in *The Century*, but more likely he only reacted to a scandal entrancing the American public.[1] At the beginning of the twentieth century, forest wilderness had returned to rural New England and New York, profoundly shaking American notions of landscape integrity, meaning, and beauty. Amidst the flowering of the republic lay a cancer.

Abandonment fails to define the complexity of change in the late-nineteenth-century New England countryside. It denotes only the end of human occupation, not the simultaneous overwhelming of once-cultivated land by weeds, brush, and forest trees.[2] English has no word that encompasses such change, no term like the German *bewüstung*, which is usually, and incorrectly, translated as *bewilderment*. By *bewilderment*, Americans understand spatial disorientation culminating in panic, not the process by which fields grow up in forest.[3] *Ortsbewüstung*, the bewildering of a specific place, has no English synonym at all.[4] The process of reforestation over agricultural land might be called *wildering*.

Turn-of-the-century Americans spoke in slang when they described the wildered countryside of the northeastern part of the nation. They referred to "run down" farms, villages that "had gone downhill," and to "one-horse farms" and "one-horse towns." Their terminology hints at the spatial change that accompanied the collapse of agriculture caused by the opening of the Erie Canal in 1830. Ambitious young men deserted family farms to try agriculture in the West, leaving behind sisters who eventually sought mill work in Lowell

The Century *view of abandonment, 1894. (Collection of the author)*

and other new industrial towns. Young people left marginal hill farms first and soon began deserting comparatively richer valley farms, too, happy to leave behind fields filled with boulders and hilly roads blocked for weeks at a time by heavy snow. By the 1840s, New Englanders had begun fleeing the hill country in record numbers, and despite optimistic editorials in agricultural periodicals, even the older generation of farmers dismissed agriculture as unprofitable at worst and desperately difficult at best.[5] For the next half century, the forest steadily regained land settlers had once wrested from it.

"At the present day, some of those mountain townships present an aspect of singular abandonment," wrote Herman Melville in 1855 of a locale that resembled "countries depopulated by plague and war." He remarked that "every mile or two a house is passed untenanted," that the house timbers "seem to have lapsed back into their woodland original," and that "the landscape is intersected in all directions with walls of uncommon neatness and strength," enclosing an aching nothingness.[6] His comments are among the earliest dealing with a scruffy landscape that profoundly disturbed his contemporaries. Hawthorne, despite a passing notice in the preface to *Mosses from an Old Manse* to the melancholic atmosphere of apple trees guarding old cellar holes, ignored the wildering New England scene.[7] Romanticism certainly deflected artistic concern to the colonial past, but disgust made certain the deflection. As early as 1859, Harriet Beecher Stowe began *The Minister's Wooing* with a chapter entitled "Pre-Railroad Times"; ten years later, when she published another retrospective novel, *Oldtown Folks*, she admitted that she hoped to depict the seminal period of New England history. "I would endeavor to show you New England in its *seed-bed*, before the hot suns of modern progress had developed its sprouting germs into the great trees of to-day."[8] What explains the curious metaphor, the connection of seedbed to mature trees, not to grain or vegetables? Stowe understood that in New England fields stood mostly trees, that the landscape of agricultural prosperity had vanished. Donald G. Mitchell struggled to find in suburbs some way to restore the remembered landscape of beauty. Stowe—and many subsequent writers—escaped into historical fiction, into the landscape of nostalgia.

Not every artist attempted an escape. A handful peered about at the wildered countryside, determined to capture the "local color" of a region not in its seedbed time, but gone to seed. In 1940, the literary historian Van Wyck Brooks surveyed the fiction of the period following the Civil War and analyzed the powerful effect of the wildered countryside on New England authors. "They wondered about the black old tenantless houses, where the windows lay in the grass and the roof had tumbled in, the houses, damp and cold, with people in them, where the rain had rotted the shingles, the barns with wooden cages in dark corners, the double houses of brothers who never spoke, the thresholds that had never been crossed since someone's death," he wrote of both well-known and obscure authors. "What lay behind the shutters of

Half-abandoned farm, ca. 1878. (Courtesy of Vermont Historical Society)

the white Greek temples, with the dark shadow-pines beside the door," he wondered of Greek Revival farmhouses.[9] Many authors found weariness, poverty, loneliness, and a sense of void utterly alien to anything in the metropolitan corridor. They found the place that reflected the absolute opposite of modern space characterized by energy, technology, speed, and affirmation of prosperous futures.

Local colorists frequently depicted the harsh life of farm women condemned to labor into old age, or else they focused on the penurious daily existence of village women. In short stories like "The Foreigner," Sarah Orne Jewett described the poverty that led townspeople to dig up the cellar of an abandoned house in a frenzied search for treasure. In tales like "A Solitary" and "The Revolt of 'Mother,'" Mary Wilkins Freeman scrutinized the lot of recluses and overworked farmwives.[10] Often the stories and novels involve physical coarseness and violence, as in Freeman's *Madelon*, in which a woman knifes a man who grabs her on a dark path.[11] Male writers also confronted the issue of life in a wildered place. William Dean Howells published *The Vacation of the Kelwyns: An Idyl of the Middle Eighteen-Seventies* in 1920, during the height of one of the tramp-menace crazes, and his nearly abandoned, wildered fictional landscape shelters not only impoverished farm folk and a few tourists, but tramps sleeping in deserted farmhouses. "He was a gigantic negro, with a sullen, bestial face, which looked the wickeder because of his vast, naked, feet," he says of one tramp encountered by the vacationers during a woodland ramble. "He faltered a moment, glaring at them with bloodshot eyes, and then lurked away into the shadow of the woods."[12] After the encounter, the vacationing men decide to arm themselves and begin target practice in an orchard. Readers of popular periodicals and novels gradually realized that something hideously wrong tormented rural New England, immune to bullets.

More than perhaps any other writer, Edith Wharton identified the creeping spiritual paralysis, the "worm in the brain," that created the wildered landscape of New England.[13] Her novels about New York City sparkle with descriptions of such urban wonders as great railroad terminals; her short stories and novels about the hill country grimly portray life far beyond the end of the metropolitan corridor. In a 1914 short story, "The Triumph of Night," a young city man discovers the absolute, almost appalling emptiness of the wildered country when he alights from a night train at Northridge Junction, "standing alone on the open platform, exposed to the full assault of nightfall and winter." He shivers with a cold unknown in cities. "The blast that swept him came off New Hampshire snowfields and ice-hung forests. It seemed to have traversed interminable leagues of frozen silence, filling them with the same cold roar and sharpening its edge against the same bitter black-and-white landscape." From within a luxury train, such an isolated station seemed totally insignificant, but away from the steam-heated, comfortably upholstered cars the barren building miles from the nearest town represented the last edge of the metropolitan corridor. Beyond lay winter emptiness and a cold that makes the man's urban overcoat seem "no thicker than a sheet of paper."[14]

Wharton's 1911 novel *Ethan Frome* captures the sterile chill of the wildered landscape and half-crazed local people. Its narrator, a man of the modern, metropolitan corridor—a builder of powerhouses—tells the story of the Fromes, and particularly of Ethan, a man who had returned from engineering school to take over the family farm on the death of his father. The loneliness of hill-farm life in winter that eventually prompts Frome's attempt to kill himself and his would-be lover is magnified by the desolation of the town, Starkfield, which Frome calls a "sidetrack" bypassed by the railroad.[15] Writing *Ethan Frome* did not satisfy Wharton's desire to examine the wildered life of the wildered landscape. Six years later she published *Summer*, a novel concerning seduction, illegitimate pregnancy, and a young woman abandoned by her lover. "There it lay, a weather-beaten sunburnt village of the hills, abandoned of men, left apart by railway, trolley, telegraph, and all the forces that link life to life in modern communities," she says of her fictional North Dormer. "It had no shops, no theatres, no lectures, no 'business block'; only a church that was opened every other Sunday if the state of the roads permitted, and a library for which no new books had been bought for twenty years, and where the old ones mouldered undisturbed on the damp shelves." The village "with all its mean curiosities, its furtive malice, its sham unconsciousness of evil" is indeed isolated both physically and intellectually, but not nearly as much as the settlement high up on the overshadowing mountain.[16] Certainly Wharton's frank treatment of rural vice derived in part from the greater liberties accorded early-twentieth-century novelists by a more permissive generation of readers, but it stemmed too from her determination to describe a rural New England vastly changed from that "half Hebrew theocracy, half ultra-democratic republic of little villages" Stowe lovingly portrayed in *Oldtown Folks*, or the turbulent, Jacksonian-era utopia of Winston Churchill's 1906 novel, *Coniston*.[17] Stowe, Churchill, and many other novelists lacked the courage of Wharton and avoided the harsh issues implicit in the ruinous houses, collapsed schoolhouses, and overgrown fields beyond the end of the metropolitan corridor. They shied away from the sterile ice-bound or sunburnt hill towns like Starkfield and North Dormer. They evaded a central question of their era: did a ruined landscape objectify the ruined character of its inhabitants?

Poets confronted the question squarely—and answered in the affirmative. Edwin Arlington Robinson addressed the social and moral decline by describing the devastated landscape. In "The House on the Hill" of 1897 he determined that

> There is ruin and decay
>   In the House on the Hill
> They are all gone away,
> There is nothing more to say.

Forested mountains announced the failure of turn-of-the-century hill farming.
(Courtesy of Vermont Historical Society)

Hill towns withered slowly and painfully. (Collection of the author)

But he found more to say, as in the conclusion to "The Dead Village": "The music failed, and then / God frowned, and shut the village from His sight." Robinson knew as clearly as Wharton that sordid violence had returned to the rural Northeast with the returning wild animals. "There was more / Than just an axe that once was in the air / Between us and the chimney, long before / Our time," he wrote in "Haunted House." "So townsmen said who found her there."[18]

Such evil figures strongly in the poetry of Robert Frost, who worked a hill farm in New Hampshire for two decades before his recognition as an artist. In "Something for Hope" he remarked on the continuing encroachment of forest:

> At the present rate it must come to pass,
> And that right soon, that the meadowsweet
> And steeple bush, not good to eat,
> Will have crowded out the edible grass.
> Then all there is to do is wait
> For maple, birch, and spruce to push
> Through meadowsweet and steeple bush
> And crowd them out at a similar rate.[19]

Many of his other poems suggest that most of the stalwart, industrious people had been crowded out of the hill country by the forest, leaving behind the deserted houses he described in "Ghost House," "The Black Cottage," and "The Need of Being Versed in Country Things" and abandoning the rocky fields he scrutinized in "The Hill Wife" and "Stopping by Woods on a Snowy Evening." Frost devoted much attention to the twisted, evil folk of the ruined farms and villages; poems like "Home Burial," "The Fear," and "A Servant to Servants" emphasized the problems of the mad farmwives, the mentally retarded locked in cages in barns—precisely as Brooks observed in *New England: Indian Summer*—and the continuing belief in witchcraft, walking skeletons, and other eldritch terrors. At least once, in "Desert Places" of 1936, Frost deliberately called the overrun winter fields of New England more empty and spiritually threatening than the vastness of interstellar space, and he used them as an image of the empty spaces of his own psyche.[20] Frost, Robinson, and other lesser writers repeatedly used the encroaching forest and abandoned houses as emblems of spiritual decay.

Not only first-rate writers discerned the seeming connection between wildness of landscape and corruption of character. H. P. Lovecraft set many of his gothic tales in rural New England and in fact created an entire fictional locale focused on the ruinous township of Arkham. West of the village, he wrote in *The Colour out of Space* in 1927, the houses "are all vacant now, the wide chimneys crumbling and the shingled sides bulging perilously beneath low gambrel roofs. The old folk have gone away and foreigners do not like to live there."[21] Lovecraft emphasized, in rather heavy-handed fashion, the topographical feature treated more delicately by Wharton, Robinson, and Frost, the tree-covered mountain. As Pullman passengers learned to perceive the beauty of the Rocky Mountains, the authors concerned with New England reverted to an old, almost medieval, morbid fear of mountain wilderness.[22] In his 1916 poem, "The Mountain," Frost analyzed a mountain that "held the town as in a shadow," remarking its forest moving slowly down upon the few remaining pastures and its stultifying effect on a local farmer, who had never ventured far up its sides.[23] In much New England local color writing, mountains became the clearest emblem for the decay of the New England spirit.

American novelists and poets consequently either ignored the abandoned-farm problem by writing about the past glories of rural New England, or else they scrutinized the ruinous landscape as the emblem of a withered, twisted people from whom little could ever again be expected. Nowhere in American literature is the meaning of environmental representation more clearly presented: industrious, thrifty, moral people create and maintain neat fields, straight walls, and snug houses in the face of wilderness, winter storms, and the temptations of the Devil—only lazy good-for-nothings abandon land shaped by their righteous ancestors and succumb to temptation. The fictional and poetical treatment of New England *ortsbewüstung* suggests that the nation's first encounters with decay shook the popular faith in a wilderness-conquering manifest destiny. Beyond that, however, the outpouring of fictional treatments suggests the rapidly strengthening suburban bias of the national press. Ordered, efficient, well-maintained space—the space of terminals, industrial zones, railroad rights-of-way, productive suburban back yards, and velvet-like lawns—had become good. All else, except natural wilderness, struck suburban newspaper and magazine readers as shabby, immoral, and bad.

Between 1880 and 1920 appeared an extraordinary number of essays treating the history, causes, and effects of abandonment and offering ideas for the retaking of the land and the perceiving of the countryside in new ways. Many essayists, perhaps under the influence of Mitchell, dismissed the causes not as economic, but moral. "The result of this exodus is that a considerable part of the present population is a sort of immovable sediment, a weedy sort of folk attached to the soil in a blind way," wrote Elizabeth Eggleston Seelye in *The Century* in 1894, "who have neither the spirit to seek new fields to conquer, nor to conquer those about them, but who seem to strive only to solve the problem of how to exist with the least possible amount of bodily exertion."[24] Most magazine writers were less caustic and more apt to search out complex economic and topographical reasons, or even to blame the climate. "The winters, in particular, are a great trial. With their cold and the blocked roads, they make the women of the family prisoners for months," observed Clifton Johnson in "The Deserted Homes of New England," a long article that appeared in *The Cosmopolitan* in 1893. "The almost inevitable result of this six months of winter loneliness is that the people's lives get a touch of hopelessness." Johnson extolled the golden age of rural prosperity in books like *The Farmer's Boy* and *The Country School in New England*, but he could not escape the changed circumstances of his favorite countryside. Although he concluded his magazine piece by observing that "it will not make life less full if these lonely hills are again possessed by the old-time forests," the tone of the essay makes clear his distaste for a shabbiness incredibly worse than that afflicting so many small towns along the railroads.[25] Poets could transform the landscape into the material of starkly beautiful poems; even novelists could use the wildered landscape as the setting for novels that somehow transformed shabbiness into literary beauty. But the essayists stunned by the wildering process had no such recourse, and over and over again, distaste suffuses their writing.

More than tone makes clear the distaste informing Rollin Lynde Hartt's 1899 *Atlantic Monthly* articles. Of his thinly disguised "Sweet Auburn," a town "sans inn, sans boarding house, sans butcher shop, sans trolley line, sans sidewalks, sans street lights, sans newspaper, sans fire brigade, sans doctor, sans—everything," Hartt concluded that there is "something patriarchal about this whole region." The ancient houses and barns "speak of ancestral interests and family history," "lichens on old stone walls afford a sense of abode." But is "the landscape kindly, gracious, pastoral," as he comments at one point, or is it the mask of something hideously disgusting? "It is not nice to have six toes on each foot," he remarks of the in-bred, sullen farm families, at the beginning of a long catalogue of genetic mutation evident not only in physical and mental retardation, but in the slovenly fields around the decrepit houses.[26] "A New England Hill Town" aroused fierce antagonism near Leverett, Massachusetts, where Hartt had sojourned as minister for two years. For the locals, "Sweet Auburn" identified—or misidentified—Leverett all too closely, and a nearby newspaper, the Greenfield *Gazette and Courier*, published a series of letters responding to Hartt's attack. At least one of the letter readers thought highly enough of the responses to paste the letters into a notebook deposited for all time in the library of Harvard College. The letters, mostly from clergymen, admitted that "liquor is slyly sold, some sexual immorality is undiscovered as everywhere" but refuted Hartt's accusations of in-breeding and agricultural catastrophe. One writer noted that "the farmers are buying some of the latest improved farm machinery," and another remarked on increased library-book circulation. But the letters *were* defensive; they admitted to problems less severe than those described by Hartt, and only rarely denied their existence. The letter writers knew that the very landscape, the wildered countryside, bespoke volumes in favor of Hartt's argument. The respondents, along with commentators in national magazines, urged repair of social life and restoration of the land, either by reestablishing agriculture or by converting the ruined farms into summer homes.[27]

Officially at least, all the New England states except Rhode Island (which refused to recognize an abandonment problem despite the poverty of such wildered areas as its northwest corner) urged the reinforcement of agriculture and published booklets advertising unworked farms for sale at low prices. As William Henry Bishop pointed out in an 1894 *Century* article, only Massachusetts used *abandoned* in the title of its catalogue; Connecticut called its list *A Descriptive Catalogue of Farms for Sale* and New Hampshire entitled its publication *Secure a Home in New Hampshire*. Despite different titles, however, the lists make the same point. A great many farms were abandoned indeed, but a larger number than the catalogues admitted, because the state departments of agriculture listed only recently deserted places. Massachusetts town tax assessors, for instance, were told to report only farms "formerly cultivated but now deserted, upon which cultivation is now abandoned, and the buildings, if any are unoccupied and permitted to fall into decay. In some cases the grass is still cut on these farms, but nothing is done in the way of enriching the soil, and the land is practically unproductive and left to run wild."[28] Assessors appear to have ignored farms so long abandoned that they had grown up completely in forest and may also have ignored farms on which people still lived but did not farm. Even allowing for the narrow definition, Massachusetts assessors turned up 1,461 such farms for the 1891 *Report*. The catalogues offer amazing glimpses at one facet of the turn-of-the-century rural landscape; even the shortest listings are usually couched in colorfully detailed language:

> Farm of 90 acres: mowing, 10 to 20; remainder mostly covered with hard-wood and young pines. Grass can be cut with a machine. One and one-half story house, with L, not in very good repair. Good-sized barn, not in first-rate repair. Stone wall around mowing, in poor condition. One or two wells. Some apple and some other fruit trees. Railroad station, Coldbrook, 1½ miles; post-office, Coldbrook Springs, 1½ miles.[29]

A number of essayists discerned patterns in the listings. The editor of the *New England Magazine* remarked that most of the farms lay too far from cities to interest market gardeners and dairymen, but ten years later, in 1901, an essayist in the same magazine noted that isolation from railroads or industrial towns was less important as a cause of abandonment than had been suspected.[30] Another magazine writer, Edward Ashael Wright, calculated that at least a third of the farms were abandoned due to their owners' old age or other occupations, not because of soil or location.[31]

But Wright, like Frank West Rollins, an ex-governor of New Hampshire who wrote a 1910 *Country Life* article entitled "The Abandoned Farm in New Hampshire: Why It Will Soon be a Thing of the Past," could not explain why young farmers failed to try market gardening or dairy farming. In tones reminiscent of Mitchell's agricultural-reform essays, Rollins blasted farmers' sloth for not raising crops for the visitors to the summer hotels: "The New Hampshire farmer looks upon the apple as he does upon the blueberry, or the wild raspberry,—a casual thing that the good Lord has sent along and which He (the Lord) takes care of or not, as He takes a notion."[32] But Rollins, unlike Seelye, believed in progress; he hoped that farmers would grow staples and delicacies for summer visitors, although how he expected them to produce crops so early in a short growing season he failed to say, and he thought that horticulture would end the flight from the farms. Other optimistic visionaries and reformers suggested settling the industrious urban poor on deserted farms, and Clarence E. Blake proposed sending unemployed college graduates to the rural regions. "We have more professional characters, merchants, and what not than we can use; but still they come," he lamented in 1901 in the *New England Magazine*. "Our college graduate can well afford to turn his attention to the country. There he will find a 'position,' sure pay and abundant opportunity to use his culture for the general good."[33] All the enthusiastic essayists determined to reintroduce efficient agriculture stressed good soil, new crops, improved machinery, and ready markets. None praised the social, religious, and intellectual life of the rural areas, none mentioned severe winters or the condition of so many derelict houses, barns, and fields. They knew what poets and novelists knew, that many of the hill folk made dull neighbors, if not worse, and that ambitious newcomers might find little encouragement for clearing tree-choked fields.[34] Indeed they ignored the absence of all metropolitan amenities, including the absence of the metropolitan corridor.

The seediest, weediest, one-horse towns gone downhill almost invariably lay far from railroads, in the high country. American slang reflected the popular understanding of the abandonment process in ways often missed by magazine essayists. Hill farms and hill towns failed first, not only for the reasons so frequently mentioned in *The Century* and other periodicals, but because such places lay miles from the nearest railroads. Certainly, poor access to markets made many such farms and towns nearly penniless within several decades following the popularization of railroads in the 1840s, but depriving people of newspapers, magazines, and other metropolitan news, including advertising circulars and mail-order catalogues, meant somehow stultifying their minds. *Downhill* entered American speech to identify places left behind by people anxious to reach the valleys in which railroads maintained agricultural prosperity. In such valleys, natives and visitors alike found few one-horse towns— towns in which everyone owned one-horse wagons and in which every road had three ruts, two made by wagon wheels and the third by the hoofs of single horses. A farm gone downhill symbolized the life-sapping power of the metropolitan corridor; just as the corridor drew trade from Main Street retailers, it sucked away prosperity from high-country farmers and storekeepers. The hilly rural Northeast first revealed to Americans the electrifying power everywhere in the corridor and hinted to all observers the likely result of abandoning a railroad almost anywhere. No small-town midwestern storekeeper returned from a visit to an ancestral New England hill town at all doubtful of the life-sapping and life-giving force of the railroad and its infrastructure.

In the late 1890s, however, a few city dwellers angered by ever-worsening pollution problems, and by the ever-present urban scurry, discovered the wildered Northeast as the place to summer. Mature trees hid many abandoned farmsteads, and whole fields had vanished into young forest. Gradually, urban people found the landscape beautiful, and they perfected the hunting of abandoned farms. In another *Century* essay, "Hunting an Abandoned Farm in Connecticut," William Henry Bishop contrasted "a journey on the elevated railway, which, in its odious overcrowding, was an epitome of all the false and wearisome conditions that made an escape from life in the metropolis seem desirable" with the poverty-stricken, railroadless rural districts where the "true rural peace still lingers, and you can drive about the well-made roads without the chronic fear of being cut in two at a grade-crossing."[35] A month later, Bishop published another, longer piece in *The Century*, "Hunting an Abandoned Farm in Upper New England," concerning a long ramble in search of a cheap deserted farm. "Not even once did I see any fine mansion or notable homestead, capable of better things, abandoned to decay, after the numerous pathetic stories to that effect with which we have grown familiar," he concluded after learning that most derelict houses were in "a condition of deplorable neglect or else had never been good for anything in the first place."[36] His articles mark a decisive turning point in the national perception of rural New England, however, a change announced by the rapidly rising prices asked by farmers for any deserted farm with decent housing. The boom in values derived from the discovery by the wealthy that a farmhouse made an excellent summer home, especially if several like-minded summer residents occupied neighboring houses, and that a few acres of open land offered the fun of gentleman-farming at a scale unavailable in most railroad suburbs. By 1900, a writer in the *New England Magazine* remarked that "the revival of interest in the antique has passed beyond what I may call the 'old china' stage" to "the popularity just now of 'colonial' residences."[37] The interest in abandoned houses as antiques or ruins remained largely a phenomenon of the upper- and middle-class educated elite. As the well-to-do hunted abandoned farms far from metropolitan corridors and grade-crossings, the rural poor deserted the remaining hill farms to seek prosperity in the industrial zones that stretched along the railroad lines. Gradually, however, magazine art and advertising made known the charms of former farms.

Photography advertised wildered regions to city people anxious to find a

A few prim hill-town houses attracted house-hunters from the cities.
(Courtesy of Vermont Historical Society)

relaxing vacation spot reasonably near railroad lines. Owners of resort hotels advertised the "environs" of their establishments as filled with dozens of "picturesque" ruins, and vacationers delighted in photographing the antiquities. Handsome photographs reproduced in magazines and vacation snapshots combined to create an "image" of the rural Northeast as delightfully isolated from railroads.[38] In the suddenly antique wildered countryside, a commuter might find a summertime respite from the metropolitan corridor.

Summer residents quickly learned that improving an old house and clearing a field or two did not lead at once to happiness. On the one hand, such isolated, restful summer retreats struck many vacationers as too isolated and too monotonously restful. On the other, the ideas and values of the newcomers, and their not infrequent displays of wealth—and their propensity for missing the long, cruel winters—irked many local residents. "They try to do the work in their own way," complained Bishop of the local handymen, "and are inclined to be cross and grumpy if you want to have it done your way."[39] Summer people sought out the best "natives," those who retained the virtues prized by magazine writers who told readers that high-quality farmers still lived comfortable, upright lives in the back-country Northeast, and they avoided the shiftless families living in decrepit shacks covered with tarpaper, the mountain people who frightened the valley folk in Wharton's novel *Summer*.[40] The continuing clash between the summer visitors, those well-to-do people fleeing the scurry of the great city in the late spring and anxiously awaiting a Pullman-equipped train at some isolated country station in autumn, and the locals, those desperate to attain the privilege of living in a metropolitan corridor, is a central theme of Wharton's novel and of Frost's 1914 poem, "The Code," in which "the town-bred farmer failed to understand" that his casual comment about carefully piling hay deeply offended his hired hand.[41] The clash gradually helped to shape scenery values.

As the mountains of the rural Northeast became a favorite vacation locale, the railroad companies serving the region offered tourist rates and advertised scenic routes not through western-type wilderness, but through antique countryside. Firms like the Rutland Company, the Boston & Maine, the Boston & Albany, the Central Vermont, the Maine Central, and even the Bangor & Aroostook published calendars, magazines, and timetables extolling the rediscovered and reevaluated countryside easily accessible from their rural stations. With care and patience, a vacationing family could ride in Pullman comfort to an isolated station, find waiting a reserved horse and buggy, and drive upward into the past, into a land of picturesque poverty. What mattered most in such vacations was not the Pullman train or the refurbished farmhouse, but the road leading from station to farm. As early as the 1900s, professional travel writers praised the few trolley-car companies operating service from depots to isolated hill towns and lamented the lack of such service in most of the region. By the 1920s, however, the dominant published pho-

Hill-country roads remained quiet only until the automobiles arrived.
(Courtesy of Stockbridge, Massachusetts, Library Historical Room)

tograph of the antique, peaceful countryside had acquired a distinctive characteristic. At its focus lay a smooth road, one fit for automobiles. Wallace Nutting became the master of the genre through his lavishly illustrated books like *Connecticut Beautiful* and *New Hampshire Beautiful*, which present carefully edited views of the countryside, almost every one organized about a motor road.

Debates concerning good roads worsened the clashes between summer people and year-rounders. Summer people fought to build and maintain roads just good enough for casual travel; year-round residents wanted well-made roads for year-round use. While as late as 1931 the United States Department of Agriculture argued that farm abandonment and wilderness encroachment continued as a serious rural problem, motor-vehicle flow occupied more attention in the hill country.[42] As roads improved, trucks competed more efficiently with trains, and, by 1929, railroad companies had abandoned more than a thousand miles of track. Summer visitors found themselves forced to drive longer and longer distances and learned bitterly that once quiet roads carried a constant stream of automobiles. To a summer resident, a good road signified urban scurry and noise; to the year-round inhabitant, it spelled salvation from winter isolation. While the clashes between the groups continued, the advocates of good roads won victory upon victory.

In the rural Northeast, therefore, Americans learned two great lessons. Between 1850 and 1910, they saw physical expression of the prosperity-sapping and prosperity-giving power of the metropolitan corridor. One-horse towns gone downhill proved the fabulous power of the corridor to draw to it trade and human energy, and to bestow on valley towns something of urban life. After 1910, and certainly after 1920, the nation learned that prosperity might come to a region lacking in widespread rail service, dependent on the automobile. No longer did a scenic postcard emphasize a railroad line or depot; by 1930, at least east of the Mississippi River, it emphasized a well-graded, often paved road. No longer did an absence of rails indicate poverty.

The wildered and rediscovered rural Northeast, once beyond the trains and trolleys of the metropolitan corridor and isolated from "live-wire" life, became the proving ground of the automobile, the testing place of a sprawling, irregular pattern of real estate development, the automobile exurb.

13: RUINS

Simpson Switch, on the main line of the Santa Fe, 1976. (JRS)

**A**UTOMOBILING DESTROYED
the prosperity of the corridor everywhere, not only in the rediscovered rural
Northeast, but near great cities and in smug, well-mowed suburbs. American
slang soon reflected the changed public perception of spatial importance. In
1900, nearly everyone called the intersection of a railroad and road a *road
crossing*; the term connotes the dominant perception of space seen from a
train.[1] By 1910, the term *grade crossing* had replaced the earlier one, except in
the speech of railroad employees and in the pages of popular railroad fiction.
Within two decades, however, *railroad crossing* had almost totally replaced
both earlier terms, announcing the newly dominant perception of space seen
from the motorcar. No longer did Americans travel along the metropolitan
corridor. Instead they drove across it, and, on weekends and on vacations,
attempted to avoid it altogether, driving far off "the beaten track." By 1940,
stiff competition from trucks, buses, and automobiles shaped more than
American speech. The corridor grew weedy, seedy, and in many rural areas
vanished totally. A great age of automobile-shaped spatial design dawned, and
the era of the corridor ended.

In its heyday, from about 1880 to about 1930, the metropolitan corridor
objectified the ordered life, the life of the engineered future. Industrial zones,
small-town depots, railway gardens, suburbs, even backyard vegetable gardens and lawns all drew characteristics from the railroad and its fabulous trains.
For one half-century moment, the nation created a new sort of environment
characterized by technically controlled order.

Henry James, among other observers, found in the corridor something
difficult to identify, but nevertheless heartening. "I had occasion, repeatedly,
to find the Pennsylvania Railroad a beguiling and predisposing influence," he
mused in *The American Scene*. "It absolutely, with a little frequentation, af-
fected as better and higher than its office or function, and almost as supplying
one with a mode of life intrinsically superior; as if it ought really to be on its
way to much grander and more charming places than any that happen to mark
its course—as if indeed, should one persistently keep one's seat, not getting
out anywhere, it would in the end carry one to some such ideal city."[2] James
wondered about the same vague characteristics that entranced Katherine Woods
in *The Broadway Limited*. The crack, modern, luxury express, speeding swiftly

End-of-track, Hingham, Massachusetts, 1982. (JR

Artifact of ruination, Point Reyes, Califonia, 197(
(Daphne Noyes)

and safely through a highly engineered space created for it, becomes more than a train. It becomes a herald of the future, as bold as any urban terminal, as any electricity-generating station, as any well-ordered suburb replete with gardens and lawns. Somewhere in the corridor, James, Woods, and others glimpsed the ideal city.

Benton MacKaye and Lewis Mumford glimpsed it, too. In a 1931 *Harper's Monthly Magazine* article, "Townless Highways for the Motorist: A Proposal for the Automobile Age," they argued that "once we have grasped the essential notion of the automobile as a private locomotive, the example of the railroad will give us a clue to its proper treatment."[3] But their vision of an American motorway system, a mesh of motor roads carefully linked with existing metropolitan corridors, made scant impact on the nation. No longer did suburbs exist as nodes along commuter rail lines; no longer did rural Main Streets focus on railroad depots; no longer did terminals act as the orderly gates of cities. Spatial change came too quickly to be ordered according to the ideas of MacKaye, Mumford, and other scarcely heard visionaries convinced of the essential sanity of the suddenly oldfashioned corridor.

As automobiles veered away from the corridor, as railroad passenger and freight traffic decreased, the corridor became the new wildered environment, a sort of vast jungle of sumac and Tree of Heaven likely to hide tramps and certain to shelter decrepit factories watched over by cold smokestacks. Trolley cars vanished, almost instantly, and once-ordered suburbs, quickly jammed with motor cars, changed character within two decades. Backyard vegetable gardens surrendered to the spatial requirements of garages; lawns gave up to driveways. Narrow streets focused on railroad stations clogged with cars, and station gardens vanished before bulldozers madly creating larger and larger parking lots—until commuters turned away from trains. In the wildered space roamed vandals, shattering the windows of idle factories and spray-painting vulgarities on the railroad scenery once so proudly painted in standard colors. After 1930 the corridor began its long decline, and while wartime traffic increases and gasoline rationing temporarily slowed the decay, by 1950 the wildering reached everywhere, although motorists driving the limited-access highways far from the corridor rarely saw it. A once-great environment, abandoned to wilderness, decayed almost unmourned.

What, then, was the sound of the locomotive whistle, if not the sound of turn-of-the-century modern space? "A train coming! A rapid chuck-a-chuck, chuck-a-chuck, chuck-a-chuck," wrote Sinclair Lewis in *Main Street* during the apogee of the corridor. "It was hurling past—the Pacific Flyer, an arrow of golden flame. Light from the fire-box splashed the under side of the trailing smoke. Instantly the vision was gone."[4] As late as 1934, such visions still attracted the discerning public. "To anyone outside, a speeding train is a thunderbolt of driving rods, a hot hiss of steam, a blurred flash of coaches, a wall of movement and of noise, a shriek, a wail, and then just emptiness and ab-

Automated interlocking tower,
Pawtucket Junction, Rhode Island (JRS)

Structure glimpsed from passenger train,
West Virginia, 1978. (JRS)

Newly refurbished, long-planted station, Kingston, Rhode Island. (JRS)

Restored station and grounds, North Easton, Massachusetts, 1982. (JRS)

sence, with a feeling of 'There goes everybody!' without knowing who anybody is," remarked Thomas Wolfe of the cinemalike vision peculiar to the corridor. "And all of a sudden the watcher feels the vastness and loneliness of America, and the nothingness of all those little lives hurled past upon the immensity of the continent. But if one is *inside* the train, everything is different."[5] Inside the train rode the future, or so it seemed.

And, perhaps, so it will seem again. If the age of the motorcar ends in a succession of fuel shortages, if Americans look once again to the railroad train for swift, reliable, luxurious travel, the corridor will emerge into public view not as wreckage, but as a wildered antique, something to be restored and modified as enthusiastically as the wildered rural Northeast in 1915.[6] Once again, its components will deserve notice, and once again the environment unique to the high iron will prosper. Once again, Americans will hearken to the locomotive whistle, the sound of the metropolitan corridor.

Beyond the corridor, ca. 1920. (Courtesy of American Automobile Association)

All titles and authors' names in the endnotes are furnished in abbreviated form. Full citations will be found in the bibliography.

PREFACE

1. Ralph Waldo Emerson, "The Young American," in *Nature*, 344.
2. Ralph Waldo Emerson, "The Poet," *Essays*, 23–24.
3. Stilgoe, *Common Landscape*, esp. 21–24, 111–21, and passim.
4. Marx, *Machine*, esp. 257–353.
5. Jackson, *American Space*, 13–38 and passim.
6. For a survey of the weaknesses of railroad-industry historiography, see Condit, *Port*, 1:4–19.
7. See, for example, Klein, *History of the Louisville*; and Stover, *History of the Illinois Central*; see also Stover, *Iron Road*.
8. Chandler, *Visible Hand*; Condit, *Port*; these are particularly valuable works.
9. White, *American Railroad*; Bezilla, *Electric Traction*; these studies offer penetrating insights into the entire range of engineering innovation. Unfortunately, no similar study exists concerning the steam-to-diesel transition of the late 1930s.
10. I have had the wonderful advantage of the Widener Library periodical collection; I have also used the Schlesinger Library at Harvard to examine women's magazines, the Baker Library at Harvard to examine trade journals, and the Boston Public Library to examine children's magazines. I have also carefully tabulated listings and numbers of listings in the *Reader's Guide to Periodical Literature* and in *Poole's Index*.
11. Railroad wrecks attracted public attention, of course; one collision sometimes generated ten articles in national periodicals, particularly in the 1870s. See, for example, Davis, "Meadow Brook" and Taverner, "Death." See also part 5, "High Iron."
12. Riegel, *Story*; see also Slosson, *Great Crusade*; Weisberger, *New Industrial Society*; Wiebe, *Search*; and Garraty, *New Commonwealth*; on Populism, see Shannon, *Farmer's Last Frontier*.
13. Wilson, "Beauty," 303.

INTRODUCTION

1. For the earlier view, see Marx, *Machine*, esp. 145–226.
2. See, for example, Malloch, "Steel Road"; Saroyan, *Human Comedy*, 3–5; Nebel, *Sleepers East*; Kipling, ".007"; Benson, *Hill Country*; Spears, "Story of a Lost Car." For a typical article on wrecks, see Prout, "Safety."
3. Spearman, "Conductor" and "Million Dollar."
4. Kerr, "Luck," 235; see also Stringer, *Power*.
5. See, for example, Warman, *Short Rails* and *Tales of an Engineer*; Lincoln, *Depot Master*; Ford, *Great K&A Train Robbery*; Denbie, *Death*; Hamblen, *We Win*; Beers, *Green Signal*; Waters, *Call* and *Pounding*; Spearman, *Nerve* and *Held for Orders*; Meigs, *Railroad West*; and Hubbard, *Railroad Avenue*. An excellent bibliography is Donovan, *Railroad in Literature*; see also his anthology, *Headlights and Markers*, and a biography of a railroad-fiction writer, *Harry Bedwell*; for the railroad in "fine" literature, see Smith, "Glamor."

6. For publication information, see bibliography.

7. New novels in the series appeared at least until 1928.

8. See also Packard, *Night Operator* and Leverage, *Purple Limited*.

9. For representative short stories, see Hoffman, "Morley" and Dellinger, "Square Peg."

10. Channing, *Elements*, 340–42.

11. Waldo, *Magic Midland*, 61–62, 66, 69–70, 71, 72, 114–15, 137, 156; see also Lewis, *Main Street*, 236, in which he says that "to the small boys the railroad was a familiar playground." Van Doren identified the urge to leave town as part of the "revolt from the village"; see his *Contemporary American Novelists*, 146–71, and *American Novel*, 294–302; see also Hilfer, *Revolt*.

12. This book does not trace the change; see Allen, *Only Yesterday*; Faulkner, *Quest*; Schlesinger, *Rise*; Slosson, *Great Crusade*; Sullivan, *Our Times: The Turn of the Century*; Weisberger, *New Industrial Society*; Freidel, *America*; Wiebe, *Search*; Garraty, *New Commonwealth*; Hicks, *Republican*; and Shannon, *Farmer's Last Frontier*. In particular, see the excellent analysis by Higham, "Reorientation."

13. Love, *Situation*, and Reid, *Hurry Home*, esp. 72–74.

14. Waldo, *Magic Midland*, 63; for a contemporary view of the heroism of freight-hopping, see Steinberg, "Superpowerless."

15. Bok, "Where American Life," 14.

16. Bailey, "Small Truck Farm," 547.

17. Hungerford, *Run*, 88.

18. Bedwell, "Sun and Silence," and Hayes, "Man Failure"; see also Spearman, "Bucks" and "Sankey's Double Header."

19. Hertz, *Riding* and Page, "Twenty Years."

20. Lionel, *Catalogue*, 23–25, 1–2, and passim. On the real railroad and education, see Hogg, *Railroad* (Hogg was superintendent of the Fort Worth school system when he published his book) and Kling, *Why Every Boy Should Learn a Trade*. Kling's book offers extraordinary insights into the position of railroads, industrial zones, and machinery in turn-of-the-century child- (or boy-) rearing practices.

21. "Miniature Trains," esp. 41–42 and "Streamline Toys," esp. 16.

PART 1. GATEWAY

1. Dos Passos, *Manhattan Transfer*, 115–16; see also Gibbs, *New York Tunnel*.

2. On the role of rivers in New York railroad development, see Condit, *Port*.

3. Wharton, *Age*, 287–88; see also "Port of New York."

4. Middleton, *Grand Central*, 11–44, reproduces period illustrations of the terminal chaos; see also "Congestion of Traffic."

5. Howells, *Lady*, 10–11.

6. On scurry, see Thompson, "Future" and "On Living"; on traffic, Shurtleff, "Traffic Control" and Goodrich, "Pedestrian."

7. Fein, *Frederick Law Olmsted*, pl. 98; Fabos, *Frederick Law Olmsted, Sr.*, 25. See also Olmsted, Jr., "Pittsburgh," and Hampton, "American City."

8. Gregory, "Nation," 609–10.

9. Hungerford, "Human Side," 11.

10. James, *American Scene*, pp. 78, 98, 105; others agreed, see New York Railroad Commission, *Report on Tests of Street Car Brakes*.

11. Crocker, "Passenger Traffic." See also Thatton, "Disappearing"; Blake, *Electric Railway*; Speirs, *Street Railway*; Gordon, *Ninety-Four Years*.

12. Lewis, *Building*; Davis, "Elevated System"; Reed, *New York Elevated*.

13. "Pace," 8595–96.

14. Condit, *Port*, 1:94.

15. Gregory, "Nation," 610.

16. Richardson, "Cutting Loose."

17. Dunn, "Problem," 419.

18. See, for example, "New Grand Central Station"; "Proposed Union Station"; "Pennsylvania Station." See also Condit, *Railroad* and, on commuting, Grow, *On the 8:02*.
19. "Congestion."
20. Suplee, "Artificial," 560.
21. Layton, *Revolt*; see also Cooke, "Spirit," and Taylor, *Shop Management*.
22. Sinclair, *Jungle*.
23. Suplee, "Artificial," 560; see also "Congestion" and "City Planning and Congestion."
24. Suplee, "Artificial," 561; see also Walsh, "Congestion."
25. Packard, *Wire Devils*, 240–41.
26. Howells, *Hazard*, 1:95–96.
27. Antin, *Promised Land*, 298.
28. Ross, *Sky Blue*, 83–93.
29. See, for example, "One Signal Tower"; "Grand Central Depot in New York"; and "Grand Central Depot Signal System."
30. "Mechanical Interlocking Switch and Signal System" and "Great Subterranean Railway Junction."
31. Condit, *Port*, 1:92–97 and passim.
32. This is not the place to chronicle the building of the terminals; see Condit, *Port* (an outstanding work); Westing, *Penn Station*; Middleton, *Grand Central*; Couper, *History*; and Cudahy, *Rails*.
33. Condit, *Port*; for maps, see Westing, *Penn Station*; Middleton, *Grand Central*; Hungerford, *Run*; see also "Terminal Trains Run by Loop System."
34. On air rights see Condit, *Port*, 2:92–100 and "Opening of the New Grand Central Terminal," 44.
35. Stone and Carpenter, "Project for Union Passenger Station," and Wilson, "Project," show the earlier thinking; for the subsequent, see Busfield, "Design"; Cary, "Proposed"; Droege, *Passenger Terminals*; City Club, *Railway Terminal*; Mayer, "Railway Pattern"; Engineer's Committee, *St. Louis-East St. Louis*; Arnold, *Report*; California Railroad Commission, *Railroad*.
36. "Electricity Aiding the Traveller."
37. On smoke abatement, see Civic League, *Report*.
38. Bezilla, *Electric Traction*; Steinheimer, *Electric Way*; for examples of the articles, see Gordon, "Electrification," and Varney, "Some Details." For the professionals' vision, see Wilgus, "Electrification"; Couper, *History*; Baxter, *Remaking*; and Condit, *Pioneer Stage*.
39. Almost nothing has been written about Manhattan Transfer, perhaps because the station was demolished when the new Newark station was electrified. See, Cudahy, *Rails*, 38–43.
40. Locomotives are still changed at Harmon and New Haven.
41. "Port of New York."
42. Cudahy, *Rails*.
43. Condit, *Port*, 2:101–216; see also Foreman, *Electrification*.
44. Baxter, *Remaking*; Gordon, "Electrification"; Condit, *Pioneer Stage*; Middleton, *When the Steam Roads Electrified*; "World's Largest Railway Terminal"; "'Pennsy' to Spend"; and "New York and Long Island Extension."
45. Lionel, *Catalogue*, 15 and passim.
46. Corbett, "New Heights."
47. "Solving" and "City's Growth."
48. "First Great Stairless Railway Terminal"; "Modern Terminal"; "Solving"; "Grand Central Terminal"; and Baldwin, "Factors." On the extraordinary, systematized post office mail-handling equipment, see Gibbs, *New York Tunnel*, 280–83.
49. "First Great Stairless Railway Terminal."
50. "Solving."
51. "Solving" and "Handling."
52. "Grand Central Terminal Opens"; "Solving"; see also "New Grand Central Terminal Station," *Engineering News*.
53. "Grand Central Terminal Opens."
54. "Solving."

55. "Examples of Railway Efficiency."
56. "New York Terminal Station"; "Columns in the New Grand Central"; "Girders in the Grand Central"; "Opening of the New Grand Central Terminal."
57. Bernard, "World's Greatest," 595; see also "Gateway to the Heart of New York"; "Pennsylvania Station"; Inglis, "New York's New Gateway"; "New Grand Central Station in New York"; and "Monumental Gateway."
58. "Terminal Trains Run by Loop System."
59. "Pennsylvania's New York Station."
60. "Pennsylvania Station," *Architectural Record*.
61. Pope, "Grand Central," 54, 59–60, and passim.
62. Thompson, "Greatest Railroad Terminal"; "New York's New Pennsylvania Railroad Terminal"; and Richardson, "Terminal."
63. "The New Grand Central Terminal, New York Central"; "The World's Largest Railroad Terminal, General Electric." On December 7, 1912, *Scientific American* presented a rare, color cover illustration of Grand Central Terminal drawn by Jules Guerin. See also "From the New Grand Central."
64. See, for example, Williams, "Gates," and Richardson, "Terminal—Gate."
65. Hungerford, "Greatest," 902, 904–05, 906, and passim.
66. Williams, "Gates," 488–89 and passim; for other illustrations, see Maurice and Bailey, *Magical City*.
67. Snow, "Day"; see also Wolfe, *You Can't Go Home Again*, pp. 46–47.
68. Lee, "Poetry," 760.
69. "From the New Grand Central."

PART 2. ELEGANCE

1. Lionel, *Catalogue*, 23–25.
2. Fitzgerald, *Great Gatsby*, 176–77.
3. Love, *Situation*, 10–25, 194–219.
4. White, *American Railroad*, 658; see also Johnson, *American Railway*, and Beebe, *Two Trains*.
5. White, *American Railroad*, 85, 87, 177, 367, 436, 442–47; see also Ross, *Sky Blue*, 12–13, and Masury, *Ready-Made*.
6. Woods, *Broadway*, 8; on the bridal suite, see Beebe, *Mansions*, 266.
7. Rideing, "Building"; "Biggest Steamship"; see also advertisements in the 1912 *National Geographic*.
8. See, for example, Chambless, *Roadtown*; Leggett, *Dream*; Peck, *World*; Olerich, *Cityless*; Forbes, "Literary Quest"; Normano, "Social Utopias"; Roemer, *America* and *Obsolete Necessity*.
9. Beebe, *Trains We Rode*; see also a typical Pullman Company advertisement, "Courtesy." See also Williamson, *When We Went*, esp. 71–85, and Rae, *Westward*; on "voluptuous" service, see Lewis, *Babbitt*, 162–63; see also Phelps, *Under*.
10. For descriptions of luxury trains, see Atlantic Coast Line, *Vestibuled Train*; Steele, *To Mexico*; Fellow of the Royal Society, *Homeward*; Pennsylvania Railroad, *New York and Chicago "Limited"*; on the development of luxurious cars, see White, *American Railroad*, an extremely fine, complete study of passenger-train equipment.
11. Woods, *Broadway Limited*, 9, 29–30, and passim.
12. Root, *Eating*, 320; Beebe, *Trains We Rode*.
13. Beebe, *Trains We Rode*, 1:97; 2:473; see also Chicago and Northwestern Railway, *Palace Dining Car*; "New Dining and Cafe Smoking Cars."
14. White, *American Railroad*, 311–42, and esp. 312.
15. Lord, *Night*, 14.
16. Mencken, *Prejudices*, 165; for a sample Pennsylvania Railroad Company menu, see Beebe, *Trains We Rode*, 2:532.
17. On earlier luxury trains, see Leslie, *California*, and Towle, *American Society*, 2:179–80.
18. White, *American Railroad*, 298–311, 316–18; for an illustration equating a Pullman ob-

servation car with luxury, see the Armour Soap Company advertisement on the back cover of the June 1912 issue of *House Beautiful*.

19. Loewy, *Industrial Design*, 77–94.
20. "Air-Minded Railroading," *Popular Mechanics*; "Twentieth-Century Limited," *Modern Plastics*.
21. "New Trains," *Architectural Forum*.
22. Meikle, *Twentieth-Century Limited*, and Bush, *Streamlined Decade*, 151–53.
23. Plummer, "Streamlined Moderne," esp. 46–48; for advertisements of "modern" trains, see "Santa Fe for 1938"; "Look Over the Great Pacific Northwest"; "Ride the Most Beautiful Train in America."
24. See the articles listed under "streamlining" in the *Reader's Guide to Periodical Literature*, 1935–40.
25. Quoted in Dubin, "20th Century," 18.
26. Dubin, "20th Century," 18–19.
27. Quoted in Dubin, "20th Century," 20.
28. Dubin, "20th Century," 22.
29. Quoted in Dubin, "20th Century," 24.
30. Dubin, "20th Century," 25.
31. Snow, "Day at Grand Central," 18.
32. See the collection in the archives of the Pennsylvania Railroad Museum, Strasburg.
33. Dubin, "20th Century," 28; Hungerford, *Run*, 17.
34. Hungerford, *Run*, 10–11.
35. Hungerford, *Run*, 27; see also Beebe, *20th Century*, 40.
36. Hungerford, *Run*, 29–31.
37. Hungerford, *Run*, 36, 42.
38. Hungerford, *Run*, 5–51, 35–36.
39. Beebe, *20th Century*, 39.
40. For photographs, see those collected in Dubin, "20th Century," and Beebe, *20th Century*.
41. Beebe, *Overland*, esp. 26–35.
42. Quoted in Beebe, *Overland*, 30.
43. Quoted in Beebe, *Overland*, 30.
44. Beebe, *Overland*, 30.
45. Beebe, *Overland*, 50–65; see also "Overland Limited." For other advertisements of luxury trains, see the 1907 issues of *Country Life in America*.
46. Reproduced in Beebe, *Overland*, 32.
47. Beebe, *Overland*, 37.
48. Beebe, *Overland*, 42, 44, 65.
49. Judging from the amateur photographs I have seen, the signboard struck many observers as more significant than the locomotive; see also Loewy, *Locomotive*.
50. In the years before movie stars, the rich attracted prolonged and penetrating scrutiny in the periodical press.
51. Beebe, *Mansions*, 359, 30–31.
52. Beebe, *Mansions*, 359.
53. Beebe, *Mansions*, 138, 159, 199.
54. Beebe, *Mansions*, 139.
55. Quoted in Beebe, *Mansions*, 177; see also 198–99.
56. Beebe, *Mansions*, 207.
57. Beebe, *Mansions*, 53.
58. Spearman, *Daughter*, 32.
59. "Going to California."
60. Oppenheim, *Olympian*, 5; for other novels, see Cather, *My Antonia*, and Dreiser, *Sister Carrie*; for a short story, see Earle, "On the Night Train."
61. Wolfe, *Of Time*, 35.
62. Wolfe, *Of Time*, 407–19, 469–76.
63. Wolfe, *Of Time*, 407–12, and *You Can't Go Home*, 46–75.
64. Wolfe, *You Can't Go Home*, 49.

65. Oppenheim, *Olympian*, 4; Bennett, in *Your United States*, 106–13, describes *The Twentieth Century Limited* as a cross between a hotel and a private club.
66. Van De Water, *Present*, 218; see also Chopin, "A Night in Acadie," *Complete Works*, 485.
67. Harriman, *Book*, 490–91.
68. Howells, *Parlor Car* and *Sleeping Car*.
69. Lewis, *Main Street*, 21–22; for another description, see Horgan, *Main Line West*.
70. Beebe, *Trains*, 1:263, and Dubin, "Panama Limited," 22.
71. "Hyde Park," 54.

PART 3. ZONE

1. Lewis, *Babbitt*, 69 and 1–70, passim. Little scholarship exists concerning the aesthetics of industrial areas; on the aesthetics of machinery, see Huisman and Patrix, *L'Esthetique*, and Pile, *Design*, ix–x.
2. Schorer, *Sinclair Lewis*, 344–45.
3. Lewis, *Babbitt*, 52, 31.
4. *Wage-Earning Pittsburgh*, esp. 279–391; see also Byington, *Homestead*, esp. 12–31; Mitchell, *Silent War*; and Wyckoff, *The Workers, East*.
5. See, for example, Taylor, "Norwood and Oakley"; Lincoln, "City"; on the era itself, see Garraty, *New Commonwealth*, and Hicks, *Republican Ascendancy*.
6. Herrick, *Memoirs*, 158.
7. Kester, *Manager*, 38. For the "high" view of the city edge (it is not clear if it is the industrial zone), see Wharton, "Atrophy," *Collected Short Stories*, 2:502.
8. Bennett, *Your United States*, 110.
9. Nelson, *Managers*, 5–10; on the change, see Wright, *Industrial Evolution* and *Factory System*; Kirkland, *Industry*; and "Factory Management."
10. "South Philadelphia Works" is an example of the genre.
11. Sturgis, "Warehouse and Factory."
12. "Standardized Factory Buildings."
13. See, for example, Wyatt, "Building the Factory."
14. Coman, *Industrial History*, esp. 313–74; Shadwell, *Industrial Efficiency*; and Cochrane, *Modern Industrial Progress*.
15. Atkinson, "Slow-Burning," 573; see also Tyrell, *Treatise* and *Mill Building*; and Wright, "Utilitarian Architecture."
16. Atkinson, "Slow-Burning," 576; see also Prince, *Modern Factory*, and Feiker, "Preventing Fire."
17. Fire Insurance Association, *Fire Insurance*; Sturgis, "Simple Ways."
18. Atkinson, "Slow-Burning," 578; Atkinson was director of the Insurance Engineering Experiment Station in Boston. See also National Board of Fire Underwriters, *Building Code*, 123–39, and Sanborn, *Chelsea, Massachusetts* and *Memphis, Tennessee*, 15.
19. Atkinson, "Slow-Burning," 569, 576.
20. The stacks still exist, all visible from trains except for that of the Court Square Press, which is near the Boston railroad yards owned by Amtrak; the others are in Mansfield, Massachusetts, Providence, Rhode Island, and somewhere south of Philadelphia along the Amtrak main line. On roofs, see Nisbet, "Machine-Shop Roofs," 153; "Appliances"; and "Prepared Composition." See also "Barrett Specification Roofs"; Merriman, *Textbook*; and Nicholson, *Looking Back*.
21. Schmidt, "Hunting," 461; Updegraff, "Prophets and Pattern Followers."
22. Wyatt, "Building."
23. Piquet, "Is the Big City Doomed?" 139–44; see also Howes, "Aesthetic Value."
24. "South Philadelphia Works," 494–97 passim; for another example, see "Jones and Laughlin"; see also Riply, *Romance*.
25. See, for example, Waddell, *Bridge Engineering*; Ammann, "Hell Gate Arch Bridge"; Lindenthal, "Rebuilding"; Tyrell, *Artistic Bridge Design*; Reeve, "Romance"; "Erection of the Blackwell's Island Cantilever Bridge"; "Young People and Bridges"; "New Susquehanna Bridge"; Henderson, "In Praise of Bridges"; Koester, "Bridges" and "Bridges of Might and

Beauty"; Davis, "Bridges"; "Brooklyn Bridge"; "Hell Gate Arch Details"; "Hell Gate Steel Arch Bridge"; "New York Central Four-Track Drawbridge"; *Opening Ceremonies*; Woodward, *History of the St. Louis Bridge*; Hutton, *Washington Bridge*; Watson, *Decade*; Reier, *Bridges*; on the earlier period, see Malezieux, *Travaux publics*.

26. Walton, "Some Notable," 202.
27. Cowan, "Freeing a City," 5712–22 passim; see also Smith, "Minneapolis." On the significance of bridges see Cather, *Alexander's Bridge*; on the freight-car problem, see Voorhees, "Freight-Car Service."
28. Fawcett, "Center," 189–203 passim.
29. For a trade-journal view, see Cowles, "Handling Ore."
30. Oppenheim, *Olympian*, 2.
31. Riis, *How the Other Half Lives*.
32. Asher and Adams, *Pictorial Album*, 5.
33. Glazier, *Peculiarities*, 332–35; "Railroad University."
34. Glazier, *Peculiarities*, pp. 416–20.
35. *Cambridge*, esp. 337–400.
36. The photograph was made in New York City.
37. Coburn intended to complete a photographic essay on Pittsburgh.
38. "Pilgrimage," 54.
39. Davis, "Bridges."
40. Dreiser, *Hoosier Holiday*, 178.
41. Ferris, "American Capitals."
42. White, "Pittsburg," 902.
43. For information concerning artificial "snow," I am indebted to Stanley B. Hersey, my late great-uncle, who at the turn of the century devoted his boyhood after-school hours to investigating the city of Boston.
44. Sinclair, *Jungle*, 34; see also the stockyard illustration drawn by Joseph Pennell in Fuller, "Chicago," 31.
45. Dreiser, *Hoosier Holiday*, 187; White, "Pittsburg," 908.
46. The original paintings from which the calendar illustrations were made are now at the Pennsylvania Railroad Museum, Strasburg.
47. On the older values and system, see Stilgoe, "Fair Fields."
48. Barr, "Necco Factory."
49. Quoted in Walther, "Railroad," 58; see also Baur, *Charles Burchfield*, and Buffalo Fine Arts Academy, *Charles Burchfield*; for earlier paintings of industrial zones, see George Bellows, "Rain on the River," and, for a European impressionist precedent, Georges Lemmen, "Thames Scene—The Elevator" [1892] (both in Museum of Art, Rhode Island School of Design). For magazine illustrations, see Chase, "Steel Mill," and Pennell, "Vulcan's Capital."
50. Sasowsky, *Reginald Marsh*; see Marsh's "Erie Railroad and Factories" and "Chicago"; see also Kane's "Homestead" and Spencer's "Steel Country."
51. See, for example, "Vanishing Backyards." In wartime, of course, armament and other factories become magnificent symbols of liberty-insuring production; see, for example, "Steel," in *Life* magazine.

PART 4. GENERATOR

1. On railroad power stations, see Gibbs, *New York Tunnel*; on Lowell, see Eno, *Cotton*.
2. "Insurance Rates and Power House Construction."
3. Titley, "Works Engine Houses."
4. On houses, see Stilgoe, *Common Landscape*, 13–18, 159–70.
5. See, for example, Whitman, "To a Locomotive in Winter," *Leaves*, 367–68.
6. H. James, *American Scene*, 104–05 and passim.
7. W. James, *Principles* 1:87.
8. See the Charlie Chaplin film, *Modern Times* (1936).
9. Kavanagh, "Some Aspects."

10. On the rise of the industry, see MacLaren, *Rise*; Passer, *Electrical Manufacturers*; and Sharlin, *Making*.
11. For the speed of design progress, see Weingreen, *Electric Power*.
12. Sharlin, *Making*, esp. 193–95, 199–202; Knowlton, "Field." Hubbard, "Unit Power Plant."
13. Knowlton, "Field."
14. Murray, *Electric Power Plant*, esp. 299–327.
15. "New Power Houses"; "Power Station Practice."
16. Hennick, *Streetcars*, 199–201; "Steam Turbine Power Plant."
17. Many such coal-carrying railroad cars were self-propelled, gathering in power from the overhead trolley line.
18. Dixon, "Planning," 909–10.
19. Murray, *Electric Power Plants*, 1–138.
20. Dixon, "Planning," 912; Fowle, *Standard Handbook*; "New York and Long Island."
21. Bushnell, "Power Station," 268.
22. Dixon, "Planning," 912–14.
23. "New Polyphase Plant," 29; see also "Electric Power Stations."
24. Knowlton, "Handling Coal."
25. Boecklin, "Storage," 228.
26. Knowlton, "Handling Coal," 481.
27. Morrow, *Electric Power Stations*, 47.
28. Dreiser, *Hoosier Holiday*, 178.
29. "Locomotive Cranes."
30. Morrow, *Electric Power Stations*, 47–72.
31. Morrow, *Electric Power Stations*, 55.
32. Morrow, *Electric Power Stations*, 36, illustrates a rotary dumper.
33. Dixon, "Planning," 860.
34. On "coal patches," see Devine, "Coal."
35. Knowlton, "Handling Coal," 481.
36. Boecklin, "Storage," 245.
37. Dixon, "Planning," 911.
38. Morrow, *Electric Power Stations*, 66.
39. Boecklin, "Storage," 247–48; Boecklin suggests using coal conveyors to move ashes although he acknowledges the possibilities of corrosion.
40. Morrow, *Electric Power Stations*, 67–70.
41. Davis, *West*, 41.
42. Fitzgerald, *Great Gatsby*, 24; for an analysis, see Marx, *Machine*, 354–65.
43. Benjamin, "Smoke Prevention," 339.
44. Randall, "Relation"; "Gloom of Useless Smoke"; Kershaw, "Smoke Abatement" and "Industrial Smoke"; "Smoke Nuisance."
45. Information from George Hart, Director, Pennsylvania Railroad Museum, Strasburg.
46. Benjamin, "Smoke Prevention," 339; see also Obermeyer, *Stop that Smoke*, and Barr, *Catechism on the Combustion of Coal*.
47. For illustrations, see Des Granges, "Designing."
48. Des Granges, "Designing."
49. Dixon, "Planning," 860.
50. For illustrations, see Des Granges, "Designing."
51. Dixon, "Planning," 860–61; Hubbard, "Unit Power Plant."
52. Des Granges, "Designing," 361–62.
53. Des Granges, "Designing," 372.
54. See, for example, Hall, "Study"; "Chauney Street Station"; "Building for Pennsylvania Power"; "Buildings of the Murphy Power Company"; "The Coalfax."
55. Dixon, "Planning," 864–65; Bushnell, "Architect."
56. Knowlton, "Reinforced Concrete," 486–87; Taylor, *Treatise*.
57. Clark, "Cement," 375–76.
58. Knowlton, "Reinforced Concrete," 489.
59. Dixon, "Planning," 861.

60. Hall, "Model," 401.
61. Knowlton, "Handling," 481.
62. "Efficiency in Power Plants," x (part of "advertising section," which is paged differently).
63. "Efficiency in Power Plants," x.
64. Knowlton, "Handling," 480; Benjamin, "Smoke Prevention," 342.
65. Hancock, "Organization," 410; Hine, "Cast" and "Some Tools."
66. Taylor, *Shop Management* and *Principles*; Gilbreth, *Motion Study*. Taylor also wrote about concrete; see n. 56 above. See also Nadworny, "Frederick Taylor and Frank Gilbreth."
67. Goodale, "Getting New Business"; Hancock, "Organization," 403; Des Granges, "Design," 372.
68. Long Island Lighting Company, *Story*.
69. Sullivan, "Power," 850, 853; see also "New York's 70,000 Horse Power" and Fife, "Fantasy."
70. Smith, "'Peak of the Load,'" 524; see also "New York Edison's Power Station" and "Electric Power Stations."
71. Smith, "'Peak of the Load,'" 515, 521, 526; see also Dawson, "Modern Electric Power Station," and Stone and Webster, *South Boston*.
72. Bennett, *Your United States*, 81–83; for an illustration of a dynamo room, see "Philadelphia Edison Station," 3.
73. Fowle, *Standard Handbook*. Remarkably little has been written concerning the engineer as a figure in fiction.
74. Lionel, *Catalogue*; see also Barnard, "Goodbye 3876."
75. Vredenburgh, "Sign"; on the effect of such promotions, see Fife, "Fantasy."
76. Goodale, "Getting New Business"; Hillman, "Electricity."
77. Kimball, "Widening Use."
78. "Modern Methods"; "Highways of Power"; Pinchot, "Giant Power." See also Nunn, "Pioneer Work"; Barton, "Niagara Falls Power"; Varney, "Some Details."
79. Frost, "An Encounter," *Poetry*, 125.
80. Thoreau, *Walden*, 84.
81. Shadwell, *Industrial Efficiency*, 266.
82. Stilgoe, *Common Landscape*, 121–28.
83. Bruere, "Giant Power."
84. Hart, "Power and Culture"; Cooke, "Long Look"; Bruere, "Pandora's Box."
85. "Splendid Opportunity for 'Live Wires.'"

PART 5. HIGH IRON

1. Lionel, *Catalogue*, 30–31.
2. Lionel, *Catalogue*, 30.
3. Rau, "How I Photograph"; see also Central Vermont, *Album*; Erie, *Album*; Great Northern, *Valley*; New York and New England, *Literature*.
4. Williams, *Pacific Tourist*; Winner, *Great Northwest*.
5. Thayer, *Marvels*, esp. 220–428; for a collection of late-nineteenth-century photographs of Arizona railroad scenery, see Hatch, "Graphic."
6. For an analysis of the painting, see Grombrich, *Art*, 66–67.
7. The trestle appears to be of the driven-pile type, which suggests that Rossiter scrutinized the structure before painting it. "The Opening of the Wilderness" (ca. 1846–50) is in the Museum of Fine Arts, Boston.
8. Cropsey's painting is dated 1865; for a 1908 drawing of the viaduct by Harry Fenn, see Baxter, "Railway Beautiful," 815. On railroads in American scenery painting, see Novak, *Nature and Culture*, 166–84, and Marx, *Machine*, esp. 88–89, 156–60, 220–21.
9. Thoreau, *Walden*, 180, 185–86.
10. Thoreau, *Walden*, 301–02.
11. Thoreau, *Walden*, 192.
12. Thoreau, *Walden*, 469–74.
13. Thoreau, *Walden*, 447–78.

14. Funnell, *By the Beautiful Sea*, 22–23; see also Smith, *Prairie Garden*. Some of the plants cited here I have identified in period photographs. See also Williams, *Pacific Tourist*, 243, and "Prairie Preserves."
15. The illusion still entrances photographers; see Plowden, *Floor*, 67.
16. Novak, *Nature and Culture*, 166–84. For other illustrations, see Brown, *Hear*, 109, 118.
17. Williams, *Pacific Tourist*, 243.
18. Central Vermont, *Album*; Great Northern, *Valley*.
19. Engineers master such natural opposition far more often than they confront social obstructions such as strikes.
20. Merwin, *Road*, 4, 26, 62; Merwin's description of pick-and-shovel work appears accurate; see Sonnichsen, "I Was Workin'."
21. Merwin, *Road*, 112, 101, 221–22.
22. I have been unable to locate the issue, to which Merwin obliquely refers in his introduction.
23. Merwin, *Road*, 203, 215.
24. Merwin, *Road*, 148.
25. Spearman, *Daughter*, esp. 3–19, 180–206.
26. Lionel, *Catalogue*, 2.
27. Paine, "From the Track-Walker's Standpoint"; Marshall, "Problem"; "Machine for Burning Weeds"; "High Speed and Good Rails"; Webb, *Railroad Construction*; Beshan, *Field Practice*.
28. Rae, *Westward*, 90.
29. Spearman's "Roadmaster's Story" in Donovan and Henry, eds., *Headlights and Markers*, 23–48, is an example of the glamor attached to bridge-building.
30. Information from analysis of photograph collections and from fieldwork.
31. Anderson, *Hobo*; London, "Hoboes that Pass"; Flynt, *Notes*.
32. London, *Road*, 122–74 and passim; see also Wyckoff, *Day with a Tramp*.
33. Flynt, "Tramp" and "Tramping with Tramps"; see also Milburn, "Poesy."
34. On life in the jungles, see Livingston, who wrote at least ten books on hoboing, using the pseudonym "A–no.1"; in particular, see his *Here and There*.
35. "The Tramp," *Harper's Weekly*; Pinkerton, *Strikers*.
36. Flynt, *Notes*; see also Lewis, "Tramp Problem."
37. Solenberg, *One Thousand*; Feid, *No Pie*.
38. Milburn, "Poesy," esp. 81–82; see also Odum, *Rainbow* and Parker, *Casual Laborer*.
39. McCook, "Tramp Census" and Caplow, "Transiency."
40. Flynt, "Tramp" and "Railroad," 266. See esp. London, *Road*, 53–73, 153–66; also Adams, "Railroads and Juvenile Crime"; Dellinger, "Lure"; Flynt, *Tramping*. For a description of boys encountering hoboes, see Horgan, *Main Line*, 115–23.
41. Wolfe, "Bums," *Short Stories*, 41.
42. Milburn, "Poesy," 82–83; for other hobo songs, see Botkin, *Treasury*, 459–66, and Milburn, *Hobo's Hornbook*.
43. Crane, *Bridge*, 23.
44. Wolfe, quoted in Botkin, *Treasury*, iii.
45. Cohen, *Long Steel Rail*, 373–81. In the mid–1950s, when many "purged" hobo ballads had become popular folk songs, the Lionel Company manufactured a freight car in which a police officer chases a hobo. By then, of course, hoboing had withered into a shadow of its 1900s self.
46. Lewis, *Main Street*, 341.
47. Willey, "Safety."
48. Odegard, "Proceed."
49. Lewis, *Babbitt*, 1.
50. Ross, *Sky Blue*, 83–84; Prout, "Railroad Signalling"; for the trainman's view of signals, see Pennsylvania Railroad, *Operating Department*, 75–135.
51. *Harper's Weekly*, May 13, 1911; the illustration is by William Harnden Foster. For a sample of the outcry, see Scott, "Railroad's Death Roll."

52. Such illustrations typically emphasize semaphore-type signals; color-light signals appear insignificant when depicted in black-and-white advertising art.
53. Hine, "What a Train-Dispatcher Does" and "Gossip"; Oakley, "In the Railway Yard"; Fagan, "Confessions"; Stratton, "Railway Disasters"; Petersham, *Story Book*, n.p.; Dayton, "On Time": Prout, "Railroad Signalling"; Fisher, *Vanishing*.
54. Willey, "Nerves"; Fagan, "Autobiography," esp. 379–81. For a detailed fictional account of the importance of signals, see Ward, "Semaphore." See also Anderson, "First Interlocking" and "First Block Signal System."
55. Information on towers and names can be gathered from fieldwork and by asking Amtrak conductors. On the early history of the towers, see Fagan, "Autobiography," esp. 224–35, 375–87, and General Railway Signal Company, *Electric Interlocking*. For the tower in fiction, see Camp, "Signal Tower," a short story included in *Best Short Stories of 1920*, and Chapman, *Ralph in the Switch Tower*. See "Mike Tower in Fort Wayne."
56. Armstrong, "All About Signals"; see also Abans, *Block System*.
57. Woods, *Broadway*, 22–25; see also Sullivan, "Pilots"; "Automatic Block Signals on the Putnam Division"; "Automatic Block Signals on the Philadelphia and New York Divisions."
58. Woods, *Broadway*, 23; the explanation is a simplified version of that in Pennsylvania Railroad, *Operating Department*, 22–25.
59. *Scientific American*, June 17, 1911.
60. I base this judgment on analysis of many photograph albums examined at auctions, farm sales, and antique shops.
61. Smith, "Empire."
62. Rau, "How I Photograph."
63. Many of Rau's photographs are collected in Greenberg and Kramer, *Handsomest Trains*; this sort of photography disappeared during the Depression but reappeared during the Second World War, when railroads moved massive amounts of military supplies. See "Railroads at War," for example. In wartime, however, the photographers emphasized the "human element."

PART 6. CROSSING

1. Pennsylvania Railroad Company, *Operating Department*, 18–21; Whiting, "Stop," 929.
2. Cochrane, *Modern Industrial Progress*, 253. For the perceived frequency of crossing wrecks near a small town, see Reid, *Hurry Home*, 73.
3. Russell, "Speed," 445. Perhaps some people wanted to be hit by trains; see "Gracious, Samuel."
4. Stuart, "People," 38.
5. Stuart, "People," 38; see also "Grade-Crossing Accidents."
6. Furnas, "Gray Hairs," 80; Russell, "Speed."
7. Whiting, "Stop," 929; see also "Grade-Crossing Scandal."
8. Willey, "Safety," 59–60; Brown, *I Travel*, 11.
9. Furnas, "Gray Hairs," 77.
10. "Grade Crossing Problem," 571.
11. Information from fieldwork.
12. Information from fieldwork.
13. "Grade Crossing Problem," 571.
14. Information from fieldwork; see also Whiting, "Stop," 928.
15. Few "tramp-problem" experts addressed this issue.
16. Stuart, "People," 126, 139.
17. Brown, *I Travel*, 11–13.
18. Stuart, "People," 126, 139.
19. Stuart, "People," 38–39; Furnas, "Gray Hairs," 9.
20. Whiting, "Stop," 930.
21. On the cover of the May 13, 1911, issue.
22. Williams, *Build Up*, 76.

23. Whiting, "Stop," 929, 931.
24. Peters, "Stop," 242.
25. The song glorifies trains running "on the advertised" schedule.
26. H. James, *American Scene*, 41–42.
27. Information from examination of period photographs.
28. Information from examination of period photographs.
29. Stuart, "People," 126.
30. Stuart, "People," 126.
31. Stuart, "People," 126.
32. Metropolitan, *Public Improvement*, 82–87; see also California Railroad Commission, *Railroad Grade Crossing*.
33. Middleton, *Time*, 129.
34. "Oldsmobile"; Whiting, "Stop," 930; see also Hall Switch and Signal Company, *General Catalogue*, for crossing protection signals.
35. Furnas, "Gray," 78–80; see also "Railway Crossing Signals That Fail."
36. "Grade-Crossing Scandal," 62.
37. I base this information on my timing of the hand-cranked gates still extant at West Medford, Massachusetts, and from interviews with gate-tenders.
38. Whiting, "Stop," 932.
39. Whiting, "Stop," 932.
40. Furnas, "Gray," 77.
41. "Grade Crossing Problem," 572.
42. Furnas, "Gray," 77.
43. Furnas, "Gray," 9; see also "Automatic Gate"; "Utilizing the Pressure"; "Shockless Railroad Crossing."
44. Russell, "Speed," 450; see also "Guarding the Country Crossing."
45. Rowsome, *Verse*, 30, 34, 35, 89.
46. Furnas, "Gray," 9; see also "Grade-Crossing Scandal."
47. Furnas, "Gray," 9.
48. I am unable to recall the name of the 1930s film in which a steam locomotive slams into a gasoline-filled trailer truck.
49. "Twentieth Century Flier in Up-State Wreck," 1, 2.
50. Peters, "Stop," 240–41; see also "Grade Crossings: A Step Backward."
51. Furnas, "Gray," 81; see also "Elimination of Grade Crossings"; Grahame, "Railroad Crossing"; "Grade Crossing Separations Increase Crashes."
52. Furnas, "Gray," 82; see also "Curbing the Crossing Maniac."
53. Stump, "Transformation," 317; see also English, "Grade-Crossing Laws."
54. *Report*, 6–14.
55. *Report*, 12–15.
56. Glasgow, *Barren Ground*, 11–12. For another novel set at a country crossing, see Manfred, *Chokecherry Tree*.

PART 7. DEPOT

1. Goldthwait, "Town"; Geiser, "Ghost Towns"; Burr, *Small Town*; Williams, *American Town*; Anderson, *Country Town*; Blumenthal, *Small-Town Stuff*; Hedges, "Colonization Work"; Fletcher, "Doom"; Jakle, *American Small Town*.
2. See also Lingeman, *Small Town*, 245–50; Hart, "Dying Village"; Marshall, "Hamlets and Villages"; Lewis, "Small Town."
3. Adams, *Success*, 1, 9; on railroad siting, see Wellington, *Economic Theory*, and Webb, *Economics*.
4. Adams, *Success*, 6–8.
5. Packard, *Wire Devils*, 219; see also Prout, "Railroad Signalling." Novelists rarely noted the isolated station; see Tarkington, *Gentleman*, 3–4, for an example.
6. Remarkably, almost nothing has been written about the isolated station; see Burt, *Railway*, 3, for a contemporaneous view.

7. Information in the foregoing paragraphs is derived from Burt, *Railway*; Droege, *Passenger Terminals*; Alexander, *Down*; Phillips, "Evolution of the Suburban Station." The volumes of *Railway Age* and other railroad-industry–oriented periodicals offer countless insights into depot operations, as does the *Bulletin* of the Railroad Station Historical Society. See also Meeks, *Railroad Station*; Lewis, *New England*; Berg, *Buildings*; Lancaster, *Waiting*; on baggage, see Hatch, *American Express*. The ballad is printed in Pound, *American Ballads*, 131–32.

8. Burt, *Railway*, 21–23, 66; Davis, *West*, 185, also make the military analogy. On systems, see Chandler, *Visible Hand*, 79–121, 144–87.

9. Burt, *Railway*, 3, 10, 32–38, 45, 132, 135, 277–88.

10. See Grant and Bohi, *Country*, and Cavalier, *Classic*.

11. Alexander, *Down*.

12. Bohi and Grant, "Country"; see also Eberlein, "Recent."

13. Chicago, Burlington, and Quincy, *Farms*, 67; see also Grant, "'Katy' Depots."

14. Vyzralek, "North Dakota Depots."

15. Grammage, "Mission"; Baxter, "Railway Beautiful," 816.

16. Grant and Bohi, *Country*, 144; "Santa Fe Concrete Depots."

17. Information from fieldwork and from interviewing railroad employees, many of whom recall former liveries with pride.

18. Quoted in Bohi and Grant, "Country," 118.

19. Burt, *Railway*, 45.

20. Corliss, *Day*; "Railway Station at Waterbury"; Babcock, "Design."

21. The clock tower is still regarded as important; see Skidmore, Owens, and Merrill Company's designs for the new Providence, Rhode Island, station.

22. Burt, *Railway*, 83. On rural free delivery and parcel post, see Cullinan, *Post Office*, and Bowyer, *They Carried*.

23. White, *American Railroad*, 472–95, and James, "Railway Mail."

24. Lewis, *Main Street*, 235; Packard, *Night Operator*, 13–45. See also Hall, "Telegraph Talk"; "Western Union"; "Send Your Letters"; Miner, "Telegraphing"; Ross, *Sky Blue*, 92; Shaffner, *Telegraph Manual*; Reid, *Telegraph*; Buckingham, "Telegraph." For the telegraph tying the small-town businessman to urban markets, and eventually enslaving him to Morse-code messages, see Faulkner, *Sound and the Fury*, 282–83, 304–05.

25. Thoreau, *Walden*, 184–85; Foss, *Back Country*, 86–89.

26. Carruth, "In Grafton," 10; Tracy, "Blizzard," 263, 265, 271, and passim.

27. Anderson, *Winesburg*, 302.

28. Burt, *Railway*, 21–23.

29. Dell, *Moon-Calf*, 393–94; for illustrations of maps, see Lewis, *New England*, 64–65, and passim.

30. Dell, *Briary Bush*, 3; for the lure of the city, see Schlesinger, *Rise*, 53–77.

31. Burt, *Railway*, 3–20, 38–40.

32. Adams, *Success*, 7.

33. Love, *Situation*, 118–24.

34. Loungers were sometimes retired railroad employees, although how frequently I do not know.

35. Tarkington, *Gentleman*, 4.

36. Vyzralek, "Standardization," 12.

37. Waldo, *Magic Midland*, 168–69.

38. F. Packard, *Running Special*, 40–69.

39. Thoreau, *Walden*, 57, 69–70.

40. Lynde, *Taming*, presents such attitudes.

41. Wilder, *Our Town*, 6–7.

42. Stilgoe, *Common Landscape*, 14–16, 343.

43. Downing, *Architecture*, 213–53; the term *cottage* also applied to the mansions of the very rich, especially those at Newport, Rhode Island; see Eyre, "Mrs. Eliza Newcomb Alexander Cottage" and Thomas Alexander Tefft, "Emily Harper Cottage, Newport, 1853," in the John Hay Library, Brown University.

44. Thoreau, *Walden*, 69–70.

45. As in Wilder's play; see also Lewis, *Main Street*, 247; Lewis understood the vacation-time nature of cottages; see 204.

46. Allen, "Our National Shabbiness," 36.

47. Hartt, "Beautifying" and Olmsted, "Village Improvement"; see also Manning, "History," and Waring, *Village Improvement*.

48. See, for example, Schott, "A City's Fight"; Manning, *Suggestions*; Schuler, "Art,"; *Let Us Make a Beautiful City*; Prince, "Beautiful City."

49. Allen, "Our National Shabbiness," 33.

50. M. Harger, "Country Store," esp. 92–94.

51. M. Sullivan, *Our Times*, 409–10.

52. Grant and Bohi, *Country*, 121; see also Slosson, *Great Crusade*, 185–86, 217.

53. Reid, *Hurry Home*, 89; for an example of the "pull" of catalogues, see McFarland, "My Growing Garden."

54. Harger, "Country Store," 95–96. Towns *did* fail; see Mott, "Abandoned Towns"; Geiser, "Ghost-Towns"; Goldthwait, "Town"; Hart, "Dying Village"; Fletcher, "Doom"; White, *In the Heart*; Holmes, "Passing."

55. See, for example, Tufts, "Prairie Cabin"; Smalley, "Isolation"; Carver, "Life"; "Destitution in Nebraska"; Wyckoff, "With Iowa Farmers." Writers linked the decline with other declines; see Tomlinson, "Decline of the Ministry," and Hume, "Are We a Nation of Rascals?"

56. See also, Suckow, *Country People*; Bailey, *York State Rural Problems*; Bowers, *Country-Life Movement*; Shumway, *Back to the Farm*. By the late 1920s, similar problems had struck small cities; see Cozzens, *Just*, 217.

57. Ward, *Andrew Jackson*.

58. Burt, *Railway*, 25–26.

59. Spearman, "Bucks," *Nerve*, 168.

60. Loewy, *Industrial Design*, 90; Evans, "U.S. Depot," 138–42.

61. Lionel, *Catalogue*, 36–37.

62. Ross, *Sky Blue*, 92. For examples of such maps, see Missouri Pacific, "Map"; Denver and Rio Grande, "Denver and Rio Grande Railroad"; Chicago and Northwestern, "Chicago, Union Pacific."

63. Grant and Bohi, *Country*, 3.

64. Lewis, *Main Street*, 272.

PART 8. GARDEN

1. Huebner, "Railroad," 288.

2. André, *L'Art*, 195–96 (my translation).

3. Mitchell, *Out-of-Town*, 147, 148, 151. On Mitchell, see below.

4. Mitchell, *Out-of-Town*, 148, 151.

5. Mitchell, *Out-of-Town*, 158–59.

6. Mitchell, *Out-of-Town*, 159.

7. Parsons, "Railway," 415–19.

8. Eliot, *Charles Eliot*, 42, 280–81.

9. Boston & Albany, *Railroad Beautiful*, n.p.; see also "Railway Stations at Wellesley."

10. On safety considerations, see Pennsylvania Railroad, *Operating Rules*, 152–53, 174–75.

11. Boston & Albany, *Railroad Beautiful*, n.p.

12. Robinson, *Suburban Station*, 3–5; "Station at Stockbridge"; "Railroad Station at Auburndale"; and "Railroad Station at Chestnut Hill."

13. Waugh, "Rural Railway," esp. 379.

14. McCrea, *Railroad*, esp. 6–14; Jacobs, "Square Deal."

15. McCrea, *Railroad*, 13–14.

16. "How to Improve Railroad Stations."

17. Sieveking and MacFarlane, "Station Beautiful"; on Pray, see below, n. 22.

18. "Station Grounds."

19. Pray, *Railroad Grounds*, esp. 6–7.

20. Phillips, "Evolution," 125.
21. On the ideal, see Veblen, *Theory*, 98–101.
22. Pray, *Railroad Grounds*, 17–21.
23. Pray, *Railroad Grounds*, 18.
24. "Beautifying the Roadbed"; see also "Machine for Burning Weeds."
25. Pray, *Railroad Grounds*, 18.
26. Robinson, *Railroad Beautiful*, n.p.
27. Bok, "My Gardens," 41–45 passim.
28. See the membership lists in the association's Eighth Annual Convention *Proceedings*.
29. Lionel, *Catalogue*, 39.
30. Scott, *American City*, 183–269 passim.
31. I base this finding on my analysis of projects reported in *Landscape Architecture Quarterly*.
32. I have found no indication that any railroad company employed a landscape architect in 1930.
33. Pray, *Railroad Grounds*, 20.

PART 9. CINEMA

1. Woods, *Broadway*, 21.
2. H. James, *American Scene*, 416–17.
3. Emerson, *Journals*, 4:296.
4. Emerson, *Journals*, 8:335.
5. Quoted in Edward Emerson, *Emerson*, 182.
6. W. James, *Principles*, 2:90–91; the blurring-zone figures are based on my observations aboard commuter and long-distance passenger trains, particularly the *Crescent*, the *Patriot*, and *The Merchants' Limited*. See also Bullough, "Psychical Distance."
7. Frost, *Poetry*, 248.
8. Crane, *Bridge*, 25–26.
9. Frost, *Poetry*, 290–92.
10. Wolfe, *Of Time*, 470–71.
11. Woods, *Broadway*, 30–32; see also Vivian, *Tour*, 92–100.
12. Wolfe, *Of Time*, 471.
13. Wolfe, *Of Time*, 32–33.
14. Cather, *My Antonia*, ix; see also her *Lost Lady*, 9–11.
15. Tarkington, *Gentleman*, 3.
16. Wolfe, *You Can't Go Home Again*, 48–49.
17. Herrick, "Background," 219–20.
18. Trumbull, "Railway Touring."
19. Brown, *I Travel*, 74.
20. The quotation is found in Spearman, *Held*, 56. See also Brown, *I Travel*, 74.
21. Vivian, *Tour*, 98.
22. For an analysis of the boredom, see Percy, "Man on the Train."
23. Davis, *West*, 4, 6.
24. Vivian, *Tour*, 124–25, 181.
25. Packard, *Running Special*, 252.
26. American Film Institute, *Catalog*, 1:1602–03. Before and during the period of railroad-film popularity, the publishers of sheet music and records had enjoyed considerable success in marketing songs concerning railroading. See Cohen, *Long Steel Rail*.
27. *Black Diamond*; *Midnight Flyer*.
28. *Night Flyer*.
29. *Signal Tower*; *Block Signal*.
30. *Danger Signal*; *Overland Limited*; *Kindled Courage*.
31. *Midnight Express*; *Midnight Special*.
32. *Warning Signal*.
33. On "rotations," see Percy, *Moviegoer*, 146–69 and passim.

34. For other examples of the view from the train, see Howells, *Suburban Sketches*, 118–19, and Crane, "The Bride Comes to Yellow Sky," 377.

PART 10. VILLA

1. Packard, "Developing," 7.
2. Williams, "Gates," 490–91; see also Stuyvesant, "Vicissitudes," 599, and Whitaker, "Country Living."
3. "Mission," 3.
4. Lionel, *Catalogue*, 34–35.
5. Burpee, *Farm*, pp. 11, 13, 28, 54, 74–75, 78, 89.
6. Darlington, *How and What to Grow*, 20–21.
7. Nutter, *Quarter Acre*, 1, 10, 13; see also Kellaway, *How to Lay Out*, and Butler, "Adventures."
8. For further information concerning model suburbs, see Stilgoe, *Forest Hills*.
9. Bailey, "Open Country," 81.
10. For an extended analysis of Mitchell's career, see Stilgoe, "Donald G. Mitchell." For Mitchell's writings, see bibliography.
11. Johnson, *Farmer's Boy*, 98; see also "Small Farms a Solution."
12. Larcom, *New England Girlhood*, and Arr, *New England Bygones*. Jones, *Age*, 219–49, discusses the growing sentimentality.
13. Garland, *Son*, 268–69 and passim; "Poverty on the Farm"; Smalley, "Isolation."
14. Emory O. Hersey, my great-grandfather, placed his records in a trunk before he died in 1920. Among the account books is one in which he pasted copies of the newspaper advertisements he inserted in the *Transcript*.
15. Downing, *Architecture*, 112, 237; see also "Roadside," 17; Cock, *American Poultry*; Lewis, *Productive*.
16. Basley, "How a California Woman Makes Poultry Pay," 17.
17. Lewis, *People's*, v–vi; see also *Palliser's Model Homes*.
18. "Inexpensive but Practical," 504; see also Beale, *Profitable*; Sands, "Housing"; "$200.00 in Six Months"; Bolte, "Profitable"; Robinson, "Good Living"; Mead, *Our Farm*; Roosevelt, *Five Acres*; Briesmaster, "Experience."
19. Samson, "Log"; Whiting, "Home-Made"; Ruggles, "Combination"; Valentine, "Poultry House"; "Among Craftsmen," esp. 501–07. See also Clift, "Chicken House"; Dunn, "Handy Home-Made Silo"; Gallup, "Model Colony House"; Fiske, *Poultry Architecture* and *Poultry Appliances*; Bennett, "Hen-House"; Newland, "Planning"; Dacy, "Two-Story Mansion"; Ballentine, "Poultry."
20. Gardner, "Back-Yard," 118–19; Powell, "Balance Sheet," 167–68; Beals, "Ten Acres"; "Profitable Milch Goats"; "Flock of Pheasants"; "Clergyman's Squabs"; Waugh, "Ten Acre Forestry"; for the quotation, see French, "Debit and Credit."
21. Jenkins, "My Experience," esp. 56, 96; Bailey, "Small Farm." Backyard agriculture long existed in small towns; see Cather, *My Antonia*, 168, and Reid, *Hurry Home*, 142–43. On adulterated food, see Sinclair, *Jungle*. Millionaires anxious for fresh, wholesome vegetables also established kitchen gardens, of course; see Bowditch, "Miss Ellen Mason Estate."
22. For an example, see "Good Living from Poultry"; see also McMahon, *Success*.
23. Folson, *Home*, n.p. (section 8); see also Wright, "Gardening"; Jenkins, "Child's Own Garden"; "Children's Gardens."
24. A. D. G., "Improvement of Lawns"; "Mowing Machines"; Jackson, "Ghosts"; Grigson, "Room"; "Deciduous Lawn Trees"; Durand, "Lawns and Grasses"; "The Lawn"; Parsons, "Lawn Planting"; "Home Lawn"; "Hydrangea"; Eliot, "Anglomania"; "Formation and Care"; Tricker, "Lawn Notes"; Troop, "Essentials"; Rice, "Making." On the early history of lawns and grasses, see Stilgoe, *Common Landscape*, 46–47, 183–84, 193, 195; on the social significance of lawns, see Veblen, *Theory*, 98–101. See also Whitman, "Song," *Leaves*, 27–28.
25. "Improved Lawn Cleaner"; "Latham's Grass Collector"; "Simpson Motor Lawn Mower";

"Lawn Mower Attachment"; "Improved Lawn Mower." On the early history of lawn mowers, see "Birmingham Lawn Mower Contest."
26. Maynard, "How to Have a Good Lawn." See also Henry, "Way"; Corbett, *Beautifying*; Waugh, *Landscape Gardening*; Bottomley, *Design*; "Motor Lawn Mower"; Dickinson, *The Lawn*; Butler, "Adventures."
27. Maynard, "How to Have a Good Lawn," 179–80; Henry, "Way," 145.
28. Bottomley, *Art*, 191.
29. Merwin, *Road Builders*, 153; see also Fitzgerald, *Great Gatsby*, 83.
30. Wright, *Garden*, 87, 118, 245, and passim.

PART 11. TROLLEY

1. Lucas, *Trolley*, 7. Trolleying produced at least one full-length novel; see Phillips, *Lee Blake*.
2. H. James, *American Scene*, 78, 98.
3. H. James, *American Scene*, 105.
4. Weltzer, "Electric"; Johnson, "Trolley."
5. Quoted in Hennick and Charlton, *Streetcars*, 23.
6. Warner, *Streetcar Suburbs*, remains the best general introduction; on New Orleans, see Hennick and Charlton, *Streetcars*.
7. Hennick and Charlton, *Streetcars*, 57.
8. Cudahy, *Change*, traces the Boston congestion.
9. Holmes, *Complete Poetical Works*, 301.
10. Grant, "Electric Traction"; the best overall accounts are Middleton's *Interurban Era* and *Time of the Trolley*, although both books concentrate on rolling stock.
11. Curtis, "Street Railways."
12. The cultural effects of rural trolleying have received little scholarly scrutiny. For a contemporaneous view, see Bogart, "Economic and Social Effects."
13. Baxter, "Trolley," 64.
14. Baxter, "Trolley," 64.
15. Howells, *Literature*, 54–56.
16. Lucas, *Trolley*, 14, 32, 60; the party car "City of Manchester" is preserved at the Seashore Trolley Museum, Kennebunk, Maine.
17. Lucas, *Trolley*, 23–24, 57; Gill, "Summer Places," 48.
18. Lucas, *Trolley*, 12, 44.
19. Lucas, *Trolley*, 18, 46–47.
20. Lucas, *Trolley*, 13.
21. Lucas, *Trolley*, 45.
22. Lucas, *Trolley*, 88.
23. Abbott, *Trolley*, 15.
24. It is difficult to be certain, but Lucas does note some landscape features accorded mention by Derrah.
25. Derrah, *Trolley through Western New England*, n.p.
26. Derrah, *Trolley through Western New England*, *Trolley through Eastern New England*, and *Official Street Railway Guide*; see also Lane, *Trolley Wayfinder*.
27. Paine, "Short," 3677–78; see also Saylor, "Garden Entrances."
28. LeGallienne, "Jitneying," 34–41.
29. Derrah, *Trolley through Western New England*, 52.
30. Abbott, *Trolley*, 27.
31. Derrah, *Trolley through Western New England*, 34.
32. Stilgoe, *Common Landscape*, 128–32.
33. Lucas, *Trolley*, 80.
34. Ingersoll, "Trolley," 756; Carelton, "Electric."
35. Rice, "Urbanizing," 534; see also Howells, *Suburban Sketches*, 91–114.
36. Rice, "Urbanizing," 535; on the effect of trolley lines on town greens, see Stilgoe, "Town Common," 33.
37. Rice, "Urbanizing," 536–37.

38. Harriman, "Trolley," esp. 138–40; see also Hilton and Due, *Electric Interurban*, and Siebert, *Northwestern*.
39. "Street-Car Houses," 64; "Tram-Car Town"; "Method of Utilizing"; "Settlement of Carville," 492.
40. Harriman, "Trolley," 143.
41. Information from field work; see also Derrah, *Official*, 207–09, and "Interurban Railroad."
42. Coburn, "Five-Hundred-Mile City," 1252.
43. Coburn, "Five-Hundred-Mile City," 1253.
44. Channing, *Student's History*, 568–70.
45. Wharton, *Collected Short Stories*, 2:385.

PART 12. BEYOND

1. Taylor, "Passing." The *Century* drawing by Irving R. Wiles appeared in Bishop, "Hunting an Abandoned Farm in Connecticut," 915; see also Paine, "Abandoning."
2. Oxford English Dictionary, s.v. "abandonment."
3. Broudy, "Lost."
4. Abel, *Wüstungen*, esp. pp. 12–58; Guyan, "Mittelalterlichen Wüstlegungen"; Beresford, *Lost Villages*; Häberle, *Wüstungen*; Roux, *Territoire*; and Percy, *Love*.
5. Wilson, *Hill Country*, esp. 97–138; Taylor, "New England"; Holbrook, *Yankee*.
6. Melville, *Israel Potter*, 18; see also "Stone Walls."
7. Hawthorne, *Mosses*, 21.
8. Stowe, *Minister's*, 1, and *Oldtown Folks*, iii; Bellamy, *Duke*.
9. Brooks, *New England*, esp. 86–87, 462–63.
10. Jewett, "Foreigner"; Freeman, *New England Nun*, 215–23, 448–68.
11. Wilkins, *Madelon*.
12. Howells, *Vacation*, 154–55.
13. Wharton, "Bewitched," *Collected Short Stories*, 2:416.
14. Wharton, "Triumph," *Collected Short Stories*, 2:325.
15. Wharton, *Ethan Frome*, esp. 1–10, 19; on tramps, 48.
16. Wharton, *Summer*, 1–12, 157.
17. Stowe, *Old Town Folks*, 1 (here she cites the "ante-railroad times"); Churchill, *Coniston*, esp. 5–37.
18. E. A. Robinson, *Selected Poems*, 375.
19. Frost, *Poetry*, 375.
20. Frost, *Poetry*, 296, 62, 89, and passim.
21. Lovecraft, *Colour*, 7.
22. See, for example, Tuan, *Landscapes*, 79–80, 108–09; Collier, *Cosmogonies*; Nicholson, *Mountain Gloom*; King, *White Hills*, esp. 50–54. See also Inness, "In the Berkshire Hills," and Durand, "Chocorua Peak."
23. Frost, *Poetry*, 40.
24. Seelye, "Abandoned," 792.
25. Johnson, "Deserted Homes," 221–22. See also Learned, "Suggestion."
26. Hartt, "New England," 569–70; see also Sanborn, "Future."
27. "Our Hill Towns," n.p.; see also Hartt, "New England: National" and "Mountaineers."
28. Bishop, "Hunting . . . Connecticut," 916–17; Laut, "Abandoned Farm"; Corbin, "Old Houses."
29. Sessions, *Farms*, 90–91.
30. Mead, "Editor's Table," 676; see also Eaton, "Abandoned Farm."
31. Wright, "Hill Town," 622; see also "Abandoned Homes."
32. Rollins, "Abandoned Farm," 532; see also "Dignity of Farming." Other observers agreed that fruit-growing might save New England farming; see Munson, "Abandoned Farms."
33. Blake, "Abandoned Farms," 583; Atwell, "Abandoned Farms."
34. On trees, see Spring, *Natural Replacement*; Buttrick, "Forest Growth"; Beckwith, "Ecological Succession."

35. Bishop, "Hunting . . . Connecticut," 915, 920; Achorn, "To a Deserted New England Farm House."
36. Bishop, "Hunting . . . New England," 36; see also Chamberlain, "Ideal Abandoned Farms."
37. Gleason, "Old Farm," 679.
38. For photographs, see Hill, *Vermont Album*, and Sandler, *This Was Connecticut*.
39. Bishop, "Abandoned Farm Found," 886–88; see also Craven, "Abandoned Farm."
40. Bryant, "Rescue"; Stuyvesant, "Vicissitudes"; Hooper, "Reclamation"; Bishop, "Abandoned Farm Found," esp. 888; Roberts, "Abandoned Farm Clubs."
41. Frost, *Poetry*, 69.
42. Clayton, "Farm Abandonment."

PART 13. RUINS

1. Packard, *Wire Devils*, 157; Tarkington, *Gentleman*, 453.
2. H. James, *American Scene*, 266.
3. MacKaye, "Townless Highways," 349.
4. Lewis, *Main Street*, 236.
5. Wolfe, *You Can't Go Home Again*, 48–49.
6. In children's literature, of course, the railroad remains important; see, for example, Bragg, *Little Engine*; Kessler, *All Aboard the Train*; and Ehrlich, *Everyday Train*.

"Abandoned Homes." *Current Literature* 29 (October 1900): 386.

Abans, Braman B. *Block System of Signalling on American Railroads*. New York: Railroad Gazette, 1901.

Abbott, Katherine M. *Trolley Trips: The Historic New England Coast*. Lowell, 1899.

Abel, Wilhelm. *Die Wüstungen des ausgehenden Mittelalters*. Stuttgart: Gustav Fischer, 1955.

Achorn, Edgar O. "To a Deserted New England Farm House." *New England Magazine* 24 (August 1901): 605.

Adams, M. E. "Railroads and Juvenile Crime." *Charities and the Commons* 15 (November 11, 1905): 203–06.

Adams, Samuel Hopkins. *Success: A Novel*. Boston: Houghton, 1921.

"Air-Minded Railroading." *Popular Mechanics* 61 (February 1934): 169–73.

Alexander, Edwin P. *Down at the Depot: American Railroad Stations from 1831 to 1920*. New York: Bramhall, 1970.

Allen, Frederick Lewis. *Only Yesterday: An Informal History of the Nineteen-Twenties*. New York: Harper, 1931.

———. "Our National Shabbiness." *House Beautiful* 37 (January 1915): 33–36.

Allen, Lewis F. *Rural Architecture*. New York: Moore, 1852.

American Film Institute. *Catalog of Feature Films, 1921–30*. Ed. Kenneth W. Munden. New York: Bowker, 1971.

Ammann, O. H. "Hell Gate Arch Bridge." American Society of Civil Engineers, *Transactions* 82 (1918): 850–56.

"Among Craftsmen." *Craftsman* 19 (February 1911): 506–08.

Anderson, J. A. "First Block Signal System in America." *Railroad Age Gazette* 46 (March 5, 1909): 457–59.

———. "The First Interlocking Plant in America." *Railroad Age Gazette* 45 (September 25, 1908): 992–93.

Anderson, Nels. *The Hobo: The Sociology of the Homeless Man*. Chicago: Univ. of Chicago Press, 1923.

Anderson, Sherwood. *Winesburg, Ohio: A Group of Tales of Small Town Life*. New York: Boni, 1919.

Anderson, Wilbert L. *The Country Town: A Study of Rural Evolution*. New York: Baker & Taylor, 1906.

Andre, Edouard. *L'Art des jardines*. Paris: Masson, 1879.

Antin, Mary. *The Promised Land*. Boston: Houghton, 1919.

"Appliances for Re-roofing Shops without Stopping Work." *Scientific American Supplement* 57 (April 2, 1904): 23621–22.

Armstrong, John. *All about Signals*. Milwaukee: Kalmbach, 1957.

Arnold, Bion J. *Report on Railroad Terminals, City of Chicago*. Chicago, 1913.

Arr, E. H. *New England Bygones*. Philadelphia: Lippincott, 1880.

Asher and Adams. *Pictorial Album of American Industry*. [1876]. Ed. Glenn Porter. Reprint. New York: Rutledge, 1976.

Atkinson, Edward. "Slow-Burning Construction." *Century* 37 (February 1898): 566–79.

Atlantic Coast Line Railroad. *Vestibuled Train to Florida*. New York [?]: Atlantic Coast Line Railroad, 1887.

Atwell, R. I. "Abandoned Farms in New England." *New England Magazine* 5 (November 1881): 404–07.

"Automatic Block Signals on the Philadelphia and New York Divisions of the Pennsylvania Railroad." *Railroad Gazette* 34 (May 16, 1902): 355–57.

"Automatic Block Signals on the Putnam Division." *Railroad Gazette* 34 (July 25, 1902): 585.

"Automatic Gate for Crossings." *Scientific American* 67 (June 12, 1909): 376.

Babcock, William S. "Design for a Suburban Railroad Station." *Building Age* 32 (April 1910): 171–72.

Baier, Leslie K. *Walker Evans at Fortune, 1945–65*. Wellesley, Mass.: Wellesley College Museum, 1977.

Bailey, Liberty Hyde. "The Open Country." *Countryside Magazine* 20 (February 1915): 81.

———. "A Small Truck Farm that Pays." *Country Life* 12 (September, 1907): 547–48.

———. *York State Rural Problems*. Albany: Lyon, 1913.

Baldwin, A. S. "Factors Governing the Design of Passenger Terminals." *Railway Age* 73 (September 2, 1922): 429–35.

Ballentine, John H. "Poultry and the Small Lot." *Countryside Magazine* 21 (October 1915): 208–09.

Barnard, C. "Goodbye 3876." *St. Nicholas* 34 (February 1907): 324–29.

Barnard, Charles. *Knights of Today*. New York: Scribner's, 1881.

Barr, Alfred H. "The Necco Factory." *The Arts* 13 (May 1928): 292–95.

Barr, William M. *A Catechism on the Combustion of Coal and the Prevention of Smoke*. New York: Henley, 1900.

"Barrett Specification Roofs." *Outlook* 102 (October 26, 1912): back cover.

Bartholomew, Hubbard. "The Removal of Grade Crossings." *Wildwood Magazine* 3 (Christmas, 1916): 21–23, 37.

Barton, Philip. "Niagara Falls Power." *Cassier's Magazine* 21 (January 1902): 179–205.

Basley, Mrs. A. "How a California Woman Makes Poultry Keeping Pay." *Suburban Life* 9 (September 1905): 17–18.

Baur, John. *Charles Burchfield*. New York: Macmillan, 1956.

Baxter, Sylvester. "The Railway Beautiful." *Century* 65 (April 1908): 805–18.

———. *Remaking a Railway: A Study in Efficiency*. Boston: New England Lines, 1910.

———. "The Trolley in Rural Parts." *Harper's Monthly* 97 (June 1898): 60–69.

Beahan, Willard. *Field Practice of Railway Location*. New York: Engineering News, 1904.

Beale, Jessie Tarbox. "Ten Acres of Ducks: How One Man Has Solved the Problem of Making a Living." *Suburban Life* 7 (July 1908): 25–26.

Beale, Stephen. *Profitable Poultry Keeping*. New York: Routledge, 1895.

Beaudette, Edward H. *Central Vermont Railway: Operations in the Mid-Twentieth Century*. Newton, N.J.: Carstens, 1982.

"Beautifying the Roadbed by Sodding." *Scientific American* 94 (December 1, 1906): 406.

Beckwith, S. L. "Ecological Succession on Abandoned Farm Lands." *Ecological Monographs* 24 (Summer 1944): 349–76.

Bedwell, Harry. "Sun and Silence." *Railroad Magazine* 23 (April 1938): 34–48.

Beebe, Lucius. *Mansions on Rails: The Folklore of the Private Car*. Berkeley: Howell-North, 1959.

———, and Charles Clegg. *The Trains We Rode*. Berkeley: Howell-North, 1966.

———. *20th Century*. Berkeley: Howell-North, 1962.

———. *Two Trains to Remember*. Privately printed, 1965.

Beers, Frank. *The Green Signal, or Life on the Rail*. Kansas City, Mo.: Hudson, 1904.

Bellamy, Edward. *The Duke of Stockbridge: A Romance of Shay's Rebellion*. [1880]. Ed. Joseph Schiffman. Reprint. Cambridge: Harvard Univ. Press, 1962.

Benjamin, C. H. "Smoke Prevention in the Power House." *Cassier's Magazine* 31 (February 1907): 339–52.

Bennett, Arnold. *Your United States*. New York: Harper, 1912.

Bennett, I. D. "Hen House." *American Homes* 6 (February, 1906): 21–23.

Benson, Ramsey. *Hill Country: The Story of J. J. Hill and the Awakening West*. New York: Stokes, 1928.

Beresford, Maurice. *The Lost Villages of England*. London: Lutterworth Press, 1954.

Berg, Walter Gilman. *Buildings and Structures of American Railroads*. New York: Wiley, 1900.

Bernard, Walter. "The World's Greatest Railway Terminal." *Scientific American* 104 (June 17, 1911): 594–95, 609–10.

Bettelheim, Bruno. *The Uses of Enchantment: The Meaning and Importance of Fairy Tales*. New York: Random, 1977.

Bezilla, Michael. *Electric Traction on the Pennsylvania Railroad*. University Park, Penn.: Pennsylvania State Univ. Press, 1980.

"The Biggest Steamship Afloat." *McClure's* 15 (May 1900): 64–73.

"Birmingham Lawn Mower Contest." *The Garden* 6 (July 18, 1874): 64.

Bishop, William Henry. "Abandoned Farm Found." *Century* 62 (October 1901): 884–91.

———. "Hunting an Abandoned Farm in Connecticut." *Century* 47 (April 1894): 915–24.

———. "Hunting an Abandoned Farm in Upper New England." *Century* 48 (May 1894): 30–43.

Black Diamond Express. Los Angeles: Warner Brothers Pictures, 1927.

Blake, C. E. "Abandoned Farms as Homes." *New England Magazine* 24 (August 1901): 579–83.

Blake, Henry W., and Walter Jackson. *Electric Railway Transportation*. New York: McGraw-Hill, 1917.

Block Signal. New York: Gotham Productions, 1926.

Blumenthal, Albert. *Small-Town Stuff*. Chicago: Univ. of Chicago Press, 1932.

Boecklin, Werner. "The Storage and Handling of Coal and Ashes in Power Plants." *Cassier's Magazine* 34 (July 1908): 235–56.

Bogart, Ernest L. "The Economic and Social Effects of the Interurban Railroad in Ohio." *Journal of Political Economy* 14 (December 1906): 585–601.

Bohi, Charles W., and H. Roger Grant. "The Country Railroad Station as Corporate Logo." *Pioneer America* 11 (August 1979): 116–29.

Bok, Edward W. "Where American Life Really Exists." *Ladies' Home Journal* 12 (October 1895): 14.

Bolte, J. Willard. "Profitable Poultry Raising." *Country Life* 11 (February 1907): 429–31.

Botkin, B. A., and Alvin F. Harlow. *A Treasury of Railroad Folklore*. New York: Bonanza, 1953.

Bottomley, M. E. *The Art of Home Landscape*. New York: De La Mare, 1935.

———. *The Design of Small Properties*. New York: Macmillan, 1926.

Bowditch, Ernest W. "Miss Ellen Mason Estate." Brookline, Mass.: Frederick Law Olmsted National Historic Site.

Bowers, William L. *The Country-Life Movement in America, 1900–1920*. Port Washington, N.Y.: Kennikat, 1974.

Bowyer, Mathew. *They Carried the Mail*. New York: Luce, 1972.

Bragdon, Claude. "The Rochester Passenger Station." *American Architect* 104 (December 17, 1913): 237–39.

Bragg, Mabel C. *The Little Engine that Could*. New York: Platt & Monk, 1930.

Briesmaster, Charles. "An Experiment in the Poultry Business." *Country Life* 10 (September 1906): 119.

"Brooklyn Bridge." *Harper's Monthly* 66 (May 1883): 925–46.

Brooks, Van Wyck. *New England: Indian Summer*. New York: Dutton, 1940.

Broudy, Eric. "Lost on My Own Land." *Blair and Ketchum's Country Journal* 4 (February 1976): 67–70.

Brown, Rollo Walter. *I Travel By Train*. New York: Appleton, 1939.

Bruere, Robert W. "Giant Power—Region Builder." *Survey* 54 (April 1, 1925): 161–88.

———. "Pandora's Box." *Survey* 51 (March 1, 1924): 556–60.

Bryant, Harriet C. "The Rescue of an Old Colonial Farmhouse." *Country Life* 11 (April 1907): 661–65.

Bryant, Keith L. *History of the Atchison, Topeka, and Santa Fe Railway*. New York: Macmillan, 1974.

Buckingham, Charles. "The Telegraph of Today." *Scribner's* 6 (July 1889): 3–22.

Buffalo Fine Arts Academy. *Charles Burchfield*. Buffalo: Holling, 1944.

"Building for Pennsylvania Power and Light Co." *American Architect* 133 (January 5, 1928): 15–16.

"Buildings of the Murphy Power Co." *American Architect* 92 (October 12, 1907): 128.

Bullough, Edward. "Psychical Distance as a Factor in Art and as Aesthetic Principle." *British Journal of Psychology* 5 (June 1912): 87–118.

Burpee Company. *Farm Annual*. Philadelphia: Burpee Co., 1887.

Burr, Walter. *Small Towns: An Estimate of Their Trade and Culture*. New York: Macmillan, 1929.

Burt, Benjamin C. *Railway Station Service*. New York: Wiley, 1911.

Busfield, T. L. "The Design of Large Passenger Terminals." *Railway Age Gazette* 60 (May 5, 1916): 989–93.

Bush, Donald J. *The Streamlined Decade*. New York: Braziller, 1975.

Bushnell, Fred N. "The Power Station." *Electrical Age* 36 (April 1906): 268–74.

Bushnell, S. M. "Architect and the Central Station." *Cassier's Magazine* 31 (January 1907): 261–64.

Butler, Ellis Parker. "The Adventures of a Suburbanite." *Country Life* 16 (October 1909): 595–98.

Buttrick, P. L. "Forest Growth on Abandoned Agricultural Land." *Scientific Monthly* 5 (July 1917): 80–91.

Byington, Margaret. *Homestead: The Households of a Mill Town*. New York: Russell Sage, 1910.

Cambridge of Eighteen Hundred and Ninety-Six. Cambridge, Mass.: Riverside Press, 1896.

Camp, Wadsworth. "The Signal Tower." *The Best Short Stories of 1920*. Ed. J. O'Brien. Boston: Small, Maynard, 1921.

Caplow, Theodore. "Transiency as a Cultural Pattern." *American Sociological Review* 5 (October 1910): 731–39.

Carelton, Frank T. "The Electric Interurban Railroad." *Yale Review* 13 (August 1904): 179–93.

California Railroad Commission. *Railroad Grade Crossing and Terminal Investigation, Los Angeles*. San Francisco, 1922.

Carrier, Lyman, and Katherine S. Bort. "History of Kentucky Bluegrass and White Clover in the United States." American Society of Agronomy, *Journal* 8 (1916): 256–66.

Carruth, Frances Weston. "In Grafton." *Four O'Clock Magazine* 2 (April 1898): 10–15.

Carver, T. N. "Life in the Corn Belt." *World's Work* 7 (December 1903): 4232–39.

Cary, George. "The Proposed Union Station in Buffalo." *House and Garden* 7 (March 1905): 167–69.

Cather, Willa. *Alexander's Bridge*. New York: Houghton, 1912.

———. *A Lost Lady*. [1923]. Reprint. New York: Random House, 1972.

———. *My Antonia*. Boston: Houghton, 1918.

Cavalier, Julien. *Classic American Railroad Stations*. San Diego: Barnes, 1980.

Central Vermont Railroad Company. *Album of Central Vermont Railroad Scenery*. Portland: Chisholm, n.d. [ca. 1880].

Chamberlain, A. "Ideal Abandoned Farm." *New England Magazine* 16 (June 1897): 473–78.

Chambless, Edgar. *Roadtown*. New York: Roadtown Press, 1910.

Chandler, Alfred D. *The Visible Hand: The Managerial Revolution in American Business*. Cambridge: Harvard Univ. Press, 1977.

Channing, Edward. *Elements of United States History*. New York: Macmillan, 1919.

———. *A Student's History of the United States*, 3rd ed., rev. New York: Macmillan, 1917.

Chapman, Allen. *Ralph and the Train Wreckers*. New York: Grosset and Dunlap, 1928.

———. *Ralph in the Switch Tower*. New York: Grosset and Dunlap, 1907.

———. *Ralph the Train Dispatcher*. New York: Grosset and Dunlap, 1911.

Chase, J. C. "Steel Mill." *Scientific American* 104 (April 15, 1911): cover.

"Chauney Street Station." *American Architect* 117 (May 26, 1920): 647–50.

Chicago and Northwestern Railway Company. *Chicago, Union Pacific North-Western Line* [map]. Chicago, 1890.

———. *Palace Dining Car: Bill of Fare Between Chicago and Council Bluffs*. Chicago, n.d. [ca. 1890].

Chicago, Burlington, and Quincy Railroad Company. *Farms in Iowa*. Chicago, 1907.

Chicanot, E. L. "Beautifying a Railroad System." *Landscape Architecture Quarterly* 15 (April 1925): 185–94.

"Children's Gardens." *Country Calendar* 1 (May 1905): 13.

Chopin, Kate. *Complete Works*. Ed. Per Seyersted. Baton Rouge: Louisiana State Univ. Press, 1969.

Churchill, Winston. *Coniston*. New York: Macmillan, 1906.

City Club. *The Railway Terminal Problem of Chicago*. Chicago, 1913.

"City Planning and Congestion." *Survey* 25 (March 25, 1911): 1069–71.

"City's Growth Epitomized in Terminal Changes." *New York Times*, February 2, 1913, section T, 3.

Civic League of St. Louis. *Report of the Committee on Railroad Electrification*. St. Louis, 1911.

Clark, Eugene B. "Cement in Central Station Design." *Electrical Age* 34 (May 1905): 375–78.

Clayton, C. F. "Farm Abandonment Goes by Definite Stages in Vermont's Hill Towns." United States Department of Agriculture, *Yearbook for 1931*. Washington, D.C.: Government Printing Office, 1930.

Clift, M. L. "Chicken House for $3." *Country Life* 9 (February 1906): 390.

Coburn, Frederick W. "The Five-Hundred-Mile City." *World Today* 11 (December 1906): 1251–60.

Cochrane, Charles H. *Modern Industrial Progress*. Philadelphia: Lippincott, 1904.

Cock, Micahah R. *The American Poultry Book*. New York: Harper, 1843.

Cohen, Norm. *Long Steel Rail: The Railroad in American Folksong*. Urbana: Univ. of Illinois Press, 1981.

Collier, Katharine Brownell. *Cosmogonies of Our Fathers*. New York: Columbia Univ. Press, 1934.

"Columns in the New Grand Central Terminal, New York City." *Engineering Record* 67 (February 1, 1913): 125–26.

Coman, Katharine. *The Industrial History of the United States*. New York: Macmillan, 1919.

Condit, Carl W. *The Pioneer Stage of Railroad Electrification*. Philadelphia: American Philosophical Society, 1977.

————. *The Port of New York: A History of the Rail and Terminal System from the Beginnings to Pennsylvania Station*. Chicago: Univ. of Chicago Press, 1980.

————. *The Port of New York: A History of the Rail and Terminal System from the Grand Central Electrification to the Present*. Chicago: Univ. of Chicago Press, 1981.

————. *The Railroad and the City: A Technological and Urbanistic History of Cincinnati*. Columbus, Ohio: Ohio State Univ. Press, 1977.

"Congestion of Traffic at the Grand Central Station and Its Remedy." *Scientific American* 83 (December 1, 1900): 338.

Cooke, Morris Llewellyn. "The Long Look Ahead." *Survey* 51 (March 1, 1924): 600–04, 651.

————. "The Spirit and Social Significance of Scientific Management." *Journal of Political Economy* 21 (June, 1913): 485–86.

Corbett, Harvey Wiley. "New Heights in American Architecture." *Yale Review* 17 (July 1928): 690–701.

Corbett, L. C. *Beautifying the Home Grounds* [Farmer's Bulletin no. 185]. Washington, D.C.: Government Printing Office, 1904.

Corbin, Alice. "Old Houses." *Century* 94 (September 1917): 665–67.

Corliss, Carlton J. *The Day of Two Noons*. Washington, D.C.: Association of American Railroads, 1959.

Couper, William. *The History of the Engineering, Construction, and Equipment of the Pennsylvania Railroad Company's New York Terminal and Approaches*. New York: Blanshard, 1912.

"Courtesy: An Advertisement by the Pullman Company." *Outlook* 115 (April 25, 1917): 767.

Cowan, John L. "Freeing a City from a Railroad's Control." *World's Work* 9 (January, 1905): 5712–22.

Cowles, W. L. "Handling Ore at a Blast-Furnace: Some Details of a Typical American Plant." *Cassier's Magazine* 22 (June 1902): 157–74.

Cozzens, James Gould. *The Just and the Unjust*. New York: Harcourt, 1942.

Crane, Hart. *The Bridge*. New York: Liveright, 1930.

Crane, Stephen. "The Bride Comes to Yellow Sky." *McClure's Magazine* 10 (February 1898): 377–84.

Craven, A. O. "Abandoned Farms of New England." American Historical Association, *Annual Report for 1922*. New York, 1923.

Crocker, George D. "The Passenger Traffic of Boston and the Subway." *New England Magazine* 19 (January 1899): 523–41.

Crozier, William, and Peter Henderson. *How the Farm Pays: The Experiences of Forty Years of Successful Farming and Gardening*. New York: Peter Henderson, 1884.

Cudahy, Brian J. *Change at Park Street Under*. Brattleboro: Stephen Greene, 1972.

————. *Rails Under the Mighty Hudson*. Brattleboro: Stephen Greene, 1975.

Cullinan, Gerald. *The Post Office Department*. New York: Praeger, 1968.

"Curbing the Crossing Maniac." *Illustrated World* 29 (April 1918): 175–79.

Curtis, Charles E. "Street Railways and their Relation to the Public." *Yale Review* 6 (May 1897): 17–36.

Curtis, George D. *Souvenir of the Centennial Exhibition: Or Connecticut's Representation at Philadelphia*. Hartford, 1877.

Dacy, G. H. "Two-Story Mansion for Chickens." *Illustrated World* 36 (September 1921): 124–26.

Danger Lights. New York: RKO Radio Pictures, 1930.

Danger Signal. New York: Columbia Pictures, 1925.

Darlington, E. D., and L. M. Mall. *How and What to Grow in a Kitchen Garden of One Acre*. Philadelphia: Burpee, 1888.

Davis, James L. "The Elevated System and the Growth of Northern Chicago." Evanston: Northwestern Univ. Studies in Geography, 1962.

Davis, Richard Harding. *The West from a Car Window.* New York: Harper, 1892.

Davis, Theodore R. "The Meadow Brook Disaster." *Harper's Weekly* 17 (May 10, 1873): 388.

Davis, William S. "Bridges as Pictorial Subjects." *Photo-Era* 37 (September 1916): 108–12.

Dawson, P. "Modern Electric Power Stations." *Cassier's Magazine* 19 (January 1901): 211–14.

Dayton, Thaddeus S. "On Time: The Incessant Struggle of the Railroad to Prevent the Trains Falling Behind their Schedule." *Harper's Weekly* 54 (January 22, 1910): 11–12.

"Deciduous Lawn Trees." *Horticulturist* 3 (1853): 62–64.

Dell, Floyd. *Briary Bush.* New York: Knopf, 1921.

———. *Moon-Calf.* New York: Knopf, 1920.

Dellinger, E. S. "Lure of the Rails." *Railroad Man's Magazine* 1 (January 1930): 172–93.

———. "The Square Peg." *Railroad Magazine* 24 (November 1938): 86–111.

Denbie, Roger. *Death on the Limited.* New York: Morrow, 1933.

Denver and Rio Grande Railroad Company. *Denver and Rio Grande Railroad* [map]. Denver, 1890.

Derrah, Robert H. *By Trolley through Eastern New England.* Boston, 1904.

———. *By Trolley through Western New England: Connecticut Valley Edition.* Boston, 1904.

———. *Official Street Railway Guide for Eastern New England.* Boston: Derrah, 1900.

Des Granges, Donald. "The Designing of Power Stations." *Architectural Forum* 51 (September 1929): 361–72.

Desmond, Harry W. "The Work of Frost and Granger." *Architectural Record* 18 (August 1905): 115–45.

"Destitution in Nebraska." *Harper's Weekly* 39 (January 19, 1895): 59–63.

Devine, Edward T. "Coal." *Survey* 51 (November 1, 1923): 128–37.

Dickinson, Lawrence S. *The Lawn: The Culture of Turf in Park, Golfing and Home Areas.* London: Paul, 1930.

"Dignity of Farming." *Craftsman* 18 (April 1910): 134.

Dixon, A. E. "The Planning and Construction of Power Stations." *Engineering Magazine* 31 and 32 (August 1906–March 1907), 722–27, 909–34, 58–86, 227–47, 370–90, 551–71, 749–68, 860–73.

Donovan, Frank P. *Harry Bedwell: Last of the Great Railroad Storytellers.* Minneapolis: Ross and Harnes, 1959.

———. *The Railroad in Literature.* Boston: Railway Historical Society, 1940.

———, ed. *Headlights and Markers: An Anthology of Railroad Stories.* New York: Creative Age, 1946.

Dos Passos, John. *Manhattan Transfer.* New York: Harper, 1925.

Downing, Andrew Jackson. *The Architecture of Country Houses.* 1850. Reprint. New York: Dover, 1969.

———. *Rural Essays.* New York: Leavitt, 1854.

Dreiser, Theodore. *A Hoosier Holiday.* New York: John Lane, 1916.

———. *Sister Carrie.* New York: Doubleday, 1900.

Droege, John. *Passenger Terminals and Trains.* New York: McGraw-Hill, 1916.

Dubin, Arthur. "The Panama Limited." *Trains* 23 (March 1963): 16–29.

———. "The 20th Century Limited: A Chronicle of the Land's Most Famous Train." *Trains* 22 (August 1962): 16–35.

Dumjahr, Horst-Werner. *Bahnhöfe im Spiegel alter Postkarten.* Hildescheim: Olms, 1979.

Dunn, G. "Handy Home-made Silo for the Hen." *Country Life* 36 (May 1919): 136.

Dunn, Samuel O. "The Problem of the Modern Terminal." *Scribner's Magazine* 52 (October 1912): 416–42.

Durand, L. "Lawns and Grasses." *Horticulturist* 3 (1853): 310–11.

Dwight, James. "Form in Lawn Tennis." *Scribner's* 6 (August 1889): 231–39.

Earle, Mary Tracy. "On the Night Train." *Atlantic Monthly* 85 (June 1900): 748–56.

Eastman, Peggy. "Nostalgia Derailed." *Cape Cod Times*, October 13, 1982, 11.

Eaton, Walter Prichard. "Abandoned Farm in New Hampshire." *American Magazine* 72 (August 1911): 402–14.

———. "Essays on Newark." In *Newark: A Series of Engravings*, ed. Rudolph Ruzicka. Newark: Carteret Book Club, 1917.

Eberlein, Harold D. "Recent Railway Stations in American Cities." *Architectural Record* 36 (August 1914): 98–122.

"Efficiency in Power Plants." *Cassier's Magazine* 34 (June 1908): x.

Ehrlich, Amy. *The Everyday Train*. New York: Dial, 1977.

"Electric Power Stations in New York." *Engineering Magazine* 18 (February 1900): 773–74.

"Electricity Assisting the Traveller." *Scientific American* 104 (June 10, 1911): 582.

"Elimination of Grade Crossings." *Scientific American* 101 (September 11, 1909): 174.

Eliot, Charles. "Anglomania in Park Making." *Garden and Forest* 1 (April 4, 1888): 64.

Emerson, Edward Waldo. *Emerson in Concord: A Memoir*. Boston: Houghton, 1888.

Emerson, Ralph Waldo. *Essays: Second Series*. Philadelphia: McKay, 1892.

———. *Journals and Miscellaneous Notebooks*. Ed. Alfred R. Ferguson. Cambridge: Harvard Univ. Press, 1964.

———. *Nature, Addresses, and Lectures*. Boston: Houghton, 1884.

Engineer's Committee. *St. Louis–East St. Louis Railroad Terminals*. St. Louis: C. E. Smith, 1922.

English, C. H. "Grade-Crossing Laws." *Municipal Journal* 33 (September 10, 1912): 397–99.

"Erection of the Blackwell's Island Cantilever Bridge." *Scientific American* 97 (August 10, 1907): 100–01.

Erie Railway Company. *Album of Erie Railway Scenery*. New York: Witteman, 1882.

Evans, Walker. "Before They Disappear." *Fortune* 55 (March 1957): 141–45.

———. "The U.S. Depot." *Fortune* 47 (February 1953): 138–43.

"Examples of Railway Efficiency." *Outlook* 9 (December 10, 1910): 795–96.

Eyre, Wilson. "Mrs. Eliza Newcomb Alexander Cottage." Unpublished manuscript, ca. 1900. Philadelphia: University of Pennsylvania Archives.

Fabos, Julius, Milde, Gordon T., and Weinmayr, V. Michael. *Frederick Law Olmsted, Sr.: Founder of Landscape Architecture in America*. Amherst: Univ. of Massachusetts Press, 1968.

Factory Insurance Association. *Fire Insurance Plans*. Hartford, 1905.

Fagan, James O. "The Autobiography of an Individualist." *Atlantic Monthly* 110 (August–October 1912): 224–35, 375–87, 504–16.

———. "Confessions of a Railroad Signalman." *Atlantic Monthly* 101 (January–February 1908): 80–87, 225–32.

Faulkner, Harold U. *The Quest for Social Justice*. New York: Macmillan, 1931.

Faulkner, William. *The Sound and the Fury*. [1929]. Reprint. New York: Random, 1956.

Fawcett, Waldon. "The Center of the World of Steel." *Century* 62 (June 1901): 189–203.

Feid, Frederick. *No Pie in the Sky: The Hobo as American Cultural Hero*. New York: Citadel, 1964.

Feiker, F. M. "Preventing Fire in the Factory." *Factory* 2 (August–October 1908): 60–63.

Fein, Albert. *Frederick Law Olmsted and the American Environmental Tradition*. New York: Braziller, 1972.

Fellow of the Royal Society of Literature. *Homeward through America*. Chicago: Poole, 1888.

Fife, George Buchanan. "A Fantasy of City Light." *Harper's Weekly* 57 (February 8, 1913): 9–10.

"Fire Retardant Roofs." *Building Age* 32 (June 1910): 270.

"First Great Stairless Railway Terminal in History." *New York Times*, February 2, 1913, T, 5.

Fisher, Marvin. "The Iconology of Industrialism, 1830–60." *American Quarterly* 13 (Fall 1961): 347–64.

Fisher, Ralph. *Vanishing Markers*. Brattleboro: Stephen Greene, 1977.

Fiske, G. B. *Poultry Appliances and Handicraft*. New York: Orange Judd, 1902.

———. *Poultry Architecture*. New York: Orange Judd, 1910.

Fitzgerald, F. Scott. *The Great Gatsby*. [1925]. Reprint. New York: Scribner's, 1953.

Fleming, Ronald Lee, and Lauri A. Halderman, eds. *On Common Ground*. Harvard, Mass.: Harvard Common Press, 1982.

Fletcher, Henry J. "The Doom of the Small Town." *Forum* 19 (April 1895): 214–23.

Flynt, Josiah. *Notes of an Itinerant Policeman*. Boston: Page, 1900.

———. "The Tramp and the Railroad." *Century* 58 (June 1899): 258–66.

———. "The Tramp at Home." *Century* 48 (February 1894): 517–26.

———. "Tramping with Tramps: The American Tramps Considered Geographically." *Century* 47 (November 1893): 99–108.

———. *Tramping with Tramps*. New York: Century, 1901.

Folsom, M. V. *A Home of Your Own and What It Means to You*. Chicago: National Association of Real Estate Boards, 1922.

Forbes, Allyn Bailey. "The Literary Quest for Utopia, 1880–1900." *Social Forces* 6 (December 1927): 179–89.

Ford, Paul Lester. *The Great K&A Train Robbery*. New York: Dodd, Mead, 1897.

Foreman, Milton J. *The Electrification of Railway Terminals*. Chicago: Donnelley, 1908.

"Formation and Care of Lawns." *Garden and Forest* 5 (December 28, 1892): 618.

Foss, Sam Walter. *Back Country Poems*. Boston: Lee and Shepard, 1894.

Fowle, Frank F., ed. *Standard Handbook for Electrical Engineers*. New York: McGraw, 1907.

Freeman, Mary E. Wilkins. *A New England Nun*. New York: Harper, 1903.

Freidel, Frank. *America in the Twentieth Century*. New York: Knopf, 1970.

French, George. "The Debit and Credit of a Tiny Suburban Garden." *Countryside Magazine* 20 (March 1915): 144, 163–64.

"From the New Grand Central Terminal." *New York Times*, February 2, 1913, section T, 6.

Frost, Robert. *Poetry*. Ed. Edward Connery Lathem. New York: Holt, 1969.

Fuller, Henry B. "Chicago." *Century* 84 (May 1912): 25–33.

Funnell, Charles. *By the Beautiful Sea*. New York: Knopf, 1975.

Furnas, J. C. "Gray Hairs for Casey Jones: Automobile Drivers and Grade Crossings." *Saturday Evening Post* 209 (April 10, 1937): 8–9.

Gallup, Christopher M. "Model Colony House." *Country Life* 15 (April 1909): 638.

Gammage, Grady. *Mission and Mediterranean Revival Railroad Stations*. Crete, Nebraska: Railroad Station Historical Society, 1980.

Gardner, Frank A. "The Back-Yard Profitable." *Suburban Life* 2 (March 1906): 118–19.

Garland, Hamlin. *A Son of the Middle Border*. New York: Macmillan, 1917.

Garraty, John A. *The New Commonwealth, 1877–1890*. New York: Harper, 1968.

"A Gateway to the Heart of New York." *Scientific American Supplement* 74 (December 7, 1912): 364–66.

Geiser, S. W. "Ghost Towns and Lost Towns of Texas." *Texas Geographical Magazine* 8 (1944): 9–20.

General Railway Signal Company. *Electric Interlocking Handbook*. Rochester, N.Y., n.d. [ca. 1923].

Gibbs, George. *The New York Tunnel Extension of the Pennsylvania Railroad*. New York: American Society of Civil Engineers, 1910.

Gilbreth, Frank Bunker. *Motion Study*. New York: Van Nostrand, 1911.

Gill, Brendan. "Summer Places." *The New Yorker* 54 (August 21, 1978): 33–52.

"Girders in the Grand Central Terminal, New York City." *Engineering Record* 67 (January 18, 1913): 78–79.

Glasgow, Ellen. *Barren Ground*. Garden City, N.Y.: Doubleday, 1925.

Glazier, Willard. *Peculiarities of American Cities*. Philadelphia: Hubbard, 1884.

Gleason, Herbert Wendell. "The Old Farm Revisited." *New England Magazine* 22 (August 1900): 668–80.

"Gloom of Useless Smoke." *World's Work* 17 (November 1908): 10865–66.

"Going to California." *Country Life* 12 (December 1907): 131.

Goldthwait, J. W. "A Town That Has Gone Down Hill." *Geographical Review* 17 (October 1927): 527–52.

Goodale, R. L. "Getting New Business and Holding the Old as Applied to Electric Central Stations." *Cassier's Magazine* 31 (November 1906): 58–62.

"Good Living from Poultry." *Garden Magazine* 14 (November 1911): 193.

Goodrich, E. P. "The Pedestrian in City Traffic." *Landscape Architecture Quarterly* 7 (July 1917): 195–97.

Gordon, Reginald. "The Electrification of American Railways." *Engineering Magazine* 49 (April 1915): 34–42.

Gordon, William R. *Ninety-Four Years of Rochester Railways*. Albion, N.Y.: Eddy, 1975.

"Gracious, Samuel." *Life* 38 (October 17, 1901): 303.

"Grade Crossings: A Step Backward." *Outlook* 101 (May 18, 1912): 95–96.

"Grade-Crossing Accidents Hit Six-Year High." *Science News Letter* 32 (October 2, 1937): 212–13.

"Grade Crossing Problem as Handled by the California Railroad Commission." *American City, Town and Country Edition* 16 (June 1917): 569–72.

"Grade-Crossing Scandal." *Scientific American* 109 (July 26, 1913): 62.

"Grade Crossing Separations Increase Crashes." *Science Digest* 13 (January 1943): 82.

Grahame, A. "Railroad Crossing." *Collier's* 114 (August 26, 1944): 50–55.

"The Grand Central Depot in New York: How the Trains are Handled." *Railway Age* 4 (April 1, 1880): 180.

"Grand Central Depot Signal System." *Scientific American* 33 (December 25, 1875): 399, 402.

"Grand Central Station Improvements." *Scientific American* 88 (January 17, 1907): 39–40.

"Grand Central Terminal Opens Its Doors." *New York Times*, February 2, 1913, section T, 1.

Grant, H. Roger. "Electric Traction Promotion in the South Iowa Cornfields." *Palimpsest* 58 (1977): 18–31.

———, and Charles W. Bohi. *The Country Railroad Station in America*. Boulder, Col.: Pruett, 1978.

———, and Donovan L. Hofsommer. "'Katy' Depots of Oklahoma: A Pictorial History." *The Chronicles of Oklahoma* 52 (Fall 1974): 331–41.

Great Northern Railway Company. *Valley, Plain and Peak: Scenes on the Line*. St. Paul, 1898.

"Great Subterranean Railway Junction." *Scientific American* 103 (November 19, 1910): 393, 398.

"Greatest Railroad Station in the World." *Harper's Weekly* 56 (May 25, 1912): 14.

Greenberg, Dolores. *Financiers and Railroads: 1869–1889: A Study of Morton, Bliss, & Co.* Newark, Del.: Univ. of Delaware Press, 1980.

Greenberg, William T., and Frederick Kramer. *The Handsomest Trains in the World*. New York: Quadrant, 1980.

Gregory, Eliot. "A Nation in a Hurry." *Atlantic Monthly* 85 (May 1900): 609–13.

Grigson, Geoffrey. "The Room Outdoors." *Landscape* 4 (Winter 1954/55): 25–29.

Grimm, Jacob, and Wilhelm Grimm. *German Folk Tales* [1857]. Trans. Francis P. Magoun and Alexander H. Krappe. Carbondale: Southern Illinois Univ. Press, 1960.

Grombrich, E. H. *Art and Illusion: A Study in the Psychology of Pictorial Representation*. Princeton: Princeton Univ. Press, 1960.

Grow, Lawrence. *On the 8:02*. New York: Mayflower, 1979.

"Guarding the Country Crossing." *Illustrated World* 25 (August 1916): 778–79.

Guerin, Jules. "Grand Central." *Scientific American* 107 (December 7, 1912): cover.

Guyan, Walter Ulrich. "Die mittelalterlichen Wüstlegungen als archäologisches und geographisches Problem dargelegt an einigen Beispielen aus dem Kanton Schaffhausen." *Zeitschrift für Schweizerische Geschichte* 26 (1946): 433–78.

Häberle, Daniel. *Die Wüstungen der Rheinpflatz, Beiträge zur Landeskunde der Reheinpfalz*. Kaiserlauten, 1922.

Hale, D. E. *What and How to Feed Poultry*. Mount Morris, Ill.: Poultry Tribune, 1915.

Hall, Gilbert P. "Study for a Power House." *American Architect* 136 (August 5, 1929): 183.

Hall, Keppele. "A Model Power Station." *Electrical Age* 35 (December 1905): 401–11.

Hall, L. C. "Telegraph Talk and Talkers." *McClure's* 18 (January 1902): 227–31.

Hall Switch and Signal Company. *General Catalogue* New York: Hall Signal Company, n.d. [ca. 1910].

Hallett, F. W. *Plans for Poultry Houses*. Indianapolis: Inland Poultry Journal, 1919.

Hamblen, Herbert E. *We Win: The Life and Adventures of a Young Railroader*. New York: Doubleday, 1899.

Hamilton Watch Company. "Hamilton Watches." *National Geographic* 23 (July 1912): 1.

Hancock, W. P. "The Organization of Working Forces in Large Power Houses." *Electrical Age* 34 (June 1905): 407–12.

"Handling the Baggage." *New York Times*, February 2, 1913, section T, 3.

Harger, Charles M. "The Country Store." *Atlantic Monthly* 95 (January 1905): 91–98.

Harriman, Karl E. "The Trolley Car as a Social Factor." *World Today* 10 (February 1906): 137–44.

Harriman, Mrs. Oliver. *Book of Etiquette*. New York: Greenberg, 1942.

Hart, John Fraser. "The Dying Village and Some Notions About Urban Growth." *Economic Geography* 44 (October 1968): 313–49.

Hart, Joseph K. "Power and Culture." *Survey* 51 (March 1, 1924): 625–28.

Hartt, Mary Bronson. "Beautifying the Ugly Things." *World's Work* 9 (February 1905): 5859–68.

Hartt, Rollin Lynde. "The Mountaineers: Our Own Lost Tribes." *Century* 95 (January 1918): 395–404.

———. "A New England Hill Town." *Atlantic Monthly* 83 (April and June 1899): 561–74, 712–20.

———. "New England: The National Wallflower." *Century* 93 (November 1916): 43–56.

Hatch, Alden. *American Express*. New York: Doubleday, 1950.

Hatch, Heather S. "Graphic Arts on the Arizona Frontier: Railroad Stations and Roundhouses." *Journal of Arizona History* 12 (Summer 1971): 101–11.

Hawthorne, Nathaniel. *Mosses from an Old Manse*. [1845]. Reprint. Boston: Houghton, 1882.

Hayes, William Edward. "Man Failure." *Railroad Stories* 10 (February 1933): 40–67.

Hedges, James B. "The Colonization Work of the Northern Pacific Railroad." *Mississippi Valley Historical Review* 13 (December 1926): 311–42.

"Hell Gate Arch Details." *Engineering Record* 70 (September 12, 1914): 393.

"Hell Gate Steel Arch Bridge." *Engineering News* 71 (January 8, 1914): 59–64.

Henderson, A. "In Praise of Bridges." *Harper's Monthly* 121 (November 1910): 925–33.

Hennick, Louis C., and E. Harper Charlton. *The Streetcars of New Orleans*. Gretna, La.: Pelican, 1965.

Henry, H. H. "The Way to Make a Good Lawn." *Suburban Life* 10 (March 1910): 143–45.

Herrick, Robert. "The Background of the American Novel." *Yale Review* 3 (January 1914): 213–33.

———. *The Memoirs of an American Citizen.* [1905]. Reprint. Ed. Daniel Aaron. Cambridge: Harvard Univ. Press, 1963.

Hertz, Louis H. *Riding the Tinplate Rails.* Ramsey, N.J.: Model Craftsman, 1944.

Hicks, John D. *Republican Ascendancy, 1921–1933.* New York: Harper, 1960.

"High Speed and Good Rails." *Scientific American* 107 (December 7, 1912): 476.

Higham, John. "The Reorientation of American Culture in the 1890s." In *The Origins of Modern Consciousness,* ed. John Weiss. Detroit: Wayne State Univ. Press, 1965.

Hilfer, Anthony Channell. *The Revolt from the Village: 1915–1930.* Chapel Hill: Univ. of North Carolina Press, 1969.

Hill, Ralph Nading. *Vermont Album.* Brattleboro: Stephen Greene, 1974.

Hillman, H. W. "Electricity in the Home." *Cassier's Magazine* 31 (November 1906): 25–35.

Hilton, George W., and John F. Due. *The Electric Interurban Railways in America.* Stanford: Stanford Univ. Press, 1950.

Hine, Charles De Lano. "Gossip of the Switch-Shanty." *Century* 62 (September 1901): 685–90.

———. "What a Train-Dispatcher Does." *Century* 62 (August 1901): 594–603.

Hine, Lewis W. "Cast of Characters." *Survey* 51 (March 1, 1924): 594–600.

———. *Men at Work.* New York: Macmillan, 1932.

———. "Some Tools of the Trade." *Survey* 51 (March 1, 1924): 629–33.

History of the Engineering, Construction and Equipment of the Pennsylvania Railroad Company's New York Terminal and Approaches. Ed. William Couper. New York: Blanshard, 1912.

Hoffman, Robert Fulkerson. "Morley Puts One Over." *Railroad Man's Magazine* 1 (January 1930): 194–206.

Hogg, Alex. *The Railroad as an Element in Education.* Louisville: Morton, 1897.

Holbrook, Stewart H. *The Yankee Exodus: An Account of Migration from New England.* New York: Macmillan, 1950.

Holmes, Oliver Wendell. *Complete Poetical Works.* Ed. Horace E. Scudder. Boston: Houghton, 1895.

Holmes, Roy Hinman. "The Passing of the Farmer." *Atlantic Monthly* 110 (October 1912): 517–23.

"Home Lawn." *Harper's Monthly* 66 (April 1883): 722–33.

Hooper, Charles Edward. "The Reclamation of the Old Colonial Farmhouse." *Country Life* 16 (October 1909): 617–20, 646.

Horgan, Paul. *Main Line West.* New York: Harper, 1936.

Howe, F. C. "American City of Tomorrow." *Hampton's Magazine* 26 (May 1911): 573–84.

Howells, William Dean. *A Hazard of New Fortunes.* New York: Harper, 1890.

———. *The Lady of the Aroostook.* Boston: Houghton, 1879.

———. *The Parlor Car.* Boston: Houghton, 1904.

———. *The Sleeping Car.* Boston: Osgood, 1883.

———. *Suburban Sketches.* New York: Hurd, 1871.

———. *The Vacation of the Kelwyns: An Idyl of the Middle Eighteen-Seventies.* New York: Harper, 1920.

Howes, Ethel Puffer. "The Aesthetic Value of Efficiency." *Atlantic Monthly* 110 (July 1912): 81–91.

Hubbard, C. L. "The Unit Power Plant." *Brickbuilder* 22 (March–June 1913): 33–38, 59–62, 81–84, 109–12.

Hubbard, Freeman H. *Railroad Avenue: Great Stories and Legends of American Railroading.* New York: McGraw-Hill, 1945.

Huebner, Paul. "Railroad Gardening." *Horticulture* 3 (March 10, 1906): 288–89.

Huisman, Denis and Georges Patrix. *L'Esthétique industrielle*. Paris: Presses Universitaires de France, 1961.

Hume, John F. "Are We a Nation of Rascals?" *North American Review* 139 (August 1884): 127–44.

Hungerford, Edward. "The Greatest Railway Terminal in the World." *Outlook* 102 (December 28, 1912): 900–11.

———. "The Human Side of a City Railroad." *Harper's Weekly* 53 (August 7, 1909): 10–12, 32.

———. *The Run of the Century*. New York: New York Central, 1938.

Hutton, William R. *The Washington Bridge over the Harlem River*. New York: Rosenberg, 1890.

"Hyde Park." *Life* 9 (September 23, 1940): 53–56.

"Hydrangea as a Lawn Shrub." *Country Life* 16 (October 1909): 680–82.

"Improved Lawn Cleaner." *Scientific American* 63 (September 20, 1890): 178.

"Improved Lawn Mower." *Scientific American* 73 (August 17, 1895): 100.

"Improved Lawn Mower." *Scientific American* 73 (December 14, 1895): 372.

"Improvement of Lawns." *Horticulturist* 3 (1853): 147–48.

"Inexpensive but Practical Poultry House." *Country Life* 15 (March 1909): 504.

Ingersoll, Ernest. "The 'Trolley' Near New York." *Harper's Weekly* 40 (August 1, 1896): 755.

Inglis, William. "New York's New Gateway." *Harper's Weekly* 57 (February 1, 1913): 13, 20.

Ingram, J. S. *The Centennial Exposition*. Philadelphia: Hubbard, 1876.

"Insurance Rates and Power House Construction." *Street Railway Review* 4 (March 15, 1894): 149–50.

"Interurban Railroad and Land Values." *Technical World* 21 (June 1914): 572–74.

Jackson, John Brinckerhoff. *American Space: The Centennial Years, 1865–1876*. New York: Norton, 1972.

———. "Ghosts at the Door." *Landscape* 1 (Autumn 1951): 3–9.

———. *The Necessity for Ruins and Other Topics*. Amherst: Univ. of Massachusetts Press, 1980.

Jakle, John A. *The American Small Town: Twentieth-Century Place Images*. Hamden, Conn.: Shoe String, 1981.

James, Henry. *The American Scene*. New York: Harper, 1907.

James, Thomas L. "The Railway Mail Service." *Scribner's* 5 (March 1889): 258–77.

James, William. *The Principles of Psychology*. [1890]. Reprint. New York: Dover, 1950.

Jenkins, Dorothy H. "A Child's Own Garden." *Good Housekeeping* 106 (April 1938): 222, 240–41.

Jenkins, W. H. "My Experience with a Three-Acre Farm." *Country Life* 18 (May 1910): 56, 96.

Jewett, Sarah Orne. "The Foreigner." *Atlantic Monthly* 86 (August 1900): 152–67.

Johnson, Albert L. "The Trolley Age." *Independent* 53 (April 11, 1901): 841–43.

Johnson, Clifton. "The Deserted Homes of New England." *Cosmopolitan* 15 (May–October 1893): 213–22.

———. *The Farmer's Boy*. New York: Appleton, 1894.

Johnson, Emory R. *American Railway Transportation*. Rev. ed. New York: Appleton, 1905.

Jones, C. M. "Highways of Power." *Overland* 55 (April 1910): 404–13.

"Jones and Laughlin Aliquippa Works." *Iron Age* 91 (January 2, 1913): 23–29.

Kavanagh, Charles J. "Some Aspects of the Power Problem for the Textile Industries." *Cassier's Magazine* 34 (August 1908): 371–80.

Kellaway, Herbert J. *How to Lay Out Suburban Home Grounds*. New York: Wiley, 1915.

Kellogg, Paul U. "The Play of a Big Man with a Little River." *Survey* 51 (March 1, 1924): 637–42, 658, 661, 664.

Kerr, Alvah Milton. "In Front of the Stampede: A Story of the Frontier Railroad and the Plains." *McClure's* 14 (August 1900): 510–19.

———. "The Luck of the Northern Mail." *McClure's* 14 (January 1900): 23–35.

Kershaw, J. B. C. "Industrial Smoke and Its Prevention." *Cassier's Magazine* 27 (December 1905): 109–14.

———. "Smoke Abatement." *Cassier's Magazine* 29 (June 26, 1909): 335–41.

Kessler, Ethel, and Leonard Kessler. *All Aboard the Train*. New York: Doubleday, 1964.

Kester, Vaughan. *The Manager of the B&A*. New York: Harper, 1901.

Kimball, Arthur Reed. "The Master of Edgewood." *Scribner's* 27 (February 1900): 184–93.

Kimball, Frederick H. "The Widening Use of Small Electric Motors." *Cassier's Magazine* 27 (February–March 1905): 291–302, 363–71.

Kindled Courage. Los Angeles: Universal Pictures, 1923.

King, Thomas Starr. *The White Hills: Their Legends, Landscape and Poetry*. Boston: Estes and Lauriat, 1887.

Kipling, Rudyard. ".007." *The Day's Work*. New York: Doubleday, 1898.

Kirkland, Edward C. *Industry Comes of Age: Business, Labor, and Public Policy, 1860–1897*. New York: Holt, 1961.

Klein, Maury. *History of the Louisville and Nashville Railroad*. New York: Macmillan, 1972.

Kling, Peter M. *Why a Boy Should Learn a Trade: The Workman as a Citizen; Reward for Skill and Energy*. Pittsburgh: Smith, 1906.

Knowlton, H. S. "The Field of Electric Alternating-Current Service." *Cassier's Magazine* 31 (February 1907): 353–56.

———. "Handling Coal for the Power House." *Cassier's Magazine* 27 (April 1905): 480–81.

———. "Reinforced Concrete in Power Station Construction." *Cassier's Magazine* 31 (April 1907): 486–506.

Koester, F. "Bridges and Bridge Approaches." *American City* 8 (May 1913): 467–72.

———. "Bridges of Might and Beauty." *Craftsman* 25 (February 1914): 437–46.

Kramer, Frederick A. *Pennsylvania-Reading Seashore Lines*. Ambler, Penn.: Crusader, 1980.

"Lackawanna Route." *Life* 38 (August 22, 1901): 142.

Lancaster, Clay, and Lawrence Grow. *Waiting for the 5:05*. New York: Main Street, 1977.

Lane, John J. *Trolley Wayfinder*. Boston: New England Street Railway Club, 1909.

Larcom, Lucy. *A New England Girlhood*. Boston: Houghton, 1899.

"Latham's Grass Collector for Lawn Mowers." *Scientific American* 65 (July 4, 1891): 5.

Lauis, Fred. *Building the New Rapid Transit System of New York City*. New York: Engineering News, 1915.

Laut, Agnes C. "Abandoned Farm." *Collier's* 44 (February 12, 1910): 18–19.

"Lawn." *Horticulturist* 20 (April 1865): 97–101.

"Lawn Mower Attachment." *Scientific American* 78 (March 19, 1898): 180.

"Lawn-Planting for City and Country." *Scribner's* 18 (June 1879): 249–55.

"Lawns and Tennis Grounds." *Scientific American* 74 (May 9, 1896): 295.

Layton, E. T. *The Revolt of the Engineers*. Cleveland: Case Western Reserve Univ. Press, 1971.

Learned, J. E. "Suggestion for Summer: N. S. Bachelder's Pamphlet on New Hampshire's Abandoned Farms." *Nation* 50 (March 6, 1890): 195–96.

Lee, Gerald Stanley. "The Poetry of a Machine Age." *Atlantic Monthly* 85 (June 1900): 756–63.

LeGallienne, Richard. "Jitneying in the Berkshires." *Harper's Monthly* 139 (September 1919): 534–46.

Leggett, Mortimer D. *A Dream of a Modest Prophet*. Philadelphia: Lippincott, 1890.

Leland, H. L. "The Farm and the Home." *Agriculture of Maine* 26 (1882): 80–90.

Leslie, Miriam Florence. *California: A Pleasure Trip from Gotham to the Golden Gate*. New York: Carleton, 1877.

Let Us Make a Beautiful City. Springfield, Mass.: Republican, 1901.

Leverage, Henry. *The Purple Limited: A Detective Story*. New York: Chelsea, 1926.

Lewis, Edward A. *New England Country Depots*. Strasburg, Penn.: Baggage Car, 1973.

Lewis, Harry R. *Productive Poultry Husbandry*. Philadelphia: Lippincott, 1919.

Lewis, O. F. "The Tramp Problem." American Academy of Political and Social Studies, *Annals* 40 (March 1912): 217–27.

Lewis, Peirce F. "Small Town in Pennsylvania." Association of American Geographers, *Annals* 62 (1972): 323–51.

Lewis, Sinclair. *Babbitt*. New York: Harcourt, 1922.

———. *Main Street*. New York: Collier, 1920.

Lincoln, J. T. "City of the Dinner Pail." *Outlook* 85 (February 9, 1907): 317–24.

Lincoln, Joseph C. *The Depot Master*. New York: Appleton, 1910.

Lindenthal, Gustav. "Rebuilding the Monongahela Bridge." American Society of Civil Engineers, *Transactions* 12 (1883): 353–61.

Lingeman, Richard. *Small Town America: A Narrative History, 1620 to the Present*. Boston: Houghton, 1980.

"Linking New England with the South and West." *Harper's Weekly* 53 (September 18, 1909): 25.

Lionel Company. *Catalogue for 1929*. New York, 1928.

Livingston, Leon Ray. *Here and There with A-no.1*. Erie, Penn.: A-no.1, 1921.

"Locomotive Cranes for Coal Handling." *Electrical Age* 36 (January 1906): 66–67.

Loewy, Raymond. *Industrial Design*. New York: Overlook, 1979.

———. *The Locomotive*. New York: Studio, 1937.

London, Jack. "Hoboes that Pass in the Night." *Cosmopolitan* 44 (December 1907): 190–97.

———. *The Road*. New York: Macmillan, 1907.

Long Island Lighting Company. *The Story of Our Twenty-Five Years of Service to Long Island, 1911 to 1936*. New York, 1936.

"Look Over the Great Pacific Northwest." *Good Housekeeping* 106 (March 1938): 182.

Lord, Walter. *A Night to Remember*. New York: Bantam, 1955.

Loring, George B. *The Farm Yard Club of Jotham*. Boston: Lockwood, 1876.

Love, Edmund G. *The Situation in Flushing*. New York: Harper, 1965.

Lovecraft, H. P. *The Colour out of Space*. [1927]. Reprint. Ed. Frank Belknap Long. New York: Harcourt, 1978.

Lucas, Clinton W. *A Trolley Honeymoon from Delaware to Maine*. New York: Hazen, 1904.

Lynde, Francis. *The Taming of the Red Butte Western*. New York: Grosset and Dunlap, 1910.

McCabe, James. *The Illustrated History of the Centennial Exposition*. Philadelphia: National, 1876.

McCook, J. J. "A Tramp Census and Its Revelations." *Forum* 15 (August 1893): 753–66.

McFarland, J. H. "How to Improve Railroad Stations and Their Surroundings." *American City* 9 (November 1913): 440–44.

McFarland, J. Horace. "My Growing Garden: The Planning and the Catalogues." *Countryside Magazine* 20 (February 1915): 79–80, 118.

MacKaye, Benton. *The New Exploration: A Philosophy of Regional Planning*. New York: Harcourt, 1928.

———, and Lewis Mumford. "Townless Highways for the Motorist: A Proposal for the Automobile Age." *Harper's Monthly* 163 (August 1931): 347–56.

MacLaren, Malcolm. *The Rise of the Electrical Industry in the Nineteenth Century*. Princeton: Princeton Univ. Press, 1943.

McMahon, John R. *Success in the Suburbs: How to Locate, Buy, and Build*. New York: Putnam's, 1917.

"Machine for Burning Weeds along Railroads." *Scientific American* 98 (June 13, 1908): 429.

Malezieux, M. *Travaux publics des Etats-Unis d'Amérique en 1870*. Paris: Dunod, 1873.

Malloch, Douglas. "The Steel Road." *Literary Digest* 49 (November 21, 1914): 1022.

Manfred, Frederick. *The Chokecherry Tree*. [1948]. Reprint. Ed. Delbert E. Wylder. Albuquerque: Univ. of New Mexico Press, 1975.

Manning, Warren H. *Suggestions for Beautifying the House, Village and Roadway*. Philadelphia: American Civic Association, 1910.

———. "The History of Village Improvement in the United States." *Craftsman* 5 (February 1904): 423–32.

Edwin Markham. *The Man with the Hoe*. San Francisco: A. M. Robertson, 1899.

Marshall, D. "Problem of the Broken Rail." *McClure's* 29 (August 1907): 428–33.

Marshall, Douglas G. "Hamlets and Villages in the United States: Their Place in the American Way of Life." *American Sociological Review* 11 (April 1946): 159–65.

Marx, Leo. *The Machine in the Garden: Technology and the Pastoral Ideal in America*. New York: Oxford, 1964.

Masury, John W. *Masury's Ready-Made "Railroad" Colors: The Only Standard Line*. New York: John W. Masury and Son, Co., 1880.

Maurice, Arthur Bartlett, and Vernon Howe Bailey. *Magical City*. New York: Scribner's, 1935.

Mayer, Harold Melvin. *Railway Pattern of Metropolitan Chicago*. Chicago: Univ. of Chicago, 1943.

Maynard, Samuel T. "How to Have a Good Lawn." *Suburban Life* 2 (April 1906): 179–80.

———."Laying Out the Grounds of a Country Home." *Suburban Life* 9 (August 1905): 13–14.

Mayo, Earl. "The Biggest Steamship." *McClure's* 15 (May 1900): 64–73.

Meade, C. A. "Disposal in New York." *Municipal Affairs* 2 supplement (June 1898), 101–22.

Mead, E. D. "The Editor's Table." *New England Magazine* 4 (July 1891): 675–77.

Mead, Peter B. *Our Farm of Four Acres and the Money We Made By It*. New York: Saxton, 1860.

"Mechanical Interlocking Switch and Signal System at the Grand Central Depot, New York." *Scientific American* 62 (February 15, 1890): 97, 102.

Meeks, Carroll L. V. *The Railroad Station: An Architectural History*. New Haven: Yale Univ. Press, 1956.

Meigs, Cornelia Lynde. *Railroad West*. Boston: Little, Brown, 1937.

Melville, Herman. *Israel Potter: His Fifty Years of Exile*. 1855. Reprint. Ed. Alfred Kazin. New York: Warner, 1974.

Mencken, H. L. "The Divine Afflatus." In *Prejudices: Second Series*. New York: Knopf, 1920.

Merriman, Mansfield. *A Textbook on Roofs and Bridges*. 4 vols. New York: Wiley, 1901–32.

Merwin, Samuel. *The Road Builders*. New York: Macmillan, 1905.

"Method of Utilizing Old Streetcars." *Scientific American* 84 (June 29, 1901): 409.

Metropolitan Improvements Commission. *Public Improvements for the Metropolitan District*. Boston: Wright and Potter, 1909.

Middleton, William D. *Grand Central*. San Marino, Calif.: Golden West, 1977.

———. *The Interurban Era*. Milwaukee: Kalmbach, 1970.

———. *The Time of the Trolley*. Milwaukee: Kalmbach, 1967.

———. *When the Steam Roads Electrified*. Milwaukee: Kalmbach, 1974.

Midnight Express. New York: Columbia Pictures, 1924.

Midnight Flyer. New York: R-C Pictures, 1925.

Midnight Special. New York: Chesterfield Motion Picture Company, 1930.

Milburn, George. *The Hobo's Hornbook*. New York: Ives Washburn, 1930.

———. "Poesy in the Jungles." *American Mercury* 20 (May 1930): 83–84.

Miner, W. M. "Telegraphing 1000 Words a Minute." *St. Nicholas* 37 (March 1910): 462–64.

"Miniature Trains." *Fortune* 6 (December 1932): 41–43, 110, 113.

"Mission of Country Life Magazines." *Suburban Life* 9 (August 1905): 3.

Missouri Pacific Railroad Company. "Map of the Missouri Pacific Railway." Chicago: Rand, McNally, 1894.

Mitchell, Donald G. *Bound Together: A Sheaf of Papers*. New York: Scribner's, 1907.

———. "The Country House." *Scribner's* 8 (September 1890): 313–35.

———. *Doctor Johns: Being a Narrative of Certain Events in the Life of an Orthodox Minister of Connecticut*. New York: Scribner's, 1864.

———. *Dream Life: A Fable of the Seasons*. New York: Scribner's, 1851.

———. *My Farm of Edgewood: A Country Book*. New York: Scribner's, 1863.

———. "The Farmer's Homestead, and Its Relation to Farm Thrift." *Agriculture of Massachusetts for 1876*. Boston: Wright, 1877.

———. "Fences and Divisions of Farm Lands." Connecticut Board of Agriculture, *Report, 1875–1876*. Hartford: Case, Lockwood, 1876.

———. *Fresh Gleanings, or a New Sheaf from the Old Fields of Continental Europe*. New York: Harper, 1847.

———. "Hints about Farming." *New Englander* 18 (November 1860): 889–907.

———. "Landscape Gardening." *American Review* 5 (March 1847): 295–306.

———. "Landscape Gardening and Rural Architecture." *New Englander* 1 (April 1843): 203–15.

———. "Letters." *Cultivator* 1 and 2 (November 1844–April 1845) [pagination erratic].

———. *Out-of-Town Places: With Hints for their Improvement*. [1867]. Reprint. New York: Scribner's, 1884.

———. *Report . . . on the Lay-Out of East Rock Park*. New Haven: Punderson, 1882.

———. *Reveries of a Bachelor: A Book of the Heart*. [1850]. Reprint. New York: Scribner's, 1884.

———. "A Scattering Shot at Some Ruralities." *Scribner's* 6 (October 1889): 507–12.

———. *Seven Stories with Basement and Attic*. New York: Scribner's, 1884.

———. "A Talk about the Year." *Atlantic Almanac for 1868*. Boston: Atlantic, 1868.

———. *Wet Days at Edgewood*. [1865]. Reprint. New York: Scribner's, 1894.

———. "What Farmers Should Live For." *New England Farmer* 10 (February 1858): 75–79.

"Modern Methods of Telephone and Telegraph Line Construction." *Electrical Age* 34 (May 1905): 321–25.

"Modern Terminal Supplies Patrons with Home Comforts." *New York Times*, February 2, 1913, section T, 3.

"Monumental Gateway to a Great City." *Scientific American* 107 (December 7, 1912): 475, 484–89, 499–501.

Morrow, Lester William Wallace. *Electric Power Stations*. New York: McGraw-Hill, 1927.

"Motor Lawn Mower." *Scientific American* 77 (November 13, 1897): 314.

Mott, David C. "Abandoned Towns, Villages, and Post Offices of Iowa." *Annals of Iowa* 17 and 18 (October 1930–October 1931): 435–65, 513–43, 579–99, 42–69, 117–48.

"Mount Morris Electric Light Company." *Electrical Review* 16 (March 15, 1890): 1–3.

"Mowing Machines for Lawns." *Horticulturist* 5 (June 1855): 292.

Munden, Kenneth W., ed. *The American Film Institute Catalog*. New York: Bowker, 1971.

Munson, W. M. "Abandoned Farms and Their Capabilities." *Horticulture* 3 (May 12, 1906): 620–21.

Murphy, A. "Station Grounds for Town Betterment." *House and Garden* 50 (August 1926): 88–89.

Murray, Thomas Edward. *Electric Power Plants*. New York, 1910.

"My Farm of Edgewood." *American Agriculturist* 23 (January 1864): 6.

"My Farm of Edgewood." *Country Gentleman* 6 (1864): 137–38, 325.

Nadworny, Milton J. "Frederick Taylor and Frank Gilbreth: Competition in Scientific Management." *Business History Review* 31 (Spring 1957): 23–24.

National Association of Real Estate Boards. *A Home of Your Own and What It Means to You*. Chicago: Folsom, 1922.

National Board of Fire Underwriters. *Building Code.* [1905]. Rev. ed. New York: National Board, 1922.

Neal, David. *The History of New England.* London: J. Clark, 1720.

Nebel, Frederick. *Sleepers East.* Boston: Little, Brown, 1933.

Nelson, David. *Managers and Workers: Origins of the New Factory System in the United States.* Madison: Univ. of Wisconsin Press, 1975.

"New Dining and Cafe Smoking Cars for the Burlington." *Railroad Gazette* 40 (March 2, 1906): 207.

"New Grand Central Station in New York." *House and Garden* 7 (February 1905): 63–65.

"New Grand Central Terminal." *Scientific American* 107 (December 7, 1912): 473.

"New Grand Central Terminal Station." *Engineering News* 69 (May 1, 1913): 883–95.

"New Grand Central Terminal Station." *Scientific American* 99 (December 5, 1908): 410–12, 417–18.

"New Polyphase Plant of the Commonwealth Electric Company." *Western Electrician* 27 (January 12, 1901): 29–34.

"New Power Houses of the West Chicago Street Railroad Company." *Street Railway Review* 4 (May 15, 1894): 285–89.

"New Susquehanna Bridge, Pennsylvania Railroad." *Scientific American* 97 (November 16, 1907): 362–63.

"New Trains." *Architectural Forum* 69 (September 1938): 175–82.

"New York and Long Island Extension of the Pennsylvania Railroad: The Long Island City Power Station." *Electrical Age* 36 (April 1906): 295–301.

New York and New England Railroad Company. *Literature of the Road.* Philadelphia: Baker, 1882.

"New York Central Four-Track Drawbridge over the Harlem River." *Railroad Gazette* 28 (February 21, 1896): 122–24.

"New York Edison Power Station." *Scientific American* 87 (September 6, 1902): 147, 152.

New York Railroad Commission. *Report on Tests of Street Car Brakes in 1899.* Albany: Brandow, 1900.

"New York Terminal Station of the Pennsylvania." *Railroad Gazette* 37 (September 23, 1904): 359–62.

"New York's New Pennsylvania Railroad Terminal." *Collier's* 45 (April 16, 1910): 12.

"New York's 70,000 Horse Power." *Scientific American* 82 (January 13, 1900): 26.

Newland, J. J. "Planning a Poultry House." *American Homes* 9 (August 1912): 1.

Nicholson, John Eliot. *Looking Back 100 Years.* New York: Nicholson and Galloway Roofing Company, 1947.

Nicholson, Marjorie Hope. *Mountain Gloom and Mountain Glory.* New York: Norton, 1962.

Night Flyer. New York: James Cruze, Inc./Pathé, 1928.

Nisbet, D. F. "Machine Shop Roofs." *Cassier's Magazine* 29 (December 1905): 152–54.

Normano, J. F. "Social Utopias in American Literature." *International Review for Social History* 3 (1938): 287–99.

Norton, John P. "Letter No. VIII." *Cultivator* 4 (October 1847): 306.

Novak, Barbara. *Nature and Culture: American Landscape and Painting, 1825–1875.* New York: Oxford, 1980.

Nunn, P. N. "Pioneer Work in High-Tension Electric Power Transmission: The Operations of the Telluride Power Company." *Cassier's Magazine* 27 (January 1905): 171–200.

Nutter, Frank H. *Quarter Acre Possibilities.* Minneapolis: Kimball and Storer, 1898.

Oakley, Thornton. "In the Railway Yard." *Century* 73 (January 1907): 338–41.

Obermeyer, Henry. *Stop that Smoke.* New York: Harper, 1933.

Odegrad, Gordon. "Proceed, Prepared to Stop." *Model Railroader* 43 (September 1976): 54–57.

Odum, Howard, W. *Rainbow Round my Shoulder*. New York: Bobbs-Merrill, 1928.

"Oldsmobile." *Collier's* 45 (May 14, 1910): 37.

Oglesby, Paul. "The Ideal Country Home." *Horticulture* 3 (January 6, 1906): 16–17.

Olerich, Henry. *A Cityless and Countryless World*. New York, 1893.

Olmsted, Frederick Law, Jr. "Village Improvement." *Atlantic Monthly* 95 (June 1905): 798–803.

———. "Pittsburgh City Plan." *Survey* 25 (February 4, 1911): 733–53.

"One Signal Tower Controls Seventy-Nine Acres of Tracks." *New York Times*, February 2, 1913, section T, 8.

Opening Ceremonies of the New York and Brooklyn Bridge, May 24, 1883. Brooklyn, 1882.

"Opening of the New Grand Central Terminal." *Engineering Record* 67 (February 8, 1913): 144–48.

Oppenheim, James. *The Olympian*. New York: Harper, 1912.

"Our Hill Towns." Letters from the Greenfield, Massachusetts, *Gazette and Courier* deposited in the Harvard College Library.

"Overland Limited." *House Beautiful* 18 (November 1905): 64.

Overland Limited. New York: Gotham Productions, 1925.

"Pace that Kills." *World's Work* 13 (March 1907): 8595–96.

Packard, Frank L. *The Night Operator*. New York: Doran, 1919.

———. *Running Special*. London: Hodder and Stoughton, 1925.

———. *The Wire Devils*. New York: Doran, 1918.

Packard, Winthrop. "Developing a Suburban Colony." *Suburban Life* 9 (January 1905): 7–11.

Page, John. "Twenty Years of Model Railroading." *Model Railroader* 21 (January 1954): 41–45.

Paine, Albert Bigelow. "Short Vacations by Trolley." *World's Work* 6 (July 1903): 3673–78.

Paine, George S. "From the Track-Walker's Standpoint." *Scientific American* 100 (March 20, 1909): 222–23.

Paine, Ralph D. "Abandoning the Old Farm." *Colliers* 42 (June 12, 1909): 14–15.

Palliser's Model Homes . . . also Farm-Barn, Hennery, Stable. Bridgeport, Conn.: Palliser, 1878.

Parker, Carleton H. *The Casual Laborer and Other Essays*. New York: Harcourt, 1920.

Parsons, Samuel. "Lawn Planting for Winter Effect." *Atlantic Monthly* 47 (May 1881): 690–95.

Passer, Harold. *The Electrical Manufacturers, 1875–1900*. Cambridge: Harvard Univ. Press, 1953.

Peck, Bradford. *The World a Department Store: A Story of Life Under a Cooperative System*. Lewiston, Me., 1900.

Peckham, Howard H. *The Colonial Wars, 1689–1762*. Chicago: Univ. of Chicago Press, 1964.

Pennell, Joseph. "Vulcan's Capital." *Century* 80 (July 1910): 349–56.

"'Pennsy' to Spend $100,000,000 on Electrification." *Christian Science Monitor*, November 1, 1928, 1.

Pennsylvania Railroad Company. *The New York and Chicago "Limited."* Chicago [?], 1890.

Pennsylvania Railroad System. *Operating Department Rules*. Philadelphia, 1925.

"Pennsylvania Station." *House and Garden* 7 (January 1905): 56.

"Pennsylvania Station." *Architectural Review* 30 (August 1911): 65–74.

"Pennsylvania's New York Station." *Architectural Record* 27 (June 1910): 518–21.

Percy, Walker. *Love in the Ruins: The Adventures of a Bad Catholic at a Time Near the End of the World*. New York: Farrar, Strauss, 1971.

———. "The Man on the Train: Three Existential Modes." *Partisan Review* 23 (Fall 1956): 478–94.

———. *The Moviegoer*. [1960]. Reprint. New York: Avon, 1980.

Peters, R. H. "Stop, Look, and Listen." *Forum* 92 (October 1934): 239–43.

Petersham, Maud, and Miska Petersham. *The Story Book of Trains*. Chicago: Winston, 1935.

Phelps, Henry P. *Under the Turquoise Sky*. Chicago: Chicago, Rock Island, and Pacific Railway, Co., n.d. [ca. 1902].

"Philadelphia Edison Station." *Electrical Review* 16 (March 29, 1980): 2–3.

Phillips, J. H. "The Evolution of the Suburban Station." *Architectural Record* 36 (August 1914): 123–27.

Phillips, Roland Ashford. *Lee Blake, Trolley Man*. New York: Street and Smith, 1911.

Pile, John F. *Design: Purpose, Form, and Meaning*. Amherst: Univ. of Massachusetts Press, 1979.

"Pilgrimage to the Secession Shrine at Pittsburgh." *Camera Work* 2 (April 1904): 54–56.

Pinchot, Gifford. "Giant Power." *Survey* 51 (March 1, 1924): 561–62.

Pinkerton, Allan. *Strikes, Communists, Tramps, and Detectives*. New York: Carleton, 1878.

Piquet, John A. "Is the Big City Doomed as an Industrial Center?" *Industrial Management* 68 (September 1924): 139–44.

Plowden, David. *The Floor of the Sky: The Great Plains*. San Francisco: Sierra Club, 1972.

Plummer, Kathaleen Church. "The Streamlined Moderne." *Art in America* 62 (January 1974): 46–54.

Pope, Robert Anderson. "Grand Central Terminal Station, New York." *Town Planning Review* 2 (April 1911): 55–64.

"Port of New York and the Hackensack Meadows." *American Architect* 72 (June 15, 1901): 82.

Pound, Louise. *American Ballads and Songs*. New York. Scribner's, 1922.

"Poverty on the Farm." *Harper's Weekly* 46 (May 24, 1902): 676.

Powell, E. P. "The Balance Sheet of a Country Home." *Suburban Life* 3 (October 1906): 167–68, 194.

"Power Station Practice of the West Jersey and Seashore Railroad." *Street Railway Journal* 30 (October 12, 1907): 615–17.

"Prairie Preserves and Railroads." *Iowa State Parks Bulletin* 4 (July–August 1926): 25–26.

Pray, James Sturgis. *Railroad Grounds: A Study of their Design, Planting, and Relation to Community*. Minot, N.D.: American Institute of Park Executives, n.d. [ca. 1914].

"Prepared Composition Roofing." *Engineering Magazine* 45 (May 1913), 265–68.

Prince, William L. "The Beautiful City." *Craftsman* 17 (October 1909): 53–57.

Prout, H. G. "Safety in Railroad Travel." *Scribner's* 6 (September 1889): 258, 327–50.

———. "Railroad Signalling." *Harper's Weekly* 53 (October 16, 1909): 8.

Rae, W. F. *Westward by Rail: The New Route to the East*. London: Longmans, 1870.

"Railroad Station at Auburndale, Massachusetts." *Garden and Forest* 2 (March 13, 1889): 124–25.

"Railroad Station at Chestnut Hill." *Garden and Forest* 2 (April 3, 1889): 159–60, 63.

"Railroads at War: Southern Pacific Does a Tough Job." *Life* 13 (September 21, 1942): 112–23.

"Railroad University: Altoona." *Engineering Magazine* 33 (May 1907): 74.

"Railway, Church-Yard, and Cemetery Lawn-Planting." *Scribner's* 22 (July 1881): 415–19.

"Railway Crossing Signals that Fail." *Literary Digest* 33 (March 22, 1930): 104.

Railway Gardening Association. *Proceedings, Eighth Annual Convention*. New York, 1915.

"Railway Station at Waterbury, Connecticut." *Brickbuilder* 18 (September 1909): 119–23.

"Railway Station at Wellesley." *Architecture and Building News* 21 (February 26, 1887): 103–04.

Randall, D. T. "Relation of the Character of Coals to the Prevention of Smoke." *Scientific American* 67 (June 26, 1909): 402–03.

Rau, William H. "How I Photograph Railroad Scenery." *Photo-Era* 36 (June 1916): 261–66.

Reed, Robert C. *The New York Elevated*. Cranbury, N.J.: Barnes, n.d.

Reeve, Arthur B. "The Romance of Tunnel Building." *World's Work* 13 (December 1906): 8338–8352.

Reid, James D. *The Telegraph in America*. New York: Derby, 1879.

Reid, Loren. *Hurry Home Wednesday: Growing Up in a Small Missouri Town, 1905–1921*. Columbia: Univ. of Missouri Press, 1978.

Reier, Sharon. *The Bridges of New York*. New York: Quadrant, 1977.

Report of the Special Committee on Grade Crossing. Winchester, Mass., 1906.

Rice, Frederick. "Urbanizing Rural New England." *New England Magazine* 53 (January 1906): 528–41.

Rice, J. H. "The Making of a Lawn." *Suburban Life* 6 (April 1908): 244–45.

Richardson, Alfred Talbot. "Cutting Loose from the City." *Country Life* 18 (September 1910): 537–39.

Richardson, W. Symmes. "The Terminal—The Gate of the City." *Scribner's* 52 (October 1912): 401–16.

"Ride the Most Beautiful Train in America." *Good Housekeeping* 106 (March 1938): 167.

Rideing, William H. "The Building of an 'Ocean Greyhound.'" *Scribner's* 5 (April 1889): 431–42.

Riegel, Robert Edgar. *The Story of the Western Railroads*. New York: Macmillan, 1926.

Riis, Jacob. *How the Other Half Lives: Studies among the Tenements of New York*. New York: Scribner's, 1897.

Ripley, Charles M. *Romance of a Great Factory*. Schenectady, N. Y.: Gazette, 1919.

"Roadside." Ed. Donald G. Mitchell. *Atlantic Almanac for 1869*. Boston: Atlantic, 1869.

Roberts, M. "Abandoned Farm Clubs." *Country Life* 10 (June 1906): 176.

Robinson, Charles Mulford. *Suburban Station Grounds*. Boston: Boston & Albany Railroad Company, 1905.

Robinson, Edwin Arlington. *Selected Poems*. Ed. Morton Dauwen Zabel. London: Collier, 1965.

Robinson, John H. "The ABC of Poultry Keeping." *Suburban Life* 2 (March 1906): 128–30.

Roemer, Kenneth M. *America as Utopia*. New York: Burt Franklin, 1980.

———. *The Obsolete Necessity: America in Utopian Writings, 1888–1900*. Kent, Ohio: Kent State Univ. Press, 1976.

Rollins, F. W. "Abandoned Farm in New Hampshire." *Country Life* 18 (September 1910): 531–34.

Roorbach, Eloise. "A Seaside House that Fits Its Site." *House and Garden* 16 (June 1914): 453–55, 485–86.

Roosevelt, Robert B. *Five Acres Too Much*. New York: Harper, 1869.

Root, Wendy, and Richard de Rochemont. *Eating in America*. New York: William Morrow, 1976.

Ross, Olin J. *The Sky Blue: A Tale of the Iron Horse*. Columbus, Ohio, 1904.

Roux, Jean-Michel. *Territoire sans Lieux*. Paris: Dunod, 1980.

Rowsome, Frank. *The Verse by the Side of the Road*. Brattleboro: Stephen Greene, 1965.

Ruggles, P. B. "Combination Poultry, Tool, and Feed House." *Country Life* 23 (April 1913): 67–68.

Russell, C. E. "Speed." *Hampton's Magazine* 27 (October 1911): 444–57.

Russell Sage Foundation. *Wage-Earning Pittsburgh*. New York: Survey Associates, 1914.

Samson, A. L. "Log Chicken House." *Country Life* 19 (March 1, 1911): 370.

Sanborn, Alvan. "The Future of Rural New England." *Atlantic Monthly* 80 (July 1897): 74–83.

Sanborn Map Company. *Chelsea, Massachusetts*. New York: Sanborn-Perris, 1894.

———. *Memphis, Tennessee*. New York: Sanborn-Perris, 1897.

Sandler, Martin W. *This Was Connecticut: Images of a Vanished World*. Boston: Little, Brown, 1977.

Sando, R. B. "Housing and Yarding Poultry." *Outing* 60 (April 1912): 61–66.

"Santa Fe for 1938." *Good Housekeeping* 106 (April 1935): 225.

Saroyan, William. *The Human Comedy*. New York: Harcourt, 1943.

Sasowsky, Norman. *Reginald Marsh: Engravings, Lithography*. New York: Praeger, 1936.

Saylor, Henry H. "Garden Entrances." *Country Life* 11 (March 1907): 501–06.

Schivelbusch, Wolfgang. *Geschichte der Eisenbahnreise zur Industrialisierung von Raum und Zeit im 19. Jahrhundert*. Munich: Hanser, 1977.

Schlesinger, Arthur Meier. *The Rise of the City: 1878–1898*. New York: Macmillan, 1933.

Schmidt, L. W. "Hunting for Factory Locations." *Industrial Management* 55 (June 1918): 461–64.

Schorer, Mark. *Sinclair Lewis: An American Life*. New York: McGraw-Hill, 1961.

Schott, Henry. "A City's Fight for Beauty." *World's Work* 11 (February 1906): 71–91.

Schuyler, Montgomery. "The Art of City Making." *Architectural Record* 12 (May 1902): 1–26.

Scott, Leroy. "The Railroad's Death Roll." *World's Work* 9 (January 1905): 5699–5705.

Seeley, Elizabeth Eggleston. "Abandoned Farm Again." *Century* 48 (September 1894): 791–93.

"Send Your Letters by Telegraph." *Outlook* 94 (March 19, 1910): 598–99.

Sessions, William R. *Farms in Massachusetts, Abandoned*. Boston: Wright and Potter, 1893.

"Settlement of Carville." *Country Life* 11 (March 1907): 492–92*b*.

Shadwell, Arthur. *Industrial Efficiency*. New York: Longmans, 1909.

Shaffner, Taliaferio P. *Telegraph Manual*. New York: Pudney, 1859.

Shannon, Fred A. *The Farmer's Last Frontier: 1860–1897*. New York: Rinehard, 1959.

Sharlin, Harold. *The Making of the Electrical Age*. New York: Abelard-Schumann, 1964.

Shaughnessy, Jim. *The Rutland Road*. Berkeley, Calif.: Howell-North, 1980.

"Shockless Railroad Crossing." *Literary Digest* 50 (June 12, 1915): 1399.

Shumway, Merline Henderson. *Back to the Farm*. Minneapolis: Univ. of Minnesota Agricultural Extension Division, 1915.

Shurtleff, Arthur A. "Traffic Control and its Application to the Re-Design of Copley Square, Boston." *Landscape Architecture Quarterly* 6 (January 1916): 61–71.

Siebert, C. L. *Northwestern Pennsylvania Railway*. Camp Hill, Penn., 1976.

Signal Tower. Los Angeles: Universal Pictures, 1924.

"Simpson Motor Lawn Mower." *Country Life* 12 (June 1907): 246.

Sinclair, Upton. *The Jungle*. New York: Doubleday, 1906.

Single Track. New York: Vitagraph Company of America, 1921.

Slosson, Preston W. *The Great Crusade and After, 1914–1928*. New York: Macmillan, 1930.

"Small Farms a Solution for the Evils of Overcrowded Cities and Unnatural Living." *Craftsman* 20 (June 1911): 305–12.

"Small Railroad Station." *American Architect* 100 (October 4, 1911): 293.

Smalley, E. V. "Isolation of Life on Prairie Farms." *Atlantic Monthly* 72 (September 1893): 378–82.

Smith, Arthur H. "Peak of the Load: What It Means to Light New York City and Transport Her Crowds." *Putnam's* 6 (August 1909): 519–26.

Smith, Charles C. "Empire State Express." *Photo-Era* 37 (September 1916): 130.

Smith, D. J. "The Glamor of the Glittering Rails." *Midwest Quarterly* 11 (Spring 1970): 311–26.

Smith, J. Robert. *The Prairie Garden*. Madison: Univ. of Wisconsin Press, 1980.

Smith, Rollin. "Minneapolis and the Northwest." *Harper's Weekly* 58 (April 19, 1913): 14–15.

"Smoke Nuisance." *Outlook* 90 (September 12, 1908): 53–54.

Snow, Franklin. "A Day at Grand Central Terminal." *Christian Science Monitor*, November 1, 1928, 18.

Solenberg, Alice W. *One Thousand Homeless Men*. Philadelphia: Russell Sage, 1911.

Solotaroff, William. "The City's Duty to Its Trees." *American City* 4 (March 1911): 131–34.

"Solving the Greatest Terminal Problem of the Age." *New York Times*, February 2, 1913, section T, 2.

Sonnichsen, Eric. "I Was Workin' on the Railroad." *American Mercury* 20 (June 1930): 218–22.

"South Philadelphia Works of the Westinghouse Company." *Industrial Management* 55 (June 1918): 494–97.

Souvenir Hand Book. Pittsburgh: Krebs, 1890.

Spearman, Frank H. "Bucks: A Story from the Train-Dispatcher's Office." *McClure's* 14 (November 1899): 147–53.

———. "Conductor Pat Francis." *McClure's* 15 (August 1900): 330–39.

———. *The Daughter of a Magnate*. New York: Scribner's, 1904.

———. *Held for Orders: Stories of Railroad Life*. New York: Burt, 1901.

———. "The Million Dollar Freight Train: The Story of a Young Engineer on his First Run." *McClure's* 14 (February 1900): 380–86.

———. *The Nerve of Foley and Other Railroad Stories*. New York: Harper, 1902.

———. "The Roadmaster's Story." In *Headlights and Markers*, ed. Frank P. Donovan and Robert S. Henry. New York: Creative Age, 1946.

———. "Sankey's Double-Header." *McClure's* 14 (March, 1900): 456–59.

Spears, John R. "The Story of a Lost Car." *Scribner's* 6 (July 1889): 102–15.

Speirs, Frederick W. *The Street Railway System of Philadelphia: Its History and Present Condition*. Baltimore: Johns Hopkins Univ. Press, 1897.

"Splendid Opportunity for Live Wires." *Collier's* 46 (January 7, 1911): 25.

Spring, S. N. "The Natural Replacement of White Pine on Old Fields in New England." United States Department of Agriculture, Bureau of Forestry, Bulletin No. 63. Washington, D.C.: Government Printing Office, 1905.

"Standardized Factory Buildings." *Industrial Management* 55 (April 1918): 329–30.

"Station at Stockbridge, Massachusetts." *American Architect* 41 (September 23, 1893): 187.

"Steam Turbine Power Plant of the New York, New Haven, and Hartford Railroad at Warren, Rhode Island." *Street Railway Journal* 25 (January 21, 1905): 111–12.

"Steel." *Life* 13 (October 19, 1942): 68–76.

Steele, James W. *To Mexico by Palace Car*. Chicago: Rand, McNally, 1886.

Steinberg, Alan. "Superpowerless." *Yankee* 46 (June, 1982): 52–55, 114–21.

Stilgoe, John R. *Common Landscape of America, 1580 to 1845*. New Haven: Yale Univ. Press, 1982.

———. "Donald G. Mitchell and the American Landscape." In *Public Space: Environmental Awareness in the Nineteenth Century*, ed. Peter Trowbridge. Cambridge: Harvard University Department of Landscape Architecture, 1976.

———. "Fair Fields and Blasted Rock: American Land Classification Systems and Landscape Aesthetics." *American Studies* 22 (Spring 1981): 21–33.

———. *Forest Hills Gardens*. Cambridge, Mass.: Vision, Inc. (forthcoming, 1983).

———. "Suburbanites Forever: The American Dream Endures." *Landscape Architecture* 72 (May 1982): 88–93.

———. "Town Common and Village Green in New England, 1620 to 1981." In *On Common Ground*, ed. Ronald Lee Fleming and Lauri A. Halderman. Harvard, Mass.: Harvard Common Press, 1982.

———. "The Wildering of Rural New England." New England and St. Lawrence Valley Geographical Society, *Proceedings* 10 (1980): 1–6.

Stone and Webster Engineering Corporation. *South Boston Power Station*. Boston, 1912.

"The Stone Walls of New England." *Country Life* 11 (April 1907): 690, 692.

Stover, John F. *History of the Illinois Central Railroad*. New York: Macmillan, 1975.

———. *Iron Road to the West: American Railroads in the 1850s*. New York: Columbia Univ. Press, 1978.

Stowe, Harriet Beecher. *The Minister's Wooing*. New York: Derby, 1859.

———. *Oldtown Folks*. Boston: Field, 1870.

Stratton, G. M. "Railway Disasters at Night." *Century* 74 (May 1907): 118–23.

"Streamline Toys." *Fortune* 11 (January 1935): 16, 20.

"Street-Car Houses." *House Beautiful* 18 (November 1905): 64.

Stringer, Arthur. *Power*. Indianapolis: Bobbs-Merrill, 1925.

Stuart, R. "People Act as if They Wanted to Be Killed." *American Magazine* 92 (September 1921): 38–39.

Stump, F. V. "Transformation of a Grade Crossing." *American City* 15 (September 1916): 317.

Sturgis, Russell. "Simple Ways of Fireproofing." *Architectural Record* 13 (February 1903): 119–33.

———. "Warehouse and Factory in Architecture." *Architectural Record* 15 (January–February 1904): 1–17, 122–33.

Stuyvesant, Jared. "The Vicissitudes of a Colonial Farmhouse." *Country Life* 16 (October 1909): 599–602.

Suckow, Ruth. *Country People*. New York: Knopf, 1924.

Sullivan, Alan. "Pilots of the Night." *Harper's Weekly* 56 (May 18, 1912): 14–15.

———. "The Power that Serves." *Harper's Monthly* 126 (May 1913): 848–53.

Sullivan, Mark. *Our Times: The Turn of the Century*. New York: Scribner's, 1926.

———. *Our Times: The War Begins*. New York: Scribner's, 1932.

"Sunset Limited." *National Geographic* 23 (December 1912): 2.

Suplee, Henry Harrison. "Artificial Congestion Center in Cities." *Cassier's Magazine* 34 (October 1908): 559–62.

T., R. M. "Color for the Lawn in November." *Garden and Forest* 5 (November 23, 1892): 555–56.

Tarkington, Booth. *The Gentleman from Indiana*. New York: Doubleday, 1899.

Tatum, George B. *Andrew Jackson Downing: Arbiter of American Taste, 1815–52*. State College: Pennsylvania State Univ., 1950.

Taverner, Jules. "Death on the Rail." *Harper's Weekly* 17 (May 10, 1873): 388.

Taylor, Frederick Jackson. "New England, 1830–1850." *Granite State Monthly* 61 (November 1929): 411–21.

Taylor, Frederick Winslow. *The Principles of Scientific Management*. New York: Harper, 1911.

———. *Shop Management*. New York: Harper, 1900.

———. *A Treatise on Concrete, Plain and Reinforced*. New York: Wiley, 1905.

Taylor, G. R. "Norwood and Oakley." *Survey* 29 (December 7, 1912): 287–301.

Taylor, W. L. "The Passing of the Farm." *Ladies' Home Journal* 18 (June 1901): 5.

"Terminal Trains Run by Loop System." *New York Times*, February 2, 1913, section T, 5.

Thatton, Steven D. "The Disappearing Car Track." *Harper's Weekly* 58 (January 11, 1913): 22.

Thayer, William M. *Marvels of the New West*. Norwich, Conn.: Henry Bill, 1890.

Thompson, Hugh. "The Greatest Railway Terminal in the World." *Munsey's Magazine* 45 (April 1911): 27–40.

Thompson, Warren S. "On Living in Cities." *American Mercury* 20 (June 1930): 192–201.

———. "The Future of the Large City." *American Mercury* 20 (July 1930): 327–37.

Thoreau, Henry David. *Walden*. [1854]. Reprint. Boston: Houghton, 1898.

Titley, Arthur. "Works Engine Houses." *Cassier's Magazine* 34 (July 1908): 195–201.

Tomlinson, Everett T. "The Decline of the Ministry." *World's Work* 9 (December 1904): 5635–40.

Towle, George. *American Society*. London: Chapman and Hall, 1870.

Tracy, Frank B. "The Blizzard at Imogene." *McClure's* 14 (January 1900): 263–72.

"Tram-Car Town." *Collier's* 45 (August 27, 1910): 15.

"The Tramp." *Harper's Weekly* 20 (September 2, 1876): 718–19.

Tricker, William. "Lawn Notes." *Garden and Forest* 6 (October 11, 1893): 427.

Troop, J. "The Essentials of a Good Lawn." *Garden and Forest* 9 (March 11, 1896): 106.

Trumbull, Frank. "Railway Touring in the United States." *Outlook* 115 (April 25, 1917): 744–46.

Tuan, Yi-Fu. *Landscapes of Fear*. New York: Pantheon, 1979.

Tufts, G. E. "Prairie Cabin." *New England Magazine* 24 (April 1901): 174–80.

"20th Century Flier in Up-State Wreck." *New York Times*, December 9, 1923, section 1, 7.

"Twentieth Century Limited." *Modern Plastics* 15 (July 1938): 21–23, 62, 64.

"$200.00 in Six Months from 20 Hens." *Suburban Life* 7 (November 1908): 241.

Tyrell, Henry Grattan. *Artistic Bridge Design*. Chicago: Clark, 1912.

———. *Mill Building Construction*. New York: Engineering News, 1901.

———. *Treatise on the Design and Construction of Mill Buildings and Other Industrial Plants*. Chicago: Clark, 1911.

Updegraff, Robert R. "Prophets and Pattern-Followers: How Great Industries Plan for the Next Generation." *Harper's Monthly* 139 (July 1919): 225–33.

Updike, John. "First Wives and Trolley Cars." *New Yorker* 58 (December 27, 1982): 36–39.

"Utilizing the Pressure on Railroad Rails to Operate Electric Crossing Signals." *Scientific American* 115 (November 4, 1916): 418.

Valentine, F. H. "Poultry House on the Country Place." *Country Life* 28 (October 1915): 58.

Van De Water, Virginia. *Present Day Etiquette*. New York: Burt, 1924.

Van Doren, Carl. *The American Novel, 1789 to 1939*. New York: Macmillan, 1920.

———. *Contemporary American Novelists, 1900 to 1920*. New York: Macmillan, 1922.

"Vanishing Backyards." *Fortune* 1 (May 1930): 77–81.

Varney, Theodore. "Some Details of High-Pressure Line Construction for Alternating Current Railways." *Electrical Age* 34 (May 1905): 356–60.

Veblen, Thorstein. *The Theory of the Leisure Class*. [1899]. Reprint. New York: New American Library, 1962.

Vivian, H. Hussey. *Notes of a Tour in America*. London: Stanford, 1878.

Voorhees, Theodore. "The Freight-Car Service." *Scribner's* 5 (May 1889): 568–85.

Vredenburgh, La Rue. "Sign and Decorative Lighting." *Electrical Age* 34 (June 1905): 418–25.

Vyzralek, Frank E.; H. Roger Grant; and Charles W. Bohi. "North Dakota's Depots: Standardization on the Soo Line." *North Dakota History* 42 (Winter 1975): 4–25.

Waddell, John A. L. *Bridge Engineering*. New York: Wiley, 1916.

Waldo, Harold. *The Magic Midland*. New York: Doran, 1923.

Walsh, George Ethelbert. "Traffic Congestion in New York." *Cassier's Magazine* 34 (June 1908): 151–55.

Walther, Susan Danly. "The Railroad in the Industrial Landscape." In *The Railroad in the American Landscape: A Catalog of an Exhibition*, ed. Susan Danly Walther. Wellesley: Wellesley College Museum, 1981.

Walton, James G. "Some Notable American Railway Bridges." *Cassier's Magazine* 29 (January 1906): 202–08.

Ward, Herbert D. "The Semaphore." *Scribner's* 14 (December 1893): 760–76.

Ward, John William. *Andrew Jackson: Symbol for an Age*. New York: Oxford, 1953.

Ware, John. *Home Life: What It Is, and What It Needs*. Boston: Spencer, 1868.

Waring, George. *Village Improvement and Farm Villages*. Boston: Osgood, 1877.

Warman, Cy. *Short Rails*. New York: Scribner's, 1900.

———. *Tales of an Engineer with Rhymes of the Rail*. New York: Scribner's, 1895.

———. *The White Mail*. New York: Scribner's, 1899.

Warner, Sam Bass. *Streetcar Suburbs: The Process of Urban Growth in Boston*. Cambridge: Harvard Univ. Press, 1962.

The Warning Signal. New York: Ellbee Pictures, 1926.

Waters, Don. *The Call of the Shining Steel*. New York: Chelsea House, 1928.

———. *Pounding the Rails*. New York: Chelsea House, 1928.

Watrous, A. E. "Railroad Safety Appliances." *Harper's Weekly* 37 (March 4, 1893): 203–04, 206–07.

Watson, Wilbur J. *A Decade of Bridges, 1926–36*. Cleveland: Jansen, 1937.

Waugh, F. A. *Landscape Gardening*. New York: Orange Judd, 1899.

———. "Ten-Acre Forestry." *Suburban Life* 3 (October 1906): 175–76.

Webb, Walter Loring. *Economics of Railroad Construction*. New York: Wiley, 1906.

———. *Railroad Construction: Theory and Practice*. New York: Wiley, 1900.

Weingreen, Joshua. *Electric Power Plant Engineering*. New York: McGraw-Hill, 1910.

Weisberger, Bernard A. *New Industrial Society: 1848–1900*. New York: Wiley, 1968.

Wellington, Arthur Mellen. *Economic Theory of the Location of Railways*. New York: Wiley, 1904.

Weltzer, Joseph. "The Electric Railway of Today." *Scribner's* 7 (April 1890): 425–43.

Westcott, Thomas. *Centennial Portfolio: A Souvenir of the International Exhibition at Philadelphia*. Philadelphia: Thomas Hunter, 1876.

"Western Union vs. the Pennsylvania." *Outlook* 73 (January 31, 1903): 235–36.

Westing, Fred. *Penn Station*. Seattle: Superior, 1978.

Wharton, Edith. *The Age of Innocence*. New York: Random House, 1920.

———. *Collected Short Stories*. New York: Scribner's, 1968.

———. *Ethan Frome*. [1911]. Reprint. New York: Scribner's, 1960.

———. *Summer: A Novel*. New York: Appleton, 1917.

Whitaker, John H. "Country Living in Westchester." *Country Life* 15 (March 1909): 431–34.

White, Charles Henry. "Pittsburg." *Harper's Monthly* 117 (April 1908): 901–08.

White, John H., Jr. *The American Railroad Passenger Car*. Baltimore: Johns Hopkins Univ. Press, 1978.

White, William Allen. *In the Heart of a Fool*. New York: Macmillan, 1918.

Whiting, Frank V. "Stop, Look, and Listen." *Outlook* 104 (August 23, 1913): 927–33.

Whiting, Percy H. "Home-Made Chicken Coop and Run." *Country Life* 20 (August 1, 1911): 50.

Whitman, Walt. *Leaves of Grass and Selected Prose*. Ed. John Kouwenhoven. New York: Modern Library, 1950.

Wiebe, Robert H. *Search for Order: 1877 to 1920*. New York: Hill and Wang, 1967.

Wight, Peter B. "Utilitarian Architecture in Chicago." *Architectural Record* 27 (February 1910): 189–98.

Wilder, Thornton. *Our Town*. [1938]. Reprint. New York: Harper, 1968.

Wilgus, William J. "The Electrification of the Suburban Zone." American Society of Civil Engineers, *Transactions* 61 (December 1908): 73–155.

Wilkins, Mary E. *Madelon*. New York: Harper, 1896.

Willey, Day Allen. "The Nerves of a Railway: Block Signalling Systems on American Railways." *Cassier's Magazine* 28 (August 1905): 251–68.

———. "Safety in American Railway Travel." *Cassier's Magazine* 28 (May 1905): 55–62.

Williams, Henry T. *The Pacific Tourist*. New York, 1878.

Williams, James M. *An American Town: A Sociological Study*. New York: James Kempster, 1906.

Williams, Jesse Lynch. "The Gates of the City." *Century* 74 (August 1907): 487–500.

Williams, William Carlos. *The Build-Up*. New York: Random House, 1952.

Williamson, Ellen. *When We Went First Class*. Garden City, N.Y.: Doubleday, 1977.

Wilson, Albert Frederick. "Ik Marvel and Edgewood Farm: A Revery Come True." *Outlook* 90 (October 24, 1908): 391–96.

Wilson, Edward D. "Beauty in Ugliness." *Photo-Era* 64 (June 1930): 303.

Wilson, Howard Fisher. *The Hill Country of Northern New England: Its Social and Economic History*. New York: Columbia Univ. Press, 1936.

Winser, Henry J. *The Great Northwest*. New York: Putnam's, 1883.

Wolfe, Thomas. "The Bums at Sunset." In *Short Stories*. New York: Penguin, 1947.

———. *Of Time and the River*. 1935. Reprint. New York: Scribner's, 1935.

———. *You Can't Go Home Again*. 1940. Reprint. New York: Harper, 1968.

Woods, Katherine. *The Broadway Limited: 1902–1927*. Philadelphia: Pennsylvania Railroad Company, 1927.

Woodward, C. M. *A History of the St. Louis Bridge*. St. Louis: Jones, 1881.

Worcester, Joseph E. *A Comprehensive Dictionary*. Boston: Swan, 1861.

"World's Largest Railroad Terminal, General Electric." *Scientific American* 107 (December 7, 1912): 474.

Wright, Carroll. *The Factory System as an Element in Civilization*. Boston: Williams, 1882.

———. *The Industrial Evolution of the United States*. Meadville, Penn.: Flood and Vincent, 1897.

Wright, E. A. "The Hill Town Problem." *New England Magazine* 24 (August 1901): 622.

Wright, Mabel. *The Garden of a Commuter's Wife*. New York: Macmillan, 1902.

Wright, Richard Little. "Gardening as a Sport." *House and Garden* 45 (March 1924): 70, 104.

Wyatt, J. A. "Building the Factory." *Harper's Weekly* 55 (May 20, 1911): 16.

Wyckoff, Walter A. *A Day with a Tramp*. New York: Scribner's, 1901.

———. "With Iowa Farmers." *Scribner's* 29 (May 1901): 525–36.

———. *The Workers: An Experiment in Reality: The East*. New York: Scribner's, 1897.

———. *The Workers: An Experiment in Reality: The West*. New York: Scribner's, 1898.

"Young People and Bridges." *St. Nicholas* 39 (September 1912): 1035–37.